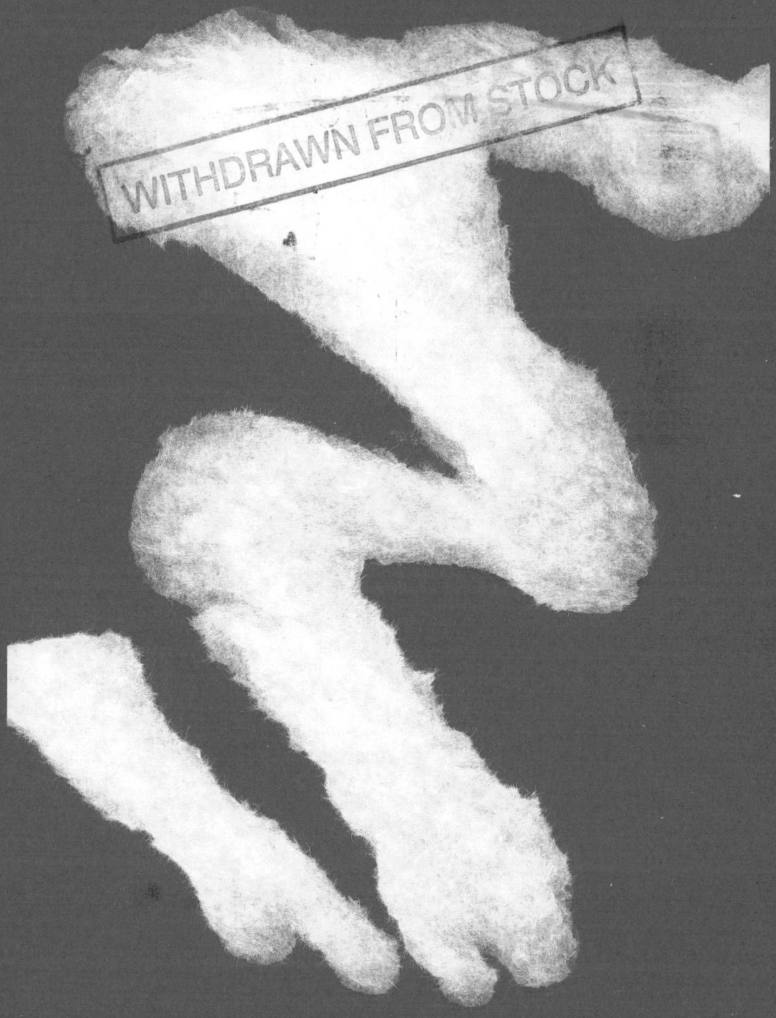

WITHDRAWN FROM STOCK

The Art of the Book in India

by Jeremiah P. Losty

The British Library

Contributors to the Exhibition

H.M. The Queen 77, 82, 133
H.H. Prince Sadruddin Aga Khan 18

Ahmadabad	Lalbhai Dalpatbhai Institute of Indology 15, 16, 24, 29, 39
Alwar	Government Museum 67, 108, 109, 138
Baltimore	Walters Art Gallery 63, 66, 72
Berlin	Staatsbibliothek Preussischer Kulturbesitz 33, 34, 78
Bhubaneshwar	Orissa State Museum 115
Bombay	Prince of Wales Museum of Western India 37, 45, 91
	The Asiatic Society 38
Cambridge	Christ's College 104
	University Library 2, 3, 4, 31
Delhi	National Museum 12, 28, 30, 42, 56
Dublin	Chester Beatty Library 47, 50, 60, 68, 71, 74, 80, 112
Gauhati	Department of Historical and Antiquarian Studies 120
Jaipur	Maharaja Man Singh II Museum 128, 129
London	British Library 1, 7, 8, 10, 11, 14, 19–23, 26, 35, 40, 43, 44, 51–3, 55, 59, 62, 65, 69, 70, 73, 75, 76, 79, 81, 84–8, 92, 94, 96–101, 103, 105, 107, 110, 113, 116–9, 121–2, 124–7, 130–2, 135–7, 139–40
	British Museum 13, 32, 36, 54, 89, 111, 114, 123
	India Office Library 25, 41, 48, 95, 106, 134
	Royal Asiatic Society 9, 58, 83
	School of Oriental and African Studies 57
	Victoria and Albert Museum 6, 27, 32, 49, 114
Manchester	John Rylands University Library 46
Oxford	Bodleian Library 5, 64, 102
Pontresina	The Keir Collection 17, 61
Poona	Bhandarkar Oriental Research Institute 90
Udaipur	Rajasthan Oriental Research Institute 93

Catalogue of an exhibition mounted at the British Library, Reference Division, from 16 April–1 August 1982

Published by the British Library
Reference Division Publications
Great Russell Street
London WC1B 3DG

British Library Cataloguing in Publication Data

Losty, Jeremiah P.
The art of the book in India.
1. Illustrated books 2. Illustration of books – India
I. Title
741.64′0954 NC992.1/

ISBN 0-904654-78-8

Produced for the British Library by Lund Humphries Publishers Ltd
Designed by Graham Johnson and Cathy O'Neill of Lund Humphries
Printed in Great Britain by Lund Humphries, Bradford

Contents

Preface

The exhibition *The Art of the Book in India* (16 April–1 August, 1982) is the British Library's contribution to the Festival of India, held in 1982 under the joint patronage of the Rt. Hon. Margaret Thatcher, M.P., and Shrimati Indira Gandhi.

I must here express my gratitude to all those individuals and organizations which have made the exhibition possible, and first of all to the lenders who are listed on p.2. I am under a deep obligation for help and advice to the keepers of the Indian collections of many museums and libraries in Europe, India and the USA for making it possible to see their treasures and for recommending their loan. To those in New Delhi concerned with organizing the loan of manuscripts from India, to Dr Kapila Vatsyayan and her colleagues in the Department of Culture, to the authorities of the National Museum, and to the British Council Division, especially Robert Frost and Sushma Bahl, go my warmest thanks.

In an exhibition covering so many different disciplines and languages, some must necessarily lie outside the scholarly competence of any one individual. I am deeply grateful to all those colleagues in the British Library who have patiently answered my numerous queries, above all to Norah Titley, for her unstinting encouragement and advice.

I cannot conclude without expressing the debt I owe my wife for her constant support and her help in preparing the manuscript.

J.P. Losty

Notes

Only the titles of oriental works and technical terms are recorded in full transliteration.

Dates quoted from manuscripts are recorded with the year in the original era (*Saṃvat*, *Śaka*, Nepal or *Hijra*) followed by the AD date.

David Cripps supplied the photographs for 12, 15, 16, 24, 28–30, 37–9, 42, 45, 56, 90 and 91. All others were supplied by the lenders or taken in the British Library.

77, 82 and 133 reproduced by gracious permission of Her Majesty The Queen.

Introduction

What is a book? Physically, it could be said, it is a collection of pieces of paper of the same size between covers and held together by glue and string. In another sense, it is the intellectual content conveyed by the words which are written or printed on the pages. All cultures are in agreement with the latter statement; comparatively few would agree with the former. Two thousand years ago in the Mediterranean world a book was physically a long roll of papyrus or of parchment. At the same time in China it was a collection of thin strips of bamboo or pieces of silk.

In India, the earliest concept of the book was as a collection of leaves or sheets of bark strung together between covers by a cord. The Indians would have viewed with horror both the slaughtering of young animals for their skin and the writing of sacred texts on such material, while paper, which was invented in China in the 1st century, did not come into general use in northern India before the 13th century, at about the same time as in Europe, in each case the Muslim world being the intermediary. In southern India, however, palm leaves continued in general use until the 19th century as the normal writing material.

The first references to writing in India, found in the earliest layers of the Pali Buddhist Canon of about the 5th century BC, speak of various types of material used for writing, such as leaves (*paṇṇa*), wood (*phalaka*, or boards, and *śalākā*, or bamboo chips or slips), and metals. The type of leaves is unspecified, but there is no reason to believe that it is as yet actually the usual writing palm of ancient India, the talipot (*Corypha umbraculifera*), for the latter is indigenous only to the extreme south of the peninsula, of which the early Buddhist texts had no knowledge. In fact any kind of suitable leaf was probably made use of, as leaves of the plantain and *śāla* trees were used in village schools until recent times.

Since much of what is known of the social history and material culture of ancient India is deduced from the *obiter dicta* of authors actually writing about something else, any argument 'from silence' must be used with extreme caution. Nonetheless, there is, as Rhys David long ago pointed out, an absolute silence about books (as physical objects, that is) in the Buddhist Canon, despite long inventories of what monks are and are not permitted to own, which argues that literary or religious texts were not committed to writing, while the repeated assertion that *suttas* (the Buddha's discourses) could be lost through a monk's having no disciple to teach them to, argues very strongly that the mere possibility of writing down the Buddhist sacred texts could not be entertained. This is not only the Indian aversion to the written as opposed to the oral tradition, but the very real problem that no writing material known in the 6th and 5th centuries BC was usable for writing connected literary or scriptural texts, as opposed to records, letters, or accounts. It is clear therefore that the use of the talipot must have been unknown to the north of India at this time, and seems still to have been unknown by the late 4th century BC, since it is not included with the writing materials (bark and cloth) noted by the Greek companions of Alexander. It can only have been with the expansion of the Mauryan empire into the south of India in the 3rd century BC that the talipot could have become known to the northern Indians, and its possibilities exploited for the writing of literary and religious texts.

The leaves of the talipot in its natural state are arranged like a fan and are about 1·3m long and 15cm wide at their broadest, tapering off to both ends, being divided by a central rib around which the leaf naturally folds. Each fold is cut from the rib, and fashioned into its finished shape, about 6·5–9cm broad by up to a metre in length, and then subjected to several processes of boiling, drying, and rubbing. The finished leaf is a smooth and flexible, light-brown surface. The size varies very much according to the purpose for which the leaves are needed. A long religious text would be written on leaves of the maximum possible length. A shorter text would usually be written on leaves of lesser length, which would enable the breadth to be somewhat greater, if desired, but this did not necessarily follow. Precise evenness of breadth was difficult to achieve in such a medium, and whereas many of the fine-quality palm-leaf manuscripts from eastern India of the 10th to 12th centuries taper only slightly towards their ends, in those from western India the difference is much more noticeable.

Hoernle writing in 1900 states that the talipot, *Corypha umbraculifera*, grows wild fairly commonly in Ceylon and the Malabar coast, and cultivated up both coasts as far as Bombay in the west and lower Bengal in the east, although the latter very uncommonly. Inland it does not grow at all. There must have been in ancient India a flourishing trade in the leaves, either in their raw or finished states, from south to north. The western manuscripts tend to be uneven in quality and size, suggesting that supplies could be difficult to get; this is particularly true of the period from the 13th century on, after the Turkish conquest. The eastern manuscripts on the other hand tend to be much more even, suggesting availability of a good supply, and they may have been in much more intensive cultivation in Bengal then than now. All the same, the great scriptoria of Bihar and Nepal would have had to have obtained their supplies from a source at some considerable distance. Palm leaves were still obtainable after the Turkish conquest of eastern India, and were used in eastern India up to the 17th century, but always on a much smaller size of prepared leaf than in the 12th century.

In southern India, the home of the talipot, early manuscripts are extremely rare, but this type of palm leaf was used in the earliest surviving southern manuscripts, of *c.*1112, in the Digambara *bhaṇḍār* at Moodabidri. However, those manuscripts from southern India which have survived from about the 16th century on, use a different palm leaf, that of the palmyra (*Borassus flabellifer*), a fan palm similar to the talipot, but somewhat smaller as to its leaf size. This is a less tender tree than the other, able to stand the colder winter climate of northern India, and was introduced from East Africa. According to Hoernle, the earliest reference to such a tree in India is dated 1328, but the evidence seems to suggest that the leaves were not widely used for writing until the 16th century. Manuscripts of this material are much less broad, about 3·75cm being the maximum.

It is clear then that round about 1500 there was a decided change from the one palm to the other. The talipot is useful only for its leaves, but the palmyra for all its products including fruit and sap, giving *tāḍī* or toddy, as well as being far easier to cultivate. In the course of a few centuries it completely ousted the widespread cultivation of the talipot in southern India, so that palmyra leaf had to be adopted as a writing material *faute de mieux*. This changeover also coincided with the introduction of paper

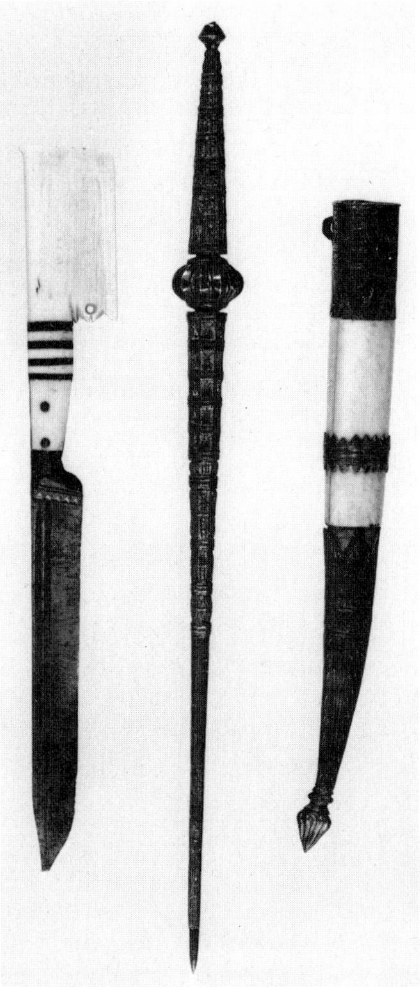

Iron stylus for incising palm leaves, with knife for trimming and erasing, and sheath. Andhra Pradesh, 18th century. Bodleian Library, Ms. Sansk. a. 1.

into the plains of northern India, so that the flourishing export trade of talipot leaves from south to north ceased and the commercial cultivation of talipot groves of the sort described by Hsüan Tsang in the 7th century became uneconomic. Only in Ceylon and Burma where the talipot grows far more readily, were its leaves still generally used for the production of manuscripts.

It is undeniable, however, that the leaves of the palmyra are inferior as writing material to those of the talipot, being less flexible, smaller, and more difficult to write on, while not taking ink well at all. The changeover from the one to the other involved also a change in the method of writing. All the talipot manuscripts known from northern India, as well as the much earlier fragments found in Central Asia, are written on with a reed pen (*lekhanī*) using ink (*maṣī*), although it would seem from Rājashekara's evidence (writing in Kanauj about 900) that they could also be incised with an iron stylus (*loha-kaṇṭaka*). The former method was used right up until the cessation of writing on palm leaves in northern India, an area which for the purposes of this discussion may be taken to be north of a line from Goa to Calcutta. However, with the exception of the early Jaina manuscripts of *c.*1112 referred to above, all the manuscripts from India south of this line, have their texts written on the leaves through incision with an iron stylus. After inscribing, the leaves were usually, although not invariably, smeared with ink (usually carbon based) and then cleaned with sand, leaving the ink in the incised letters which otherwise would have been almost invisible. As it was difficult to write directly on to the leaves of the palmyra, the method of inscribing became the only one used in southern India after its widespread adoption as the normal writing palm. However, before its introduction into the Indian subcontinent only shortly before this, all the earlier southern manuscripts must have been on the talipot, as we find in the manuscripts in Moodabidri; and as in the north, it is probable that both methods of writing were used. It is perfectly possible to use the incision method with a talipot, as most Burmese and Ceylonese manuscripts are written in this fashion, although in neither instance are the leaves rubbed as fine and smooth as the ancient talipot manuscripts with surface writing from northern India.

The finished pile of leaves whether talipot or palmyra was normally strung on a cord (*sūtra* or *nāḍī*) through pre-bored holes, and protected by a pair of covers (*paṭa* or *paṭlī*), usually wooden, at top and bottom of the pile. The earliest palm-leaf manuscripts tend to have a single hole bored about one-quarter of the way from the left edge. The odd position of the hole in these early manuscripts suggests that the format is based on an earlier one using different materials, probably wooden strips with holes at one end and kept strung together, as known from Khotan in the 2nd century. These were used as letters and accounts, not for literary purposes. Very long manuscripts at a later date have a similar hole one quarter of the way from the right edge. This second hole does not appear to serve any useful function, as long manuscripts are traditionally bound up with the string passing through only the left holes. It is wound round the pile several times, then passed diagonally across to the position of the right holes, but only wound round the outside and fastened in a loop. Sometimes the cord is replaced by two metal spikes fastened to one cover. The manuscript could then be protected by a square piece of cloth wrapped round it, or put in a specially made wooden box if important

Tamil Ms. on palmyra leaves enclosed by a brass frame in the shape of a tortoise. 18th century. British Library, Add.6780.

enough. Over the centuries the hole in manuscripts which had only the one tended to move nearer and nearer the natural position for it, *i.e.* the centre of the leaf. In addition to wood, the covers could be of metal or ivory or other materials, or sometimes no more than strengthened leaves. Wooden covers could be painted or carved and inlaid with precious stones or ivory, while metal ones could be sculpted with images. The Sanskrit term for the physical form of such a manuscript is *pustaka*, usually translated as 'book'. The Hindi derivative *poṭhī* is used to describe this type of book, for the format of the palm-leaf manuscript was used also for many other materials – bark, ivory, metals, cloth – and was retained for many centuries in northern India after paper had generally replaced the talipot. Palm leaves could however also be cut into different shapes, making manuscripts in the shape of a cow, or a Shiva *lingam* or a rosary, often with minutely incised writing. Special covers might also be required, such as the brass tortoise enclosing an 18th-century Tamil manuscript.

The palm leaf is a writing material which was in universal use at one time or another across the length and breadth of the Indian subcontinent, yet it seems almost certainly not to have been the earliest material so used. That the talipot was unknown in north-western India when Alexander invaded the Panjab is clear from the contemporary Greek accounts now lost but quoted in later sources. We are told firmly that the Indians used as writing materials the inner bark of trees, and well-beaten cotton cloth. The former is of course the inner bark of the common birch *Betula utilis*, which known as the *bhojapattra* or *bhūrja* grows freely in the Himalayan regions, and which provided the Hindu Kashmiris with their writing material until the 18th century.

The shape of birch-bark manuscripts varies considerably over the centuries. The earliest known, the 2nd-century Ms. Dutreuil de Rhins in Paris and Leningrad, is in the shape of a long scroll, with strips of birch bark pasted together. For other manuscripts, on the other hand, the original sheet was cut into long narrow strips conforming to the *poṭhī* format, with stringholes, which are of doubtful utility in such a manuscript due to their friability. Many of the Gilgit manuscripts (4th–8th centuries) conform to this pattern, but this cache of manuscripts also contained magnificent manuscripts on large sheets of bark far larger than any palm leaf, though again in the *poṭhī* format (No. 1). These originally would have had long wooden covers, perhaps decorated.

All these manuscripts come from a quite wide area of the western Himalayan regions through into Afghanistan, but we know from al-Bīrūnī and Rājashekara that birch bark was used over a much wider area of northern India. After the Turkish conquest, the vale of Kashmir, long renowned for its Sanskrit learning, was left isolated as the only centre for the production of birch-bark manuscripts; and even there the introduction of Muslim manuscripts into the valley after the 14th century radically affected the format of this the last period of their production. The sheets of bark were cut to fairly large rectangles and then about eight to ten at a time were folded in two and sewn into sections, and the sections sewn together into a codex shape; the whole was then covered with a binding which sometimes was of rough leather. This radical departure from traditional Hindu practice would seem to have begun as early as the 15th century, as all birch-bark manuscripts after this date are in this upright format, even though few still have their original bindings. All birch-bark manuscripts were written on with pen and ink, that used in the later Kashmiri manuscripts being famous for its indelible properties.

The birch was not the only tree whose bark was used as a writing material. At the other end of the Himalayas in that other enclosed valley, the Assam valley of the Brahmaputra, the inner bark of the aloe tree (*Aquilaria agallocha*) known locally as the *sāñcī* was used as a writing material. Although no extant manuscript appears to be earlier than the 15th century, it is known from Bāna's 7th-century account, when King Bhāskaravarman of Assam sent as presents to the great King Harsha of Kanauj, jewels, silks, and 'volumes of fine writing with leaves made from aloe bark, and of the hue of the ripe pink cucumber'. This lovely description fits perfectly well the 18th-century manuscripts commissioned by the Ahom Kings (No. 121). These sheets of bark when suitably prepared were written on with pen and ink. Unlike the large sheets of birch bark they bear a hole in the centre of the leaf, often ornamented, and traditionally were threaded with a string or *nāḍī*. The *sāñcīpāt* leaves have a tendency to split at the edges, but are otherwise tough and durable. The upper and lower covers were usually thick leaves of the same bark, still with the outer layer on.

The other early writing material referred to by Nearchos (quoted by Strabo) is well-beaten cotton cloth, a material (*paṭa* or *kārpārsika paṭa*) to which reference is made in early Sanskrit legal literature being used for official documents. Texts for engraving on stone or copper plates were written on cloth before being handed over to the engraver. None has survived from a very early period, but it may be assumed that, as in later times, it had to be made writable on by first stiffening it with paste and then covering it with a suitable ground. The earliest surviving example appears to be a solitary leaf from a *poṭhī* manuscript on silk found in Sinkiang, but probably of Indian origin, datable on palaeographic grounds to the 8th century and in a northern Indian hand (British Library Or.8212/1594). Such manuscripts are extremely rare; a complete one dated 1351 is reported to be preserved in a Jaina library in Patan in Gujarat.

The cloth scroll is a format of considerable antiquity, and was used almost exclusively for horoscopes and almanacs. The soothsayers summoned by Siddārtha to expound the meaning of his wife's dreams are shown on the illustrated *Kalpasūtra* manuscripts with long scrolls of cloth (No.26) from which they make their pronouncements. The writing on these scrolls commences parallel to the short side, proceeds to the end of the scroll, and if more space is required proceeds back along the reverse side. The same format is seen in the 2nd-century birch-bark scroll from Gandhara. The ancient tradition of painting on large squares of cloth is found continued, remarkably, in the great manuscript of the *Ḥamzanāma* commissioned by the Mughal Emperor Akbar about 1570 (No.54). This huge project involved the preparation of 1400 paintings on separate sheets of cloth, with the text normally written on the reverse.

These materials – birch bark, cloth, aloe bark, and palm leaf – were the normal materials of which books were made in ancient India. But faced with their impermanence in the Indian climate, the ancient Indians turned naturally to stone and metal when they wanted to record a text for all time. Everlasting stone, used widely for inscriptions from the 3rd century BC, was occasionally used by a royal author to demonstrate his literary as well as his martial talents. Buddhist tradition records that the

A treaty between the Zamorins of Calicut and the Dutch East India Company engraved on a gold strip 2·03m long in 1691. India Office Library, Malayalam Ms. 12.

Land-grant on seven plates of copper, AD664, with seal of the Eastern Chālukyas. British Library, Ind. Ch. 6.

Canon was inscribed on sheets of gold in Ceylon in 88 BC, and on sheets of copper in Mathura in the reign of Kanishka (?1st century AD). None of these has survived, but from a very early period are found votive offerings on gold or silver inscribed with the Buddhist creed, which would appear to have been placed in *stūpas* or buried in the foundations of monasteries or similar religious foundations. Buddhist texts were frequently inscribed on metal plates, and strung between covers as if they were palm-leaf manuscripts. The practice of writing on long strips of palm leaf kept in spirals which was prevalent in southern India, Nepal, and Ceylon, for letters and official documents, was imitated in at least two spectacular instances in gold and silver, in a pair of treaties exchanged between the Zamorins of Calicut and the Dutch East India Company engraved on long strips of gold and silver in 1691 and *c.* 1711.

Another precious material used for manuscripts is ivory sheets, with the text incised. Due to its extreme fragility in the Indian climate, little of this material has survived from an early period, but several manuscripts are known from the 18th and 19th centuries.

More ubiquitous even than the stone inscriptions are the copper-plate charters (*tāmraśāsana*), which record the granting of land to individuals from the king, represented by his chief minister or chief of staff, of which examples survive from the 4th century. These records were first copied out on cloth, birch bark or palm leaf, before being handed over to the copper smith (*ayaskāra*) for engraving. The originals were apparently kept in the royal chancellery and the plates were given to the donee.

The smiths copied not only the letters but also the shapes of the original, the charters from southern India being long and narrow in imitation of palm leaves, from northern India being comparatively wider. The text was incised parallel to the long side. Usually several sheets were required to complete the text, and these were written in the usual *poṭhī* format, with blank first and last sides, and then strung through a hole on a ring to which could be affixed a large bronze boss cast from a mould bearing the royal seal. Some dynasties of northern India preferred to issue grants in large single sheets with the seal welded or riveted on. They were usually kept not in secure storage but buried at the boundaries of the land which had been granted. They were especially important as the only permanent records of land holdings and were frequently altered by beating out the important details and reincising: and in later centuries entirely spurious grants are commonplace. The largest grant so far discovered is on 55 plates weighing 216lb with over 2,500 lines, issued by Rājendra Cola in AD 1024.

Most of these materials, apart from palm leaves, birch bark and *sāñcī* bark, were used for special purposes for which the newest material, paper, could not be substituted. This material, officially invented according to Chinese annals by one Tsai Lun in AD 105, was formed by pulping and shredding materials of vegetable origin in a solution of water and gum and catching the suspended fragments on a fine mesh; when allowed to dry, a malleable and durable sheet of considerable strength is the result. The Chinese after perfecting the process used the bark of the paper mulberry as the vegetable basis of their paper. The process was learnt by the Arabs after the conquest of Samarkand in 751, and spread throughout the Middle East, but linen rags were substituted for the mulberry bark. This sort of paper was introduced by the Turks after their conquest of northern India, in the early 13th century. There is some

Single copper plate issued at Monghyr in c.AD854, with Pāla seal riveted on. Iveagh Bequest.

evidence, however, to show that another kind of paper was in use at least in the Himalayan regions long before this.

Numerous examples of paper manuscripts in Indian scripts were discovered in the various archaeological expeditions sent to Central Asia in the early years of this century. The paper used in these manuscripts is of poor quality and in no way compares with the many specimens of beautiful papers used for Chinese manuscripts found, for example, in the Cave of the Thousand Buddhas at Tunhuang. It is usually unbleached, off-white or dirty-brown in tone, and suggests that its makers while knowledgeable in the techniques of papermaking were either insufficiently skilled to be capable of the manufacture of, or simply indifferent to, such a high-quality product. They are all in the *poṭhī* format and in a variety of hands, one of them being a large calligraphic variety of the Gupta script used exclusively in Central Asia. Examples of paper manuscripts from Central Asia such as the Weber and Macartney Mss. (in the Bodleian and British Libraries) include, however, texts written in scripts of undeniable Indian origin, the northern and western varieties of the Gupta script, which were thought to have been copied by Indian scribes in Central Asia. However, the discovery of a large cache of paper manuscripts in Gilgit in 1931 along with birch-bark manuscripts suggests that papermaking was practised at least in the Himalayan regions of the Indian subcontinent by the 6th century AD. Knowledge of the process may have spread to Gilgit across the Karakorum, or perhaps along the Himalayan trade route from Nepal.

Papermaking in another part of the Himalayan region, the valley of Nepal, was undertaken since at least the 12th century, since two manuscripts dated 1105 (now in the Asutosh Museum in Calcutta) and 1185 (No.11) are now known. The earlier manuscript is on a greyish-brown paper, the later on a paper dyed dark blue and written in gold and silver ink, a style that was especially popular in Nepal in later centuries. In place of the mulberry, Nepalese papers all used the bark of the daphne as the raw vegetable material, which grows on the high hills surrounding the Kathmandu valley.

It is perhaps extraordinary that if papermaking was practised as early as the 6th century, its use should not have been more widespread. However, these ancient papers depended on the use of plants which grow only in the Himalayas, so that its manufacture was severely localized. The same of course is true of birch bark, but by the middle of the first millennium AD its use was sanctified by centuries of traditions, so that there was little incentive to change to a new material which involved an even more laborious preparation and was not especially suitable to the climate of the north Indian plains. Even in Nepal where papermaking was clearly well-established by the 12th century, the number of palm-leaf manuscripts surviving far outstrips those on paper until the 16th century.

It was the Middle Eastern type of paper made from shredded cloth rather than bark which began to undermine the pre-eminence of the traditional materials in northern India from the 13th century, and this happened comparatively quickly in the west so that scarcely any palm-leaf manuscripts from this area are later than the 15th century. But traditionalist concepts asserted themselves in the formats of the Hindu and Jaina manuscripts in their *poṭhī* format, and like the Nepalese paper manuscripts they are cut to the same shape as the earlier materials. At first in the height : width ratio of 1 : 3. they gradually increase the height to 1 : 2 by the 15th century and this shape is maintained until the 18th century for most types of manuscripts.

For manuscripts in Arabic and Persian, and those Indian languages like Urdu normally written in the Arabic script, no material was thought suitable other than paper, and at the earliest Muslim court in Delhi, historians were soon hard at work writing up the conquest on paper which was first imported from Iran, but which was later produced in India in centres like Daulatabad, Ahmadabad, Lahore, and Kashmir. The centres of excellence of paper manufacture were by the 16th century producing beautiful papers of thick and durable quality, capable of being highly burnished and decorated. Until the 18th century the production centres and methods for manufacturing paper for Muslim and Hindu manuscripts were different. Hindu papermaking was apparently much more localized, and the sheets of paper produced were much smaller, normally the size of the folio required for a manuscript, rather than the much larger sheets requiring cutting favoured by the Muslim centres. In good-quality Persian manuscripts the text is written in the centre of the page and margins in gold and colours drawn all round, forming a central text panel. The sharpness of the tools needed for the marginating often caused the panel to split from its borders. Also the borders suffered far more than the central panels from normal wear and tear, and could easily be replaced.

Manuscripts in languages written in the Arabic script were bound and covered in the normal Middle Eastern way, *i.e.* leather over boards. These bindings differ somewhat from western ones in that they are 'roundback', *i.e.* the front and back covers flow smoothly round into the spine without a strengthening ridge, and are never 'hollowback', *i.e.* the spine is always stuck to the backs of the sections. They also lack a square, a protrusion of the covers beyond the edges of the folios on three sides, and often have a flap, a leather piece attached to the front edge of the rear cover which covers the front of the folios and rests beneath the front cover. There are very few surviving early examples, of which some have rudimentary tooling. At least from the late 16th century, in the Mughal studio, much more elaborate bindings were attempted, with gold-tooling, stamping, gilding, and also pasteboard covers painted and lacquered instead of being covered with leather (Nos.65, 66).

The earliest imitations of such bindings on Hindu manuscripts are from Kashmir, where birch-bark sheets were folded into sections, sewn together and bound with a leather cover from at least the 15th century.

A compromise between the Hindu *poṭhī* and the Muslim codex format was reached in the 17th century, in which a pile of paper folios in the *poṭhī* format was folded in two, and sewn in a single section, each bifolium being sufficiently wide for even half of it, the single folio, to be in a landscape format. The cover could be made of board covered with cloth or leather, or even nothing but a piece of leather (as No.99), and was united with the rest of the manuscript in the single sewing, a fairly heavy cord being used. The pages were protected in this rather rudimentary binding by several flyleaves at beginning and end, and very stiff pieces of paper or card inserted under the cord in the centre. Later in the 18th century, manuscripts in this format but vertical rather than horizontal were produced (No.101). The text areas are however still between side margins, and not yet contained within frames. This final approximation

Oriya Ms. on palmyra leaves wrapped in a gazelle skin. 18th century. British Library, Add.5033.

occurs in manuscripts of the late 18th century from Kashmir and in certain northern traditions based on those of Kashmir, as at Jaipur, where fine-quality papers were used. In these traditions the folios are now sewn section by section, and stitched at the back, and a cover usually with a flap attached. Even in these manuscripts, however, the sewing is only rarely at the long edge at right-angles to the line of the text (No.126). More usually the text is parallel to the long-edge of the paper, and the sewing is therefore at the top, still keeping to the *poṭhī* format (Nos.128–9). Occasionally the sewing is along the short side, which means that the text even on a *poṭhī*-shaped leaf has to be written the same way up on both recto and verso.

The covers of this type of manuscript usually include a flap called a *jihvā* (tongue); often a cord attached to the tip of the flap is meant to be wound round the manuscript for added security. Cloth was normally used to cover the boards – brocade, velvet, silk, or cotton, often gorgeously embroidered with coloured threads or gold and silver wire (Nos.128–9). Leather was also used as well from the 18th century, usually deerskin, but sometimes a more exotic material such as tiger skin could be used (British Library Add.26539).

Finally, as an added protection against the ravages of insects (termites, white ants, silverfish) and the extremes of temperature and humidity, manuscripts of all different formats were wrapped up, usually in large square pieces of cloth, and sometimes committed to boxes. The cloth traditionally used was cotton dyed with an orpiment preparation containing arsenic, in which bundles of paper or palm-leaf *poṭhīs* would be wrapped up. Occasionally another material is used, such as a deer skin round a very long palm-leaf *poṭhī* (British Library Add.5033). Fine quality manuscripts would have their own individual cloths and the richer the manuscript the more elaborate the cloth, which could be of silk stitched over a tougher coarser cotton as in Nepal, or the most elaborate brocade. The imperial *Pādshāhnāma* in Windsor Castle (No.82) is still kept in its fine brocade cover from the royal library in Lucknow. Sometimes specially decorated boxes would be made; a tradition associates the name of the great 15th-century Assamese Vaishnava reformer Shankaradeva with the painting of a manuscript container.

India's literary tradition is older by 1,000 years than the earliest references to writing in the Buddhist scriptures. The culture of Vedic

India was an oral one, in which poetry and religious literature were handed down from generation to generation by word of mouth, remembered word perfectly by a complex mnemonic system devised specially for the purpose from about the 15th century BC. When writing was introduced into India, doubtless by traders, probably about the 6th or 7th century BC, from some as yet unidentified Semitic alphabet, it was regarded as a practical tool for keeping accounts and inventories, but the idea of actually writing books with it seems not to have occurred to the ancient Indians, as the oral tradition was still all-powerful for all types of literature, whether religious, poetical or technical. The belief in the superiority of the spoken to the written word is one of the most long-lasting of Indian cultural traditions, and has survived to the present day.

The ancient Indian grammarians had, by the 5th century BC, scientifically analysed the phonetic system of the Sanskrit language, and arranged the letters of their alphabet on a thoroughly rational system, vowels before consonants, the latter being grouped according to their class – all the gutturals, palatals, labials, etc., together. This they had probably achieved without the help of writing, so the introduction of the written alphabet caused them no difficulties in relating sounds to symbols. The *Brāhmī* (Divine script) used in the inscriptions of Ashoka in the 3rd century BC is found all over the subcontinent, and from it developed all the multitudinous scripts of India and their offshoots in Central Asia, Tibet and south-east Asia, with the exception of Kharoshthi, derived from Aramaic, used in north-western India for a few centuries.

There is nothing that is fixed or sacred about any script in India, for Indian culture regarded the oral tradition as far superior to the written, unlike for example the Arabs. To the latter, the Koran is the word of God revealed to His Prophet and its written form therefore was beautified by the arts of calligraphy and illumination. The Indians took a different standpoint – the *Vedas* were God's revelation and couched in *devabhāṣā*, the language of the gods, *i.e.* Sanskrit. For 1,000 years, the *Vedas* had been handed down orally, each teaching and recitation being the recreation of precisely the same sounds as the original revelation. The ability to commit the eternal revelation on to transient leaf or bark or even stone seemed at best irrelevant, and, at worst, blasphemous. Hence Sanskrit has no script of its own, uniquely associated with it; it can be written in any Indian script, ancient or modern, with equal facility. There was no standard form of letter to which developments of different styles in different parts of India could be compared, and without this standard of reference, local developments became entrenched. Thus from century to century in a dozen different parts of India, the scripts changed and developed at their own pace, until they became mutually unreadable.

As a record of their sacred books, writing was of no use to the ancient orthodox followers of the Vedic religion. But when heterodox movements broke away from the sacrificial cult of the *Vedas*, when it became necessary to remember precisely the words spoken by the Buddha, and by Mahāvīra and his predecessors who founded the Jaina system, then writing was seen to have a purpose other than that of recording inventories. In the Indian manuscript tradition there was henceforth a division between the heterodox Buddhists and Jainas and the orthodox Hindus.

As we have seen, it would seem to have been physically impossible to commit large texts to writing in the early Buddhist period, as there was no suitable writing material; and that it was culturally impossible is demonstrated by the fear, expressed several times in the Canon, that a given *sutta* or discourse of the Buddha might be lost forever if an old monk had no one to teach it to. Yet as the generations passed, and divisions arose among both the Buddhists and Jainas, it became of the first priority to establish precisely what their human teachers had said through the memories of those who had known them and passed on their teaching to disciples. The accounts necessarily varied, and it was to reconcile these versions that councils met to fix the canonical texts, *i.e.* the words of the founders, and to ensure that they could not be lost by committing them to writing. From this gigantic step away from the Vedic tradition it was but an easy further step, common to all mankind, to want to do it as beautifully as possible, to develop the arts of calligraphy and manuscript decoration. Tradition records that the texts fixed by the Buddhist councils were engraved on sheets of gold, and there is no need to doubt this, as engraving important documents and religious texts on sheets of the precious metals is relatively common in later periods. The early Buddhist manuscripts recovered from both Central Asia and the Indian subcontinent include superb examples of calligraphy. From about the 11th century calligraphy was enhanced by illustrations in both Buddhist and Jaina manuscripts.

The orthodox followers of the Vedic cult were not unaffected by the powerful Buddhist and Jaina sects, and had their own literature of withdrawal and asceticism, the Upanishads. But the primacy they accorded to sound rather than to writing did not allow them to be seduced from the oral tradition, which affected not only religious and philosophical texts, but also works of literature, the law, and numerous other fields. Perhaps an exception was made for technical literature such as medicine or astronomy, as the only ancient Indian manuscripts so far recorded which are not specifically Buddhist are in these fields. Yet the tradition changed, most probably after AD 1200, with the collapse of the Hindu kingdoms before the armies of Shihab ad-Dīn Ghorī and the wholesale destruction of cities, temples, monasteries, and the apparent imminent loss of the entire Hindu tradition. Writing was seen to have a purpose in transmitting knowledge that would otherwise be lost for ever. Yet starting so late, the Hindus had missed 1,000 years of calligraphic development, and their task was one of urgently recording literature that might disappear for ever rather than of writing texts as beautifully as possible. Yet even in more settled and prosperous times, when there was occasion to prepare illustrated copies of Hindu texts, as in the late 15th and 16th centuries, the writing is pedestrian at best, but often full of deletions and corrected mistakes. Even in the Rajput courts in the 17th century, apparently so completely secure that no time and effort was spared on the production of superbly illustrated copies of Hindu texts, there is no improvement in calligraphy. It is only in the 18th century that we find Hindu manuscripts which have any pretensions to calligraphic elegance, and this only under direct influence of illumination as perfected at the Mughal courts, consequent upon the dispersal of the imperial library from the early 18th century onwards and of its artists and scribes.

Like most visual arts, those of the book could flourish only when there was patronage. Many manuscripts bear no evidence of the cause of their existence, but from those which do, it is possible to build up a picture of the different kinds of patronage found in India. The earliest surviving illuminated manuscripts are those of the sacred scriptures of the two heterodox religions of Buddhism and Jainism. Sometimes, the colophons state the name of a commissioner, who would have paid for the work to be done for his spiritual benefit (*puṇyārtham*) and that of his parents and other members of the family. The manuscript was written and illuminated by monks in their monastery, and remained in the institutional library or temple. The merit accrued by the commissioners counted as a good deed to enter on the balance sheet which determined their status in their next incarnation according to the laws of *karma*. Where no commissioner is mentioned, the book must have been illuminated for the benefit of the monks themselves. The beautification of sacred texts because of their divine origin, as an end in itself, was an idea foreign to all Indian conceptions. The Hindus would not seem even to have shared the Buddhist–Jaina view of the spiritual merit to be gained from the commissioning of illuminated manuscripts.

The Muslim conquest at the end of the 12th century introduced into India the Iranian tradition of court patronage and of court studios of book-production, and some at least of the Sultans of Delhi and the successor sultanates in the provinces established studios in their own capitals. It seems probable that a few powerful Hindu princes of northern India did the same. But their efforts seem paltry when compared with the immense studio established by the Mughal Emperor Akbar (1556–1605), and it was under this influence that later Hindu and Muslim courts set up their own studios, whose standard of work so very often depended on the interest shown by the royal patron.

The major arts of the book are fourfold – calligraphy (fine writing), illumination (embellishment with abstract designs in gold and colours), illustration (the addition of figural paintings), and binding (the adornment of the covers between which the leaves are protected). Other crafts involved include the preparation of the writing material (paper, palm leaf or bark in an Indian context); burnishing the written leaves; sewing or stringing them together; the mounting of paintings in album leaves; marginating in gold and colours; and remargining of worn-out leaves. We do not propose to treat any of these arts separately, as could be done when dealing with the book-arts of a unitary culture, such as for example the Muslim world, for India's traditions embrace too many cultures for an overall view to be as yet possible, while our knowledge of some of these arts is rudimentary. Indian calligraphy, for example, as opposed to palaeography is a totally uncharted area, where absolute canons of judgement in the form of native critiques and treatises do not exist. We propose instead to develop these themes as occasion arises as we survey the Indian tradition of the art of the book from the earliest survivals right up to the 19th century, bearing in mind that for the early period up to 1500 so much has been lost that our knowledge can never be more than partial.

For although the manuscript heritage of India is enormous, with huge libraries filled with millions of manuscripts, they represent but a small part of the tradition. Manuscripts dating from before 1000 are pitifully few, yet the first millennium AD was the greatest period of India's culture, when her literature, drama, painting, sculpture and architecture had reached their greatest heights. Literary works from these centuries have

Corrections to colour section

PLATE I *for* distinguished *read* distinguishing

PLATE IV *for* Indira *read* Indra

PLATE XI *transpose* (above) *and* (below)

PLATE I **6** f.89b (detail). A Bodhisattva, perhaps Ratnapāni, holding a white lotus, on which the distinguished object is no longer visible. Hayagrīva is in attendance.

PLATE II **14** f.2. The Goddess slaying the Buffalo-demon; with the donors of the manuscript in praying attitudes.

PLATE III **7** ff.163b, 164. The Bodhisattvas Avalokiteshvara Simhanāda (above) and Maitreya (below) mark the end of the 11th chapter of the *Prajñāpāramitā*.

PLATE IV **5** ff.92b, 93 (detail). The Jina Vajrasattva and Bodhisattva Vajrapāni (above) and the Buddha teaching Indira and the Bodhisattva Jālinīprabhā (below).

PLATE V **12** Prince Vessantara gives away his elephant (left), goes into exile with his family (centre), and gives away his chariot (right).

PLATE VI **11** ff.1b, 2. The Buddha in *dharmacakra mudrā* (above) and the six-armed Vasudhārā (below).

PLATE VII **16** (detail). The Jina Mahāvīra, lustrated by elephants, with attendants and worshippers.

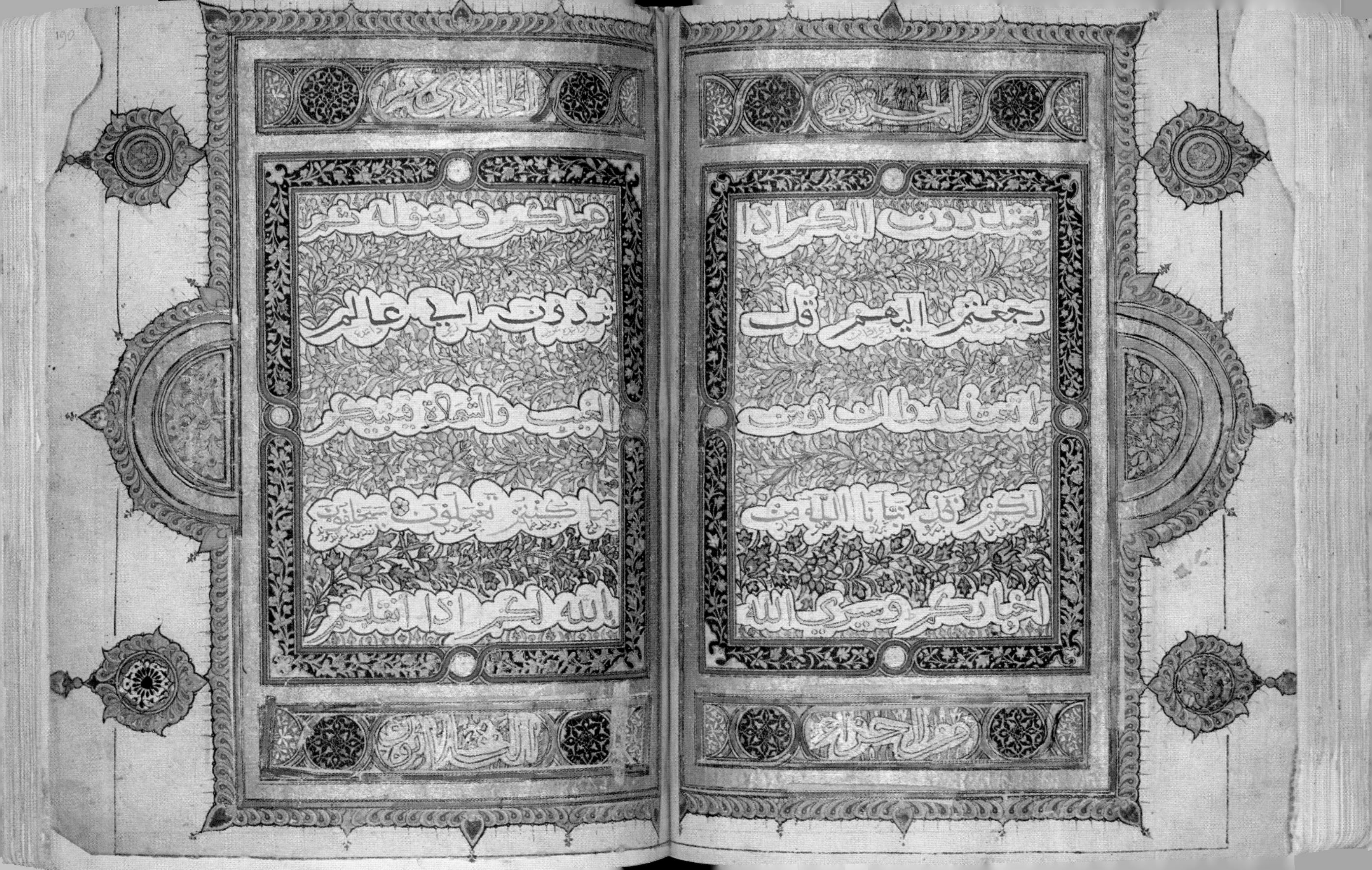

الجزء
يعتذرون اليكم اذا
رجعتم اليهم قل
لا تعتذروا لن نؤمن
لكم قد نبأنا الله من
اخباركم وسيرى الله
الحادي عشر
عملكم ورسوله ثم
تردون الى عالم
الغيب والشهادة فينبئكم
بما كنتم تعملون سيحلفون
بالله لكم اذا انقلبتم

PLATE IX **26** f.19b. The soothsayers consult their scrolls to determine the meaning of Queen Trishalā's 14 dreams, and write their opinions.

PLATE X **28** f.15b. The parents of the Jina Mahāvīra, Siddhārtha and Trishalā. The Queen is dreaming her 14 dreams which foretell the Jina's birth.

PLATE VIII (opposite) **18** ff.189b, 190.

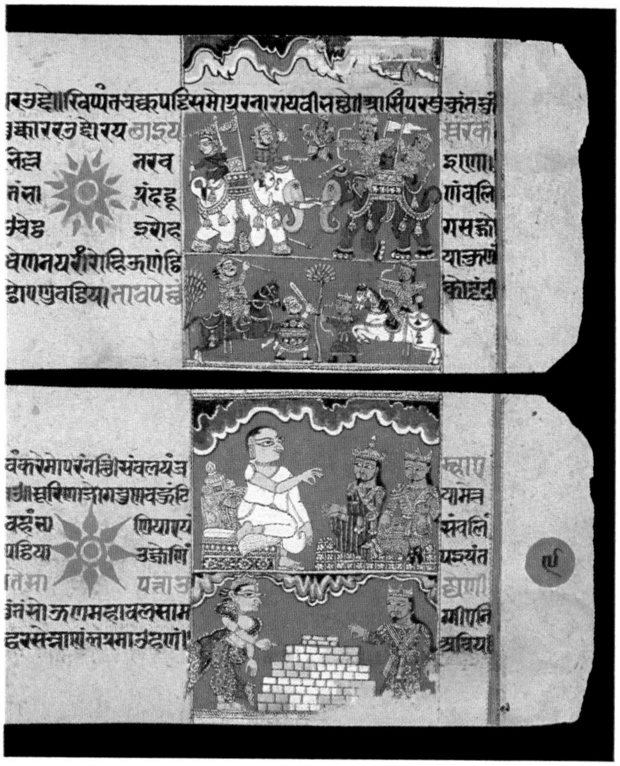

PLATE XI **29** ff.9b, 10. Kālaka turns the bricks to gold, for supplies for the Sāhi's army (above); and the battle between the armies of the Sāhi and the King of Ujjain (below).

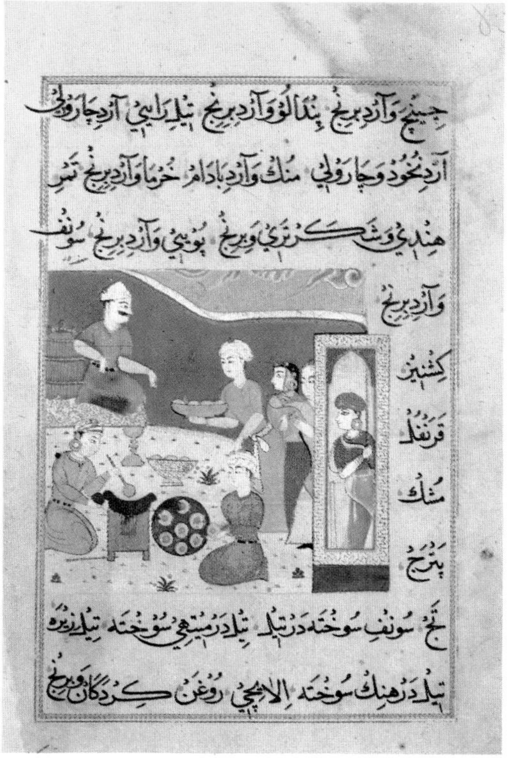

PLATE XII **41** f.83b. Preparation of sweets for the Sultan of Mandu.

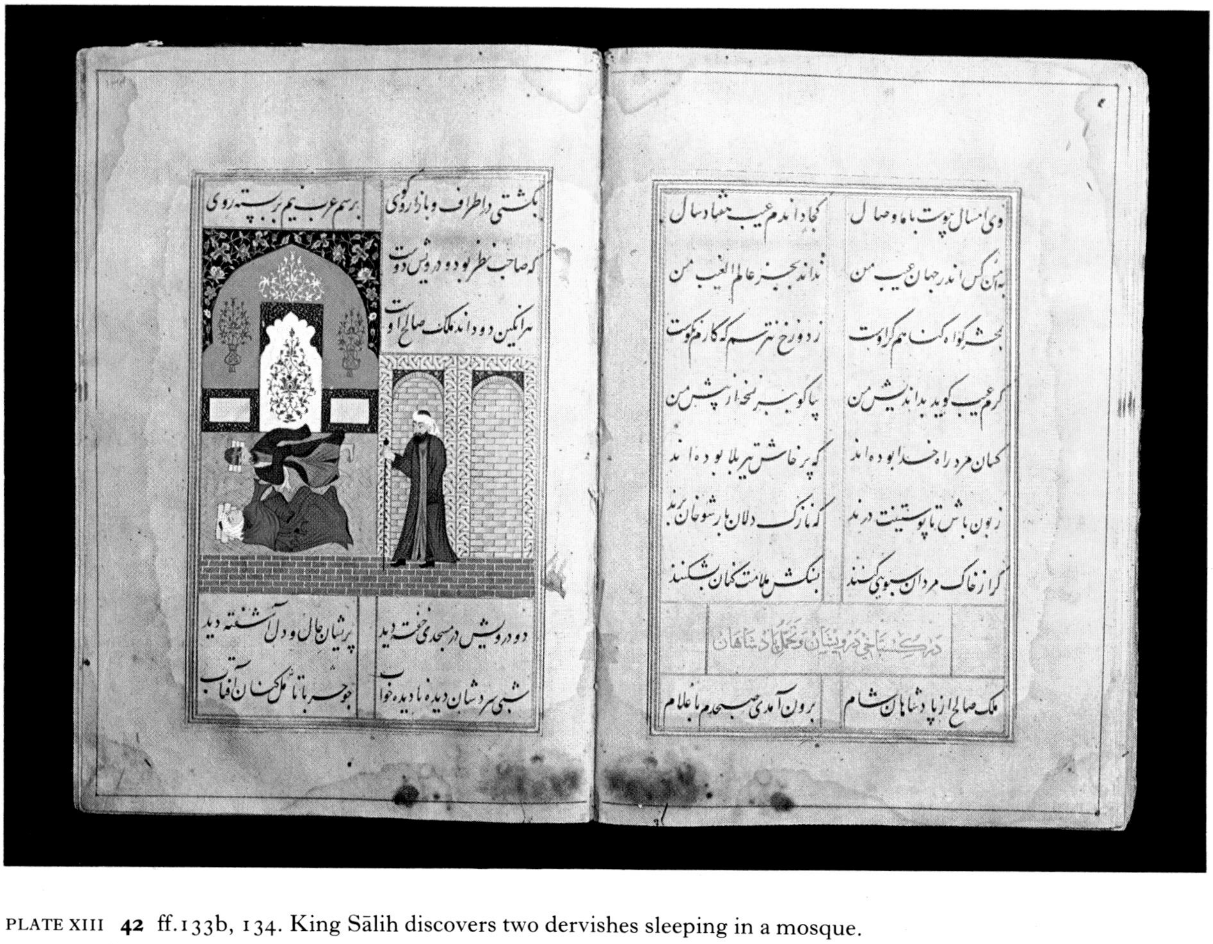

PLATE XIII **42** ff.133b, 134. King Sālih discovers two dervishes sleeping in a mosque.

PLATE XIV **37** Rādhā addresses her confidante in the groves of Brindaban.

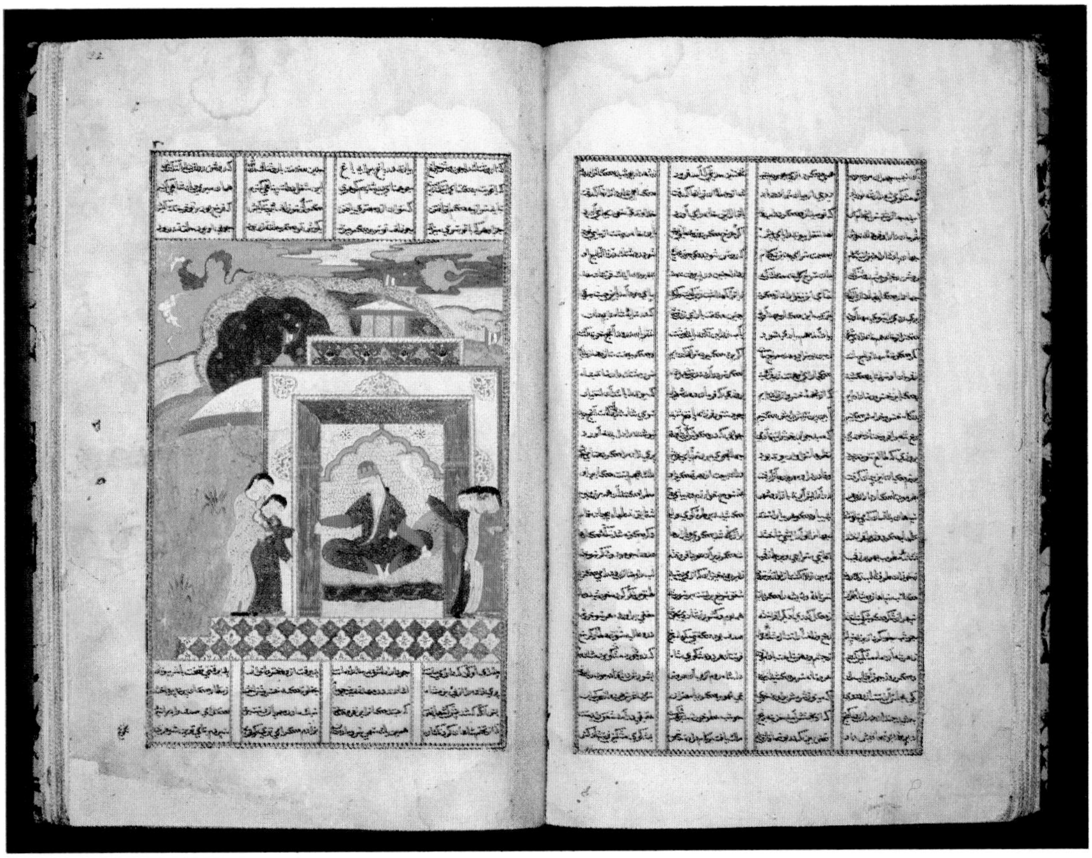

PLATE XV **44** ff.31b, 32. Alexander receives Roshanak, the daughter of Darius.

PLATE XVI **45** f.49. Mainā asks the caravan leader to convey a message to her husband Laurak. Below, the number of cattle is recorded on a *takta*.

PLATE XVII **52** f.89b. Ratan Sen asks the King of Ceylon for his daughter, whose image he already carries on his heart.

PLATE XVIII (below) **59** ff.66b, 67. Gifts being brought from the besieged fortress to Dārāb, including an elephant on wheels. Right-half by Sānvala, left by Kānhā (Nānhā).

۱۱۹ عمل سانوله

و بی ساخته چنانکه هرکه بدیدی پنداشتی که او خود میرود و عماریی بر زبر او پنج گز بالای وی همه از زر سرخ تعبیه کرده
بر صفت سرکاری و چشم وی از پیروزه الماسی و بحد جواهر و مروارید و از آن عماری او تخته و چهار بالشی در میان
عماری نهاده و تاجی از بر وی او تخته و دو نرگس دان و تن بر داشته در هر یکی شاخی مرجان نهاده به بالا پنج گز
بر میان درختی و هر مرواریدی در وی او تخته چند بیضه کبوتری و تختی زرین ده من گرفته می آوردند و پیش سر دیبت
ساخت می آوردند و ده غلام شنشلیون از حصار بیرون آورد داراب را خبر کرده اند که رسولان آمده اند
از نزدیک فصطلیفون گفت بیارید شان در حال رسول را در آوردند و داراب نشسته بود و شراب میخورد
حاجبان رسول را در آوردند داراب و خرطینوس و هرقالیس و طمروسیه هر چهار بنشستند و تدبیر کردند
داراب گفت این حصار را چگونه گیریم طمروسیه گفت هرچه من بگویم آن کن تا حصار ترا گردد گفت بگوی گفت
این مرد عم بنسبت مرا نشناسد که دیر است که مرا ندیده است تدبیر آنست که فردا مرا جامه مردان پوشانی و تو که
دارابی مرا بر زبر سر خود جای ده تا بایستم چنانکه جانداران بایستند تا عمم بیاید مرا ببیند بر بالای سر تو چون او مرا دید و دانست که
من جاندار توم مرا با خرطینوس سوی او فرست تا من بروم و جان کنم این حصار را بتو دهند داراب گفت ای طمروسیه نباید که ترا
بدانند طمروسیه گفت ندانند داراب گفت مگر تو بهانه میکنی تا نزدیک او در روی بدر شوی و باز نیایی طمروسیه گفت هرگز این خیانت که
این خواستی که دیگر نزد تو نزدیک نیامدمی داراب گفت روا بود چون آن شب بر ایشان بگذشت روز دیگر داراب بر تخت بنشست

۶۶

۱۲۰ عمل کانها

و طمروسیه بر زبر سر او بایستاد قبای دیبا پوشیده و کلاهی بر سر نهاده و تیغ حمایل کرده و هرقالیس
بر کرسی و خرطینوس همچنان شنشلیون را باز دادند تا در آمد چون پیش تخت رسید هرقالیس را بدید
بشناخت که یکسال قرین او بود و یکسال بود تا او برفته بود چون در آمد چهار جای خدمت کرد و نامه
پیش داراب نهاد و سر در پیش در هرقالیس مانده بود که او اینجا چگونه افتاده است اما مولف اخبار
و گزارنده اسرار ابوطاهر طرسوسی چنین روایت میکند که چون شنشلیون نامه بداراب داد
اول نامه نوشته بود که بسم الله الملک الحق المبین اما بعد نامه تو که دارابی بدین جزیره آمدی ترا چنین
گمان خیال بسته است که مگر این جزیره چون جزیرهای دیگر است و ما چون کسان دیگریم این هوس از دل
بیرون کن که این هوس فاسد است و اندرین حصار صد هزار مرد شمشیر زنست و اگر صد سال ترا
زندگانی بود و تو بر در این حصار بنشینی بجز دیواری که از بیرونست دیگر ترا هیچ چیز بهره نیست
این اندک مایه چیزی فرستادیم بستان و برخیز همچنان که آمدی برو و اگر نه من از این حصار لشکر بر دارم

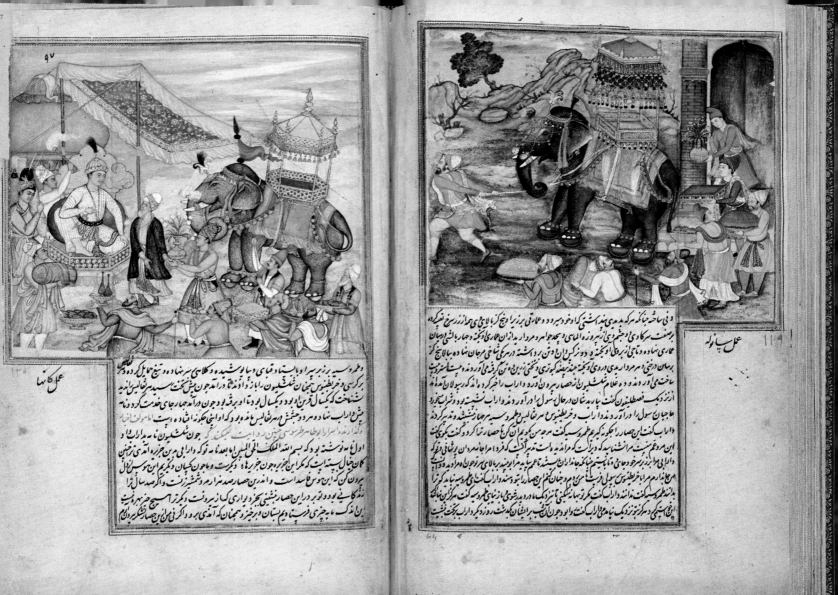

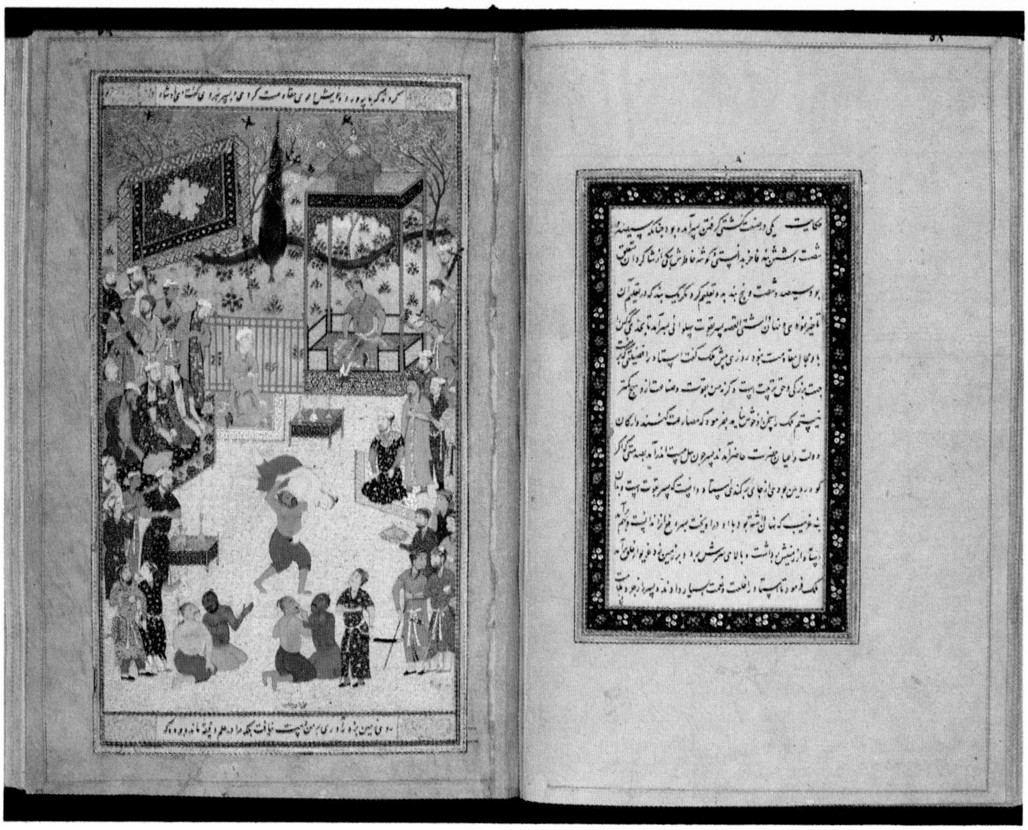

PLATE XIX **55** ff.29b, 30. The old wrestler who kept back his best trick in order to defeat his arrogant pupil. Akbar is depicted in the guise of the king. By Shahm.

PLATE XX **56** ff.28b, 29. A fiery horse is brought before Prince Khizr Khān.

PLATE XXI **65** f.325b. The scribe ʿAbd ar-Rahīm 'Amber-pen' and the painter Daulat, with their professional tools – pen-box, pens, inkpots, a roll of gold-sprinkled paper, brushes, pots of paint. By Daulat.

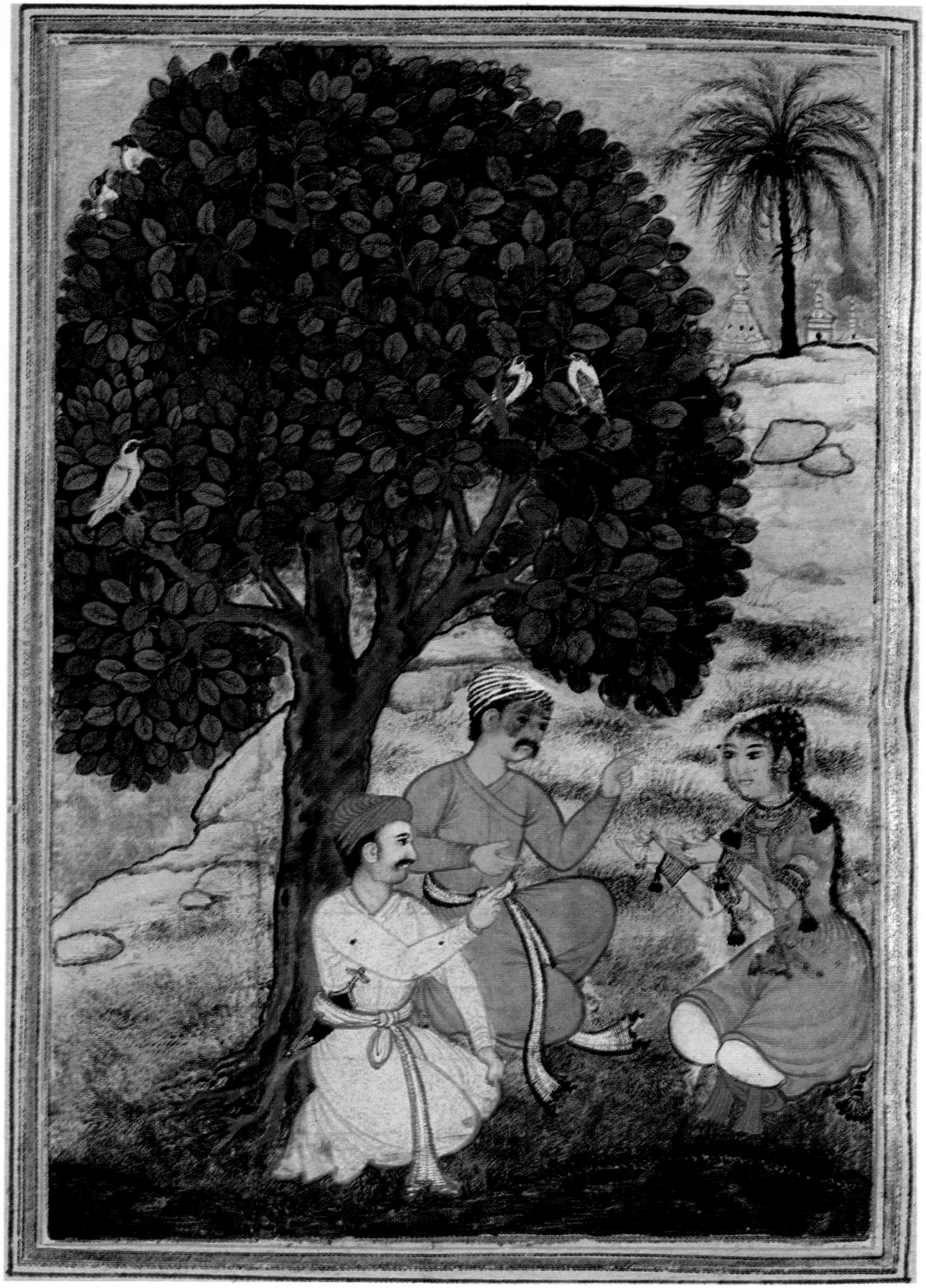

PLATE XXII **60** f.74. The virtuous wife, with her husband and the man who had impersonated him in his absence.

PLATE XXIII **61** f.157b. Laylā visits her distracted lover Majnūn, who keeps company with the wild beasts in the wilderness. By Muhammad Sharīf.

PLATE XXIV **64** f.9 (right). The dervish is rebuked by the Mulla for his pride in his darns. By Basāvan.
64 f.42 (left). The unfaithful wife enjoys the company of her lover, while the young man she persuaded to take her place in her tent is attacked by her husband. By Miskīna.

PLATE XXV **68** f.230. Shiva and his wife Pārvatī appear to the sage Vasishtha in his hermitage.

PLATE XXVI **72** f.109b. Prince Salīm hunting with his companions.

PLATE XXVII **75** f.320. The Sultan of Baghdad's infatuation with a Chinese slave-girl causes him to neglect his duties. By Bishndās.

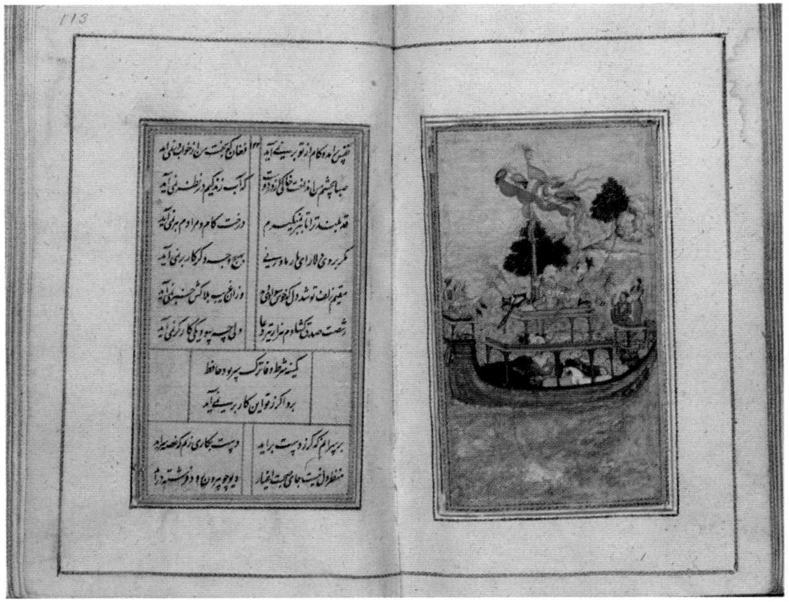

PLATE XXVIII **73** ff.112b, 113. Noah and his family in the Ark.

PLATE XXIX **76** f.194b (left). Jahāngīr plays polo with his sons Parvīz and Khurram and brother-in-law Mīrzā Abu'l Hasan.
76 f.249 (right). Jahāngīr in darbar – Khurram is presenting or receiving a gift of jewels.

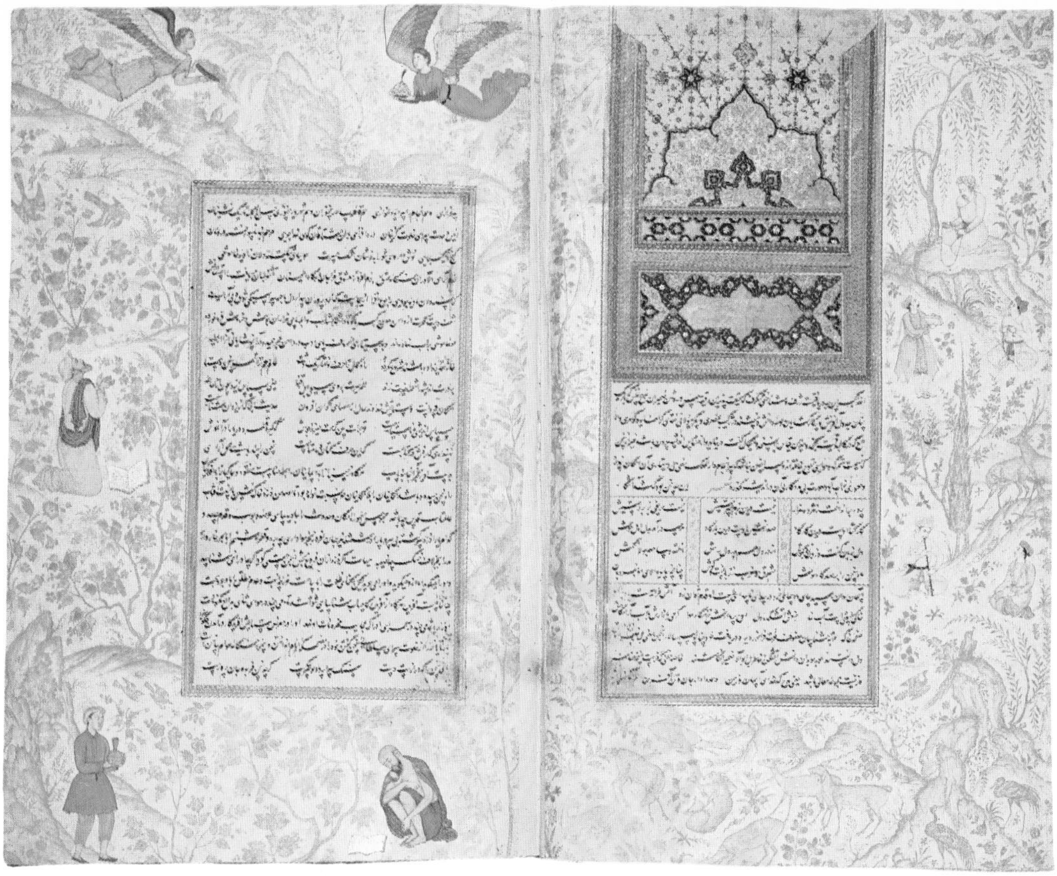

PLATE XXX **70** ff.1b, 2. Ascetics, saints and angels surround the opening phrases of the *Akbarnāma* in praise of Speech. The *sarlavḥ* is by Mansūr.

PLATE XXXI **77** f.5b (right). The Last Judgement and Resurrection of the Dead. By Nānhā and Manohar.

77 f.6 (left). Seven couples in a garden. By Narsingh.

PLATE XXXII **82** f.43b. Jahāngīr bids farewell to Khurram at the start of a military campaign. The courtiers are all identified and the artist is depicted in the bottom left-hand corner. By Bālchand.

PLATE XXXIII **90** f.5b. The beautiful Mount Trikūta (Triple-peaked), the dwelling of various heavenly beings, to the lake at the foot of which comes a herd of rampaging elephants. By Sāhīb Dīn.

PLATE XXXIV **90** f.6. The leader of the elephants has his leg seized by a powerful crocodile who dwells in the sacred lake.

PLATE XXXV **89** f.52. *Vasanta rāga*, celebrating the coming of spring.

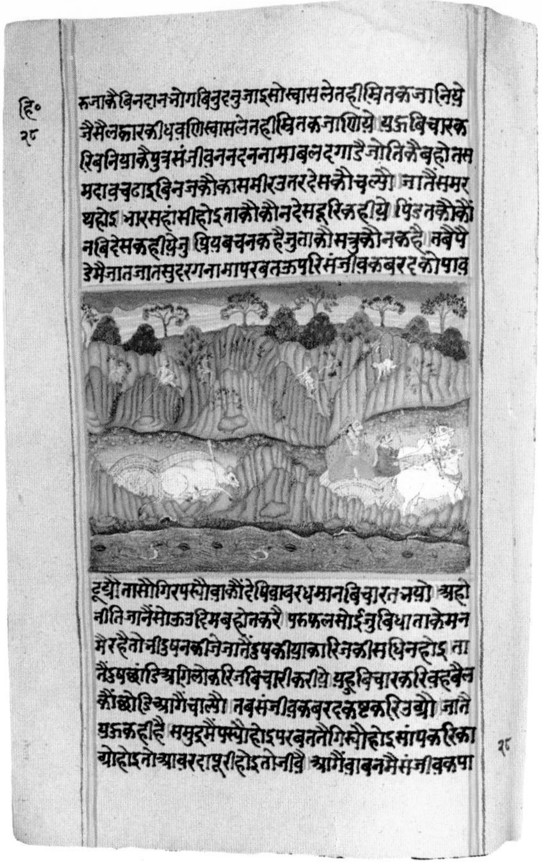

PLATE XXXVI **101** f.28b. The merchant abandons his injured ox Sanjīvaka in the wilderness. By Dhano.

PLATE XXXVII **96** f.202. Rāma and the exiles return in triumph to Ayodhyā. By Sāhīb Dīn.

PLATE XXXVIII (overleaf) **122** f.10b (above). Vyāsa milking the *Purāṇa* out of the *Kāmadhenu*, the Wish-fulfilling Cow.
122 f.11 (below). Sauti begins the narration of the *Purāṇa* to Shaunaka in the latter's hermitage of Naimishāranya. Both by Durgārāma Betha.

নাৰায়ণনৰনৰোত্তমকনমিয়া ।। দেৱীসৰস্বতিবেদব্যাসকোবন্দিয়া ।।
শ্ৰীৰাম্ভাৰতমাদিজতসাস্ত্ৰগণ ।। সাস্ত্ৰৰমাদিতকৰিবক্তড়াদিৰন ।।
বেদগনকৰিবৰসেহজদুগ্ধদে পোষন ।। স
বস্তুতিকামধেনুকৰিল দোহন ।। ৪৫ ।।
মতিৰুচিকৰজহ্মবৰ্দ্ধ পৰ্বান ।। দু
গ্ধতৈলজ্ঞযনাহিমম ৎসমান ।।
হেনযদুগ্ধকপীয়ালো কনিৰত্নৰ ।।
জীতোৰজন্মাস্বাদয়সেহি সেচন্তৰ ।। ৪৬ ।।

নৈমিষাৰণ্যতসৌনকাদিঋষিগণে ।। নিত্যক্ৰিয়াকৰিব
সিলন্তকুশাসনে ।। এনসময়তৰোমহৰ্ষতনয় ।।
আসিলন্তপ্ৰশ্ৰয়েসূতমহাসয় ।। ৪৭ ।। দেখিঋষিগণেতাঙ্ক
আসনকদিল ।। ঋষিগণনমিসূতেআসে
বেসিল ।। ঋষিসমাজতশ্ৰেষ্ঠসৌনকে
সাদৰি ।। কুশলপুছিলন্তাঙ্কসতকাৰকৰি ।।

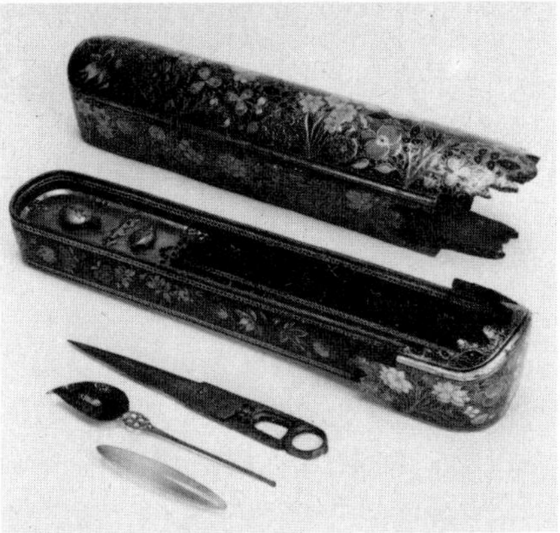

Painted and lacquered pen-box (*kalamdān*) containing inkpots, scissors, spoon and polisher. Kashmir, 19th century. Victoria and Albert Museum, I.S. 1119, A-D–1874.

of course survived through later manuscripts. But we have only a small proportion of the dramatic and poetic literature of these centuries and scarcely anything from even earlier periods. Much of the vast Buddhist literature in Sanskrit, whether of the Lesser or Greater Vehicles, has disappeared, while even the Jainas, who early took recourse to writing, managed very early to lose the most ancient strata of their sacred literature. The reasons are clear. The inability of the materials to withstand the rigours of the Indian climate, the heat and humidity, with its attendant superfluity of voracious insects meant that a century or two was the most any manuscript could generally be expected to survive. And the Indian scholar of old, who had worn-out manuscripts copied afresh, would not keep the old one or send it to the temple library but committed it to the sacred waters of the rivers, for both substance and content to be reabsorbed into the seamless web that is the universe. Also wholesale destruction occurred in the 13th and again in the 18th centuries in periods of invasion and civil wars. So that when secular manuscript libraries were established in India, there was little that was very ancient left to collect. Most of the royal libraries were composed principally of new manuscripts, many of them beautifully written and illustrated. It was not until the establishment of British rule in India that systematic searches were undertaken for the assembling of manuscripts in great repositories, so that the literary history of India could be written. But the study of the history of book-illustration, with which we are chiefly concerned, has hardly begun. So much in the early period has been lost, and so much of the medieval period is controversial, that new discoveries are anxiously awaited. And each new discovery only tells us how little we know and how much more complicated the picture is than we can yet comprehend. And even the Mughal period, outwardly so well documented and well represented, is at its beginning mysterious and controversial. So this book is full of doubts and possibilities, and puts forward theories with which many other scholars would disagree. Our purpose is to trace the development of the art of the book, by which we mean manuscripts of beauty whether on account of their format or their calligraphy, their illumination or illustrations, or binding, from the earliest discoveries known to us to the end of the traditions of manuscript production and illustration in the 19th century caused by the twin modern invention of the printing press and the camera. We shall discuss them in terms of religions and cultures and formats and patrons of apparently great diversity. Yet at the end of the day we shall see that India has absorbed, as she always has done, the ways of her invaders and turned them to her own purposes without losing her essential Indianness in the process.

CHAPTER I

Early Manuscript Illumination

It is not yet possible to determine precisely when the Indians began to treat their manuscripts as something other than mere purveyors of information, and to treat them as physical objects capable of being made beautiful both in the way the information was written and in decorations applied over and above the actual textual matter. Calligraphy is an art which finds no mention in ancient Indian literature; certainly there is no surviving treatise on the subject. Yet from the earliest manuscript survivals it is clear that some scribes took immense pains to produce beautiful and measured harmony with their pen, to invest the page with dignity through the use of majestically large and separate letters or of lines proceeding in measured, rhythmic tread across the great width of a page. The former of these devices is found only in Buddhist manuscripts on paper from Central Asia about the middle of the first millennium AD, such as the Kashgar Lotus Sūtra, which must have been a conscious imitation of large-lettered Chinese calligraphy. Yet the manuscripts are totally Indian in character, being in the *poṭhī* format but on paper, and resemble large-scale birch-bark manuscripts from India. They conform in shape to no Chinese model. Likewise the script is the Central Asian variant of the Gupta script, used also for the Iranian languages of the area. With what devotion these scribes must have sat down to copy with the utmost beauty known to them the Lotus Sūtra or the Perfection of Wisdom in language as remote to them as Hebrew to us.

In the Indian subcontinent itself, examples of early manuscripts of similarly majestic size have been found only in the excavated *stūpas* of Gilgit. Here they are on large birch-bark sheets, but the script is much smaller than their Central Asian counterparts, being remarkable for the regularity of the spacing of the letters and lines, achieving a dignified, rhythmic whole (No.1). These manuscripts also are of Buddhist origin, as are all calligraphically noteworthy early manuscripts. Their only decorative elements are concentric roundels of considerable size, and a few elaborately designed versions of the Buddhist *dharmacakra*. An early tradition refers to the copying of Buddhist texts in golden letters, but there is no evidence of such a technique being practised in early India. The tradition in Nepal of writing with gold ink on blue-black paper may now be dated comfortably to the 12th century (No.11), but this type of paper seems never to have been used in India. The reference in the Nepalese *Vaṃśāvalīs* (Chronicles) to one Yashodharā fleeing in the reign of Shankaradeva with the *Prajñāpāramitā* written in the year 225 in letters of gold must refer to the Nepal era (the date equals AD 1105), rather than to the chronicle's explicit citation of the Vikrama era (*i.e.* AD 170), when only palm leaf and birch bark were available for manuscripts. The occasional attempts to fix gold on to palm leaves as in the miniatures of the *Pañcarakṣā* dated *c.*1057 (No.4) show how difficult it was; an entire manuscript in gold script would have been impossible to fix. So the reference must be to paper and hence corroborates the early dates for the two 12th-century manuscripts on paper from Nepal (No.11).

The earliest illustrated manuscripts are found from the last two centuries before the collapse of the old Hindu states system about

1200 – a few pairs of manuscript covers from Kashmir in a style more related to Central Asian painting than to that of India, a considerable number of illustrated palm-leaf manuscripts and covers of Buddhist texts from eastern India under the Pāla dynasty and from Nepal in a closely related style, whence come also a few Hindu ones, and a much smaller number of Jaina examples from Gujarat and Rajasthan, with one isolated Jaina example from Karnataka. Are they merely the accidental survivals of a much more widespread tradition, with many centuries of development behind them? Or are they the earliest survivals of a tradition that only began at about the same time?

The Indian texts of the first millennium AD are full of references to painting. We read of pictures painted on walls, of picture galleries, of painted wooden panels or paintings on cloth, of the art of portraiture. There are various technical manuals besides, on how to prepare surfaces and means of achieving certain technical effects such as foreshortening. We can still see the pitifully few remnants of the classic art of fresco painting at sites such as Ajantā and Ellora, and see that the manuals and artistic practice usually agree. The Tibetan historian Tāranātha has given us a valuable account of the different styles of painting practised in ancient India. There are, however, no references whatever to the illustration of manuscripts, whether of palm leaf or birch bark. Any *argumentum ex silentio* is not necessarily decisive in an Indian context, and since so few Indian manuscripts pre-date the 11th century we would still perhaps be justified in keeping our options open. However, the evidence of Central Asia may perhaps be taken into account, where innumerable leaves and fragments of Indian-language manuscripts, on palm leaf, birch bark and paper, in date from the 2nd century to the 10th, have been discovered. Not one of them bears an illustration. It is immaterial in this context whether these manuscripts were actually written in India or in Central Asia. Had the art been at all widespread in India we could legitimately expect some evidence to turn up in Central Asia, either in a fragment of Indian provenance, or in a Central Asian imitation of an Indian manuscript, for where in script and format the Central Asian scribes imitated Indian exemplars, they would surely have imitated illuminations also. It is noteworthy that the only illustrated manuscript material to be unearthed in Central Asia is either of Chinese inspiration or of Manichaean origin, and we know from Arabic sources of the habit of the Iranian Manichaeans of illustrating their manuscripts, an art learnt from the Byzantines. It is quite possible, however, that the illustration of wooden covers would have had a period of some development before 1000, especially in western India and Kashmir, and our remarks here apply only to the actual folios of manuscripts.

If then it would seem unlikely that the illustration of palm-leaf manuscripts did not occur much before about the year 1000, what was the inspiration that started them along this path? The earliest decorated Jaina manuscripts from 1060 contain drawings and diagrams, with coloured miniatures not appearing until the 12th century, so that we must suppose that the art originated in eastern India and Nepal, and spread to other areas of western and southern India, *i.e.* it originated in a specifically Buddhist environment. Now it is noteworthy that none of the early manuscripts are in fact 'illustrated' in the sense of the pictures illustrating events described in the text. The most favoured Buddhist text by far, the *Prajñāpāramitā*, is a work of the most abstruse metaphysics, on the nature of Buddhahood, Bodhisattvahood, and of Wisdom. The miniatures used to illustrate it are usually of the Buddhas, transcendental (the Jinas) or Mortal, the Bodhisattvas, goddesses, and fearsome divinities, and the eight great events in the life of Gautama the Buddha. Their presence in the manuscript has no connection with the text itself, which is far earlier than the developments of the Mahāyāna which led to the proliferation of these divinities. The manuscripts were generally commissioned by pious laymen as acts guaranteeing spiritual merit, the greatest rewards coming from manuscripts of the greatest beauty. In the Tantric school of Buddhism prevalent in eastern India at this time, the act of painting a *maṇḍala* or an equivalent was more a spiritual than an artistic exercise, and meditation on the depicted divinities for the initiate served to concentrate the mind on one or other aspects of the divine. It was these developments in Vajrayāna Buddhism which would seem to have precipitated the illustration of manuscripts to form, as it were, *maṇḍalas* in miniature, bringing divine aid to the protection of the manuscripts and to the spiritual well-being of both donor and artist.

Technically, the possibilities of decorating palm-leaf manuscripts are limited by the nature of the medium itself. The decorative elements apart from calligraphy are threefold. Firstly, small figurative paintings occupying the centre of a leaf, or sometimes two or three such paintings occupying the centres of the two or three columns of text into which a large leaf would be divided, the number of stringholes being the deciding factor in the arrangement of the columns. Such paintings invariably occupy the full height of a leaf, but rarely exceed that measurement in width, and are usually contained within painted margins. If larger compositions were essayed, utilizing the entire width of the leaf, none has survived; it is improbable that this could have been a standard feature as the tension generated by the turning of leaves in such manuscripts results in flaking of the painted surface to a far greater extent than in painted paper leaves of a manuscript in codex format.

8 ff.136b, 137 (details). The Bodhisattvas Maitreya (?) and Avalokiteshvara (?) – by the 12th century, iconographical standards had collapsed in painting (No.8, p.33).

A second decorative possibility was afforded by the margins between the columns of text and at the edges. Many surviving manuscripts have painted geometrical and arabesque designs on at least all those leaves which contain paintings (Nos.5–9); while a very few have little figures of monks, worshippers, the Buddha, *caityas* etc. in these positions (No.10). Related to this type of decoration is the provision of little vignettes of animals or flowers or diagrams to mark chapter endings as in No.8 where it is restricted to those leaves which already have central paintings on them. The third element was the wooden binding-boards (*paṭa*) at top and bottom of the manuscript, both inside and outside, on which could be painted much larger compositions than was possible on the leaves.

The most usual cycle in Buddhist manuscripts is of 18 paintings arranged in groups of six, with three per side, at beginning, middle, and end of the manuscripts of the *Prajñāpāramitā*, consisting usually of the eight great miracles in the life of the Buddha, some of the five Jinas (transcendent Buddhas), the goddess Prajñāpāramitā, and some of the great Bodhisattvas (Nos.2, 5–6, 9). One Pāla manuscript of this text originally had no fewer than 78 paintings, with in addition to the cycle of 18, a pair of paintings marking the end of each of the 32 chapters (No.8), forming perhaps a most complex *maṇḍala*. Other Buddhist texts have different cycles. The *Pañcarakṣā*, a set of five charms dedicated to five different protective goddesses, is illustrated with their images, and sometimes in addition those of the five Jinas to whom they are linked (No.4). The illustrations of the *Kāraṇḍavyūhasūtra* are known only from an incomplete manuscript; here each of the 53 surviving folios (which comprise the bulk of the text) contains two paintings, and uniquely among Pāla manuscripts, some of the narrative episodes in the *sūtra* are illustrated (No.10). The Lotus Sūtra, despite the immense popularity of the scripture, is usually illustrated only by one or two introductory paintings, as are a few other Buddhist texts.

The wooden covers gave much greater scope and freedom to the artist than the restricted space available on one of the folios, but only rarely was the opportunity taken to depict a fully integrated painting (No.12). More usually the covers were divided into compartments, with scenes from the life of Buddha on one, and Prajñāpāramitā with attendants and worshippers on the other. However, there are very few examples of a Pāla manuscript surviving complete with its original painted covers, which were the parts of the manuscript most exposed to damage; the *Prajñāpāramitā* in the Museum of Fine Arts in Boston dated *c.*1134 is perhaps one of them. It is quite possible that none of the 11th-century manuscripts had illustrated covers, as the covers must have been deemed less intimately connected with the text itself, and less capable of imparting magical protection. Only two sets of covers are of possible 11th-century date, both of Nepalese origin, enclosing unillustrated manuscripts dated 1028 and 1054 – however, these covers do not fit into the stylistic development of Nepalese painting between two securely dated manuscripts of 1015 (No.3) and 1071 and are more likely to be 12th century; it was in this century and the next that many Nepalese covers were given to earlier Nepalese and Pāla manuscripts (see Nos.2, 3, 5, and 9).

Turning to the Jaina manuscripts, we can see that again the miniatures do not illustrate the text but are rather images of Jaina divinities. The Tantric element that led to the illustration of Buddhist manuscripts is apparent in Jainism to a much lesser extent, but even so the *Vidyādevīs* (goddesses of wisdom), the Jaina equivalent of the Buddhist Prajñāpāramitā, occur in two of the surviving documents, on a pair of covers (No.15) which show significant influence from Pāla art and on the leaves of a manuscript dated 1161, where their function can only be magically protective. The earliest surviving illustrated Jaina manuscript is dated 1060, and has delightful drawings of the goddess Shrī and the love-god Kāma, with elephants, vases etc., and other manuscripts of this date have drawings of lotuses and diagrams in similar style. They apparently continue a tradition found in birch-bark manuscripts (No.1). Illustrated manuscripts with paintings are not found before the 12th century, and have just a few opening illustrations of the Jinas, the gods and goddesses, various monks, including sometimes possibly the authors of the work, and the patrons of the manuscript. No large-scale iconographic sequence is attempted, except possibly for the *Vidyādevī* sequence, nor in any 12th-century manuscripts is there any attempt at a narrative sequence illustrating the texts. The texts chosen for illumination are not confined to a few favourites as with the Buddhists, but include various parts of the Jaina Canon or its commentaries. It is only by accident that these illustrated manuscripts have survived rather than others, but it is not without significance that they are all canonical texts, and that the miniatures in them have no connection whatever with the text. In other words, they must be serving the same purpose as the Buddhist miniatures, that of magical protection of the text and the bestowing of benefits on the donor. The same is true of the only known illuminated Digambara palm-leaf manuscript, a group of semi-canonical works on *karma* dated *c.*1112 from southern India which has the same set of miniatures – divinities, donors, monks, etc. The earliest miniatures which actually occur in texts capable of illustration are of early 13th-century date in works on the lives of Mahāvīra and Neminātha, but the opportunity so to do is not taken, and the miniatures are simply of the Jinas and the donors. In fact, the earliest manuscript with narrative paintings is dated 1288, a *Subāhukathā*, with 23 miniatures, and the earliest such manuscript of the *Kalpasūtra*, the life of the Jina Mahāvīra which was the standard text for illustration and presentation in the 15th and 16th centuries, is not for another century, and is dated 1370. Even this has only six miniatures, and it is not until the roughly contemporary *Kalpasūtra* from Idar that there is a manuscript with a set of 34 miniatures fully illustrating the narrative portions of the *Kalpasūtra*. By this time of course there was considerable influence from the Islamic world on the arts of India, and it is quite possible that narrative paintings in Jaina manuscripts are in imitation of the Persian book-arts. From the subject-matter of the miniatures in these Jaina manuscripts which we have traced from 1060 to 1370, it would appear that the art of manuscript illustration must have begun in western India only in the 11th century, and doubtless under the stimulus of emulating Buddhist manuscripts. The drawings in the 11th-century manuscripts, the lack of fixed iconographical schemes in those of the 12th century, the slow realization of the possibilities of narrative illustration, all point to this conclusion.

On the other hand, the paintings on the covers (*paṭlīs*) of Jaina manuscripts seem infinitely more assured than those on palm leaves, and it is possible that there is a longer tradition behind them. There are indeed references in Jaina literature to painting *paṭṭakas*, which may be cloth or wood panels. The Jaina covers from western India are concerned quite often with historical events of importance to the Jainas, such as the meeting between the Shvetambara Jaina polymath Vādi Devasūri and the Digambara scholar Kumudachandra for the purposes of theological debate in 1124 at the court of Siddharāja Jayasimha of Gujarat, or the consecration of the temple of Mahāvīra at Marot in Marwar by the famous Jaina *ācārya* Jinadatta Sūri (No.16). Quite a large proportion of the 20 or so surviving Jaina *paṭlīs* do not depict either historical events or standard divinities, but on one of their sides include a flowering creeper motif which loops around a large variety of birds and animals – monkeys, geese, elephants, even a giraffe – revealing a delight in nature that is one of the enduring motifs of western Indian painting (No.15).

Calligraphically these manuscripts are of great beauty, especially the Buddhist ones. The script used in the latter is the ornamental *Siddhamātṛkā* ('Perfect-measure') or *Kuṭila* (crooked) script, so called from the marked twist at the bottom of the vertical stroke of each character ending in the finest of points. At its best the characters proceed with measured and even tread across the leaf, the heavy horizontal and vertical strokes being balanced by the lighter curves between of the characteristic portions of the letter, by the sublinear twist and by the flourishes of vowel indicators above the line, most markedly above the top line. This script was already archaic by the 11th century. In this particular form it is found only in manuscripts from the Buddhist monasteries. The Buddhist manuscripts from Nepal tend to use the early *Nāgarī* script to much lighter effect, although some have the *Siddhamātṛkā* (No.3). However, in Nepal from the 15th century there was an archaistic revival of the *Kuṭila*, called *Rañjanā*, using gold ink on blue-black paper. Although the effect of these manuscripts is of great richness, the *Rañjanā* is a complex character of no great calligraphic beauty, being heavy in effect without comparable dignity. It is moreover an almost unreadable character, and was probably never intended to be otherwise, for the texts written in it are of a very limited range and copied for pious purposes of donation to monasteries. There they remained wrapped and unread – like the earlier *Kuṭila* manuscripts brought from India, except for the annual *pustakapūjā*, or book-worshipping day, when they were placed on public view and their covers anointed with sandal-paste, which still adheres to many of them (No.7).

The script used in the western Jaina manuscripts was an early form of *Nāgarī* with characteristics that mark it out as Jaina — special forms of certain letters and diphthongal signs which normally protrude above the line always occurring before the letter (e and o) or with a combination of both (ai and au). It is an elegant rather than monumental script, and remained characteristic of the Shvetambara Jainas until the 18th century. The southern Digambara Jaina manuscripts used an early Kannada hand, of no particular beauty.

All the early illustrated palm-leaf manuscripts which have survived from eastern India are of Buddhist texts, while all those from western and southern India are of Jaina ones. The Buddhist manuscripts owe their survival to having been taken to Nepal by monks fleeing the destruction of their monasteries by the Turkish invaders about 1200, and deposited usually in temple libraries there. The Jaina ones were in any case deposited in *bhaṇḍārs* or libraries attached to temples in Jaina strongholds in western and southern India such as Jaiselmer, Patan, Cambay and Moodabidri, and they and their contents have survived to the present day. There are no survivals of a Hindu tradition of manuscript illustration in India from this time, but there certainly was one in Nepal, represented by documents from the 12th and 13th centuries (Nos.13, 14). The dated Buddhist documents from India are all in the regnal years of the Pāla monarchs, who were Buddhist, except for one manuscript dated in the reign of the Hindu monarch of south Bengal, Harivarman, to which area one more manuscript can be assigned on stylistic grounds (No.10), but it would be dangerous on account of the paucity of early manuscript material from Hindu Bengal to argue that Hindu illustrated manuscripts should also have survived had any been done there. Jaina *bhaṇḍārs* in western India have a catholic content that includes early and important manuscripts of Buddhist and Hindu texts, but no early Hindu illustrated manuscript is to be found in them. Again one can argue no case for this that the Hindus of western India did not decorate their manuscripts as the number of Jaina illustrated ones is in any case extremely small. We have argued above that the Hindus of India did not have a proper manuscript and library tradition until later, so it is in any case unlikely that there would have been many illustrated ones from this time, but we cannot at this stage rule out the possibility. From the Nepalese evidence it is clear that Hindu illustrated manuscripts are far outweighed in number by Buddhist ones, as is to be expected, even though it would appear that the number of adherents of both religions in Nepal at this time was roughly equal.

From the evidence presented by later illustrated manuscripts of Hindu, and Muslim, texts from Bengal (No.43), Assam (Nos.119–22) and Orissa (Nos.115–8), in which there are stylistic continuities of the Pāla tradition, the most striking being the placing of figures under scalloped arches or their derivatives, whether in interior or exterior scenes, it is possible to argue that the Pāla style could not have been confined just to artists working in Buddhist monasteries, but must have been widespread throughout eastern India, at least in wall paintings, if not in manuscripts, and that likewise it must have been used for Hindu paintings, even though the earliest of these manuscripts is of 16th-century date. The former point is indeed proven by the covers of the 1446 Buddhist manuscript from Arrah in Bihar (No.31), which are descended in style directly from the Pāla tradition, but 250 years after the destruction of the monasteries of Nālandā and Vikramashīla.

If, as we believe, manuscripts were first illustrated in India about AD 1000 specifically to add magical power and protection to the manuscripts of the *Prajñāpāramitā*, it is hardly to be wondered at that there are so few Hindu manuscripts illustrated, as there would have been hardly any occasion to do so. The precise iconographic depiction of a deity as an aid to meditation did not have the same force or rationale in Hinduism as in Tantric Buddhism. Those Hindu illustrated manuscripts which have survived from Nepal are identical in style to the Buddhist ones, coming often perhaps from the same brush, but painted without the same religious and philosophical significance. The pair of covers (No.13) showing the avatars of Vishnu, for example, is decidedly odd iconographically; the image of Vishnu *Anantaśayana* (lying on the snake Ananta) seems to be confused with Brahmā in the multi-headed form of the recumbent divinity, while some of the avatars are conventional Bodhisattva representations. The hand which painted them was more used by far to Buddhist manuscripts.

Any discussion of the style of the Pāla Buddhist manuscripts is hampered by the paucity of securely dated and provenanced material. The dated manuscripts are all given in the regnal years of kings, with no distinctions between them even if there be more than one king of the same name – three Gopālas, two Mahīpālas, etc. Opinion is also divided as to the chronology of the Pāla monarchs, both relative and absolute. Only five of the illustrated manuscripts give their provenance – three come from the great monastic university of Nālandā (Nos.5, 9) one from the monastery of Vikramashīla (No.7), and one much damaged, from Uddandapuri (Bodleian Ms. Sansk. c.13(R). Absolutely fixed are the manuscripts dated in the reigns of Nayapāla (*c*.1043–58), Rāmapāla (*c*.1082–1130), and Govindapāla (1161–*c*.1170), which group includes two of the manuscripts from Nālandā.

The styles employed vary considerably. On the one hand is a style which employs a sinuous and flowing line able of itself to suggest volume, which is also achieved through gradations of colour tone, in harmoniously composed groups of figures (usually exemplified by part of the Mahīpāla manuscript in the Asiatic Society Library, Calcutta); on the other is a style which uses an angular and distorted line and flat colour planes with only the most perfunctory attempts at modelling, in

2 ff.127b, 128 (details). The Buddha is offered honey by the monkeys, and tames the elephant Nalagiri, two of the eight great episodes from his life (No.2, p.30).

simplified groups (the other Mahīpāla manuscript in Cambridge University Library) (No.2). Attempts have been made to classify the first of these styles as 'early Pāla' because of its affinity with the classical frescoes at Ajantā, and the brittle style as 'late Pāla' because of its affinity with the norm in medieval Indian painting from the 14th century on. However, neither Mahīpāla manuscript can be later than *c.*1070, firmly in the centre of the probable time span covered by the surviving manuscripts (*c.*1000–1170), while manuscript paintings of unquestionably later date (those dated in the reigns of Rāmapāla and Govindapāla, Nos.5, 6, 9) show in their handling of modelling and line more of an affinity with the so-called 'early' style than with the 'late' one.

A more profitable line of enquiry towards establishing a relative chronology lies perhaps in an analysis of the iconographic content of the paintings, and the way in which certain conventions from the first half of the period are misunderstood by painters in the latter half. A notable example is the use of thrones, cushions and haloes. It is usual for seated divinities in manuscripts dated in the Rāmapāla period to have a lotus or double-lotus base beneath them, and a cushion behind them, which hides the lower part of a throne-back, the top of which protrudes above the cushion on either side of the divinity's head. They can also have a double halo, a small one round the head and a larger one around the entire body encompassing also the small halo. The earliest securely dated manuscript to show the double halo is the Nayapāla manuscript in Cambridge (No.4) of *c.*1057, but this has no throne-backs or cushions. Of the two manuscripts dated in the reign of Mahīpāla I (*c.*995–1043) or II (*c.*1075–80) which are either slightly later than the Nayapāla manuscript or 50 years earlier, the Calcutta manuscript has double haloes while the Cambridge manuscript (No.2) has a small, single one. As for the throne-backs, in the Rāmapāla period, artists either no longer recognized them for what they were or else deliberately ignored their real nature, for the throne-top is tilted at right angles to the axis of the divinity's head. They have often been termed flames issuing from the divinities' shoulders. Moreover, the standing Buddha and the Buddha lying down in his *parinirvāṇa* scene are each encumbered with cushion and throne-top, and with double haloes also in the latest manuscripts. The standing Buddhas in the Calcutta Mahīpāla manuscript display the accompanying throne-back and cushion, while many of the divinities also display the double halo, features which would seem to argue against the early date (*c.*1000, in the reign of Mahīpāla I) suggested for it. With the possible exception of one miniature, that of the birth of the Buddha, there is nothing in this manuscript that necessarily places it much earlier than Rāmapāla manuscripts, with which it is stylistically linked. On the other hand, the Cambridge Mahīpāla manuscript does not display any of these features, so that on iconographic grounds we arrive paradoxically at the conclusion diametrically opposite to that usually propounded for these two manuscripts on stylistic grounds, namely that the Calcutta manuscript belongs to the Mahīpāla I period and the Cambridge to Mahīpāla II. We believe the precise opposite to be true, and date them *c.*1080 and *c.*1000 respectively. An early dating for the Cambridge manuscript is suggested by other arguments also (see No.2).

An examination of the evidence from Nepal reinforces these arguments. There are two incontrovertibly 11th-century illustrated manuscripts from Nepal, dated 135/1015 in Cambridge University Library

(No.3) and 191/1071 in the Asiatic Society, Calcutta. These display the same format, the same type of text as the Pāla manuscripts, except that the paintings are mostly accompanied by a caption identifying the subject as a divinity from, or worshipped in, such and such a locality. Frequently, the painting shows the divinity as an image, *i.e.* as a painted representation of a statue, with accompanying small worshippers. Where this is not the case, we may take the painting to be the iconographic representation of the particular aspect of the divinity worshipped in a particular location.

Stylistically, the two manuscripts vary greatly. The earlier is a vigorous, but crude, provincial style, the latter the most perfect of all surviving illustrated manuscripts of the period, in line, modelling, colouring and composition. Both, however, are distinctively and unmistakably Nepalese, even though they have not yet developed the characteristics of the true Nepalese style of the 12th century, as they are presumably closer to the vanished Indian school of painting from which both the Nepalese and Pāla styles spring. In both are missing the conventions of throne-backs and cushions which have been discussed above, while in neither has any divinity more than one, small halo. It would be an extreme position to argue from Nepalese evidence that all Pāla paintings displaying these characteristics must be later than 1071, but it is nonetheless a powerful piece of corroborating evidence that they are so.

The crudity of the Nepalese manuscript of 1015 strikes a chord when compared with that of the Cambridge Mahīpāla manuscript, the crudity not of provincial backwardness but of stylistic innovation, and it is possible that these two manuscripts (Nos.2, 3) represent the earliest attempts to produce illustrated palm-leaf manuscripts in Nepal and eastern India. We have seen that there are no literary references to the illustration of manuscripts in earlier works mentioning paintings, but art-historians have argued that the comparative perfection of the Calcutta Mahīpāla manuscript proved a definite stylistic link with a school of post-Gupta fresco painting in eastern India. However, if we accept the re-ordering of the illustrated Pāla manuscripts proposed here on iconographic grounds, there are only three manuscripts earlier than the Calcutta 'classic' manuscripts of 1071 from Nepal and the Mahīpāla manuscript of *c.*1080, viz. the Cambridge Mahīpāla manuscript (*c.*1000) and Nayapāla manuscript (*c.*1057), and the Cambridge Nepal manuscript of 1015, all of which are experimental in style. The first of these (No.2) employs garish colours, a jerky, unfluent line, with faces fixed in perpetual grimaces. As for the so-called crudity of the paintings of the Nepalese manuscript of 1015 (No.3) they are in an extremely vigorous style that lacks the classical harmony displayed by the 1071 manuscript in Calcutta; an artist is coming to grips for the first time possibly with the problems of reducing to a tiny scale paintings on a much larger scale, and he is tempted to cram too much in. The paintings in this manuscript are astonishingly detailed for their tiny compass, and in addition to the main figure and its shrine, often contain numerous other figures or objects or details of landscape. By the time of the 1071 manuscript a truer art of manuscript illustration had been developed. It had been realized that it was not possible to cram so much in without sacrificing plastic qualities which the artists also valued; thus in the later manuscript the central figures are much larger, the architectural elements have been greatly

4 ff.19b, 20 (details). Two of the group of divinities accompanying Mahāmāyūrī – the Bodhisattva Maitreya, and the goddess Tārā (No.4, p.31).

reduced, and the subsidiary figures much more sensibly organized. The result is a truer art of book illustration, even though at the sacrifice of the vigour of the earlier style. No material is available between these two dates to enable us to see this process in transition. The Nayapāla manuscript (No.4) is a definite improvement technically, but experiments with the gilding of the flesh of all the human figures, a none too successful experiment as most of it has disappeared. It was not apparently repeated in the later Pāla manuscripts. We are here, it seems, witnessing early attempts to translate styles used in fresco or other large-scale paintings into a miniature compass, and it is not to be supposed that the techniques to do so could be acquired immediately or that the translation could be accomplished without a crashing of gears. From the available evidence it took about 70 years to evolve both the classic Pāla style which we associate with the reigns of Mahīpāla II, Rāmapāla, and Gopāla III, covering the period *c.*1075–1143, and the classic Nepalese style.

The iconographic peculiarities of the Pāla school such as throne-backs and cushions accompanying the standing Buddha argue a school that was becoming increasingly atrophied and decadent, and they are common to all the later manuscripts. No doubt the earlier manuscripts contained paintings that were scaled-down versions of larger frescoes or *paṭas*, but once an iconographic norm had been established the evidence suggests that the paintings were copied from existing patterns almost by rote. Mistakes of iconography that crept in by misunderstanding were irreversible. Many of the Bodhisattvas in the later manuscripts are unidentifiable, they have no attributes peculiar to themselves. Colours can be arbitrarily changed, even in the lovely manuscript dated in the 36th year of Rāmapāla (No.6) where the artist has adopted a colour scheme of blue throughout and sticks rigidly to it, despite the clear weight of tradition and evidence from other manuscripts that green is required.

Nonetheless, if we ignore the peculiarities of some of the miniatures depicting the scenes from the life of the Buddha, these tiny miniatures in the classic Pāla period of painting (Nos.5–9) are of a grace and beauty which belies the decline of the religion they serve, having arrived at a peak of classical perfection. The crudities of the earlier manuscripts have been ironed out. Only the bare essentials for iconographic comprehensibility are included now in the miniatures. The Bodhisattvas sit in graceful pose on lotus seats with often no background other than the halo which is their radiant emanation of light. Flaking of the paint reveals the beauty and sureness of the line, its superb expression of the mercy and compassion which is the essence of Bodhisattvahood.

The Pāla kingdom was reduced by rival Hindu dynasties to a small territory round Gayā by the reign of Govindapāla (commencing in 1161), and even this was destroyed soon afterwards. There are no illustrated Indian Buddhist manuscripts dated after this last reign, although there are some undated ones assigned to this period. The Buddhist monasteries and with them the traditions of Pāla painting were destroyed by the Turkish onslaught which swept across the north Indian plain after the Battle of Tarain in 1192. Of the rest of eastern India outside the Pāla dominions, only one illustrated manuscript has so far been published. Dated in the reign of Harivarman, one of a Vaishnava dynasty which ruled in south-eastern Bengal about 1100, it is a Buddhist manuscript of the *Prajñāpāramitā* in one of its longest recensions. In a related style, but linked architecturally more to the Sena dominions of south-western Bengal, is a newly discovered manuscript of the *Kāraṇḍavyūhasūtra* (No.10) which even in an incomplete state is the most heavily illustrated manuscript to survive from this period. Both are in a simplified Pāla style, with neatly drawn figures, but eschewing any attempt at the sophisticated modelling practised under the Pālas. The *Kāraṇḍavyūha* is however remarkable for its being the only Buddhist manuscript of the period to attempt narrative illustration – a few of its miniatures actually represent the events described in the text.

In Nepal, the 12th century was a kind of plateau in her achievement in the art of manuscript illustration. The heights reached in the 1071 manuscript were not attained again, but a number of very fine manuscripts and covers survive from the period, including two on paper (No.11). From the 13th century on, the best painters in Nepal must have found even the comparatively large paintings in the 1185 manuscript (No.11) too cramping, and concentrated exclusively on large-scale paintings on cloth (*paṭa*), while manuscript illumination developed a rigidity that argues a dying art even in so fine a piece of painting as the Devī in No.14. The technique here is brilliant, but the effect is cold; the pliancy and fluency of line and colouring in earlier Nepalese work has disappeared, leaving a hardness of line and a monotonous approach to colour modelling that is impressive in so tiny a compass but ultimately unsatisfying. Similar rigidity is to be observed in all later manuscript illustrations, but largely without compensatory brilliance. The collapse of the Hindu and Buddhist kingdoms of northern India after 1192 left Nepal isolated culturally as well as politically. Removed from the Indian states system, she continued in isolation for many centuries, and her manuscript traditions need not concern us again.

The much greater rarity of illustrated Jaina manuscripts on palm leaves does not permit us to indulge in any large-scale discussion of stylistic development. All these manuscripts were preserved in the Jaina *bhaṇḍārs* of Rajasthan and Gujarat, with the exception of a group from Moodabidri in Karnataka, and in the absence of evidence to the contrary we must assume that the manuscripts concerned were produced in these areas of western and southern India. The Jainas in the 11th and 12th centuries were by no means unrepresented in other areas of India, and may have illustrated their manuscripts. But it is only where safe refuges could be provided in the underground *bhaṇḍārs* that any have survived, and it is to the latter that these manuscripts owe their survival.

We must first separate on grounds of style the painted wooden covers from the illustrated palm leaves. This we can easily do as there is in fact no connection between them. None of the surviving covers is now attached to a manuscript, illustrated or otherwise; none of the manuscripts with illustrations has a painted cover. This separation of the two seems to have been largely the case in eastern India also, where only one Pāla manuscript has survived with its original cover. Now the Jaina covers, of which the earliest appears to be late 11th century, are painted with a technical assurance that argues an already existing school of *paṭa*-painting. The style is somewhat more angular and linear than Pāla art at this time, but it is still capable of expressing considerable plasticity through modelling and indeed through the line itself. The narrative technique is fluent, as in the great Devasūri–Kumudạchandra confrontation, with the different episodes of the story spaced out along both sides of the cover but interlocking.

The miniatures on the 12th-century palm leaves on the other hand are of much greater crudity, even though they use the same basic technique and artistic vocabulary, and this crudity is a constant factor throughout the manuscripts of this and the next century. In the 13th century, the basic vocabulary has practically disintegrated and it took another century to fashion a new one, as we see in the 1370 *Kalpasūtra* in the Ujjamphoi Dharmasāla Bhandār in Ahmadabad. Attempts at plasticity have disappeared, the linear technique has triumphed, but it is now one that also imposes fixed distortions and angularities. The further projecting eye, of which there are hints as early as the Ajantā and Ellora frescoes, occurs in the book-covers as well as the palm-leaf illustrations; in the former it co-exists happily with the generally plastic approach, in the latter it becomes part of the angularity and distortion. The free rendition of the human figure in the earlier work is impossible in the later, figures must stand, sit or lie in only the one position, their clothing disposed in only the one way. To compensate for these conformings to stereotypes, artists were allowed freedom of colouring and textile design which in the hands of the master who painted the Ujjamphoi *Kalpasūtra* afford it a grace and delicacy not achieved before. In this manuscript and the approximately contemporary Idar *Kalpasūtra* we can see that the narrative iconography of the *Kalpasūtra* is fixed and is the same as the Bombay paper manuscript of the same date, but we cannot as yet determine the source for it. This must have occurred in Gujarat during the course of the 14th century, doubtless at a centre like Pattan which could impose it on others. Although palm leaves continued to be illustrated in western India for another century, new developments occur only in the paper manuscripts.

1 'Vinayavastu' of the Mūlasarvāstivādins

The rules of monastic discipline in Sanskrit of the Mūlasarvāstivādins, one of the schools of Hīnayāna Buddhism, compiled about the 4th century AD. This school seems to have had its stronghold in Kashmir and Gandhara. Its *Vinaya* contains in addition to the usual monastic regulations a large number of illustrative stories (*avadānas*) and *sūtras* so that it forms one of the most important sources for the study of early Indian narrative literature. The discovery of almost the entire work at Gilgit in its Sanskrit original (being previously known only from its Tibetan and Chinese translations) was one of the greatest literary discoveries of this century.

The whole Ms., consisting apparently of some 423 almost perfectly preserved leaves of birch bark of great size (12 × 66cm), superbly written in the Gupta characters of the 7th–8th century, was dug out of a collapsed *stūpa* at Gilgit in 1931. This is a Ms. of the finest quality, of austere grandeur. The birch bark is of good quality, smooth and of even colour, with attractive darker brown lenticels running across the leaf. Of decorative elements there are only large circles which mark the end of one of the major divisions of the *Vinaya* (as on f.53a), and the smaller circles which mark off verse passages. The final folio contains three very large decorated circles, apparently *dharmacakras*, the Buddhist Wheel of the Law.[1] The folios are numbered on the recto, on the left. The stringhole is a third of the way along from the left, and sits in solitary splendour in a blank square, four lines deep. Its undamaged state suggests the whole Ms. was little used, as constant friction of the leaves over the cord would in course of time have produced considerable damage. It was doubtless a presentation Ms., given to the Buddhist monk whose relics were enshrined in the *stūpa* at Gilgit along with his library. The remainder of the Ms. is in the National Archives, New Delhi, and a private collection in Lahore.

British Library, London, Or.11878A.

ff.11 (numbered 43–53); 12 × 66cm; birch bark; ten lines of north-western Gupta script; in glass.

Bibliography: Lévi 1932.

[1]See reproduction in Vira and Chandra 1974.

1 f.53. Birch-bark folio, with roundels noting chapter ends.

2 'Aṣṭasāhasrikā Prajñāpāramitā'

Illustrated on p.25.

The Perfection of Wisdom in 8,000 Sections, one of the earliest works of Mahāyāna Buddhism, originating probably in the Andhra country of southern India about the 2nd century AD. The 32 chapters are of metaphysical speculation on the nature of Buddhahood, Bodhisattvahood, and of Wisdom. This is the earliest text of the Perfection of Wisdom cycle; in subsequent centuries it was both expanded (to 25,000 sections) and contracted (to a few brief verses).

This palm-leaf manuscript was copied in the fifth regnal year of the Pāla monarch Mahīpāla. The rest of the colophon is much rubbed, but the Ms. was commissioned by one Lāḍākā (?), the daughter of Bahubhūti. The Ms. originally had six illustrated folios, with three paintings on each, of which only five have survived, the opening leaf being a later replacement without illustration. The covers are slightly larger, with interior paintings, and are replacements of 12th-century date from Nepal.

The date of this Ms. is controversial, owing to the colophon's not stating which of the two Pāla monarchs named Mahīpāla is meant; the fifth year of either being equivalent to *c.*1000 or 1080. Bendall in his Catalogue is inclined to identify the difficult to read Lāḍākā, the donor of this Ms., with the Queen Uḍḍākā, who is the donor of No.4, which is firmly dated in the 14th year of Nayapāla, *c.*1057, where she is described as *paramopāsikārājñī*, the 'devoutly Buddhist Queen'. If she is the same woman, then her description as Bahubhūti's daughter necessarily must precede chronologically her description as Nayapāla's queen, so that there can be no question of her donating a Ms. in the reign of Mahīpāla II which occurred after the reign of Nayapāla. Stylistically this fits very well, for reasons advanced above, on the comparative crudeness of these miniatures. Early features include details such as the single halo only, the possibility that the round-headed arches under which the figures sit are the prototype of the large body haloes of later Pāla painting, and the absence of the characteristic Pāla dip in the upper eyelid (a universal feature of the Rāmapāla-period manuscripts) and of other late features such as moving thronebacks and cushions.

The painted covers are both slightly larger and were made for some other manuscript in Nepal in the 12th century. They are extremely beautiful, with wonderfully-fluent figure modelling; on one is the Buddha and attendant Bodhisattvas, on the other Prajñāpāramitā with attendants.

University Library, Cambridge, Add.1464.

ff.227; 5 × 53·5cm; talipot leaves; *Kuṭila* script, six lines; 15 miniatures, 5 × 4·5cm; wooden boards, 5·5 × 54cm.

Bibliography: CUL 1883 pp.100–1, and pl.II, 1. Saraswati, 1977, figs. 261–3 in colour.

3 'Aṣṭasāhasrikā Prajñāpāramitā'

The Perfection of Wisdom in 8,000 Sections (see No.2).

This manuscript was copied by one Sujātabhadra in the Nepalese year 135/1015 in the ancient and famous monastery of Śrī Hlam, the whereabouts of which is not known to us, in the joint reigns of Bhojadeva, Rudradeva and Lakshmīkāmadeva (the Nepalese king often adopted the system of joint reigns with sons and other relatives). It is written in a transitional *Kuṭila* script, in which the angle at the bottom of the vertical strokes is scarcely noticeable. Another hand, that of Karunavajra, added a second colophon in 259/1139, stating that the *Prajñāpāramitā* was rescued by him when fallen into the hands of unbelievers. This note is in the hooked Nepalese script or *Bhujmoli*, one of its earliest attestations. A third hand, probably the original scribe, has added notes in a more cursive script, almost a *Bhujmoli* underneath most of the 85 paintings in the manuscript, informing us of the name of the divinity and the whereabouts of the shrine containing this particular image. Similar inscriptions occur in the manuscript of the same text dated 191/1071 in Calcutta, and these two documents are unique in their importance in this respect for their evidence of iconography and the main shrines of Vajrayāna worship. Foucher has noted that the first 26 of the inscriptions all end with the phrase – *āriṣasthāna*, *i.e. ālekhyasthāna*, the scribe's note to the illuminator to insert a miniature here of the deity so indicated, and that the appropriate chapter end is likewise indicated. In the later miniatures he simply wrote the name of the deity involved, the purpose by then being obvious. The miniatures were obviously added after the text was written, as the paint occasionally goes over the edges of letters. There is however no good reason to doubt that these miniatures are contemporary with the original date of the colophon, although doubts have recently been expressed on the grounds of the painting's comparative crudity and resemblance to certain manuscripts of the 13th and 14th centuries.[1] However, the possibility of their being so late is excluded, as Foucher pointed out, by the writer of the second colophon in 1139 actually writing over the paint of some of the miniatures on the last page. The substance of the text of the inscriptions at the beginning of the Ms. is a sufficient indication that they were instructions to a painter, either from the scribe or someone competent to choose an iconographic scheme for the Ms. Nor need this very early attestation of the *Bhujmoli* script in the inscriptions deter us from accepting this date of 1015 for the paintings. Bendall's earliest Ms. in this script is dated 1165; the second colophon of the 1015 Ms. in *Bhujmoli* is dated 1139. Earlier examples still are found in the *Pañcarakṣā* dated in the 53rd year of Rāmapāla (*c.*1135)[2] and of course the inscriptions under the paintings of the 1071 Ms. in Calcutta, whose date no one doubts, are in a hand similar to the 1015 Ms. in Cambridge.

The 85 paintings of the latter Ms. occur at chapter ends and at the beginning of the entire Ms. The first chapter is an exception, with five single paintings occurring at various intervals throughout – the original first folio is missing so it is not known how many paintings it would have had, although we may guess at three. The ends of the chapters are marked by two paintings on the same folio, until the end of the 12th chapter, which is marked by three. Two pictures then mark the end of each chapter (apart from chapter 14 which has three) until the 31st chapter, four folios of which have two paintings each. The end of the 32nd chapter and of the work proper (f.222a) has three paintings. The next and final folio (f.223) carries on the recto the colophon and the extra colophon inserted in 1139, and on the verso a short text in the same hand as the main manuscript entitled *Vajradhvajapariṇāma* on the virtues of reading the *Prajñāpāramitā*. This leaf has three paintings on the recto and no less than five on the verso. No Pāla Ms. adopts this arrangement of the miniatures, which again argues for experimentation in this manuscript. The 1071 Ms. from Nepal has simply a single miniature at chapter ends, and three to end the work.

As for the subjects of these paintings, they are in general different from their Indian Pāla counterparts. Apart from the last eight on the colophon folio, which are of the eight great scenes from the life of the Buddha, they are all of specific iconographic representations of the Buddha or Bodhisattvas or other divinities, or of important *stūpas* or *caityas*. The majority of places designated are in eastern India, but there are some from far off places – China, Java, Ceylon, Gujarat, southern India. The specific locations extend even to different temple types or caverns around and over the divinities.[3] It need not be assumed that the painter was personally familiar with the specific appearance of these temples. Rather he was copying from earlier materials, either another manuscript, as Foucher believed, or larger-scale wall paintings or *paṭas*. The covers are later additions of the 12th century, with fine paintings of the *Pāramitās*[4] spread over the two interior covers.

University Library, Cambridge, Add.1643.

ff.223; 5·25 × 54cm; talipot leaves (first folio a paper replacement); six lines of transitional *Kuṭila* in three columns, with stringholes in the central margins, which on the illustrated leaves and some others have large *vajras* painted on them; 85 paintings (out of 88?), about 5·25 × 6cm; wooden covers, later additions, with *pūjā* marks on outside, and painted interiors, 5·4 × 54·5 and 6 × 56cm.

Bibliography: CUL 1883, pp.151–2. Foucher 1900. Saraswati 1977 (with numerous col. repros. of Add.1643).

[1] Pal 1978, p.34.
[2] Banerjee 1969.
[3] Saraswati 1975 discusses them.
[4] The cover published by Pal (1978, fig.16) as belonging to this Ms. actually belongs to Add.1464 (No.2). One of the Pāramitās is reproduced in Foucher 1900 pl.IX, 4.

3 f.127a (detail). The Bodhisattva Samantabhadra, and the marginal decoration of a *vajra* (thunderbolt).

4 'Pañcarakṣā'

Illustrated on p.27.

Five hymns addressed to five Buddhist protective goddesses.

These hymns are among the most ancient of Buddhist *dhāraṇīs* or hymns, fragments of the text having been found in Central Asian Mss. of the early first millennium AD. The goddesses addressed are protective – thus hymned, they ward off evils. The text was extremely popular in Nepal from at least the 10th century, as numerous manuscripts of it have survived, many of them illuminated. It appears to have been used at least in more modern times as a sacred book on which oaths could be sworn. This Ms. of these hymns was copied in the 14th year of King Nayapāla of the Pāla dynasty, on the orders of Queen Uḍḍākā (see No.2), in a fine *Kuṭila* hand. The date is equivalent to *c.*1057. There are 36 miniatures in an elaborate iconographic scheme that is at present somewhat obscure. *Pañcarakṣā* Mss. are usually illustrated by paintings of the five goddesses, with or without their equivalent Jinas. Here this pattern is not adhered to. Pratisarā is accompanied by five of the Mortal Buddhas (ff.1b, 2a); Mayūrī by the remaining two Mortal Buddhas, Maitreya, Vajrapāni and Tārā (ff.19b, 20a); Sāhasrapramardanī by four Bodhisattvas and a *stūpa* being worshipped by two figures (ff.45b, 46a); Sītavatī by Manjushrī, Padmapāni and three other goddesses (ff.64b, 65a); and Mantrānusāranī by five demonic figures of yoginīs (ff.66b, 67a). The final group round the end of the text (ff.69b, 70a) is the same five terrifying yoginīs around the last of the Mortal Buddhas, Maitreya.

All the figure drawing in this Ms. is of great simplicity and elegance. The artist of these paintings experimented with gilding the flesh of all these figures, none too successfully as little of it remains. However, its presence on this early manuscript demonstrates that gilding on paper manuscripts need not necessarily be taken as a late feature as has sometimes been claimed. Most of the figures have both head and body haloes, a development since the Mahīpāla I Ms. (No.2), but none of them is seated on a throne with vertical throne-back as is found in later manuscripts. Some have large cushions behind them, and others triangular projections above their shoulders which are a feature of the Bodleian manuscript dated *c.*1100 (No.5). These must be rudimentary versions of the backs of thrones found in later Pāla manuscripts, but their curious shapes which change direction haphazardly suggest that the artists are copying from a prototype whose precise language they no longer comprehend.

University Library, Cambridge, Add.1688.

ff.70; 5·2 × 56cm; talipot leaves; *Kuṭila* script, five lines; 36 miniatures, 5·2 × 5–6cm; lotus designs at end of chapters; plain wooden boards.

Bibliography: CUL 1883, p.175. Saraswati 1977, col. figs.203–6, 259–60.

5 'Aṣṭasāhasrikā Prajñāpāramitā'

COLOUR PLATE IV

The Perfection of Wisdom in 8,000 Sections (see No.2).

The Pāla empire was in decline from the middle of the 9th century, but under monarchs like Mahīpāla (*c.*995–1043) was able to check and even counteract this tendency. Rāmapāla (*c.*1082–1130) was another such monarch, about whom we know far more than most other medieval Indian kings, as he is the subject of a contemporary political biography (*Rāmacarita* by Sandhyākaranandī). He came to the throne after his father (Mahīpāla II) had perished in a rebellion, and the imperial hold on Bihar and Bengal was very shaky, but he succeeded in countervailing the fissiparous tendencies of the Pāla dominions and exerting strong central rule for most of his long reign. And it was during his reign that Pāla painting seems to have reached its peak of classical perfection – three extremely fine manuscripts have survived, as well as several others.

The Bodleian Ms. is dated in the year 15 of Rāmapāla (*c.*1097) and was copied at the famous monastery-university of Nālandā by the scribe Ahunakunda Bhattāraka. It is illustrated with 18 paintings and has painted covers as well, most of it being in superb condition. It has the usual cycle of 18 miniatures in three sets of six each, the middle one marking the end of the 12th chapter. The eight scenes from the life of the Buddha are symmetrically disposed for once, being the outer pairs of the first and last sets, although they are not here, nor anywhere else, in their natural order. There are three extra miniatures of the Buddha and the remaining ones are of Prajñāpāramitā and the Bodhisattvas.

The style of this manuscript is not reflected in the two other known manuscripts from Nālandā (the Calcutta Ms. dated in the year 5 of Mahīpāla and the Royal Asiatic Society's Ms. in the year 4 of Govindapāla, No.9). The line is superb, especially in the drawing of the Bodhisattvas of the central pair of illustrated leaves; the outline of their faces and of the Buddha in three-quarter profile with the curve towards the lower part of the face is unique in Pāla painting. Of especial interest also is the triangular shape of the throne-backs visible over the shoulders, which slopes and tilts with the figures. This is found in more pronounced form in the contemporary Bengal Mss. (see No.10). Absent are the elaborate throne-backs and cushions of the standing Buddha.

The covers have been published as Pāla[1] but are in fact superb specimens of Nepalese painting of the 12th century. On one, the more damaged, the temptation of the Buddha forms the centre-piece for the other scenes from his life; on the other is Prajñāpāramitā with the nine other Pāramitās and Varendra Tārā surrounding her[2], a theme that is apparently found also on the covers of No.3.

Bodleian Library, Oxford, Ms. Sansk. a.7. Provenance: Hoernle Collection.

ff.188; 6·1×55·7cm; talipot leaves; text in fine *Kuṭila* hand in six lines in three columns (15, 17, and 15 cm wide); 18 miniatures, about 6×6cm; illuminated folios have margins decorated in arabesque and geometric designs; wooden covers 6·1×55·5cm, with painted interiors.

Bibliography: Bod 1905, p.250. Conze 1948. Mallmann 1965.

[1]Barrett and Gray, 1963, pp.52–3 (col. repro.).
[2]Identified by Mallmann 1965.

6 'Aṣṭasāhasrikā Prajñāpāramitā'

COLOUR PLATE I

The Perfection of Wisdom in 8,000 Sections (see No.2).

This famous manuscript is perhaps the most clasically perfect of the great manuscripts associated with the name of Rāmapāla[1]. It was copied at a place unspecified in the 36th year of his reign, *c.*1118, at the expense of one Udayasimha for the benefit of his parents' souls. Only the illustrated pages plus one other survive from the whole Ms. which originally had 179 folios, and was illustrated with a cycle of 18 miniatures, at beginning, middle (beginning of chapter 12) and end. Unlike all the other similar cycles, it lacks an image of Prajñāpāramitā herself, and also any of the scenes of the life of the Buddha, who is represented only by the red-coloured Amitābha Buddha, and Vajrasattva. It is the images of the Bodhisattvas which are the especial glory of this manuscript, nine of them in all, drawn with a perfectly controlled line fully expressive of volume, so that even where the paint has flaked on the yellow and white Bodhisattvas the figures still seem fully modelled.

Not the least remarkable aspect of these miniatures is the uniform colour scheme which is preserved throughout the Ms. The images are, apart from the red Amitābha, all yellow, white or different shades of slate-blue, which is used as a substitute for green on the images of Samantabhadra, Ratnapāni, Vajrapāni, Shyāmatārā and Parnashabarī. The large body haloes are all red, while the ground beyond is very dark slate-blue. Apart from the occasional pink head halo, all other details of dress, throne-backs, cushions, lotuses and so on conform to this basic scheme of white, yellow, red and slate-blue. Even more remarkably, the square *maṇḍala* in which sits Vajrasattva, in the middle position of f.89b, is divided by diagonals into four triangles, each of which is coloured in one of these basic colours. There can be no doubt that this is deliberate, that the artist was deliberately restricting his colour range, and indeed colouring his subjects in accordance with his scheme rather than with iconographical demands.

Victoria and Albert Museum, London, I.S.4–10, 1958.

Provenance: Vredenburg Collection.

ff.7 (numbered 1, 2, 89, 90, 178, 179 and one without illustration apparently unnumbered); 6·2×54cm (ends slightly broken, and some pieces missing from upper and lower edges); talipot leaves; six lines of *Kuṭila*, with marked twist to the bottom, in three columns, 14, 17 and 14cm wide; four margins on each folio; the illustrated pages have margins decorated with foliate and geometric designs in yellow and white and touches of colour, and with red borders; 18 miniatures, 6–6·2×7–8·2cm, including their red borders; no covers; now mounted under glass and framed.

Bibliography: Vredenburg 1927 (col. repro. of nine miniatures). AB No.45 (col. repro.).

[1]The colophon of this one seems incomplete, as Rāmapāla does not have his full imperial titles, and indeed one of them, *mahārājādhi*, breaks off in the middle of a word and carries on without interruption into the king's name *Śrīmadrāmapālasya* etc.

7 'Aṣṭasāhasrikā Prajñāpāramitā'

COLOUR PLATE III

The Perfection of Wisdom in 8,000 Sections (see No.2).

This Ms. is on 337 palm leaves, and was copied in the 15th year of Gopāladeva at the monastery of Vikramashīla. This great monastic-university establishment was founded by Dharmapāla (*c.*781–821) to teach the *Prajñāpāramitā* doctrine, and was destroyed along with the other Buddhist monasteries at the end of the 12th century. Its site has recently been discovered at Antichak east of Bhagalpur in Bihar.

The precise king named in the colophon is a matter of some controversy, as there were three kings named Gopāla in the dynasty, but it is now becoming clearer that it must be the third of that name, whose reign began *c.*1130. The Ms. is illustrated with six miniatures, arranged in facing pairs at the beginning, middle (beginning of the 12th chapter) and end of the work. All but one of these divinities are seated within a shrine under a trefoil or cinquefoil arch surmounted by three diminishing horizontal courses in pyramidal form surmounted by an *amalaka* and supported by pillars with vase bases, representing the cella of a Pāla shrine. The details are picked out minutely in red, blue, green and yellow.

One other illustrated Ms. is known from the reign of Gopāla III, dated in his 4th year (*c.*1134), with 18 miniatures, and now in the Boston Museum of Fine Arts.[1] The divinities are similarly located under shrines, although not elaborately decorated. This is the only Pāla Ms. which has survived with its original decorated covers, and on these the architecture is as detailed as on Or.6902.

British Library, London, Or.6902.

ff.337; 6·8×41cm; talipot leaves; six lines of fine *Kuṭila* script in three columns 11·5cm wide; four margins on each side, 2cm wide, decorated with arabesque and geometrical designs; six miniatures approx. 6·8×6·5–7·00cm; two stringholes in inner margins, 13·5cm from edge; wooden binding boards, undecorated, covered with *pūjā* marks.

Bibliography: AB, p.39 [the present author has revised his views on the dating of this Ms. to *c*.970 as presented there]. JRAS 1910, pp.150–1.

[1]No.20.589, published Bulletin BMFA, LXIII, 1965.

8 'Aṣṭasāhasrikā Prajñāpāramitā'

Illustrated on p.20.

The Perfection of Wisdom in 8,000 Sections (see No.2).

This undated manuscript is the most heavily illustrated surviving Pāla manuscript, with 69 miniatures. It has lost a few folios, and would originally have had 78 miniatures. The disposition of the miniatures is complex, combining the normal cycle of 18 miniatures, which consists of six paintings each at the beginning and end of the work and another six at the beginning of chapter 12 (ff.149b/150a), with another cycle which consists of a pair of miniatures on facing folios at the beginning of each of the 32 chapters not illuminated in the first cycle, *i.e.* all the chapters apart from Nos.1 and 12. It is not yet clear whether the precise iconographic scheme is to be interpreted as a single enormous *maṇḍala*, or if not, what are the reasons for the choice of divinities in their coupling and relative positions within the framework of the overall scheme. It begins with the five Jinas around Prajñāpāramitā, followed by the *Jina-śaktis*, and then a sequence of important Bodhisattvas and four of the Mortal Buddhas. The six paintings at the beginning of chapter 12 are of six of the eight great events from the life of the Buddha, the remaining two beginning chapter 25. Between these two points, the subjects of the miniatures are mostly the terrifying divinities of the northern Buddhist pantheon, with some more Bodhisattvas, resulting in some apparently very odd couplings – Marīcī with Lokanātha, Dīpankara Buddha with Samvara etc. The final group from chapter 26 on is of mostly benificent deities again, with the remaining three Mortal Buddhas. The last surviving miniatures beginning chapter 32 are of Vajrasattva and Vajradhātvīshvarī; they would have been followed by six miniatures at the end of the chapter concluding the whole cycle, but these last two folios are missing.

There are two styles represented in the miniatures of this Ms. One is an angular, linear style in which the scenes from the life of the Buddha are painted, with flat colour planes and hardly any modelling. The Buddha, when standing, carries his throne-back and cushion around with him. The other style is somewhat more modelled, and there are some lovely Bodhisattvas painted in pink, green and dark blue, fully modelled, but still with rather angular features and pointed chins. Even these are not so fully modelled as the figures in the Rāmapāla Ms. of *c*.1118 (No.6) or the Govindapāla Ms. of 1165 (No.9), both from Nālandā. It could of course be later than this last Ms. but since no Mss. of comparable size or beauty are known from this period, between the collapse of the Pālas and the destruction of the Buddhist monasteries, it seems safer to date it to the late Pāla period in the middle of the 12th century, from a monastery other than Nālandā or Vikramashīla (No.7.).

British Library, London, Or.12461.

ff.325 (five folios missing, numbered originally 29, 104, 105, 324, 325); 6·2 × 39cm; talipot leaves (ff.321–4 are yellow paper replacement leaves in an 18th-century Nepalese hand – they have the text from the end of chapter 31 to the finish); six lines of *Kuṭila* script in an elegant hand in three columns; text area 4 × 34·5cm; 69 miniatures, mostly 6·2 × 4·5–6·5cm; pages with miniatures are decorated with geometric and arabesque designs mostly in red and yellow in the four margins, while the end of each chapter in the text area is usually marked with a small coloured animal or design – a peacock, deer, elephant, hare, rabbit etc. of singular charm; stringholes in both inner margins, 12cm from edge; undecorated bevelled wooden boards 6·6 × 39·8cm with red interiors, and copious *pūjā* marks on upper cover; brass lotuses were added in Nepal in the 18th century to cover the holes of the lower cover – these would have had spikes attached to secure the leaves.

Bibliography: AB No.46. Lewis 1959–60.

9 f.101b (detail). The Buddha descends from the 33rd Heaven accompanied by Brahmā and Indra, one of the eight episodes from his life.

9 'Aṣṭasāhasrikā Prajñāpāramitā'

The Perfection of Wisdom in 8,000 Sections (see No.2).

This Ms. marks practically the end of the Pāla tradition of manuscript illustration. It is dated in the 4th year of Govindapāla, whose reign commenced in 1161 and hence is equivalent to 1165. There is no epigraphic evidence linking this ruler to the main line of the Pāla kings, the last of whom is usually thought to be Madanapāla (1143–61) and under whom most of the empire was annexed by neighbouring Hindu kingdoms. It is not even certain that Govindapāla's reign began when Madanapāla's ended, but since the former assumes the full imperial titles of the Pālas and is regarded in all Buddhist Ms. colophons up to 1199 as the legitimate Buddhist king, it seems logical to assume that he was the legitimate successor of Madanapāla. Govindapāla's rule, however, was confined to the area around Gayā and Nālandā in Bihar. Even this limited power collapsed early in his reign, for all the records in his reign apart from this, the first one, speak of his 'vanished' or 'destroyed' reign.

The colophon is now somewhat damaged and almost illegible, but after the date comes a mention of the monastery of Nālandā, which in such a position can only mean that it was copied there. It has 15 illustrations, the original opening folio being missing along with its three miniatures, in the standard cycle of 18. The style is a continuation of the Rāmapāla style and is still at a high level of sensitivity in line and modelling, although exhibiting the standard conventions of the standing and lying Buddha with throne-backs and cushions.

Royal Asiatic Society, London, Hodgson Ms.1.

ff.204; 6·25 × 57cm; talipot leaves; six lines of transitional *Nāgarī* script, in three columns; 15 miniatures; all four margins on illuminated leaves are decorated, stringholes in both inner margins; Nepalese covers with interiors painted with Buddhas and Bodhisattvas, 12th century, 6·6 × 57·5cm.

Bibliography: RAS 1876.

10 'Kāraṇḍavyūhasūtra'

A comparatively late Buddhist *sūtra* in Sanskrit, concerned to exalt the Bodhisattva Avalokiteshvara through recounting his compassionate journeys to the underworld, Ceylon, etc. The Ms. is incomplete, having only 53 surviving leaves from a putative 70, but is the most heavily illustrated surviving Buddhist Ms. from India. All 53 leaves have a miniature in the centre of each side, while all four margins on each side also bear little vignettes of the Buddhas, worshippers, etc., under *caityas*. The outer margins have however mostly been broken away. The miniatures are in a fluent, almost purely linear style, that is different from the known styles associated with the Pālas or with Nepal, and closely related to the only known illustrated Buddhist Ms. from eastern India done outside the Pāla empire, *i.e.* the Ms. of the *25000 Prajñāpāramitā* with 22 miniatures in the Baroda Museum dated in the eighth year of Harivarman, *c.*1100.[1] The Varmans were a Hindu Vaishnava dynasty who ruled over south-eastern Bengal (now Bangladesh) between about 1080 and 1150, and appear both to have tolerated and indeed patronized Buddhism.

In both Mss. the neatly drawn figures are usually under trefoil arches below pyramidal roofs with horizontal courses, with crowning *amalaka*, as in the Vikramashīla Ms. (No.7), but in a much more simplified style, while two stylized trees protrude above the top of the temple structure. But whereas the Harivarman Ms. has wide-opened eyes on all its faces, the *Kāraṇḍavyūha* has the characteristic Pāla dip in the upper eyelid, suggesting a provenance nearer the Pāla empire than the extreme edge of Bengal. A further clue is provided by the unusual type of temple architecture seen in a few of the miniatures, which instead of the types analysed by Saraswati[2] in other manuscript illustrations of the period, is in fact a *śikhara* or *deul* type of temple consisting of a single tower with vertical sides, and a top curving into a crowning *amalaka*. This is not an architectural type seen in any other Buddhist Ms. It is exemplified by the surviving temples of Orissa in particular, but it was also fairly common in the Bankura District of West Bengal bordering on Orissa.[3] It is not axiomatic in these Mss. that such features are necessarily based on local architectural types – both the 11th-century illustrated Nepalese Mss. (No.3) bear labels to all their illustrations giving the whereabouts of the particular image, but it is doubtful whether the different architectural types thus represented in fact conform to reality. However this Ms. is in a different position; there is no attempt to suggest that the images of Avalokiteshvara and the other divinities are localized anywhere in particular, so it is probable that any architectural oddities represent actual conditions. Stylistically the Ms. may be dated to the first half of the 11th century, when the Bankura area along with all south-western Bengal was under the control of the Hindu Sena dynasty.

British Library, London, Or.13940.

ff.53; much damaged at edges, maximum 5·5 × 36cm (originally about 5·5 × 39cm); talipot leaves; six lines of early *Nāgarī* in four columns, text area 3·5 × 35cm; 106 miniatures, each in centre of page, measuring 5 × 4·75cm (all damaged at top and bottom); both inner and outer margins of each page decorated with vignettes, the outer ones mostly broken off; stringholes in both inner margins..

Bibliography: Unpublished.

[1]Bhattacharya 1944. [2]Saraswati 1975. [3]Saraswati 1976.

11 'Vasudhārādhāraṇī' and 'Nāmasaṅgīti'

COLOUR PLATE VI

Two hymns in Sanskrit to the Buddhist goddess of wealth, Vasudhārā, and to the Buddha, in a pair of linked manuscripts. They are both on stout Nepalese paper, dyed blue-black, and written in alternate lines of gold and silver ink. This type of Ms. is fairly common in Nepal from the 16th century onwards, but it is now becoming clear that there is a small group of much earlier manuscripts in this style – a Ms. of the *Prajñāpāramitā* in the British Library, datable palaeographically to the 12th century,[1] another, in the National Archives, Kathmandu, with an apparent date of 1225[2], and one in the Heeramaneck

10 ff.49b, 43b (details). The goddess Parnashabarī in an Orissan type of temple, and the Bodhisattva Avalokiteshvara as Simhanāda, mounted on a lion.

13 Inner covers. The avatars of Vishnu.

Collection in Los Angeles *c.*1250,[3] which scholars have been reluctant to accept in the absence of corroborating evidence as to the antiquity of papermaking in Nepal. However, the Ms. of the *Vasudhārādhāraṇī* contains miniatures of superb quality which are unquestionably of 12th-century date, as well as a secure colophon dated in year 305 of the Nepal era (*c.*1185), in the reign of Someshvaradeva (reg. *c.*AD1180–5). Palaeographically the Ms. is in a securely 12th-century hand, and it is the earliest known dated example of such blue-black paper. An even earlier Ms. dated 1105 on normal Nepalese yellow paper is in the Asutosh Museum in Calcutta.[4]

The Ms. has two miniatures at the beginning on facing folios, of the Buddha seated on a lion-throne with attendant Bodhisattvas, and of the six-armed form of Vasudhārā seated similarly with two near-naked urchins above pouring out bags of money. Both display naturalistic modelling and a plastic use of colour of the greatest sensitivity. The companion text, *Nāmasangīti*, is in the same calligraphic hand, and has four miniatures of slightly less refinement by a different hand.

British Library, London, Or.13971A and B.

ff.21 and 28; 9·1 × 26cm, and 8·9 × 26cm; blue-black paper; five lines of *Kuṭila* script in alternate silver and gold ink; stringhole offset to left 10cm from edge; A has two paintings 9·1 × 9cm on right side of page, with decorated squares around stringholes on these pages; B four miniatures 8·9 × *c.*9cm; unbound.

Bibliography: BL1980–81.

[1]BM1902, Or.2202.
[2]Trier 1972, fig.118.
[3]Pal 1978, plate 27.
[4]Mookerjee 1947.

12 Manuscript cover

COLOUR PLATE V

A single wooden cover to a palm-leaf Ms, with painted inner surface representing the story of the *Vessantara Jātaka*. One of the most famous of the early Buddhist birth-stories, which recount the lives the *Bodhisattva* (Buddha-to-be) led in his former existences, probably dating from the 5th century BC, they are part of the literary heritage of southern Buddhism. A version of this famous story however survived in the Mahāyāna tradition, under the title of *Viśvambhara Jātaka*, included in several of the Sanskrit collections of *avadānas* and *jātakas*. The story concerns the Bodhisattva's incarnation as Prince Vishvambhara, who embodied the virtue of charity, and whose disinterestedness is tested by the gods to such an extent that he gives away his goods, his house, his kingdom, and eventually his wife and children.

This is an extremely rare example of narrative technique used on the cover of a manuscript. If the divinities painted in the Pāla and Nepalese Mss. are to be regarded as scaled-down versions of icons as wall paintings, it would follow that this cover is a version of a full-size fresco of this subject, and indeed with its fluid transitions from one episode to the next it recalls the narrative technique employed in large-scale wall paintings as in Ajantā. It is datable to *c.*1100, from Nepal.

National Museum, New Delhi, 51.212.

Wooden cover, bevelled top; 5·6 × 32·8cm; plain top, painted interior.

Bibliography: ICMAA p.114 and cited references.

13 Pair of manuscript covers

A pair of covers illustrated with the incarnations of Vishnu.

This pair of Nepalese covers must once have enclosed a Hindu manuscript; they are datable to the 12th century.

The upper cover is divided into three groups of three panels divided by the stringholes with their decorated margins, representing the Fish, Tortoise, Boar; Man-lion, Bali at the sacrificial fire, Bali and Vāmana; Vishnu Trivikrama, Parashurāma and devotees, and Rāma. The lower cover has eight panels, showing a four-armed blue Krishna with devotee, Buddha with devotee, Kalki on a green horse, then a panel which probably represents Vishnu lying asleep on Ananta (*Anantaśayana*), but in which the god appears to have three heads and a male attendant rather than Lakshmī; the next is a double-width panel, showing Vishnu being worshipped by two devotees. After the second stringhole, the last three panels show Vishnu with Lakshmī on his lap, a pair of devotees and apparently the consecration of a king. The background colour alternates between blue and red, and many panels have the curtain roll and hanging tassels usual in Nepalese painting at this period.

This interesting pair shows considerable iconographic freedom in the depiction of the avatars, including charming representations of the Fish and Tortoise avatars as precisely that, without any human attributes at all. Particular attention is shown to the Dwarf incarnation (Vāmana) which has three panels devoted to this theme. It is noticeable in fact that the iconography of the avatars is closest to the norm when the subject had already been depicted in stone in Nepal – Varāha, Narasimha, Vāmana and Trivikrama,[1] while the other avatars after the first two animal ones are often no more than conventional Bodhisattva representations. It would seem therefore that the covers were painted by a Buddhist monk, none too familiar with the correct representations of some of the avatars of which he would have seen no sculptural representations.

British Museum, London, 1965, 6-14, 2.

Two wooden covers, bevelled tops; 4·6 × 56cm; plain outsides, painted interiors; stringholes match only if one cover is reversed.

Bibliography: Pal 1978, pp.55–7, fig.51.

[1]Pal 1974, figs.1–3, 92–3, 95–7. The famous Vishnu Anantashayana of AD 642 at Budhanilakanth (fig.12) does not have an attendant Lakshmī, so hence perhaps our artist's confusion on this score, but he is apparently confusing Vishnu with the four-headed Brahmā who is meant to be sitting on the lotus growing from Vishnu's navel in the standard iconography of this scene.

14 'Devīmāhātmya'

COLOUR PLATE II

The *Devīmāhātmya* (Glorification of the Goddess) is a lengthy hymn from the *Mārkaṇḍeya Purāṇa*, in which the Devī, the Goddess, is worshipped as the supreme principle of the universe, and an account given of her origin, of her superiority to all other gods, and of her victories

15 Eight of the 16 Jaina *Vidyādevīs*, with royal devotees on right.

over demons who tyrannize the world, in particular, her victory over Mahīshāsura the Buffalo-demon.

Three palm leaves, each with a painting of the Goddess slaying the Buffalo-demon to the left of the central hole, are all that is left of this manuscript. The second of the two leaves in their present arrangement has a male and female devotee on the right of the hole. There is no text, other than a damaged inscription in Sanskrit in Nepalese *Bhujmoli* script of the 13/14th century on the reverse of the third leaf, which appears to record details of the drawing of the miniatures, but which has so far eluded precise decipherment. The precise function of these leaves is puzzling. They may be fragments of a manuscript of the *Devīmāhātmya*. They may possibly be an artist's preparatory studies for a larger painting on cloth or on a wall, but in this case their format remains puzzling, as there is no obvious reason for painting such studies on palm leaves when cloth and paper were both available, and the shape of the leaf prevented its full utilization. But there can be no doubt of the provenance of these leaves, which is Nepal, of the 13th century. The subject is identical in all three paintings, save that the Goddess's colour is respectively blue, green and red. With one foot firmly planted on her lion vehicle, and the other on the back of the decapitated demonic buffalo, she stands serenely holding the weapons given her by the gods, while lassooing with her snakes the demons Chanda and Munda.[1].

British Library, London, Or.13860.

ff.3; 4·9 × 18·4cm; talipot leaves; no text on verso, two lines of *Bhujmoli* script on reverse of f.3; three miniatures, 4·9 × 8·8cm, with extension on f.2a; central stringhole.

Bibliography: Unpublished.

[1]See Pal 1974, fig.278, for an almost contemporary version in stone, and Pal 1975, fig.73, for a 16th-century bronze realization of the same subject.

15 Manuscript cover

A wooden cover (*paṭlī*) of a palm-leaf Ms. with on the inner surface representations of eight *Vidyādevīs*, and two female devotees.

The *Vidyādevīs*, goddesses of wisdom, of whom there are 16 in the Jaina tradition, seem to be related to both the Buddhist *Prajñāpāramitās* and the Hindu conception of the mother-goddesses. This is one of a pair of covers, the other being badly damaged, showing the 16 *Vidyādevīs*, together with a pair of female devotees – one labelled Devaśrī Śrāvikā, the other Padminī, the implication of the former title being that the lady is a royal devotee.

The rendering of the *Vidyādevīs* seems to be partly dependent on influences from the Pāla Buddhist manuscripts, in their frontal viewpoint, in the attributes which they carry and the arches under which they sit, which are unique in Jaina painting at this period. The artist was none too clear about whether these arches were in fact arches, throne-backs or haloes, as they tilt about depending on the inclination of the *devīs*' head. If these are dependent on Pāla models, then it is impossible to date them before the second quarter of the 12th century, to which time the two royal ladies would seem to belong. They differ markedly from the set of *Vidyādevīs* published by Moti Chandra[1] in a Ms. dated 1161, in which none of these Pāla characteristics is apparent.

The outside of the cover is decorated with a charming creeper design, issuing on two sides from the mouth of a *kīrttimukha* in the centre of the board, with elephants and strange beasts depicted in the loops of the creeper. This is one of several such decorations known from this period.[2]

Lalbhai Dalpatbhai Institute, Ahmadabad.

Provenance: Jaina *bhaṇḍār*, Jaiselmer.

Wooden cover, with bevelled edges; 7·5 × 58cm; two stringholes; both sides decorated.

Bibliography: Punyavijaya and Shah 1966.

[1]Moti Chandra 1949, figs.17–42.
[2]*ibid*, figs.201–3; see Punyavijaya and Shah 1966, pp.40–1, for a description of others.

16 Manuscript cover

COLOUR PLATE VII

A wooden cover (*paṭlī*) of a palm-leaf manuscript.

This is the only part of this manuscript that is known. Its upper surface is divided into two unequal portions. It depicts on the left a conversation between two Jaina monks, who are labelled as Shri Jinadatta Sūri and Shri Gunasamudra Ācārya, with two laymen in respectful postures, and on the right, beyond the stringhole, an image of the Jaina *Tīrthāṅkara*, Mahāvīra, with four lay devotees, and two chowrie-bearers. Jinadatta Sūri was one of the greatest Jaina teachers of Rajasthan in the 12th century. Born in Dholka in 1075, he became the pupil, and ultimately successor, of Jinavallabha Sūri, the 43rd Pontiff of the Kharataragaccha. During his pontificate he made frequent tours throughout Rajasthan and Gujarat, one of the most famous being to consecrate a temple of Mahāvīra at Marot in Marwar. This forms the subject of a *paṭlī* formerly in one of the Jaiselmer *bhaṇḍārs*[1], which is probably contemporary with the event. Three similar *paṭlīs* in all involving Jinadatta are now known, and it would be rash to assume that all of them must be contemporary with the great Jaina pontiff or have some personal connection with him. However, stylistically they all belong to the 12th century, and this small one probably to the latter part of the period. It seems to have been copied from, or at least to belong to the same school as, the contemporary version referred to above. This latter depicts the consecration scene in the centre of a much longer panel, with a conversation between Jinadatta and Jinaraksita on the left, and on the right between Jinadatta and a monk whose name has been somewhat damaged, but which has been read as Śrīguṇa(caṃ)-drācārya. It would be possible however to read it as Śrīguṇa(samu)drācārya, and hence be the same subject as in this smaller version. Indeed the two *akṣaras* (syllables) of '*samu*' would fit the available space better than the one of '*caṃ*'. This small cover could then be seen as a version of part of the larger one. Both covers have the identical lotus pattern round the stringhole, with margins of a chain of small, white flowers, and the same *marvārī* leaf pattern forming a border round the cover.

Lalbhai Dalpatbhai Institute, Ahmadabad.

Provenance: Jaina *bhaṇḍār* in Jaiselmer.

Wooden cover, bevelled edges; 5·5 × 29cm; stringhole one third of way from left; painted exterior; plain interior, with flower designs added later.

Bibliography: Punyavijaya and Shah 1966.

[1]Moti Chandra 1949, figs.190–2.

CHAPTER II

Manuscript Illumination during the Delhi Sultanate

The conquest of northern India by the armies of Shihāb ad-Dīn Ghorī after the battle of Tarain in 1192 and the establishment of Muslim rule over the major part of the subcontinent for the next 500 years, although initially, and at intervals thereafter, destructive, yet enriched India's society with new blood and her art forms with new concepts and ideas.

Muslims are a people of the book, the revelation of God, the Holy Koran. By 1200 they had carried the arts of calligraphy and book illumination to supreme heights and were shortly to embark in Egypt and Iran on the most monumental period of book illumination ever known, in copies of the Koran produced on the most majestic and expansive scale, and embellished with gold and lapis lazuli. To this same period belong the earliest illustrated manuscripts of Arabic, and in the 14th century of Persian, literature. The Mongol conquest of much of the Middle East in the 13th century opened up its arts to the influence of China, particularly its book arts, and by the late 14th century there had emerged the classical norms of Iranian book illumination, which had such profound effect on the Indian book arts.

To copy the Holy Koran was in itself a most pious act; to do it superbly was an act that brought earthly praise and reward as well. The calligrapher was the highest artist known in the Islamic world, his primacy depending on his writing down the word of God. The illuminator and painter stood far beneath him. The Arabs, of course, frowned on both painting and sculpture as contrary to the Prophet's commandment and very rarely illustrated their manuscripts. The Iranians, who had much earlier traditions of manuscript illumination, probably before the Arab conquest, and certainly before the Mongol invasions which destroyed nearly every library in Iran, had fewer inhibitions about painting; but it was usually a private art, for the delectation of rulers and their courts. To the frontispieces and chapter-headings taken from Koranic illumination they added miniatures – true miniatures, illuminated with gold. And as no other people, they truly illustrated the text, interweaving script and paintings.

The rulers set up studios at their courts to produce books – to make the beautifully glazed and burnished paper, to write the text, to illuminate it, to paint the miniatures, and finally to bind the result in soft leather and to decorate it. This courtly bibliographic tradition was not fully established in Iran until the end of the 14th century. But the new Muslim rulers of India immediately introduced their own concepts of books. They, of course, had no truck with palm leaves and to begin with must have imported paper from Iran and elsewhere (there are early references to Syrian paper being used in India), before setting up their own production centres.

Very few manuscripts in Persian or Arabic have survived from the first two centuries of Muslim rule, perhaps because of the sack of Delhi in 1398 by Tīmūr. It is also a great problem distinguishing Indian Islamic manuscripts from Iranian ones, before the emergence of a distinct Indian

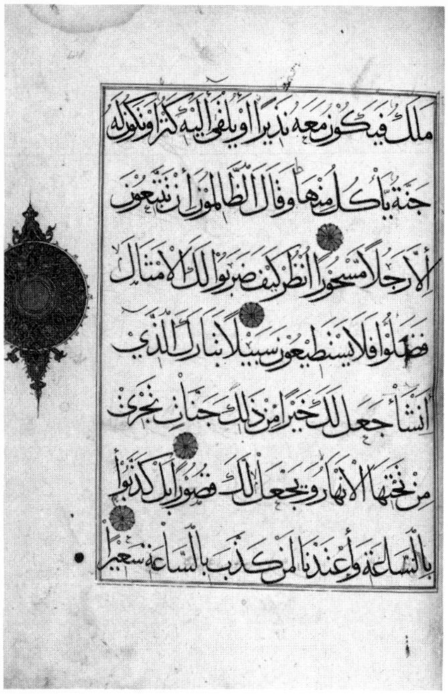

21 f.438. A Koran page in Indian *Thuluth* script (No.21, p.57).

calligraphic tradition and of schools of manuscript illumination. It is inconceivable that the 13th- and 14th-century rulers of Delhi, to whose capital flocked scholars and literati from the rest of the Islamic world, would be willing to tolerate anything but the finest work. Illuminated manuscripts of these first two centuries of Islamic rule in India would then, at their finest, probably be indistinguishable from Iranian work. However, a solitary page from what appears to be a 14th-century Koran does indicate some independent development. Three lines of excellent large *Rayḥānī* script in black are surrounded on the three outer sides by inscriptions in red Kufic with knotted red and black motifs in the outer corners. This displays the dignity of the Īl-khānid Korans combined with a massiveness altogether suited to the Tughluq dynasty at the height of its power in the mid-14th century. But when the centralized Muslim culture of India collapsed towards the end of the 14th century, being given its death-blow by Tīmūr's invasion of 1398, the independent states which emerged were able to develop their own cultures free both of Delhi and the outside Islamic world, and it is then that we first find radical developments in the book arts in the direction of an Indian identity of their own.

This first finds expression in the calligraphic arts. There developed in India a variety of *Naskhī* called the *Khaṭṭ-i Behār*, or *Behārī* script, which employs long horizontal flourishes of the pen on the line, with comparatively short verticals, and has quite large intervals between words, giving an oddly hesitant look to this combination of flowing and staccato rhythms. The meaning of the term *Behārī* is obscure – attempts have recently been made to link it to the Arabic word for spring, but this fanciful explanation is inferior to one which explains this purely Indian phenomenon in Indian terms, *i.e.* the script of Bihar. Why it whould be named after this region of India, however, is unclear, for no great Islamic centre flourished there, unless Jaunpur could also be included in Bihar in Persian terminology. However this may be, why *Naskhī* should have developed in this way is obscure also; *Behārī* is neither elegant nor monumental, and possibly arose out of Indian scribes' first efforts at *Naskhī*, a schoolroom script for provincials, which, when Tīmūr's invasion destroyed the unity of the Delhi Sultanate and Delhi's metropolitan claims and contacts with the rest of the Islamic world, became elevated to the status of a Koranic script. The earliest known Koran in this script is dated 801/1399, from Gwalior (No.18), a provincial fortress in central India, and displays a great variety of ornamental motifs, taken both from Iranian and Indian sources. These shed little light on Tughluq illumination, although from the geometrical frontispiece it may be inferred that 14th-century Delhi had studios in which the Īl-Khānid type of illumination was practised, and that some of this work was known in the provinces. Likewise it would appear that in Delhi Kufic was used in the headings and inscriptional panels of Korans, and that this was known also in the provinces, but, like the geometrical frontispieces, knowledge of, and ability to use, these elements of illumination must have practically disappeared with the destruction of Delhi. They are found in no manuscript of the Koran from India after 1399. The scribe must have been a provincial calligrapher, practising a script that would not have been tolerated for royal Koran manuscripts in Delhi, and it is he who doubtless attempted the shaky Kufic of some of the inscriptional panels. Another, and far superior calligrapher, wrote

20 f.110b. *Sūrah* heading (*sarlavḥ*) and marginal decoration (*shamsa*). The *Behārī* script is fully developed (No.20, p.56).

the other Kufic headings and probably also the fine *Thuluth* inscriptions on all the other illuminated pages. There was no shortage of fine calligraphers using *Thuluth* in 15th-century India (No.21).

The basic structure of the illumination of the Gwalior Koran, in which central panels of the text beginning each of the 30 *jūz* into which the Koran is divided, are surrounded by four panels of illuminations with prolongations of the upper and lower ones into the margin, with large projecting *ansas* between, is echoed in several other fairly crude Korans of the 15th century which all have some 30 illuminated double-pages, and use the *Behārī* script. This group of Korans is usually of medium height, on very crude paper which the acidic green pigments have invariably eaten away, and generally does not have any marginal illuminations marking the passage of the verses. It is difficult to believe that they are of royal provenance, and they were probably made for patrons of no great social standing. The general style of the Gwalior Koran of 1399 may, however, have spread to Delhi in the early 15th century, which under the Sayyid and Lodī dynasties (1414–1526) remained a sad shadow of its former self for much of the century and incapable of supporting much artistic endeavour, far less than the other courts. This group of Korans then possibly represents the Delhi school of the period.

A Koran manuscript in *Behārī* script in the Salar Jung Museum, Hyderabad, with a dated colophon gives us the key to the chronology of another group of these manuscripts. The date is slightly obscured, but probably reads 926/1520. The calligrapher has employed various devices which are typically Indian, including using the margins for subsidiary matter in a decorative manner. The illuminative content is again typical of several other Korans, consisting of five illuminated margins around the beginnings of key chapters of the text, of double frames, the inner of blue and crimson with gold tracery, the outer of a creeper, with alternate full and expanding lotuses, either in colours or in gold tracery over blue; of marginal medallions either pear-shaped with finials above and below, in blue or blue and crimson, with gold tracery, or circular with heavy use of orange with dark orange flower designs; and of chapter headings usually of gold script over blue or a pink criss-cross design, with orange in-fill designs at either end of the panel, and rudimentary palmettes almost disappearing behind the frame.

By and large this particular manuscript is crude, and suggests that it is at the end of a tradition rather than the beginning. Another Koran, undated, also in the Salar Jung Museum, is in the same tradition, but suggests because of its much higher quality and subtle differences a somewhat earlier date. The heavy use of crimson in the 1520 manuscript is paralleled by a similar development in illustrated Jaina manuscripts of the period after 1500; crimson is a costly pigment, sparingly used in the 15th century, which suddenly became much more widely used in the 16th. This second Koran uses crimson much more sparingly. The arabesque and creeper designs are much bolder, freer and far more beautiful, the medallions much more inventive in their illuminative content, many of them being suggestive of the textile designs seen in Jaina paintings of the 15th century. It is to the latter part of this century that it may be dated, along with a less ambitious Koran in the British Library (No.20). There are enough of such Korans surviving to suggest a definite school flourishing in the latter part of the 15th and first part of the 16th centuries. A *terminus ante quem* is provided by the absence of such

19 f.153. Illuminated verbal puzzle (No.19, p.56).

23 f.40b. The evil Zuhhāk is brought before Farīdūn. The attendant appears to think the tent is a parasol (No.23, p.58).

manuscripts from the Mughal period, with its renewed powerful influence from Iran in the book arts. Comparison with other manuscripts of the period around 1500, suggests that only Delhi itself and Jaunpur are possible provenances, to the former of which we have already assigned the crude school of Koranic illumination mentioned above. Jaunpur, however, on the evidence of a manuscript produced there in 1400 with a very individual illuminative content (No.19) may be considered a distinct possibility for this type of work. The development of this school in the neighbourhood of Bihar may also explain the title *Behārī* given to the script.

Normal Middle Eastern *Thuluth* was a serpentine, static script, used mostly for chapter-headings and inscriptions. In India there developed in the early 15th century a more dynamic variety, with tall slanting uprights and onward-sweeping sub-linear curves and flourishes, used for large one-volume Korans. Everything about the Koran known to have been in the library of Sultan Mahmūd Bigarha of Gujarat in 1488 (No.21) points to a Gujarati origin *c.*1425–75, since its illumination contains decorative motifs found in contemporary Gujarati illustrated manuscripts. An even more ambitious and better preserved manuscript in the Rampur State Library is in this same majestic *Thuluth* and has four illuminated double-pages with frames of rich floral and arabesque designs, as well as chapter-headings and marginal ornaments in the same style.

These three groups of Korans are the surviving evidence for independent schools of illumination which we have assigned to Delhi, Jaunpur and Ahmadabad. Nonetheless the different types of Koranic illumination may have been practised in other centres also, or have been more widespread. The rich kingdoms of Bengal, Malwa and the Deccan must have produced schools of Koran illumination, but at the moment we have no knowledge of them whatsoever.

Although the rulers of Delhi before 1400 were able to attract to their court scholars and poets from other parts of the Islamic world, there is no evidence that they were able to attract artists. Yet painters must have flourished in Delhi: the institutes of Firoz Shāh Tughluq (1351–88) state that he had the wall paintings in the palace covered up, while the *Candāyana* of Maulānā Dā'ūd written in the same reign refers to palace wall-paintings with Hindu themes (No.46). Although there is not a single reference to manuscript illustration being practised at the Delhi court in this period, there is now known a considerable number of illustrated Persian and Avadhi manuscripts from the period between 1400 and the advent of the Mughals. These manuscripts may be divided into three broad groups. The first, work in basic Iranian styles, is in two parts, the earlier being a controversial group of mid-15th-century manuscripts of the Persian classics, which are in a simplified or provincial Timurid idiom, with characteristics which are archaic or provincial but not necessarily Indian (Nos.22–3). This type of work, basically metropolitan Persian but executed in India, is better documented by the second part of this group, manuscripts securely linked to Mandu, Bengal and Golconda in the 16th century, in which the Indian characteristics are more pronounced (Nos.40–4, 47–9). A second group consists of a small number of manuscripts probably not connected with any Muslim court but produced for other patrons, in which are found archaic elements from the 14th-century Mamluk and Inju styles as well as medieval Indian characteristics. They date from the mid-15th century (Nos.33–4). The third group consists of two lovely 16th-century manuscripts of the *Candāyana* of Maulānā Dā'ūd, in which Persian and Indian elements are thoroughly synthesized (Nos.45–6).

All aspects of Indian painting in the 15th and 16th centuries are hotly disputed, even the terminology. It is proposed here to use the term Sultanate to refer to all the above groups collectively, with further subdivisions as necessary. The Delhi Sultanate is a convenient term coined by historians to differentiate the period *c.*1200 to 1526 from the old Indian states system which preceded it and the Mughal imperium which followed it, and we propose to use the term here to mean all manuscripts and painting done by or for Muslims during this period.

The briefest outline of events in Iran is necessary here. Despite general Muslim disapproval of the art of painting, it flourished in the form of manuscript illustration in the various courts of Iran under royal patronage. The earliest styles have been lost, but were doubtless similar to Arab painting at Baghdad in the 13th century. The conquest of Iran by the Mongols in this same century brought considerable Chinese influence to bear, particularly at Tabriz in the first half of the 14th century, although in the south, in Shiraz, work continued in the old way. Most of this 14th-century work is based on a horizontal viewpoint without a landscape tradition. However, towards the end of the century, in the Jalayrid courts at Baghdad and Tabriz, and at the Shiraz court of the Muzaffarids, the normal viewpoint was lifted, thus affording to the painter a new world of landscape (now terminated by a high horizon) and new possibilities of spatial relationships between figures. The conquest by Tīmūr at the end of the century did nothing to upset this development, and indeed under his descendants in the 15th century, the Timurids, Iranian painting reached its greatest heights.

Our first group of manuscripts with miniatures based on the Timurid style of Shiraz of the early 15th century, have been attributed by various scholars to 15th-century India, although none has a provenance. They are linked together by a generally simple appearance. They are usually in horizontal format across the page, or sometimes squarer in shape with text columns on either side, towards the bottom of the page, both formats recalling 14th-century Persian painting. Other archaicisms and oddities have also been pointed out by Ettinghausen and Fraad, which, while mostly incontrovertible, do not actually point to India rather than to any other provincial centre away from the Timurid courts of Iran; archaicisms and provincialisms also occur in 15th-century Iranian paintings, such as in the British Library's Dunimarle *Shāhnāma* from Mazandaran or in the Central Asian styles. Nonetheless, there is a basic core of material which does suggest an Indian provenance, of which the Mohl *Shāhnāma* (No.22) has perhaps the best claim, as stylistic arguments are in this instance backed up by other evidence.

However, it is difficult to reconcile the apparent existence of these Timurid styles in the first half of the 15th century with the facts of Indian history and with the proven examples of Indian Muslim painting produced at the same time and in the early 16th century (see below). The most important group of these Timurid manuscripts of suggested Indian provenance are dated during the period 1420–50. Delhi may be ruled out as a provenance, and there is no evidence of the provincial sultans patronizing artists until later in the century. However, the *Sharafnāma*

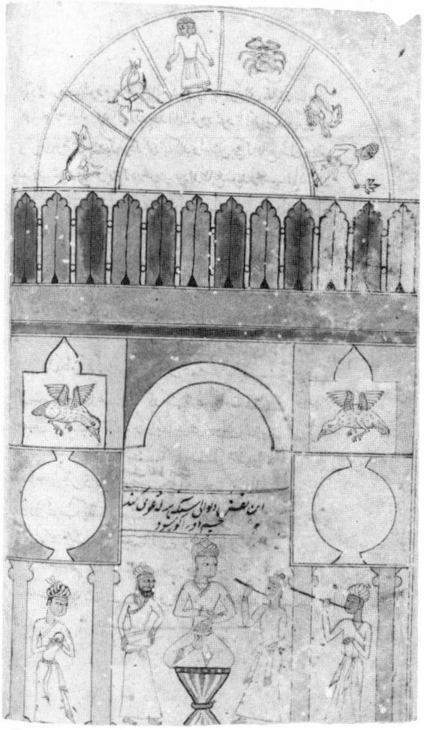

43 f.7b. Diagram illustrating the façade of a water-powered clock, in which musicians sound the hours (No.43, p.68).

produced in Bengal in 1531 (No.44), whose style is based on that of early 15th-century Shiraz and incorporates Mongol archaicisms, argues that Bengal at least had a Timurid school.

The picture becomes much clearer by 1500. A group of manuscripts (Nos.40–3) is known from Mandu *c*.1490–1510, in which the direct influence of new Iranian styles is visible, *i.e.* those of the Turkman style of Shiraz, and of Herat. The Khaljī Sultans of Malwa would seem to have imported artists and possibly manuscripts from Iran, and had the style copied by their own artists. Ghiyāth ad-Dīn Khaljī on coming to the throne in 1569 announced that henceforth his life would be one not of statecraft but of pleasure, and his biographer records with admiration his single-minded devotion to this principle. Although he had hundreds of women taught the various arts and sciences to amuse him, there is no mention of painting being one of them. However, the facts speak for themselves, for four illustrated manuscripts are associated with the Khaljī rulers. The earliest, a lectionary by a Mandu author, is illustrated in the purest Turkman style of Shiraz (No.40), and the artist must have come to Mandu about 1490. While there, he would appear to have trained at least two Mandu artists in the Shiraz style, and their work, much more Indianized, is seen in the cookery-book, the *Niʿmatnāma* (No.41), begun for Ghiyāth ad-Dīn and completed under his successor Nāsir ad-Dīn (1500–10). For the latter was illustrated about 1500–02 a *Būstān* of Saʿdī (No.42) in the Herati manner with the artists, again at least two, copying from a Herat manuscript but with improvisations of their own. The last of the four manuscripts, dated in 1509 (No.43), is a copy of an Arabic automata manuscript, but gives some hints as to the origin of the early Deccani styles. All these manuscripts indicate direct recent exposure to Iranian influence. A different situation obtained in Bengal where a *Sharafnāma* (No.44) was illustrated in 1531. It is the sole survivor and end-product of a flourishing independent school, for the style of the manuscript is based ultimately on that of Shiraz a century previously, combined with some 14th-century archaicisms – the Mongol type of rocks for instance. The Golconda manuscripts will be discussed below.

In Iranian painting the lifting of the viewpoint and the adoption of the high horizon occurred as the inevitable concomitant of attempting a fully realized picture on a scale larger than in earlier 14th-century schools. In India of course where the native tradition of painting recognized no necessity to open out in this manner, the adoption of the high viewpoint for paintings in Persian manuscripts can only be seen as an adoption of the latest foreign technique, with no structural necessity behind it forcing the move. Nonetheless, if we are to posit Indian artists as the painters of the Timurid-style group they managed the transition effortlessly. The older technique of the horizontal viewpoint is henceforth seen in Sultanate manuscripts only of marked crudity which have been termed 'bourgeois'. These form our second group, which is attributable to the period 1450–1500 and is of no immediately obvious ancestry, and certainly not from the Timurid Shirazi manuscripts. Their format of painting across the centre of a page of text is strongly suggestive of the 13th- and 14th-century schools of the Middle East and Iran, as is the viewpoint, from the horizontal plane as opposed to the high viewpoint of Timurid painting.

Although the dispersed Amīr Khusraw manuscript, the Berlin *Ḥamzanāma* (No.33) the vanished *Sikandarnāma* and now the newly discovered Berlin *Candāyana* (No.34), are usually regarded as the main manuscripts of this group, there is a marked difference in style between the first and the others. The former is based on some 14th-century style, probably Mamluk, but exhibits little that is specifically Indian in style. An origin in Gujarat seems likely in view of the commercial links of the area. We are prevented from dating it very early in the 15th century, as we would be inclined to do on the evidence of style alone, by the use of a crude *Nastaʿlīq* hand in the accompanying text that must be assumed to be somewhat later than the reputed inventor of this script Mīr ʿAlī, in the late 14th century. The other three by contrast are hardly removed from the context of Jaina painting.

Any discussion of manuscript illustration in the Sultanate period must involve Jaina and Hindu painting as well as that in Persian manuscripts, as developments in one influenced the others throughout this period. We must return now to discuss the development of paper manuscripts in western India and the developments of illumination made possible by the new material. Palm leaf was speedily abandoned as a writing material in western and northern India during the 13th century, but the format of the new paper manuscripts kept at first to the proportions of the palm leaf, before gradually increasing the height of the folio. No attempt was made however to abandon the *poṭhī* format. Western Indian palm-leaf manuscripts are either in two or three columns of text, depending on the width of the leaf and the number of necessary stringholes. The early paper manuscripts all invariably conform to the one-hole, two-column pattern, with margins ruled in red, and red roundels marking the spot where the hole would have been in the off-centre 'central' margin, both on obverse and reverse. The reverse also has an additional red roundel in each of the outer margins; these occur also in palm-leaf manuscripts and are the places where the foliation is marked, the letter system in the left margin, and the numeral one in the right. On paper manuscripts the letter system was abondoned, and the numeral notation usually written in the bottom right-hand corner underneath the red roundel. This basic type of decoration survives in Jaina manuscripts well into the 17th century.

The earliest surviving Jaina paper manuscript with paintings appears to date from the middle of the 14th century, and is the hagiographical work on the founders of Jainism, the *Kalpasūtra*. In fact, the earliest illustrated manuscripts of this work in both palm-leaf and paper formats are contemporary, of the mid-14th century, and argue from their iconography that they represent the beginning of the tradition. A few isolated Jaina illustrated narratives are known from earlier centuries, but it is very probable that the Iranian tradition of narrative illustration was the catalyst which occasioned the very large number of illustrated versions of this text which have survived from the 14th- to 16th-century period. They were generally commissioned by pious laymen to donate to the temple library or *bhaṇḍār* of their spiritual teacher. The quality of the paintings varies tremendously. The earliest illustrated paper manuscripts are of high quality, but from 1400 on there are increasing stylistic exaggerations and rigidity. The human figure is more distorted, with exaggerated sharpness of features and protrusions at chest, bust and hips, and most disturbing of all, the further eye of figures in the invariable three-quarter profile is fully drawn and protrudes into space. This protrusion is already observable in many Jaina paintings in the palm-leaf period (Nos.15, 16), and indeed it also occurs in incipient form in much earlier frescoes at Ajantā and Ellora. We are lacking, however, in the crucial documents of the earlier centuries which turn this occasional slight exaggeration into an invariable one fully realized.

Various attempts have been made to explain this phenomenon in religious and metaphysical terms, but it is more satisfactory to regard it as a technical problem that was not solved until the 15th century. What we are witnessing is a stage on the road between the early habit of having all faces in three-quarter profile and the later one of having them all in strict profile. Why Indian artists should have gone along this road is at present an unanswerable question; but what is obvious is that they had technical difficulties in so doing. In the early period, the head is only slightly to one side, and the further eye ends just round the corner, with eyelashes protruding into space. By the 12th century in western India and somewhat later in the east, the head has shifted round somewhat further, the earlier occasional tendency to finish off the corner of the eye in space has gained the mastery and invariably half of it now protrudes (No.16). In the course of the 15th century, the head has shifted round still further, so that in some manuscripts people are really in profile with practically the entire further eye protruding (Nos.28–9). By the end of the century it was generally realized that this protruding eye was dispensable and there are several examples of illustrated manuscripts where the eye was first painted in, and then washed over with the background colour (No.35). From this time on it is only deliberately archaic, conservative Jaina paintings which keep this protruding eye; in progressive Jaina painting and in Hindu painting people are in strict profile. They are not necessarily so of course in Sultanate painting or in the Akbar and early Jahāngīr periods; but by 1610–15 most people in any school are in strict profile and remain so until European influences intruded at the end of the 18th century.

Another distinction between the palm-leaf and paper illustrated Jaina manuscripts is the abandonment in the latter, at least in the mass-produced varieties, of any attempt at modelling with colours – all is now flat planes of colour, contained within a sometimes brilliant but always brittle line. Paper is seen as a surface to be decorated with colours in patterns, yielding in the best examples a brilliant jewel-like surface. The number of pigments used has increased – costly pigments such as ultramarine, crimson, gold and silver are used in increasing quantities. The iconography of the *Kalpasūtra* becomes completely rigid by about 1400, and from this century and the next have survived large numbers of illustrated manuscripts of this text, practically identical in their subject-matter and colouring, based on originals of about 1400 (No.24). In these, against first a red background and later in the century one of ultramarine, figures are all in gold with details picked out in other colours. The carelessness and roughness of all these stereotyped manuscripts are evidence of flourishing centres for their mass production at the great Jaina centres of Pattan and Ahmadabad, superficially rich in appearance but in reality costing much less than the much rarer and far more beautiful manuscripts individually created by professional artists for discerning patrons. Examples of the latter are found from a much wider area, produced at Mandu (No.28), Idar, Jaunpur as well as Gujarat (No.30), but none is later than the very early 16th century, whereas the mass-produced type continues in production until a much later date.

24 f.16. Harinaigamesin transfers the foetus of the Jina Mahāvīra to Trishalā (No.24, p.58).

There are very few Jaina manuscripts which give us much information about their artists. Most colophons in which a scribe is named indicate that the writing was done by a Jaina monk. He may also have been the artist who painted the illustrations – the word *likhitam*, meaning 'written', can by extension also mean 'painted'. However, many of the mass-produced Jaina manuscripts have little notices by the side of the illustrations with the subject of the miniatures. These are notes by the scribe to inform the illustrator of the subject to be painted in the blank space which has been left. Clearly scribe and illustrator must have been distinct in these instances, but almost certainly the illustrator was another monk. Other colophons however can be read to indicate that the scribe and the illustrator are identical, for example in the famous *Kalpasūtra* from Jaunpur dated 1465, which was written and illustrated by a member of the Hindu caste of *kāyasthas* (professional scribes) from Bengal. Such a person was responsible for illustrating the *Mahāpurāṇa* from Palam of 1540. It is remarkable that in the small group of half-a-dozen Jaina manuscripts which mark stylistic advances between 1400 and 1540, the only two which have colophons naming scribes and artists both name Hindu *kāyasthas*. A Buddhist manuscript from Bihar dated 1446 (No.31) with illustrated covers has a Hindu *kāyastha* as scribe and probably artist. And the most important dated Hindu manuscript in a progressive style in this period, the *Āraṇyakaparvan* of 1516 (No.38), is likewise painted by a Hindu *kāyastha* from Bengali stock. The conclusion from the limited evidence available would seem to point to Hindu *kāyastha* artists being responsible for many of these stylistic advances. Yet if we look for other Hindu manuscripts of the period, we find only one or two dated or securely datable manuscripts of the 15th century from Gujarat, in style close to the Jaina, and a few documents from eastern India, to indicate the work which they were doing for Hindu patrons. That no high-quality Hindu manuscripts apart from the 1516 manuscript should have survived from this period to parallel the Jaina manuscripts is difficult to believe. Yet there is an abundance of first-rate undated Hindu material. To this problem we shall return.

The gradual change in the human profile throughout the 15th century has already been noted; it is accompanied by other innovations. The style as we find it about 1400 is already hidebound – there exist a number of almost identical manuscripts of good quality from the early 15th century. There have survived a very few manuscripts which show the loosening of these traditional chains – the 1439 *Kalpasūtra* from Mandu (No.28), and the 1465 one from Jaunpur for example – in which, visibly, first-rank artists apply their own intelligence to solve stylistic and technical problems. The Mandu artist, who is unnamed, had probably never painted a *Kalpasūtra* before, as he makes numerous mistakes in the iconography. He had, however, seen examples of Iranian painting. The movement is towards a style still linear but in which the artist can design his own paintings as he chooses without falling back on time-worn clichés. Significantly both these superb manuscripts come from outside the Jaina stronghold of Gujarat. From there comes another stylistic innovation towards the close of the 15th century, the direct incorporation of motifs from Iranian painting. Its significance will be discussed below. There is an absence of any progressive Jaina manuscript of the *Kalpasūtra* after about 1500 which suggests that professional artists went on to other things thereafter. Monkish painters on the other hand were

33 f.277b. A celebration at the marriage of Hamza and Mihrafrūz (No.33, p.63).

not concerned about the latest stylistic innovations, but continued right up to the 17th century with the traditional iconic representations.

Up until the 17th century, Jaina manuscripts show little development. They continue the good calligraphic hand found in the palm-leaf manuscripts with little significant variation other than a gradual enlargement and coarsening. In the 16th century there is a tendency for the red roundels to become diamonds, often with blue scroll-work around them. Blue scroll-work is also applied to the margins of the first few folios at this period; the more these extra decorations are in evidence, the later must be the manuscript. There is a surprising absence of binding boards; none has survived from before the 18th century. It is possible, however, that the decorative patterns imitating the medallions of leather bindings, or possibly ex-libris medallions, found on the first and last folios of many manuscripts of this period may indicate that no other covering was thought necessary. This pattern of a large central medallion with four surrounding smaller ones is seen on both Jaina manuscripts (Nos.26, 39) and on the opening folios of some Korans in *Behārī* script (No.20). It was discovered in the 15th century that it was possible to do far more to paper than was possible with palm leaves. Thus paper could be dyed various colours – red and dark blue were the two colours used – and the text could be written in gold or silver ink (Nos.25, 28, 30). This technique may be a reflection of an earlier tradition known in Nepal in the 12th century (No.11). Miniatures could also be included in this sort of manuscript; and all the margins could have their own decorations, either ornamental or figurative (No.30). It was even possible to use an entire page for a single painting on a large scale, which first occurs in a manuscript dated 1423. And in a few gloriously extravagant Gujarati manuscripts towards the end of the 15th century, every square millimetre of every page is covered with pigment (No.30).

Direct Iranian influence on Jaina painting is obvious only in two instances. One of the characters in a popular Jaina story, the *Kālakācāryakathā*, the Sāhi (king) of the Saka tribes who lived originally beyond the Indus and invaded western India about the beginning of the Christian era, was traditionally depicted as a figure derived from Middle Eastern art. The precise source has not yet been pinpointed but is usually ascribed to 13th-century Iranian ceramics. It is noticeable, however, that many of his followers often wear Mongol hats, so that influence from painting in early 14th-century Tabriz may also be possible. The king is depicted in Jaina painting wearing a long *qāba*, with a heavily embroidered collar, and long boots. He and his followers are always in full or three-quarter profile but the further eye never protrudes (Nos.25, 29). Ceramics with this sort of figure must have been imported into Gujarat in considerable quantities for it to be used in painting and to be recognizable as a foreign type. The image remains constant throughout the period of the production of these manuscripts (*c.*1370–1600), untouched for the most part by later Iranian influence. This latter is most apparent in a small number of richly illuminated manuscripts produced in Gujarat towards the end of the 15th century, in which Persianate figures are included in the marginal decorations. The *Kalpasūtra* now in the Devasenopāda Bhandār (No.30) is the most famous example of this style, in which horsemen apparently derived from Turkman painting in Iran are found in great abundance. These direct influences are of only secondary interest and importance in that they had no visible effect on the

34 f.54. Laurak in Chandā's bedchamber – her maidservant waits outside (No.34, p.63).

basic conceptions of Jaina painting which remained set in its mould until the mid-16th century and only relaxed after coming under the influence of a new Hindu style. They are of significance though in that they demonstrate that in the 15th century, Persian manuscripts were being imported into India, presumably to the courts of the independent Sultans. But that they had a wider influence than simply on court artists is proved by the 1439 *Kalpasūtra* from Mandu (No.28), which already incorporates a high round horizon even though not using it as an Iranian artist would. The flow of Persian manuscripts into Mandu must have been in existence long before the Khaljīs at the end of the 15th century when it first can be proved by documentary evidence.

We have referred above to some of the Sultanate manuscripts of the 'bourgeois' type being scarcely removed from the context of Jaina painting. In the figural type of the *Ḥamzanāma* (No.33), for example, the male, usually seen in three-quarter profile, without the projecting eye, is based directly on the realization of the Sāhi King seen in Jaina manuscripts, with long oval eyes, pupils to one side, heavy hooked eyebrows, moustache and pointed beard, and dressed in a *jāma* (gown); the main female type, apart from her long tight dress, is the female Jaina type but seen in the same three-quarter profile as the male, and she wears her hair in a long braid down her back, while her *oṛhnī* (wimple) stands out stiffly in wings. There is no model for this type in Iranian painting, and she must be an individual artist's creation based on the male Sāhi type. The conclusion is obvious that the artist was trained originally in the Jaina tradition, and, given the task of illustrating a Persian text needing Iranian-type figures, he turned for his models to the only source known to him, the Sāhi King in manuscripts of the Kālaka story. He can never have seen an illustrated Iranian manuscript. This, of course, is treating this manuscript as the earliest example of its type; the development from the Sāhi figure may have happened earlier, while the *Ḥamzanāma* is a later manuscript using the same style. In addition to this female type, the *Ḥamzanāma* has another, usually of dancing girls, always in profile, who have large almond eyes and heavy eyebrows, and huge round earrings; these are the dancing girls of such Jaina manuscripts as the Jaunpur *Kalpasūtra* of 1465 minus the projecting further eye, which in the Jaunpur manuscript is structurally otiose. There is no known Iranian model for these figures. All of them without exception display the characteristic Jaina distortion of the chest underneath one armpit. The *Ḥamzanāma* probably dates from about 1450. The contemporary *Candāyana* (No.34) is in a primitive style not far removed from a Jaina original. The projecting further eye is still used, the distortion of the chest is still apparent, but, divorced from the familiar iconography of Jaina stories, the artist has been free to experiment in composition. The women are still the Jaina type, apart from the representation of the bosom, and the men with square heads and crowns are based on the Sāhi King in the Kālaka illustrations, although less obviously so than in the *Ḥamzanāma*.

The only parallel Jaina manuscripts in which similar freedom is noticeable are certain Digambara 15th-century manuscripts from Delhi and Gwalior, and it is possible that other developments of this sort were occurring in this area of northern India giving rise to this type of illustration for Persian and Avadhi texts. We are inclined to ascribe the *Hamzanāma* to Delhi and possibly the *Candāyana* also.

We have so far discussed 'Jaina' painting without going into the vexed question of terminology. The style of a typically Jaina manuscript with its projecting eye, bodily distortions, and flat colour planes is also that used for certain Hindu manuscripts of the 15th century, and indeed in two instances for Buddhist ones (No.31), so that this purely sectarian nomenclature is inaccurate. Nor are other proposed solutions to this problem any better. We propose to keep to the quite erroneous sectarian nomenclature, bearing firmly in mind that 'Jaina' painting was quite frequently the work of Hindus.

In turning to the illustrated manuscripts produced by the Hindus in these early centuries of Muslim rule over northern India, we enter into an area of scholarly controversy in which facts are few and opinions multifarious. We have seen that no illustrated Hindu manuscripts on palm leaves survived the fury of the first onslaught of the Muslims, but that the existence of such manuscripts in Nepal argues that they must have been produced in India also. However, there is no sign of any before the middle of the 15th century. We must suppose that just as it was only Buddhist manuscripts which survived the wreck of the Pāla university libraries through being taken to Nepal, so it was only Jaina illustrated manuscripts which were preserved in the temple libraries of Gujarat and Rajasthan. It was after all only Jainas who would present illustrated copies of their sacred texts to the *bhaṇḍār*; the other manuscripts preserved thereby were of the Jaina sacred texts, religion and philosophy. Non-Jaina material seems to have been preserved if accepted as part of a scholar's library. Although some Hindu temples did have libraries, none seems to have survived in the crucial areas of northern India where we would expect illustrated paper manuscripts to have been produced.

The earliest such manuscript to have survived is in fact a Buddhist manuscript (No.31) but written by a Hindu at Arrah in Bihar in 1446, and with wooden painted covers probably by the scribe, in a style which has adapted the Pāla idiom to the angularities and distortions of the medieval school. After this comes a long cotton scroll manuscript of the *Vasantavilāsa*, a Gujarati poem on the amours of Krishna with the *gopīs* which is now in the Freer Gallery of Art. Dated 1451 from Ahmadabad, its style is indistinguishable from contemporary Jaina manuscripts. The next important examples are two pairs of book covers, one from Bihar dated 1491 (No.35) in which the characters are in strict profile and the other from Bengal dated 1499 (No.32), the latter in an angular, eastern idiom which need not concern us here other than to note its difference from the western and northern styles. Then there is a manuscript of the Forest-Book of the *Mahābhārata* dated 1516 (No.38), and an undated copy of Qutban's Avadhi romance *Mṛgāvatī* in the Benares Bharat Kala Bhavan, written in the Kaithi character very probably in Jaunpur or Bihar. These are in a style considerably removed from the *Vasantavilāsa*, in which the further projecting eye has disappeared and all the figures are shown in strict profile, while a more naturalistic view is taken of humans, animals, landscapes, etc. without the distortions and exaggerations to which the Jaina style is subject. The 1491 Bihar covers are also showing elements of this style, and lead logically on to the *Mṛgāvatī* from the same area, which we would date about 1510. The crucial question about which opinions differ is whether these are forerunners of a much more important group of undated manuscripts (the *Caurapañcāśika* in the

N.C. Mehta Collection in Ahmadabad, the *Candāyana* divided between the Lahore and Chandigarh Museums, the dispersed *Bhāgavata Purāṇa* (No.36), the *Gītagovinda* in the Bombay Museum (No.37), and the *Rāgamālā* now in the J.P. Goenka Collection, Bombay), or whether they are 'bourgeois', cruder, provincial derivatives from a style already in existence by 1500. This *Caurapañcāśika* group of manuscripts can only have developed stylistically after it had been found possible to turn the human head around into strict profile and drop the further projecting eye. It has been assumed that this occurred at the end of the 15th century, for there are two manuscripts, the 1491 Bihar covers (No.35) and the now vanished but fully published undated *Sikandarnāma* of *c.*1475–1500, in which the projecting eye was first painted in and then covered over with a wash of the background colour. It has been argued that the progression then leads logically to the 1516 *Mahābhārata* (No.38) and the 1540 *Mahāpurāṇa* and, if one believes this last to be the forerunner of the true *Caurapañcāśika* group, on to this important group last of all, to be dated 1525–75, which dating is reinforced by the presence of a crucial garment, the four-pointed *jāma*, in Mughal manuscripts as well as in the major ones of the *Caurapañcāśika* group.

There are however several important problems and pieces of evidence of which this argument takes no note. In an Indian context it is rarely the case that comparatively crude manuscripts, like the 1516 *Mahābhārata* which is dated from a village near Agra in the dominions of Sikandar Lodī (1489–1517), and its successor Jaina manuscript, the *Mahāpurāṇa* dated 1540 from Palam (probably a village near Delhi), are the forerunners of an advanced courtly style, rather than provincial derivatives from it. By assuming a non-royal provenance for the masterpieces of the *Caurapañcāśika* group, a precise location can be avoided other than the vaguest reference to a Delhi–Jaunpur belt, the latter city argued for on the basis that since one of the manuscripts in the group, the *Candāyana*, is in Avadhi Hindi, it can only have been copied in an area where this language is spoken. There are, moreover, elements of the *Caurapañcāśika* style apparent in the *c.*1450 Berlin *Ḥamzanāma*, the 1491 Bihar covers and the *c.*1500 *Ni'matnāma*, while the Mandu and Jaunpur Jaina manuscripts between 1439 and 1465 are on the point of giving birth to major stylistic developments. The Hindu artist of the Jaunpur manuscript has indeed modified his own style to accommodate Jaina traditions like the projecting eye. And the argument for as late a date as the early Akbar period for the major examples of the style, on the grounds that both the latter and the earliest examples of Mughal painting show the four-pointed gown, which is to be seen in no earlier dated manuscripts, ignores all the references to this particular costume in Mughal sources as a garment peculiar to the Hindus.

Now it seems to us that starting from a viewpoint without preconceived ideas on the dating of the group it is perfectly possible to arrive at very different conclusions. Starting from the major manuscripts themselves, they are of such superb quality that it is difficult to conceive of their being other than of royal provenance. We know from the *Āraṇyakaparvan* the taste of a wealthy Hindu patron and the result – an excellent manuscript, but as a work of art in a totally different class, with indifferent composition and a weak line. One is impressed with the major manuscripts on the other hand by their absolute sureness and confidence of line and colour, and by their ability to convey not merely the story they are illustrating, but the mood as well. First-class work of this sort in an Indian context can only be of royal provenance. Looked at from the point of view of content, there is a demonstrable intimate connection between these manuscripts, particularly the *Gītagovinda* (No.37), and the *Rāgamālā* from Chawand in Mewar dated 1605, in compositional techniques, landscape and particularly the method of dividing the sky into light and dark halves that is unique to Mewar. But on the other hand the Chawand *Rāgamālā* is so much less sure in technique that this argues for a considerable distance between the two. Goetz has rightly pointed out how all Mewar art and architecture from the first half of the 17th century is decidedly old-fashioned, being about 50 years out of date, and often harkening back to the days of her greatness under Rānās Kumbha (1433–68) and Sanga (1509–28). It is not surprising then to find this close resemblance and to see in the Chawand *Rāgamālā* an archaistic revival of a much earlier style.

Looking at the *Caurapañcāśika* group from another angle, we find that its simple compositional structures of a group of figures beside or in a pavilion at one side of the painting, with plain ground and a dark/light sky above, finds earliest expression in the two much-mentioned *Kalpasūtras* of 1439 and 1465. Moreover, the profile of the women in the latter manuscript, as has often been pointed out, is, with the removal of the further eye, precisely the profile of Champāvatī in the *Caurapañcāśika* – a square face, a huge, backward sweeping eye, a large triangular nose, with nostrils carefully delineated, and a sharp protruding chin which curves softly down into the neck. Some of the ladies in this 1465 manuscript, moreover, wear the *paṭkā* hanging in front of their skirt with a projecting point, and the *oṛhnī* or wimple standing stiffly out in a wing, the garment of the ladies in the *Caurapañcāśika* group. Now we know that the illustrator of the 1465 manuscript was a Hindu *kāyastha* named Venīdāsa, who presumably earned his living illustrating Hindu as well as Jaina manuscripts. We also know from two other manuscripts from eastern India, the *Kālacakratantra* from Arrah of 1446 (No.31) and a crude *Kāraṇḍavyūha* from Hoündi of 1455, that the projecting further eye was still usually there in the mid-15th century, but we learn from the *Piṅgalatattva* covers of 1491 (No.35) and the *Viṣṇupurāṇa* covers of 1499 (No.32) that it had disappeared by the end of the century. The whole of this area was under the control of the Sultans of Jaunpur and Bengal, with the exception of Mithila, so that we would not expect the latest developments in Hindu painting to originate there. But the artists were obviously aware of the latest artistic developments from elsewhere and introduced them where they could – into the traditionally conservative format of a *Kalpasūtra* in 1465 for example – and abandoned the further projecting eye some time in the 1470s and 1480s. And it is precisely in the area of eastern India least under Muslim control, Mithila (Bihar north of the Ganges), that the artist comes nearest to the *Caurapañcāśika* style proper in 1491 (No.35). If these developments in Hindu and Jaina painting occur in Muslim-ruled areas of eastern India by the 1460s–80s, we are surely justified in assuming that they had occurred in Hindu-ruled areas sometime before this. And for northern India, the only major Hindu kingdoms at this time were Mewar and Orissa, while numerous other smaller states maintained a precarious independence in other parts of Rajasthan, in Bundelkhand and Gujarat, and in the Panjab Hills.

It is for all these reasons that we accept the very early dating of a

39 f.14b (detail). One of the different kinds of *vimānas* (chariots) used by the gods (No.39, p.66).

controversial manuscript in the Simla Museum, a manuscript of the *Devīmāhātmya* dated in a chronogram *Śāka Tvaṣṭaguṇarasendu*, *i.e.* in the *Śāka* year 1361/1439–40, which was produced in Jaisinghnagar, probably in the Panjab Hills. The paintings are in the margins around a central text panel, and in a style which is a somewhat more desiccated version of the main *Caurapañcāśika* style, in which the females, although in the latter style's costume, have obvious affinities with the females of Jaina manuscripts, particularly in posture, with one leg extended and the other bent, for example, and is arguably a stage in the development of the style between its 'Jaina' origins and its climax.

It need hardly be said at this stage that we are lacking the crucial documents which would fix the development of the *Caurapañcāśika* style to a time and place. But indeed it is doubtful if such was the way it developed. Far more likely is that it developed out of earlier styles in different parts of northern India in the early decades of the 15th century, and that it reached its peak of expressiveness shortly afterwards with the *Caurapañcāśika* and Lahore–Chandigarh *Candāyana* manuscripts, both of which come from the same studio and at the same time, which we would judge to be 1450–75. Both these manuscripts maintain in their facial profiles precisely the same elements as occur in the Jaunpur *Kalpasūtra*, and have a wiry strength in their line that suggests rather than actually contains the distortions to the human figure found in earlier manuscripts. The line has been smoothed out in the dispersed *Bhāgavata Purāṇa* (No.36), which we would date about 1500, while in the *Gītagovinda* (No.37) there are significant new developments in the facial characteristics that would make a date nearer 1525 seem probable. In the minor manuscripts of the group, the Vijayendra Sūri *Rāgamālā*, the 1516 *Mahābhārata* (No.38) and the 1540 *Mahāpurāṇa*, the line is less angular, but weaker and rather nervous. Dated Gujarati Jaina manuscripts (No.39) of the later 16th century continue the latter tradition. As to the provenance of the major manuscripts of the group, although it seems likely that the *Gītagovinda* was done in Mewar, it is not inevitable that all were done there. Gwalior under Man Singh Tomar has long been considered a probable provenance by Skelton, while the Panjab Hills, other areas of Rajasthan and Bundelkhand, even Orissa, are all possibilities.

It is undeniable that Iranian painting introduced some new compositional structures to Hindu artists, yet what they took from it was solely what could be adapted to suit their purpose. Faced with a high horizon, the Indian artist rejected it out of hand as a means of expanding the compositional depth of his paintings, preferring to keep firmly to his traditional horizontal viewpoint with a monochrome ground, on to which he grafted a horizon and a sky. Where it was necessary to show foreground and middleground action, he preferred to divide up his composition into separate registers. Nor did he greatly care for the careful balance in a Persian manuscript between text and painting. In the palm-leaf period he was forced to use only a small area for his paintings with text beside it, and this remained so in the earlier Jaina paper manuscripts. Hindu artists and patrons grasped the possibilities a larger surface gave rise to, and quickly established a tradition of illustrated manuscripts, foreign to the Iranian bibliographic tradition, which are more picture-books with accompanying text than true illustrated manuscripts. This is true whether the manuscripts are Hindu, for which the

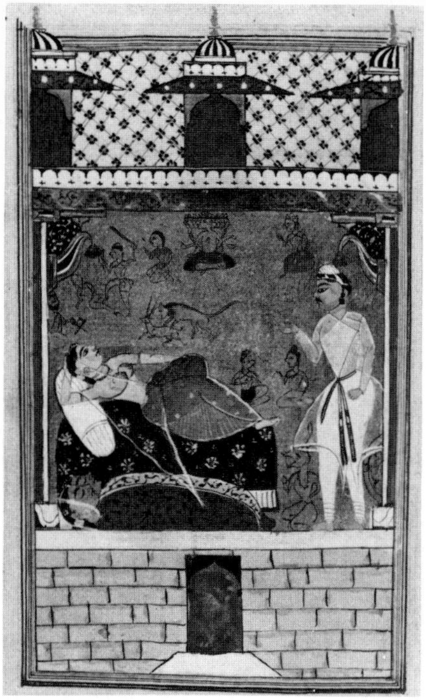

46 f.160. Laurak gains access to Chandā's bedchamber, on the walls of which are painted scenes from the *Rāmāyaṇa* (No.46, p.69).

poṭhī format was retained, or Muslim, such as the Avadhi Hindi *Candāyana* (Nos.34, 45–6) for which an upright vertical format was preferred, as more in keeping with Muslim bibliographic traditions. For all five surviving Sultanate-period manuscripts of this text are composed mostly of vertical full-page paintings with the text in the Arabic script written on the reverse, and this is true also for the Lahore–Chandigarh pages obviously done for a Hindu patron. For the *Caurapañcāśika* and *Gītagovinda*, a single verse is inscribed at the top, and the intention was to illustrate each verse of the text in this way. The *Bhāgavata Purāṇa* has only a label for the painting at the top, and the main text on the verso. We do not know for certain why this type of manuscript was produced, and it is difficult to think of possible antecedents for it; but in view of three of these manuscripts being in Sanskrit, with which by the 15th and 16th centuries patrons might not necessarily be too familiar, it could be argued that linguistic incomprehension might be a contributing factor. Avadhi Hindi might also not be readily familiar elsewhere in northern India, especially in the Arabic script. Since the *Candāyana* was dedicated to the Vizier of Firoz Shāh Tughluq in Delhi, it is probable that the original presentation manuscript of 1389 was also in this format. No doubt they were meant to be looked at in private with wives in a harem, who might not be able to read. We know from Abu'l Fazl's account of the Mughal library that the finest illustrated books were kept within the zenana. However, the existence of such a format in the second half of the 15th century for at least two of the surviving early *Candāyana* manuscripts (the Berlin manuscript, No.34, and the fragments in the Bharat Kala Bhavan, Benares) argues that it was not an isolated phenomenon, and that other manuscripts might also be in this format; this indirectly provides evidence of at least the potential existence of manuscripts of the *Caurapañcāśika* group in the 15th century.

We are now at last in a position to examine our third group of Sultanate manuscripts, a pair of manuscripts of the *Candāyana* (Nos.45, 46). They are the most beautiful surviving Sultanate manuscripts, and are the products of a sophisticated Muslim court, in which earlier influences from Iranian, Sultanate, Hindu and Jaina painting have all been assimilated, elements from each having been taken and used as required. The high round horizon is present in both but the viewpoint remains the horizontal, and middleground elements are usually placed on a different register. So the horizon and the ground and the sky above are sometimes realistically depicted, but more often used as elements in decoration, being coloured and decorated with gorgeous arabesques. Of the two, the Bombay manuscript (No.45) is the more beautiful and decorative, while the Manchester manuscript (No.46) more successfully integrates its various elements. Both, however, are sufficiently related to come from the same school with perhaps a quarter-century interval between them. It is clear that the wide variety of styles in which this text is illustrated, ranging from primitive, almost Jaina, paintings (No.34) to products of sophisticated Muslim courts (the Rylands and Bombay manuscripts Nos.45–6), and of a Hindu court (the Lahore/Chandigarh pages), renders untenable the argument that because the story of Laurak and Chandā is an eastern story and in an eastern Hindi dialect (Avadhi), all the manuscripts of the text must come from the eastern region where Avadhi was spoken. The only court in the region was at Jaunpur, and it is not possible that so many artistic styles could have been practised at the

51 f.174b. *Hastābhinaya* (hand-gestures) (No.51, p.72).

court, or in the city around it. The original text as we have seen was dedicated to the Vizier of the Sultan of Delhi, and we have argued that the format for illustrating this particular text was devised specifically to overcome the problem of linguistic incomprehensibility.

The Bombay *Candāyana* is linked closely to the *Niʿmatnāma* from Mandu in colouring, certain human types, details of landscape, etc., and it is not difficult to think of the *Candāyana* as from Mandu, *c.*1520–30. A *terminus ante quem* is provided by the presence of so many characteristics of this style in the *Ṭūṭīnāma* manuscript produced in Akbar's studio *c.*1560. The Manchester *Candāyana* has moved on another quarter-century from the Bombay manuscript, and is possibly from Mandu closer to its final fall before the Mughals in 1562. We have in Mandu at this time precisely the right type of sophisticated court milieu under Bāz Bahādur (1555–61) and his mistress Rūpmatī, a final brief flowering of an independent Mandu culture before its extinction by the armies of Akbar in 1561–2. The Bombay *Candāyana* style had time to spread from Mandu, and hence is widely represented in the *Ṭūṭīnāma*. Not so the Manchester manuscript, which is the last effort of a Sultanate court before being overwhelmed by the Mughal armies and by Mughal culture.

The three kingdoms of the Deccan remained independent of Mughal rule, in the case of Ahmadnagar until 1600 and of Bijapur and Golconda until 1686–7. No independent Sultanate school has yet been proved to have existed for any of these or the first independent sultanates in the south after 1400, although it is inconceivable that such rich and flamboyant realms did not support studios; it is possible that some of the at present unattributable Sultanate manuscripts may yet turn out to be from the Deccan, while we have noted above the possible influence from Mandu on later Deccani painting. However the earliest documented manuscripts from the Deccani kingdoms are the *Tarīkh-i Husayn Shāhī* from Ahmadnagar of 1565–7 and the *Nujūm al-ʿUlūm* of 1570 from Bijapur (No.50). Both display many of the characteristics of mature Deccani painting in their love of daring colour clashes – purples and yellows, pinks and greens, browns and blues – their rich and sumptuous character, the traditional Deccani costume, all of which argue by themselves a pre-existence for the style.

It has been proposed that certain of these elements may come from the art of the kingdom of Vijayanagar, the Hindu rival of the Muslim kingdoms of the Deccan, where wall-paintings at least flourished, and whose final destruction by the combined forces of the three was encompassed in 1565. Part of the loot from the destruction of the city may have been the painters carried off to new cities. However, no evidence has yet appeared in support of this theory in the form of manuscripts or paintings from Vijayanagar, and a more realistic solution is to postulate an earlier Sultanate school whose work has not yet been discovered. The *Niʿmatnāma* from Mandu does in fact display already in 1500–10 many of the Deccan's favourite colours.

The *Tarīkh-i Husayn Shāhī* also shows in the occasional detail, such as the faces of one or two of its women, a resemblance to the typical female profile of the *Caurapañcāśika* group, while its total misunderstanding of various motifs of Iranian painting, such as the invariable use of canopies emanating from windows to cover the royal hero and his womenfolk argues an original Iranian model for the style considerably earlier than 1565. It is not without significance in this respect that the earlier work

48 f.154. The unmasking of the deceitful damsel who tried to ruin the king's son. The domes are treated as if they were *ansas* (No.48, p.70).

49 f.116. The merchant of small means returns to his untrustworthy friend the son whom he had taken away to teach his friend a lesson. Note the fantastic architectural designs (No.49, p.71).

from the third kingdom, Golconda, which took part no less eagerly in the destruction of Vijayanagar, is under purest Iranian influence and shows no trace of the characteristic Deccani traits until much later. These earliest Golconda manuscripts display influence from Bokhara (Hatīfi's *Khusraw va Shīrīn* of 1569, in Bankipore), Herat (the frontispiece to the medical encyclopaedia of 1572, No.47) and Shiraz (the *Anvār-i Suhaylī* of 1582, No.49, and *Sindbadnāma*, No.48). Direct Iranian influence continues at Golconda in the *Kulliyāt* of Muhammad Qulī Qutb Shāh (1580–1611), this time from the Safavid style, but it is difficult to believe that the Safavid baton turban, which died out in Iranian painting about 1560, could still be in use in Golconda painting as late as 1600, the date suggested for the manuscript in its single published appearance. Within its highly Persianized style, but with some original Deccani characteristics now at last appearing in Golconda painting, we would like to assign it as early a date as is consistent with the admittedly confused chronology of the royal author's poems, *i.e. c.*1590. To this same period, following Douglas Barrett, we would assign the five Golconda paintings now in the British Museum showing Muhammad Qulī Qutb Shāh in his court, which display the developed early Golconda style fully for the first time, with its density of composition, built up often in layers, and lovely collisions of pinks and greens.

Little is known of the school of Ahmadnagar from the later 16th century apart from a few portraits, although it may have contributed artists to the Mughal studio (No.59). From the school of Bijapur has survived one magnificent manuscript (No.52) the *Pemnem* of the Bijapuri poet Hams, which at once contains three separate strands of Bijapuri painting *c.*1591. It is noteworthy that increased Mughal penetration of the Deccan from the late Akbar period onwards, together with possible sojourns of Mughal artists at the Deccani courts to which Skelton has drawn attention, resulted in a much denser Deccani style in the early 17th century in which landscape elements are much more important and are treated in much greater depth in the Mughal manner. However, there are no surviving manuscripts illustrating the superbly sumptuous quality of Deccani painting at this period, as the best artists poured their finest work into individual paintings. These must also have been done for the monarchs, who were by and large an immensely cultivated and civilized group; unlike most of their northern equivalents, they were conversant, and indeed favoured and wrote, in the languages of their people, Dakhni and Telugu – Muhammad Qulī Qutb Shāh's poems in his *Kulliyāt* are in Dakhni, not Persian, as is the *Pemnem* of Hams, the Bijapuri manuscript of 1591 (No.52). Hams' putative patron, Ibrāhīm II ʿĀdil Shāh (1580–1627), was the author, again in Dakhni, of a work on Indian music, and may possibly have commissioned the various sets of *Rāgamālā* paintings known from this period. They collected books and patronized poets and scholars – one of the great histories of Muslim India, Ferishta's *Gulshān-i Ibrāhīm* was written under court patronage in Bijapur, while innumerable poets and scholars in Arabic and Persian from many parts of the Muslim world flocked to their courts.

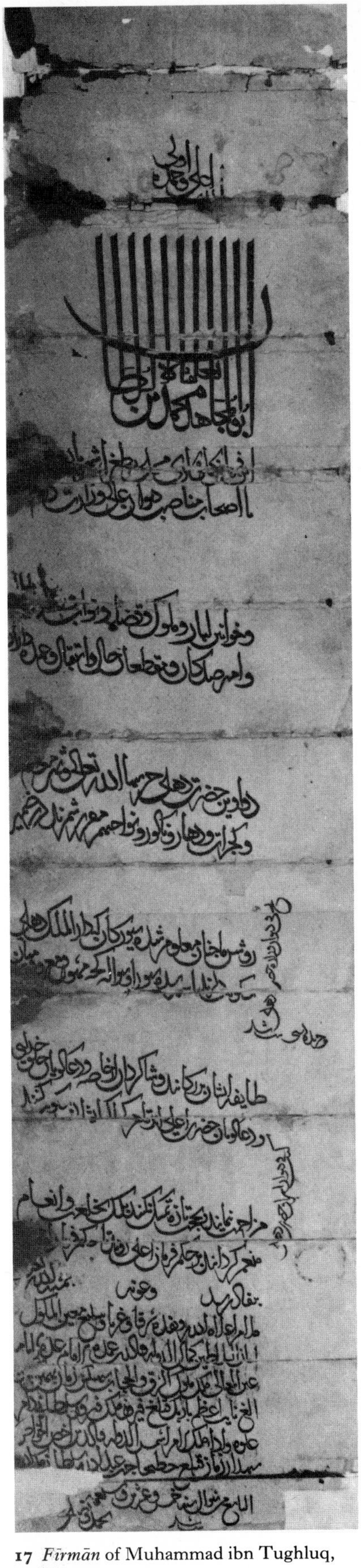

17 *Fīrmān* of Muhammad ibn Tughluq, Delhi, 1325.

17 'Fīrmān' of Muhammad ibn Tughluq

A proclamation issued on the orders of Muhammad ibn Tughluq, Sultan of Delhi (1325–57) dated Delhi 725/1325, to ensure good treatment by officials of loyal non-Muslims. It is in the form of a long scroll, with the Sultan's name and titles in *tughra* form at the top. It is the only unquestionable surviving document from the period of the undivided Delhi Sultanate.

The Keir Collection, Pontresina, Switzerland.

One scroll; 116×27·5cm; paper backed with cotton; 20 lines of *Naskhī-divānī* (chancellery) script, with heading in *tughra* form.

Bibliography: Keir 1976, pp.283–4.

18 'Qur'ān'

COLOUR PLATE VIII

The Holy Koran, copied by Mahmūd Sha'bān, in the fort of Gwalior, in 801/1399.

This manuscript marks the end of the Tughluq period of domination of India, as it was written just after Tīmūr destroyed Delhi. It is also, despite its damaged and much restored condition, one of the most beautiful of the material remains of this period of Indian culture, but presents considerable difficulty in the interpretation of its evidence. The colophon on f.550b seems unimpeachable as to date, being obviously in the same hand as the text, while Gwalior is the obvious interpretation of Gālyūr or Kalyūr. It is in the *Khaṭṭ-i Behār*, or *Behārī* script, in gold, red and blue, the former for the first, middle and last line and the other two alternating in between these two. Scribes hesitated over *Behārī* at the best of times, and it is difficult to think of this scribe, with his irregular strokes and variegated rhythms as being anything other than an inexperienced calligrapher and possibly a new user of this script.[1] He also included an interlinear translation in Persian in small *Naskhī* underneath the Arabic words.

There are 34 illuminated double-pages, marking the passage of the 30 *jūz* into which the *Qur'ān* is divided, plus four other double-pages, three at the beginning. The basic pattern of the illuminated pages is of text panels of five lines in gold, red and blue in white clouds over a ground of pink or brown cross-hatching, over which are drawn either lively floriated tendrils or simpler crown motifs or dots and crosses in red and blue. There may or may not be side panels of illumination, but always an upper and a lower panel with an inscription, the majority in a large and elegant *Thuluth*, of considerable sophistication, in marked contrast to the provincial character of the main text. Sometimes the side-panels also contain *Thuluth* inscriptions, at right angles to the body of the text. Usually an outer border of arabesques surrounds the whole, with its own border of lotus petals. There are always marginal medallions, either a central one or two nearer the inscriptional panels, and in this latter case usually an *ansa*, triangular, semi-circular, or half an octagon with points, protruding into the margin, with half versions of itself at top and bottom along the extension of the upper and lower edges of the panel of illumination. The pattern of this illumination is based on that of 14th-century Persian and Mamluk Koran manuscripts,[2] and is also known from later Indian Korans in *Behārī* script, which retained this pattern in a frozen state.[3] In Iran of course it went on developing with a multiplicity of palmettes and their incorporation into the marginal arabesques in the Safavid period (No.53).

As for the content of the illumination, there are the usual motifs of the arabesque (spirals and chains with leaves and tendrils in gold and colours) and leaf sprays, but with more varied colours and in different shapes from Iranian or Arab illumination. But more exotic, and hence presumably Indian, are the sprays of flowers found in many of the panels, as well as the elegant patterns of leaves and flowers forming the ground in the text panels. The basic motif in the latter is a five-petalled flower seen from the side, rather like a hand, which is seen again and again throughout the illumination. This is met with also in a much damaged, earlier Indian Ms.[4] Considerable use is made of the spray of unoutlined leaves seen in Shirazi illumination from about 1370, but here in various colours, quite often a lighter on a dark shade of the same colour, or vice-versa, which is seen in other Sultanate illumination (Nos.19, 20). The colourist has, in comparison with the Middle Eastern Korans' normal range of golds and blues, heavily emphasized the subsidiary colours – red and green and especially black.

The manuscript with a double-page geometric frontispiece in the Īl-Khānid and Mamluk manner of the 14th century, formed by lines radiating from a central star, with Kufic inscriptions in the panels above and below. No other such illumination is known from any other Indian manuscript, not even in the 15th-century manuscripts in *Behārī* based on this model. It is the dying gasp of an earlier, now vanished, Īl-Khānid style of the Tughluqs. This pair of illuminated pages, and the next two likewise, use an extremely clumsy and ill-articulated Kufic for the inscriptional panels, over illumination that, despite much damage and repair, seems in consonance with the rest of the manuscript. Suddenly, in the next two double-pages of illumination, the fumbling amateur becomes the master of a bold and vigorous style of Kufic, which is repeated on the penultimate illuminated double-pages. All other inscriptional headings are in *Thuluth*, in a hand much finer than that of Mahmūd Sha'bān.

Detailed comparative work within the manuscript itself reveals that some time between its writing in 1399 and the large-scale and clumsy restoration in the 19th century, it underwent another large-scale process of overpainting. Many of the colours used and colour combinations essayed are, simply, unbelievable for 1399, whether in India or anywhere else in the Islamic world. They make no sense whatever in terms of what is known of Indian painting around 1400 – the flaming reds, yellows and oranges in which this Koran abounds are never seen in western Indian painting for example, of which we have continuous examples from 1060 through to 1600. We must of course make allowances for provincialisms – not only was India provincial in terms of the totality of Muslim culture, Gwalior was itself provincial within Indian Muslim culture. Thus we may readily accept the strange outline of the content of the illumination – the odd flower shapes and tendrils, and arabesques.[5] Nonetheless, in medieval societies, artists do not suddenly create works out of their imaginations without reference to their artistic and cultural milieu, so evidence which contradicts these principles of comparison may be assigned to the repainting.

Space does not permit here a detailed account of this process of repainting. Suffice it to say that comparison between the two pages of a double-page composition frequently reveals a feature that has been overpainted on one side and not the other, and that for virtually every feature that shocks by its virulent and unharmonious colouring, there may be found elsewhere in the Ms. the same composition but painted in colours which are perfectly consonant with what may be expected from northern India about 1400. When and where the overpainting was done is not clear. It happened some time before the large-scale clumsy restoration, as it, like the original illumination, has been subjected to the same process. There must have been a fairly rapid deterioration of the condition of the Ms. between the two events, the former of which may be placed in the 18th century and the latter in the 19th. There is no especial reason to suppose that the first overpainting was done in India – indeed it seems more consonant with Middle Eastern work of the period.

Collection of H.H. Prince Sadruddin Aga Khan, Geneva, Ms.32.

ff.550; 29 × 22cm; good polished paper; 13 lines *Behārī* script in gold, blue and red in panels 22·5 × 16cm with margins ruled in gold, red and blue; 34 double-page illuminations; *sūrah* headings in gold *Thuluth* or *Behārī*; all marginal ornaments later repaintings; much damaged, and repaired; modern binding.

Bibliography: AI, p.370. Welch 1979, No.75 (f.40b in black and white, f.41a in colour).

[1]Scribes in the 15th and 16th centuries became much more purposeful when using *Behārī* script, and extended the horizontal sweeps in a much more pleasing curve. See Safadi 1978, p.29. A page from what appears to be a Tughluq Koran is published in Spink 1980, No.59 (see p.38 above)

[2]See BL 1976 Nos.73, 112 etc.

[3]As the damaged Koran in the India Office Library (Storey 1051) dated 1453.

[4]British Library Add.26189 (BM 1879 pp.71–3) has a badly damaged frontispiece with this kind of illumination.

[5]The openhanded floral motif referred to above is found in the Jaunpur *Kalpasūtra* of 1465, while there is a close similarity between some of the strangest flower shapes in arabesques in this Ms. and in the Devaseno Pādo Bhandār *Kalpasūtra* (No.30).

19 Anthology

Illustrated on p.40.

An anthology of Persian verses, without title or author's name, compiled in the reign of Sultan ash-Shārq Mubārak Shāh of Jaunpur (1400–1).

The anthology, known only from this Ms., is incomplete and has many lacunae, the poets quoted ranging in date from Firdausi to Hāfiz, and include some Indian poets unknown to Persia. The author of the anthology speaks of Mubārak Shāh as still living, in the heading he uses to introduce a poem addressed to that sovereign by Malik 'Azīzallāh. It is possible therefore that this Ms. is the autograph of the work and in fact dates from 1400–1. The hand is a 15th-century Indian *Naskhī*; the illuminated headpieces, in which the title is written in white on gold in a cartouche or medallion, with blue borders surrounded by an orange ground with flower and leaf designs in a darker shade of orange, are typical of the period. A *terminus ante quem* is in any case provided by a note in a later hand dated Delhi 935/1529.

The illuminations are rather crude, but shed light on this obscure period in the history of book production in India. The most interesting passages from this point of view occur in folios 152b–156a, eight pages of illuminated verses written in fanciful shapes, including circles, the spokes of a wheel, branches of a tree and so on. In these pages are seen further examples of the sprays of leaves in two tones of orange, white sprays on blue, lotus petals around medallions, cross-hatching and basket patterns in red, and the five-petalled flower viewed from the side, all of which occur in the Gwalior Koran of 1399 (No.18).

British Library, London, Or.4110.

ff.445; 25 × 15·5cm; creamy, slightly burnished paper; 25 lines of black *Naskhī* with headings in red, in various arrangements in panels 17·5 × 10cm, with margins, columns, headpieces etc. ruled in red in two thin lines; numerous headpieces, white script on gold, with blue and orange surrounds; eight pages of more elaborate illumination; modern binding.

Bibliography: BM 1895, pp.232–3.

20 'Qur'ān'

Illustrated on p.39.

The Holy Koran.

This manuscript is a good example of the type of Koran illumination which we associate with Jaunpur. It is undated, but assignable to about 1500, and is copied in a comparatively good *Behārī* script, which has now fully developed the horizontal curving sweep that particularly marks this script, and which in the 1399 Koran (No.18) is only just developing. The Koran begins with a now covered-over diamond medallion with four surrounding roundels, a pattern we find repeated on the first and last folios of some Jaina manuscripts.

There are four double-pages of illumination consisting of frames of blue, crimson and gold around eight or nine lines of text on a pink cross-hatching. The frames are either plain crimson or blue, with a slight pattern of dots, or a combination of these two colours divided by a wavy line down the centre of the frame; or blue with gold arabesques and circular medallions. The pink ground is dotted with crown motifs. There are panels at top and bottom, usually with blue cartouches with a gold heading in *Thuluth* with orange endpieces. The chapter-headings are disposed like these panels, but sometimes do not actually have the titles inscribed on the central cartouches. Verse markers in the margins consist of roundels in orange with gold borders (for ten verses), more elaborate roundels with an outer ring of alternate segments of blue and black (for 50 verses) and a pear-shaped medallion in blue and gold round a roundel with prolonged finials for 100 verses. The most used decorative element in all this illumination is of an orange ground with a darker orange or blue spray of leaves on it. The pear-shaped medallions contain the same motif of a gold arabesque with medallions as in some of the frames of the double-pages. The Koran seems transitional between the Jaunpur Ms. of 1400 (No.19) and larger, early 16th-century Korans such as those in the Salar Jung Museum which are much expanded versions of this one. At some stage the Ms. was split up and bound in four separate volumes, without regard to correct division.

British Library, London, Add.5548–51.

Provenance, purchased in 1794 from the collection of Capt. Charles Hamilton of Calcutta (d.1792).

ff.192, 187, 192, 190; 28 × 20cm; paper, creamy-brown; 11 lines of *Behārī* script, with margins ruled in red and black in panels 20 × 13cm, with similar outer margins; interlinear Persian translation in red *Naskhī*; rebound in 4 vols. in red with stamped medallions and corner-pieces, with painted black frame, 17–18th century; late 18th-century spines.

Bibliography: BM 1846, p.57.

21 'Qur'ān'

Illustrated on p.38.

The Holy Koran, unascribed, but before 893/1488.

This much damaged volume is datable to the middle of the 15th century, prior to the date of the seal (893/1488) impressed on f.338a, an 'ex-libris' from the library of Mahmūd Shāh 'Bigarha', Sultan of Gujarat, 1459–1511. This however applies only to part of the work, ff.123–637; folios 1–122 and 638–752 are 19th-century replacements.

The original part of the Ms. is copied in a superbly vigorous hand, in Indian *Thuluth*. The illumination of this Ms. was never completed, the illuminated folios extending now only from ff.394–490; it was originally intended to include panels for the *sūrah* headings with marginal palmettes, as well as verse markers of both circular and pear-shaped form. There have survived only one *sūrah* heading and 33 marginal ornaments, of which 15 have been removed from the discarded original pages at the time of refurbishment and stuck on to the new folios, as well as traces of a few other headings, and outline drawings for some more headings and marginal ornaments. The content of the illumination affords a further demonstration of the originality of early Muslim art in India. Doubt has been cast[1] on its 15th-century origin, because of its unusualness for this date, when compared with contemporary Timurid illumination in Iran, but everything we know now about Koranic illumination in India demonstrates the remoteness of the illuminators from Middle Eastern models and their ability to utilize new motifs, derived from the basic repertoire of Indian designs. They already favoured the use of more than blue and gold, and considerable areas were coloured in black, red and green. The motifs of the illumination in this Ms. are of two basic kinds: one is a chain of arabesques around a central circle of green and gold diamonds of different colours against a background usually blue, but sometimes divided between blue and black; the other is derived from the Iranian motif of a spray of gold leaves against blue, popular in Shirazi illumination of the 14th and 15th centuries.[2] Here the illuminator has again added red and green to this basic colour scheme, centring it round a central medallion of green and gold. The solitary surviving *sūrah* heading of f.457b consists of a simple arabesque of gold picked out in red against which the heading is set, also in gold, surrounded by margins of green, gold and blue, with a palmette. The verse dividers are gold rosettes picked out in red and blue. An elegant *tughra* in the margin makes the beginning of many of the chapters.

At some stage the manuscript was given as a *waqf* (religious endowment), as this is written every ten folios across the top of the page from f.139b to f.310, and intermittently thereafter, presumably after it left the library of Mahmūd 'Bigarha'. All the *waqf* marks have been defaced. The 19th-century refurbisher has attempted to imitate the original hand, unsuccessfully, and provided a double-page frontispiece of stunning vulgarity.

The obvious place of origin for the Ms. is Gujarat itself, which the powerful Sultan Mahmūd 'Bigarha' made one of the most important powers in the Indian system. The colours used in the illuminations are the same as those used in contemporary Jaina painting and are in fact the same pigments,[3] while there is a basic similarity of illuminative motifs.[4]

British Library, London, Add.18163.

ff.752; 37 × 26cm; thin paper, original, ff.123–637; ff.1–122 and 638–752 creamier paper, 19th century; seven lines in Indian *Thuluth* in panels 26 × 18cm ruled in blue and gold; 19th century *'unvān*; red morocco binding with gilt margins, with flap, 19th century.

Bibliography: BM 1871, No.807. BL 1976, p.82 [reproduction of f.457b, the illuminated *sūrah* heading].

[1]*ibid.*, p.76.
[2]*ibid.*, pl.xx. This motif remained popular in India up to the 16th century – the illumination of Nusrat Shāh's *Sharafnāma* from Bengal, 1531 (No.44) also contains it.
[3]cf. Nos.24–7.
[4]cf. M. Chandra 1949, figs.93–8.

22 ff.9b, 10. Dervishes dancing before a *shaykh* (right); and a holy man apparently taking a class (left).

22 'Shāhnāma'

The Book of Kings, the Persian epic poem on the ancient kings of Iran, which was completed by Firdausī in 400/1009–10 under the patronage of Mahmūd of Ghazni.

The most famous work of Persian literature was the most frequently illustrated manuscript produced in the ateliers of the Iranian rulers, no expense being spared for the copies produced for bibliophiles such as Baisunghur and Shāh Tahmāsp. Innumerable copies were made for lesser patrons using much inferior materials, among which is this manuscript dated 841/1438, one of the prime candidates of provincial Timurid appearance for inclusion in a group of suspected Indian provenance.

This *Shāhnāma* is generally in a provincial Shirazi style in a sub-Timurid idiom, with 94 paintings of small format mostly occupying horizontal bands across the page. It is in many instances naive to the point of quaintness, and its extreme remoteness from Shiraz undeniable. A provenance in India is suggested by two pieces of evidence. The text of the preface, which is the old one prior to that prepared by Prince Baisunghur of Herat for his 1430 edition of the *Shāhnāma*, and the one almost universally used since, has the additional information that the author Firdausi, when fleeing from his patron Mahmūd of Ghazna, took refuge in India at the court of the King of Delhi, who eventually sent him back to Tus, the poet's birthplace, with rich gifts. This passage is unique, and strongly suggests an Indian provenance for the Ms. This is further supported by the evidence of the pigments, since the yellow mostly used throughout is Indian yellow or *peori*, a pigment prepared from the urine of cows fed on mango leaves.[1] This pigment in the 18th century, when first discovered and used by Europeans, was made only in a village near Monghyr in Bengal. Its manufacture and use may have been more widespread in earlier centuries, but this pigment was not used in Iran at all.

Given the distinct possibility of an Indian origin for this Ms., it is possible to use it to determine criteria for assigning an Indian provenance to other manuscripts. The illumination is ambitious, but comparatively crude, using poor-quality ultramarine. The unoutlined spray of leaves characteristic of Shirazi illumination from about 1370 is used extensively but crudely, with some details added in red. The double-page *ʿunvān* (ff.10b–11a) employs unequal panels on either side of the central text columns, and utilizes the type of broad straps of blue typical of later Indian illumination. The use of a heavy crimson flourish also perhaps points to India. The complete absence of the delicate curvilinear arabesques which are so typical of Iranian illumination under the Timurids and later the Safavids allows us perhaps to make distinctions between the type of illumination practised in India and Iran, the former being largely based on 14th-century models until the Mughal school. The unoutlined leaf sprays of Shiraz were still in vogue in Bengal in 1531 (No.44).

Although the artist uses the high horizon generally, he is reluctant to take advantage of it to increase the height of his paintings. In this archaicism we may see an incomprehension of the point of the high horizon, and of the possibilities of composition in depth it gives rise to. Only in the mysterious double-page frontispiece (ff.9b–10a) is the latter possibility utilized (this has suffered some damage, and the eyes have been largely repainted). It is the work apparently of a different artist to the rest of the paintings – his outline of the head for instance has a distinct squareness to the jaw lacking on all the other paintings.

The basic vocabulary of the artist's style is still that of Shiraz – figures, trellises, rolled curtains, clouds in TV aerial shape – and it would be unwise to assume that all sub-Timurid manuscripts employing these clichés must be Indian in the absence of other corroborating evidence.

British Library, London, Or.1403.

Provenance – Collection of Jules Mohl.

ff.513; 27×16·5cm; thin light-brown paper; four cols. *Nastaʿlīq*, margins, in panels 19·5×12·5cm within gold-ruled margins; one *sarlavḥ*, and ogival gold medallion, one double-page *ʿunvān*; 93 miniatures, mostly 7–8·5×12·5cm; many repairs; defaced seals; modern binding.

Bibliography: BM 1879 p.534. BL 1977 pp.50–1. Stchoukine 1969. Ettinghausen and Fraad 1969.

[1]Scott 1932.

23 'Javāmiʿ al-Ḥikāyāt'

Illustrated on p.40.

A large collection of anecdotes, tales, and notices, of didactic nature, by Nūr ad-Dīn Muhammad ʿAufī. ʿAufī was born in Bokhara, and travelled extensively before coming to work in Sind and Gujarat for Nāsir ad-Dīn Qubācha. The consolidation of centralized Turkish rule in India under Qutb ad-Dīn Aibak (1206–10) and Iltutmish (1210–36) meant the destruction of semi-independent chiefs like Nāsir ad-Dīn Qubācha, whose power-base was in Sind and the Panjab and on the capture of the latter's fortress of Bhalkar in 1228 by Iltutmish's Vizier, al-Junaydī, ʿAufī transferred to his entourage in Delhi and dedicated to him his collection of anecdotes which he had previously begun at his former master's request. He seems to have remained in Delhi thereafter.

Several copies of this work are known from the 14th century, but this Ms. appears to be the first illustrated copy. Dated 843/1439–40, but with no other details of provenance, it displays features which have been thought to indicate Indian as opposed to Iranian origin. Unlike the group centred round the Mohl *Shāhnāma* (No.22) which display features from Timurid Shiraz, this Ms., to which the Chester Beatty anthology of 1435–6 (p.124) may also be linked, has features possibly direct from the earlier Muzaffarid school of Shiraz, and not filtered through the Timurid style – the large, oval faces for example, and the fondness for building compositions of people in rows. The links of this Ms. with India are somewhat more tenuous than those of Or.1403, the chief one being the confusion of the artist between a royal parasol and a tent, as on f.40b where the attendant holds a guy rope in the apparent conviction that it is a parasol. Certain aspects of the illumination seem Indian – the old-fashioned heavy use of unoutlined leaf-patterns, with red highlights, the absence of Timurid arabesques, oddities in the geometric construction of the illuminative pattern, the use of broad blue bands in the *sarlavḥs*, while the illumination of architecture in the miniatures seems in places distinctly un-Persian (the mosque on f.113a, for example).[1]

The 12 original miniatures of this Ms. use the 14th-century format of an almost square shape towards the bottom of the page, and sometimes extending beyond it. Another ten blank spaces left in the same shape were painted in about a century later in a Bokharan style.

The Ms. was certainly in India in the late 18th century, as three more paintings were added in a provincial Mughal style, in an archaicizing format, while many of the margins and vacant side panels were filled in with animal paintings and floral decoration (this was a practice the Mughal Emperors favoured – see Nos.58, 76). If the 12 original miniatures are to be regarded as Indian, it would follow from the presence of the Ms. in India from 1440 to the 18th century that the ten 16th-century paintings were also done in India. These are in the style traditionally associated with Bokhara, but there is now considerable evidence that Bokhara-trained artists were working in India in the mid-16th century so that this causes no difficulties (Nos.55, 57). An interesting inscription on the painting on f.430b in the Bokharan style refers to the 'mighty Sultan who rules over all peoples, the master of the kings of the Turks and the Arabs and the Persians' without further identification. Such an inscription in itself suggests an Indian provenance.

British Library, London, Or.11676.

ff.572; 32·5×23cm; paper, creamy-white; remargined; original panels 21×16cm; 25 lines good-quality *Nastaʿlīq*, marginated in gold, with red and blue lines added on remargining; one ogival medallion, one double-page *ʿunvān*, four *sarlavḥs*; 25 miniatures; modern binding.

Bibliography: BM 1966 p.46. BL 1977 pp.35–6.

[1]Meredith-Owens 1965, pp.16–17, pl.IX.

24 'Kalpasūtra' and 'Kālakācāryakathā'

Illustrated on p.44.

The correct Prakrit title of this work is Pajjosanākappasutta, the Book of the Paryushanā Ritual, and it is the 8th

25 f.129. Kālaka and the Sāhi, on a fully illuminated page.

section of the 4th *Chedasutta* of the Shvetāmbara Jaina Canon, the *Daśāśrutaskandha*, and ascribed to the authorship of the sage Bhadrabāhu (fl.300 BC). The *Kalpasūtra* as it is now extant consists of three parts, *Jinacarita*, the lives of the *Tīrthāṅkaras* (the 24 founders of the Jaina religion), *Sthavirāvali*, the succession lists of the Jaina pontiffs, and *Samācārī*, rules for monks at the Paryushanā festival.

This manuscript of the work has a problematic dating, in a different hand, of 1403/1346–7, in itself inherently unlikely as the true date as there is no scribal colophon at all on which this addition could be based. Nonetheless, the shape and style of the Ms. denote a relatively early date of about 1400, as does its fine calligraphic hand. Another note in a third hand says the Ms. was presented to the Mahāvīra temple library (*citkoṣa*) in 1505/1448–9. Doubts[1] have been expressed that in fact the latter date is the true date of the Ms. We would argue that both miniatures and calligraphy are sufficiently elegant to make an earlier dating more likely.

There are 49 miniatures in all, a cycle of 36 in the *Kalpasūtra* and 13 in the appended story of Kālaka (No.25). They are in an early version of the popular style which was so abused later in the 15th and 16th centuries with mass production for undiscriminating patrons, but here it still retains its pristine charm. Against a red ground, the figures have their flesh coloured in dulled gold leaf, with details of clothing and architecture coloured blue, green, carmine, and black. The paintings are small in relation to the size of the leaf, which is long and narrow, not too far divorced from a palm-leaf model, and it still retains the off-centre margin and the division of the text into two columns.

Lalbhai Dalpatbhai Institute, Ahmadabad, Ill. Ms. No.105.

ff.132; 8·5 × 28cm; paper, smooth and lovely beige colour; six lines of Jaina *Nāgarī*, in two columns, eight and 12cm wide, with margins painted in red; single off-centre red roundel on recto, in all three margins on verso; 49 miniatures, within red and blue borders, about 8·5 × 6cm; unbound.

Bibliography: M. Chandra and Shah 1975, pp.41–4, figs.1–7, col. pl.1A.

[1]Khandalavala and Doshi in JAA p.406, on the basis of its similarity to a Ms. in the National Museum, Delhi, securely dated 1509/1452–3, of exactly the same shape and format.

25 'Kalpasūtra' and 'Kālakācāryakathā'

The *Kalpasūtra* (Book of the Ritual, see No.24) has often appended to it the story of the Jaina monk Kālaka, who changed the date of the Paryushanā festival at which the *Kalpasūtra* was recited. The story of Kālaka used for this purpose is known in many versions in Prakrit and Sanskrit, all of them comparatively late, and in them several different persons with the same name have been confused. The monk who changed the date of the Paryushanā in the 6th century is different from the Kālaka who instigated the invasion of western India by Saka tribes in the 1st century. In the Jaina version of this event Kālaka's sister was abducted by the wicked king of Ujjain, and in order to rescue her Kālaka persuaded the Saka king to invest the city of Ujjain with his forces.

Dated 1428 and copied in the city of Anahillapattan in Gujarat, this manuscript of both texts belongs to the type of lavishly illuminated manuscripts appearing from the beginning of the 15th century, in which the text is written in gold or silver ink on a crimson or blue-black ground, and the margins all decorated with geometrical and arabesque designs, as well as numerous miniatures. The standards of this type vary greatly, depending on what patronage was available. This one was produced for a patron of some taste, who wanted a rich effect but was not willing to pay the highest price for it. The Ms. ends with the verses giving us the patron's name, Nālha Sādhu, and a eulogy of his good works, his wives, his ancestors and his friends.

India Office Library, London, Skt. Ms. 3177.

ff.154; 8·5 × 28·5cm; paper, light-brown in tone where visible; six lines of gold or silver Jaina *Nāgarī* on crimson or black ground in two panels on either side of margin 3cm wide off-centred to the left; the panels measuring 6 × 8·25cm (left) and 6 × 12cm (right); most margins decorated with arabesque, floral or geometric designs; medallions in centre margins of both recto and verso usually decorated, with three medallions on verso; 49 paintings, 8·5 × *c*.6cm.

Bibliography: IOL 1935, pp.1254, 1261–2, 1381.

26 'Kalpasūtra'

COLOUR PLATE IX

The Book of the Ritual (see No.24).

About the middle of the 15th century, a small group of comparatively sober manuscripts is known from Gujarat, which employ gold sparingly for highlights as well as powdered mother-of-pearl, and with body pigments either yellow or a warm ochre. Their distinction lies mostly in their warm colouring rather than in any particular elegance of draughtsmanship or invention. This Ms. belongs to this group and is dated 1502/1445, with 27 miniatures; it probably comes from Cambay.

British Library, London, Or.13700.

ff.61; 11·25 × 26cm; thin paper; ten lines Jaina *Nāgarī* between red painted margins 19·5cm apart; 27 miniatures in double red

27 f.16b. A monk aiming at perfect chastity should beware of women.

and yellow frames mostly 11·25 × 6·5–8cm; red medallion on recto, three on verso; f.1b has decorative blue scrollwork among text panel and medallions, and along margins; f.1a has an elaborate pattern in red scrollwork based on a binding medallion with pendants, and with four small ornaments around it.

Bibliography: Losty 1980, fig.7 (repro. of f.2b).

27 'Uttarādhyayanasūtra'

One of the Jaina canonical texts, the last recorded utterance of the Jina Mahāvīra, in Prakrit, attributable in its present format to the early centuries AD. The text is concerned mostly with advice and admonition to the monastic community, but is accompanied usually by commentaries which illustrate the points made in the text by stories, some of them very ancient. The *sūtra* is not very often found in illustrated versions[1]; the subjects of the miniatures are usually taken from the commentator's stories, rather than the text.

This copy of the *Uttarādhyayana* is one of the earliest known illustrated versions; although undated, it must be roughly contemporary with No.26, of the mid-15th century. Several of the text folios, including the last five, are 18th-century replacements; the new colophon lacks a date, but says it was done at Stambhatīrtha, *i.e.* the Jaina stronghold of Cambay on the Gujarat coast. This appears to be copied from the original colophon, and does not refer to the place of replacement of the doubtlessly damaged folios. Cambay was known as a centre of painting, and there is no reason to doubt this.

The Ms. as it is now has 36 miniatures, and probably would have had one or two more. Usually, a single miniature illustrates each of the 36 chapters of the *sūtra*, with perhaps a concluding extra miniature. It, like No.26, is a somewhat more ambitious manuscript than the standard commercialized format of the 15th century, with a lovely palette range of yellow and red, with details in crimson, blue, green, pink, white and black, and highlights in mother-of-pearl. The standard flesh colour employed is yellow, against a red ground.

Victoria and Albert Museum, London., I.S.2–1972

ff.47; 11·2 × 30cm; thin, light-brown paper (later replacements on slightly thicker paper); 15 lines of Jaina *Nāgarī*, between margins in red, text 24·5cm wide; slightly left of centre diamond blank in text on each page; 36 paintings, about 11·2 × 10cm, including borders in red and yellow; unbound.

Bibliography: Unpublished.

[1]For other illustrated versions, see Losty 1975, and references given there, and Brown 1941.

28 'Kalpasūtra'

COLOUR PLATE X

The Book of the Rituals (see No.24)

This *Kalpasūtra* was copied in 1496/1439–40 at the fort of Mandapadurga (Mandu) in the reign of Sultan Mahmūd (1436–69) for a Jaina monk Kshemahamsa Gani. This Ms. and its companion undated Ms. of the Kālaka story (No.29) are stylistically the first considerable advance in Jaina Mss. since those of the late 14th century. The line is infinitely tighter and assured, there is a greater freedom of composition, and a wider range of colours; the artist had also seen some Persian manuscripts of the early 15th century, since he has incorporated the high round horizon into some of his paintings. The concept of a horizon, and the consequent differentiation between ground and sky, was not unknown before this to Jaina painters, since some slightly earlier Jaina manuscripts do show a triangle of blue in one upper corner. However, this is the first time that the high round Persian horizon is properly depicted, although obviously the artist was not prepared to treat it as a structural aid to composition – in some miniatures, he reverts to triangular pieces of sky at the two top corners, in others to a wavy line across the top, which is also the favoured horizon of the Kālaka manuscript (No.29).

Against the cherry-red background of the miniatures, the human figures are coloured lovely browns and ochres, against which their garments of pink, blue, white and green are set off to great advantage. The Ms. is remarkable for its range of lovely textiles, employing very different motifs from those common in Gujarati manuscripts of this period, and also for its details of contemporary furniture – thrones, beds, a lovely crib, etc.

The identity of the artist is not known, but he takes much greater liberties with the iconography and with the subjects, revealing complete ignorance in some cases. Thus Shakra is represented not as a four-armed god, but as a very human king, while in the transfer of the foetus of Mahāvīra, Harinaigamesin is carrying not the usual round object but a fully developed baby. In numerous instances he simply includes scenes never present in other manuscripts – such as Kubera's servants showering the palace with wealth, or Marudevī mounted on an elephant. The artist was obviously not a Jaina, nor did he have access to a standard illustrated version of the text.

The manuscript belongs to the class of richly decorated manuscripts, of which the earliest example is No.24 from Pattan dated 1427. However, the Mandu manuscript seems somewhat unfinished in this respect. The text is written in gold against a crimson ground, while the slightly off-centre margin is richly decorated with floral and geometric designs, but all the outer margins are left blank, in contrast to other manuscripts of this type. The edges of the leaves and most of the central margins have suffered considerable damage. The decorations of the central margins are of very large floral and geometric designs, in red, blue and green (the latter pigment being responsible for the damage). The size of these elements is in marked contrast to the decorations of the 1465 Jaunpur Ms. or that of the Devaseno Pāda Bhandār (No.30) and have little in common with other Indian decorative motifs of the period with the exception perhaps of the 1399 Gwalior Koran (No.18).

National Museum, Delhi, 49.175.

Provenance – Presented by Vijayendra Suri in 1949.

ff.73 (originally – four are missing); 10·2 × 29cm; paper; seven lines of gold *Nāgarī* on crimson ground in two panels divided by slightly left of centre margin, 2·5cm wide and richly decorated; text area in all 7·5 × 24·5cm; 30 paintings, about 10 × 7cm; unbound.

Bibliography: Khandalavala and Chandra 1959 (ff.15b, 43b, 61b. in colour). ND pp.17–21 (f.15b in colour).

29 'Kālakācāryakathā'

COLOUR PLATE XI

The story of the monk Kālaka (see No.25).

The text is the long anonymous Prakrit version.[1] The loosening of the traditional Jaina school that is observable in the *Kalpasūtra* painted at Mandu in 1439 (No.28) is also observable in this undated Ms. Like the *Kalpasūtra*, this Ms. is remarkable, within the Jaina tradition, for its depiction of real, not stereotyped, people. The projecting eye, while still present, is easily removable, leaving its bearer in full profile, while the eye in full view has an upturned rear corner as in the *Caurapañcāśika* style. A version of the high Iranian horizon is attempted, but with less knowledge of its true appearance than in the 1439 Ms. as it has a jagged edge rather than the proper circular one which is seen in the 1439 manuscript. This may possibly indicate a somewhat earlier date.

Lalbhai Dalpatbhai Institute, Ahmadabad, Ill. Ms. No.103.

ff.24; 10×29·5cm; paper; seven lines of Jaina *Nāgarī* between red ruled margins; red stellar pattern on rectos, slightly left of centre, the same plus red roundels in the margins on versos; 19 paintings, about 10×7·5cm; unbound.

Bibliography: Chandra 1967. ND, pp.21–3, col. plate 3, figs.20–2.

[1]Brown 1933.

30 'Kalpasūtra'

The Book of the Ritual (see No.24).

The tradition of richly illuminated presentation copies of this text reaches its most sumptuous heights in Gujarat itself, with this famous undated Ms. of the *Kalpasūtra* and *Kālakācāryakathā* in the possession of the Devaseno Pāda Bhandār in Ahmadabad, but from which come various dispersed folios. The Ms. has unfortunately been dispersed before being properly catalogued, so that even the total number of miniatures is not now known, nor has the colophon been fully published. The Ms. was prepared at the request of Sānā and Jūthā who lived at the port of Gandhār, near Broach (on the mouth of the Narmada) but the part of the colophon containing the date is missing. The commissioners must have been extremely wealthy and wanted no expenses spared in producing the most sumptuous effect. The text is written in gold or silver ink on grounds of red, blue, deep purple or black. The miniatures of the *Kalpasūtra* are in a good but not outstanding style of the late 15th century, usually against an ultramarine ground, with lavish use of gold in the figures, and the usual range of other colours. The miniatures of the Kālaka story on the other hand seem much more ambitious, and often occupy the full space between the side margins, although the space is not treated as a single unit but broken up into several scenes.

On all the pages, the side margins and the top and bottom margins are painted with the greatest variety of scenes both figurative and decorative. The side margins of the pages with miniatures usually contain a single female figure in a named dancing pose; she is usually in typical Jaina style in three-quarter profile with projecting eye, but occasionally the artist experiments with pulling her face round to eliminate the projecting eye, and also to show her in full face[1]. She resembles in these latter poses the type of face seen in the Berlin *Ḥamzanāma* (No.33) which similarly seems to be the result of experimenting in the depiction of the head at different angles, leaving a very round face with eyes quite close together. All the other margins are illustrated in the fullest detail and liveliest manner with animals, horsemen, landscapes, mythical beings with wings, others riding clouds (of the Chinese-ribbon variety), ships, arabesques, birds, trees, dancers, and many more, providing the greatest source of Indian decorative motifs before the Mughal period. The total effect in terms of taste is of course deplorable, but its perpetrator can only be admired.

There is obviously quite close Iranian influence on the Ms., of which the Chinese ribbon-clouds with rosettes, first seen in Timurid painting of the 15th century, is the most straightforward[2]. Many of the other decorative motifs, however, simply show the range of the Indian imagination in this field and the thorough mingling of native Indian and Iranian motifs which is first observable in the 1399 Koran from Gwalior (No.18), some of whose floral ideas reoccur here.[3] The scenes from the Kālaka story in which the Sāhi King appears show a large number of variations of turban types, which must for the most part reflect the contemporary dress of Gujarat. At least one of the turban types was still extant in Sind in 1775.[4] The Sāhi King himself has replaced his old-fashioned *qābā* with Gujarati textiles, and his followers wear a mixture of *jāmas* or *dhotī* and cummerbund. The horses they ride are of the typically Indian arched-neck variety, and are not Timurid in appearance. In short, we feel that the direct Iranian influence on this Ms. has been much exaggerated, and would argue that all of its stylistic concepts would have existed already in the syncretic culture of 15th-century Gujarat[5]. Its uniqueness is that the artist has been willing to experiment boldly while illustrating a text usually bound by conventional stereotypes. Only one other comparable manuscript has so far been found, a *Kalpasūtra* and *Kālakācāryakathā* dated 1501 from Pattan[6], which shows on the evidence of the little of it so far published a similar liveliness of invention, while the 'Persianate' revisions of the traditional concepts of the Sāhi King and his followers such as the new turban and garments are also present. The date usually ascribed to the Broach Ms. of *c.*1475 seems slightly too early, since behind it there seems to stand some quite widespread Sultanate style of illustrating Persian manuscripts, of which as yet we have no evidence for Gujarat but which could only be in its formative stages by 1475. The dispersed Amīr Khusraw is of possible Gujarati provenance *c.*1450.[7] A date nearer 1500 would seem more appropriate for this *Kalpasūtra*, although we would not seek to postulate influence in either direction between it and the Pattan Ms. of 1501.

30 f.135. Marginal decorations, including fighting pairs of animals and Muslim horsemen.

National Museum, New Delhi, 70-64 (single folio).

Provenance – ex Devaseno Pāda Bhandār, Ahmadabad.

ff.187; 11·5×26·6cm; paper; seven lines of gold or silver *Nāgarī* on coloured ground in panels, 7×15·6cm, with margins painted in red and gold or red on plain paper; gold diamond with blue scrollwork in red square, slightly left of centre, marks former stringholes; no marginal medallions on versos; all margins decorated with figurative or arabesque designs; number of miniatures unknown, from about 11·5×7·5 to 11·5×15cm; unbound.

Bibliography: Brown 1937 (Brown's suggested date is a century too late). ND, pp.29–43, col. plates 5–7, figs.45–96. JAA,

31 Upper interior cover. The eight great episodes from the life of the Buddha.

32 Inner cover. The ten avatars of Vishnu.

Vol.III, col. plates 28A and B, repro. of folio 135.

[1]ND, col. plate 5.
[2]*ibid.*, figs.66–7.
[3]Compare ND, figs.76, 80, with Welch 1979, No.75.
[4]British Library Or.8758, see Siddiqui 1969.
[5]Brown's publication, drawing attention to the Timurid and earlier elements in the Ms., appeared long before the discovery of any of the Sultanate schools of India. Scholarly criticism has been content to repeat his and Professor Dimand's views long after the new evidence ought to have modified them.
[6]Chandra and Shah 1975, figs.26–9.
[7]Ettinghausen 1961, pl.I.

31 'Kālacakratantra'

A Buddhist Tantric text on the worship of Time.

This palm-leaf manuscript, in a fine state of preservation, was copied by Jayarāmadatta of the *kāyastha* caste (scribes) at Āra in Magadha (*i.e.* Arrah in Bihar, south-west of Patna) in 1503/1446, at the instigation of the pious Buddhists Bhikshu Shrījnāna and Srika as an offering for their teachers, their mother and their father. The Ms. is unillustrated, but written in a most beautiful Maithili/Bengali hand.

The wooden covers are however painted, almost certainly by Jayrāmadatta: on the outside are ten scenes from the *Jātakas* on each cover, under simple round-headed arches with alternate red and green background, while on the upper inside cover are the eight great scenes from the life of the Buddha, all enacted under the Pāla pagoda, and on the lower the seven Mortal Buddhas with attendant Bodhisattvas, again under round-headed arches. The sides of the manuscript are decorated with a *pārśvacitra* in the form of a lotus creeper; this is one of the earliest manuscripts in which this decoration is still visible. Buddhism itself was obviously not totally destroyed by the Turkish invasions but survived among the laity without the institutionalized monasteries. The copyist, however, was a Hindu who observed the Buddhist tradition of the colophon, but whereas the Buddhist scribes had dated their work by the regnal years of the Pāla monarch, with grandiloquent titles, Jayarāmadatta is forced to use the Hindu epoch of King Vikramāditya giving him the same titles in abbreviated form. The use of Pāla stylistic idioms on the covers sheds some light on what otherwise is a long gap in the development of eastern Indian painting. Pāla idioms seen in these covers of particular note are the use of the stepped *maṇḍapa* under which divinities are depicted, and the lingering habit of showing the standing Buddha complete with throne-back and cushion which we have already drawn attention to above in late Pāla work (p.25). Combined with these Pāla motifs however is the contemporary one of depicting the further eye of faces in three-quarter profile projecting into space, also found in another crude eastern manuscript of 1455;[1] this is a motif universally found in the far more numerous western Indian manuscripts of the 14th and 15th centuries, but its presence here in Bihar shows it to have been a stylistic trait common to eastern as well as western India.

University Library, Cambridge, Add.1364.

ff.128; 5·8×33·5cm; talipot leaves; Maithili script; six lines; painted wooden covers, and decorated *pārśvacitra*.

Bibliography: CUL 1883, pp.69–70. Pal 1965.

[1]In the collection of Mr Haridas Swali in Bombay. The illustrations on covers and palm leaves are of the greatest crudity, and are little more than line drawings. The projecting further eye is very prominent. See Pal 1966 and Moti Chandra 1971.

32 Covers of the 'Viṣṇu Purāṇa'

The Sanskrit *Viṣṇu Purāṇa* is one of the earliest of this group of texts, datable to about 500, and is concerned with the legends and worship of Vishnu and Krishna. The Ms. which these covers enclose has now vanished, but the colophon is known to have been dated 1421/1499; it is a paper manuscript in the Bengali hand, shaped in close imitation of the palm-leaf format. Its extreme length and narrow width tend to confirm the dating. The covers were originally found in Vishnupur in the Bankura District of south-western Bengal.

The covers are painted on the inner surfaces with the incarnations of Vishnu, which in their angularity and disjointed articulation are the sole survivors from a late medieval Hindu school of eastern Indian painting, between the collapse of the Pālas and the early 16th century. They are the result of the development of the linear traditions of the late Pāla school (Nos.2, 8), and bear witness to the triumph of the linear over the modelled technique in eastern as well as western India. This linear treatment and marked angularity survives in later documents from Orissa (Nos.115–8) and Bengal.[1] Bankura, in south-western Bengal, adjoining Orissa, seems a very likely place of origin for these covers.

The subjects of the paintings are the incarnations of Vishnu, nine of the minor incarnations on one cover, and the ten major ones on the other, although the inclusion of both Balarāma and Krishna has led to the exclusion of Vāmana, the Dwarf. The figures are mostly in dark or light brown, against a red ground.

British Museum, London, 1955-10-8-03.
Victoria & Albert Museum, London, I.S.101-1955.

35 Inner cover. Krishna with *gopīs* (cowgirls).

Provenance: found by Ajit Ghose in Vishnupur, then J.C. French Collection; the French collection was divided between the two museums in 1955.

Two wooden covers, bevelled edges; 9×56·5cm; painted interiors, plain tops.

Bibliography: French 1927. AB, p.41 (repro. of V.&A. cover). Losty 1980, pp.13–14.

[1]A *Rāmacaritamānasa* in the Asutosh Museum dated 1772–5 (Ghosh 1945) and a *Simhāsanabattīsi* in the British Library (Or.13755 – see AB p.47).

33 'Ḥamzanāma'

Illustrated on p.46.

The Romance of the Amīr Hamza, a Persian epic on the legendary exploits of one of the companions of the Prophet, conflated with those of a 9th-century hero who fought against the infidels.

This text seems to have been especially popular among the Muslims of India, doubtless because of its topical nature. In addition to this Sultanate version, it was the first major undertaking of the studio set up by Akbar, who wanted a manuscript on a gigantic scale (No.54).

This *Ḥamzanāma* manuscript is perhaps only slightly later in date, and is decidedly more Indian in treatment, than the dispersed Amīr Khusraw Ms. The viewpoint is still the horizontal, against a plain ground. Wavy stripes sometimes denote a horizon, but it is essentially irrelevant to the composition. All the figural types as we have seen are based completely on the normal Jaina ones, in contrast to the Middle-Eastern figural type of the Amīr Khusraw Ms.

Although the artist was working in a tradition only just removed from the Jaina, we cannot follow Stchoukine and argue that the provenance must therefore be Gujarat, as the Jaina tradition was known from Delhi, Jaunpur and Mandu, as well as Gujarat and Rajasthan. Pramod Chandra more convincingly points to the resemblances between the *Ḥamzanāma* and the Digambara manuscripts of the 15th century from Delhi, and it does seem to us that a northern origin for the *Ḥamzanāma* is more likely, as the Jaina tradition from which the *Ḥamzanāma* springs seems more akin to the Delhi and Jaunpur manuscripts than the Gujarati ones. The Ms. however cannot have been illustrated in a court milieu. We would date it to about 1450.

Staatsbibliothek Preussischer Kulturbesitz, Orientabteilung, Berlin, Ms. or. fol.4181.

ff.353; 32×21·5cm; paper; 16 lines of mixed *Nasta'līq* and *Naskhī* in panels 24×16cm with margins ruled in triple red lines; headings in a large bold hand; 189 miniatures, mostly about one-third of the panel; red leather binding.

Bibliography: Kramer 1956, No.73. IIH, pp.144–63, pl.41–3, col. pl.9. ND, pp.50–3, col. pl.9, and figs.117–26. P. Chandra 1976, p.34, pl.71–2.

34 'Candāyana'

Illustrated on p.47.

Candāyana is a poem on the romance of the two lovers Laur and Chandā composed in the Avadhī dialect of Hindi by Maulānā Dā'ūd from Dolman, near Kanpur, in 779/1389 during the reign of Fīrūz Shāh Tughluq, and dedicted to his Vizier, Jahān Shāh, son of Khān Jahān Maqbūl. It was the most popular of all texts for illustration in the Sultanate period, and no less than five pre-Mughal illustrated manuscripts have survived, in five different styles (see also Nos.44–5). It is one of the earliest attempts by an Indian Muslim to write in the language of the people and not that of the conquerors.

This Ms. is the oldest of the group, and like all the others is remarkable for its format, being entirely composed of full-page paintings in the vertical format with the text, in the Arabic script in each case, written on the verso.[1] Avadhī Hindi was spoken in the present eastern districts of Uttar Pradesh, from Lucknow to Jaunpur. Dā'ūd's poem was dedicated to a high noble in Delhi, probably not familiar with the language. The original presentation copy may therefore have been heavily illustrated in this fashion, drawing on a format of Hindu manuscripts of which none has survived from the 14th century, while other manuscripts are based ultimately on this lost original. That paintings were present at Fīrūz Shāh's court we know from his orders to have them obliterated!

This earliest surviving illustrated version of the *Candāyana* is in a primitive style that is not far removed from a Jaina original and is datable to 1450–70. We have seen that we may look for the production of illustrated versions of this manuscript to areas other than Jaunpur and eastern Uttar Pradesh, and it is possible that Pramod Chandra is correct in assigning this particular copy along with the *Ḥamzanāma* (No.33) to the Delhi region.[2] However, in its almost invariable use of a pavilion-structure under which to depict the story's characters, it shows distinctly eastern characteristics derived from the Pāla style which survive until the 18th century. In this it resembles the Benares pages of this text, and it is possible that both come from eastern Sultanates such as Jaunpur or Bengal.[3]

Staatsbibliothek Preussischer Kulturbesitz, Orientabteilung, Berlin, Ms. or. fol.3014.

ff.141; 24·5×14cm; cream-coloured paper; nine lines of *Naskhī* in two columns in panels 15·5×10cm; rubrics in Persian; 140 illustrations about 21×12·5cm; dark-brown leather binding.

Bibliography: UH, p.52 (repro. of f.84a).

[1]Only this and No.46 are comparatively complete Mss. However the Bombay Ms. (No.45) has about 80 folios similarly arranged, so that we are justified in assuming this format for the more fragmentary manuscripts in the Lahore and Chandigarh Museums (24 folios) and in the Bharat Kala Bhavan, Benares (five folios).

[2]P. Chandra 1976, p.34 (with repros. of two unidentified folios, pl.69–70). For Jaina paintings from Delhi and Gwaliro, see JAA, pp.415–8.

[3]Krishnadasa 1955–6. The Benares leaves are at least 25 years later than the Berlin manuscript.

35 'Piṅgalatattvavyākhyā'

An anonymous commentary in Sanskrit on the principles ascribed to Piṅgala in the *Prākṛtapaiṅgala* on Prakrit prosody. The sage Piṅgala, of indeterminate date, but earlier than Bharata (2nd century AD?) is credited with the earliest codification of rules on Sanskrit metres, but the work on Prakrit metres is in fact a very much later work, probably not earlier than the 14th century.

This palm-leaf manuscript is important not so much for its text but for its binding boards, which have painted interiors. The colophon is dated in the year 371 of the Laksmanasena era (AD 1491–2) and the script used is the Maithili, a script very close to the Bengali; the Ms.'s provenance is thus fixed in Mithila, *i.e.* Bihar north of the Ganges, where this script and this era were much used. The scribe is one Rāmadatta. The covers are Vaishnava in content, on one being the ten incarnations of Vishnu, on the other Krishna with the *gopīs*. The style of these covers is linked to the *Āraṇyakaparvan* Ms. from Agra (No.38) of 1516 and hence to the celebrated group of Mss. surrounding the N.C. Mehta *Caurapañcāśika* Ms. These links may be seen in the square faces and almond eyes of both male and female figures and the costume and stance of the female figures, as well as in many points of detail. They are the first dated documents of medieval non-Islamic provenance in which the projecting further eye has disappeared, the technical difficulty of converting from three-quarter profile to full profile having finally been overcome, and overcome at the very moment of painting these covers as in three instances the artist changed his mind about the projecting eye, first painting it in and then overpainting it with the red background colour. One suspects that the artist was, until just before he painted these covers, a traditional Jaina-type artist who had recently come into contact with examples of the *Caurapañcāśika*-type of painting; excited by this new style, he tried it out but occasionally forgot himself and lapsed into old habits.

British Library, London, Or.13133.

ff.36; 5×36·5cm; talipot leaves; Maithili script; six lines; illustrated wooden covers.

Bibliography: Losty 1977.

36 'Bhāgavata Purāṇa'

The classic Hindu scripture in Sanskrit extolling Vishnu as Supreme Lord of the Universe. The *Purāṇa* appears to belong to about AD 900, and it has put together all the cycles concerned with Krishna, as well as all the incarnations of Vishnu. The most important part is the tenth canto, which recounts the life of Krishna in detail, his birth and romantic adventures in Brindaban as well as his exploits as adviser to the Pāndavas in the *Mahābhārata* and as king of the Yādavas.

One of the most important of the *Caurapañcāśika* group of manuscripts is the dispersed *Bhāgavata Purāṇa*, a manuscript now so thoroughly dispersed that a detailed reconstruction is urgently required. Most important collections, both public and private, in India, Europe and the USA, have examples of it. The Ms. is in the landscape format, like the *Caurapañcāśika* and *Gītagovinda*, all the known folios having illustrations on one side and the text on the reverse. In this latter aspect the *Bhāgavata Purāṇa* differs from the other two manuscripts, which have the main text above the painting on

36 Krishna's marriage.

the recto. The *Bhāgavata* illustrations in this position have only a brief description of the subject of the painting, while the versos have a varied number of verses in at least two different hands. Sometimes a small amount of the text is written in a large hand, not unlike that of the *Caurapañcāśika* inscriptions; alternatively, another scribe has written many more verses covering most of the page in a smaller hand. Sometimes the text is written the same way up as the painting, sometimes in the opposite direction, indicating some confusion as to the place of the axis of turning – on the left side, as if it were a bound volume, or at the top, in the *pothī* format.

It is not clear whether the entire *Bhāgavata* was illustrated, or only the tenth canto concerned mostly with Krishna's childhood and amours. The surviving paintings seem mostly to come from this part of the text. Even so, if the whole canto was illustrated in this way, many hundreds of paintings would have been required. There is every likelihood however that the work was conceived as a picture book first of all, as the texts appear to be explanatory verses rather than part of a continuous complete manuscript.

Many of the paintings show simultaneity of action in the composition, different parts of the story being represented in different registers, so that the paintings as a whole are less satisfying than the *Caurapañcaśika* or *Gītagovinda*. They are, however, immensely spirited in a way that these other two essentially reflective manuscripts are not – horses and chariots charge across the page, fierce battles are fought, and so on, although there can be little doubt that the *Bhāgavata* artist is from the same school, even though later, as that of the *Caurapañcāśika* artist, being linked in innumerable details of line, colour, architecture, and landscape. The *Bhāgavata* pages have the curious inscription of Sā Nānā or Sā Mīthārāma on many of the rectos. These inscriptions are in a good hand, not that of the person who wrote the heading at the top of the painting, but rather linked to the scribe who wrote in a large hand on some of the versos. As to the identity of these two persons, the most likely explanation is that they are the artists responsible for the paintings; the alternative, that they are the patrons, does not deserve much credence, as no other set has ever been found inscribed in this way.

British Museum, London, 1958,10-11,01.

Provenance: Gift of P.T. Brooke-Sewell.
1 folio; 17·5×23cm; paper, damaged at edges; *Nāgarī* on reverse.

Bibliography: Barrett and Gray 1963, pp.63–72. ND, pp.83–5.

37 'Gītagovinda'

COLOUR PLATE XIV

The Song of the Cowherd, a Sanskrit lyric poem by Jayadeva, which describes the love of Rādhā and Krishna among the arbours of Brindaban, Krishna's dalliance with other ladies, Rādhā's jealousy and anger, and the lovers' final reconciliation. It is one of the most powerful of Sanskrit poems, and its influence extended far into the early vernacular literature of northern

India. Jayadeva was the court-poet of Lakshmanasena, the last Hindu ruler of Bengal in the late 12th century.

An illustrated manuscript of this work in the *Caurapañcāśika* style has survived only in a group of ten folios in the Prince of Wales Museum in Bombay. Above the paintings is inscribed a verse from the text on the usual yellow paint, while on the border below are various mysterious coloured marks. Underneath the text inscription a different hand records the number of the folio (*patra*) in the section. The text seems to have been very heavily illustrated originally, like the *Caurapañcāśika*, with one painting per verse.

The style is somewhat removed from the three other main manuscripts of this group, in that the facial features are different – much rounder heads and smaller eyes – and a much greater involvement with landscape elements. The sky however is exactly the same format – dark below, light blue above, divided by a wavy white line. This sky convention is of course found rendered precisely in the same way in the Chawand *Rāgamālā* from Mewar dated 1605, while the semicircular bower in some of the pictures of the set is a commonplace of Mewar painting until the 18th century.

Prince of Wales Museum of Western India, Bombay, Acc.54.37–46.

ff.10; 16×21·7cm; paper; one to two lines of *Nāgarī* at top of page; paintings *c.*15×20·5cm, within yellow frames; blank versos; numeration above pictures.

Bibliography: Khandalavala 1953–4 (reproduces all of the set, two in colour; the author has since revised his views as to date and provenance). Barrett and Gray 1963, pp.63–72. ND, pp.87–9.

38 'Āraṇyakaparvan' of the 'Mahābhārata'

The Great Book of the Descendents of Bharata is the national epic of India. Embodying a core of ancient narrative from the early first millennium BC, it took over a 1,000 years to reach its present shape, a vast poem in 100,000 verses, incorporating huge amounts of didactic material: legal, religious and philosophical. The original story concerns the rivalry between cousins, the five sons of Pāndu and the 100 sons of Dhritarashtra, over the possession of the kingdom of Hastinapura. Eventually the two sides meet on the great battle field of Kuruksetra, and it is here that Krishna, the ally of the Pāndavas, delivers the homily called the *Bhagavadgītā*, the central text of classical Hinduism. The resultant slaughter is so great that the Pāndavas are left with the ashes of victory, and abandon their conquered kingdom, eventually making their way to heaven.

38 f.120 (detail). The story of Bhagīratha, through whose penance the gods were forced to let the heavenly Ganges descend to earth.

In one of the earlier phases of the struggle, the Pāndavas are exiled for 12 years. In the last year they while away the time in the forest telling stories. This is the third book of the epic, the *Āraṇyakaparvan* or Forest Book.

This Ms. of the Forest Book is a *poṭhī* Ms. on paper and is provided with a full colophon. It was copied by the scribe Bhavānidāsa of a family of *kāyasthas* (professional scribal caste) from Gauḍa (Bengal) at the behest of Bhānadāsa Chaudharī, a Vaishnava, dwelling in Chandrapurī. The scribe copied it in the year 1573/1516 in the water-fort of Kacchauva (*Kacchauvajaladurge*) when Sultan Iskandar (Lodi, 1489–1517) was reigning in Delhi. Khandalavala and Moti Chandra have identified these places as Chandawar and Kachaura on the Jumna. There can be no doubt however, that this Ms. was done in the Lodi dominion which stretched at this period from Delhi to Jaunpur.

An interesting point of comparison with the earlier Jaunpur *Kalpasūtra* of 1465 is that both Mss. were copied by Hindus, Bengal *kāyasthas*, and it may well be, illustrated as well. Whereas it might be assumed that the calligraphy in the Jaunpur manuscript deliberately took on a Jaina form, being scattered with Jaina symbols and characteristics, we nonetheless see precisely the same characteristics in this purely Hindu manuscript. The initial Jaina symbol, the frequent use of the auspicious syllable '*cha*', red medallions in the verso margins, etc.

Nearly every folio of the *Āraṇyakaparvan* is illustrated, with the miniatures in a whole variety of different sizes. Some few take up the full page, others a half or a third of the page, and often these larger miniatures are divided into registers with different scenes. Sometimes the miniatures are even smaller, occupying a corner of the page, or occasionally running in a band across the bottom. This kind of freedom is associated with a group of Jaina manuscripts of the Digambara sect, mostly done in Delhi in the 15th and 16th centuries.[1] However, the style of these miniatures is that of the *Caurapañcāśika* group, although not exhibiting all the characteristics of that style.

In the *Āraṇyakaparvan* the draughtsmanship is nervous, and still has the remnants of the Jaina distortion of the projecting chest. Occasionally there is a projecting further eye, twice on the god Shiva. The horizon is usually a wavy band of white, but sometimes it is a high curved one. Nearly all the characters and even the objects in the miniatures are identified by their names, a characteristic of the *Caurapañcāśika* Ms. itself. These labels are not in the same hand as that of the scribe, but they do seem to resemble the hand which has gone over the manuscript filling in original omissions, and the language they use is Hindi where more than a mere name is noted.

Asiatic Society, Bombay, MS.B.D.245.

Provenance: Bhaudaji Memorial Collection.

ff.235 (out of 362); 15 × 34cm; country paper, deep-beige; 13 or 14 lines of good, regular Western *Nāgarī*, between margins ruled in red; red roundels on verso margins; most folios with miniatures, of varying sizes; unbound, no covers.

Bibliography: Bombay 1930, p.292. ND, pp.64–9. Khandalavala and Chandra 1974.

[1]JAA, pp.415–8.

39 'Saṅgrahaṇīsūtra'

Illustrated on p.51.

The Book of Compilations, a summary by Maladhāri Chandra Sūri in Prakrit verses of Jaina doctrine on cosmology, the nature and number of the upper and lower worlds, their inhabitants, etc. Chandra Sūri composed the work in AD 1136.

During the course of the 16th century it would seem that even traditional Jaina manuscripts began to be affected by the new movements in painting, and to abandon their steadfast adherence to outmoded stylistic conventions. Instead the new style of the *Caurapañcāśika* group was adopted; the projecting further eye was omitted and the human figure shown in the strict profile towards which it had been working for two centuries; more up-to-date clothing was used, such as *jāmas*, turbans, and scarves, and obviously more contemporary textile patterns instead of the conventionalized rows of *haṃsas* and lotuses; and a slightly more progressive view of landscape was taken. The Ms. which best exemplifies all these trends is the *Mahāpurāṇa*, a Digambara text, dated 1597/1540–41 from Pālamva in the reign of Sher Shāh.[1] Although there is doubt about precisely where Pālamva may be (usually identified with the Pālam outside New Delhi), there can be no doubt that the Ms. was painted in the northern area under the control of Sher Shāh after he had ousted the Mughal Humāyūn from his throne in 1540. However, a slightly earlier Ms. of the *Uttarādhyayanasūtra*[2] with Gujarati notes dated 1596/1539 from Siṃganapur, which is probably the village of that name near Surat in Gujarat, shows similar stylistic changes in its two introductory miniatures, so that it may be assumed that over western and northern India as a whole there were stirrings of modernity among the Jaina artists. However the only two manuscripts of this group which name their artist, the *Mahāpurāṇa* of 1540 and the *Saṅgrahaṇī* under discussion, name Hindus, so that we may in fact be discussing a revolution in patronage in which those Jainas with the money to commission new work went to artists working in the latest styles, of whatever religious persuasion, rather than to the tranditionalist Jaina painters, probably monks, who saw no reason to change their ways.

This *Saṅgrahaṇī*, whose artist is named as Govinda, is dated 1640/1583–4 from Matar, in Gujarat. It best exemplifies the influence of the *Caurapañcāśika* style on the Jaina manuscripts, with its faces in profile, its more contemporary costume, and its lively, fluent drawing, especially of dancers in motion.[3] There is not the slightest need to posit Mughal influence on this style, as has unfortunately been done,[4] as there is nothing whatever in it that is not seen in earlier Hindu manuscripts.

Lalbhai Dalpatbhai Institute, Ahmadabad, Ill. Ms. No.195.

ff.39; 10·4 × 26·5cm; paper; ten lines of Jaina *Nāgarī* within margins in red; maps, charts, diagrams and illustrations on most folios, sometimes covering the entire page; yellow medallions with blue scroll work in outer margins of some versos; lovely scalloped medallions with pendants on outer sides of first and last folios, with four outer medallions, with arabesque designs; unbound.

Bibliography: Chandra and Shah 1975, pp.63–9, figs.41–51, col. pl.VIII–X.

[1]ND, pp.69–78.
[2]British Library Or.13476, see Losty 1975, figs.19–20.
[3]M. Chandra and Shah 1975, pl.VIII.B.
[4]*ibid.*, p.29.

40 'Miftāḥ al-Fuẓalā'

40 f.242. Illustration of a *kalla*, *i.e.* a pavilion used for entertaining, in which a king is having a party.

A glossary of rare words occurring in ancient Persian poems, by Muhammad ibn Dā'ūd ibn Muhammad ibn Mahmūd Shādiyābādī. The author was a native of Shadiyabad or Mandu, the capital of Malwa under the Khaljī dynasty, and wrote this work in 873/1468–9. His literary career continued into the next century (see No.43). The glossary frequently gives the 'Hindvi' equivalent of the word, so that it also forms a rich source of early Urdu vocabulary. This copy of the work with its 179 miniatures in the Turkman style of Shiraz seems to have been made about 1490–1500 in Mandu and is the earliest of the group of four illustrated manuscripts associated with the Mandu Sultans.

It cannot be much earlier than the *Būstān* of 1500–2, as the calligraphy, an exceptionally large and fine *Nasta'līq*, is very probably by the same scribe as the *Būstān*, No.42, *i.e.* Shāhsavār; the main headings are in large gold *Muḥaqqaq* and the sub-headings in blue *Naskhī*, while the head-words within the body of the text are in red. The whole is exceptionally clear and colourful. There seem to be no Shirazi Mss. in this style, so that this is doubtless a Mandu invention. The artist has, as Norah Titley has pointed out, exercised his ingenuity to the full in devising pictures to explain the words and has produced as charming a set of little vignettes as ever came out of Shiraz. No Indian influence is discernible except for a solitary picture (f.175a) in which a female, slate-coloured in the Persian manner to indicate her Indianness, wears a large round earring, seen in other early 16th-century Indian manuscripts, and a skirt and blouse, and the occasional architectural detail such as arches which are reminiscent of those in Mandu. There are three paintings in which a king is portrayed, on two of which he wears the normal drooping moustache of Turkman painting. On one, however, illustrating the golden sandals worn by a king on f.146b, the king has an upturned moustache with separated ends as worn by the king in the *Ni'matnāma*, and this is possibly meant to be Ghiyāth ad-Din Khalji himself.

British Library, London, Or.3299.

ff.306; 30 × 17·5cm; light-brown paper much wormed; ten lines of large *Nasta'līq* with headings in gold *Muḥaqqaq* and blue *Naskhī* in panels 20·3 × 12cm ruled in gold, black and blue; one *sarlavḥ*, in Shiraz style; 179 miniatures, usually vignettes in the text without formal framing, sometimes with stepped upper edges; covers of dark brown leather with stamped medallion and corner pieces, let into an outer frame of darker colour, rear doublure of plain red leather with painted gold frames, brown leather spine.

Bibliography: BM 1895, p.116. BL 1977, pp.151–4 [repro. of f.259b]. Titley 1964–5. Lewis 1976, pp.52–3 (col. repro. of ten of the miniatures).

41 'Niʿmatnāma-i Nāsir ad-Dīn Shāhī'

COLOUR PLATE XII

The Book of Recipes of Nāsir ad-Dīn Shāh of Mandu. A recipe book in Persian with methods for cooking all sorts of delicacies, aphrodisiacs, and other epicurean delights, which seems originally to have been for the benefit of the sybaritic Ghiyāth ad-Dīn Khaljī, Nāsir ad-Dīn's father. The text is illustrated with 50 miniatures, showing the king looking on while some of his innumerable women attendants prepare the dishes. The text is written in a large and beautiful *Naskhī* that may possibly be by the same scribe as Nos.40 and 42. The headings in red give the same colourful effect.

The miniatures are the work of two different hands, both of them using a provincial Turkman Shirazi idiom, but with significant Indian characteristics. Many of the human figures, particularly the women, are in strict profile, and wear Indian costume, while the architecture is in places totally Indian, using heavy projecting eaves supported by elaborately carved brackets, as well as the small domes typical of Mandu architecture. Many features may be found in other Indian manuscripts of the 16th century. There are occurrences of the ladies in the costume, and occasionally with the profile, of one of the ladies of the Bombay *Candāyana* Ms. (ff.100b and 136b) (No.45), and on one occasion with the profile of Champāvatī in the *Caurapañcāśika* (f.83b). The costume is the bodice, skirt with *paṭkā* with a projecting corner, and the stiff *oṛhnī* held out like a wing. Trees frequently recall the Bombay *Candāyana*. There are many misunderstandings, or rather reinterpretations, of Persian conventions. On one painting the lush Turkman vegetation is arranged in heavy vertical rows, while there is an inability to distinguish between the conventions for the ground and for the sky. In the *Niʿmatnāma*, a convention which makes the sky half gold for its lower portion and half blue for its upper, has been interpreted so that the gold half is a continuation of the ground and is sprinkled with clumps of flowers.

Many of the characteristics of this Ms. are followed up in the earliest Deccani manuscripts known to us, the *Tarīkh-i Husayn Shāhī* and the *Nujūm al-ʿUlūm* (No.50). The prevalent *Niʿmatnāma* female adornment of a heavy gold ring round the neck is seen in both these manuscripts. Also present in the *Niʿmatnāma* are men in the Deccani costume of a long gown fastened up the middle and tied with a sash about the waist; one of the insignia of royalty is a flapping scarf, as in the Deccan; while many of the colour combinations and effects are forerunners of the colour clashes seen in Deccani painting throughout its important phase. It is possible either that these two Mandu painters were recruited from an early Deccani school of which no other trace has survived, or that they or their artistic heirs migrated to the Deccan courts somewhat later in the 16th century.

The Ms. of the *Niʿmatnāma* is disarranged and incomplete. In particular the first four folios are later replacements so that the contents of the original title-page are not known. The present title of the work is based on the title inscribed in the illuminated heading on f.162b, the last section being a supplement added by Nāsir ad-Dīn. However, although the Ms. was completed in the reign of Nāsir ad-Dīn, who is spoken of as living, the main text at least, with its references to Ghiyāth ad-Dīn Shāh, was probably commenced in the reign of his predecessor. The Ms. can therefore be dated *c.*1495–1505.

India Office Library, London, Persian Ms.149.

ff.196; 31×21·5cm; light-brown paper; first four folios later replacements, some lacunae; ten lines of bold *Naskhī* with headings in red in panels 22·5×15cm, with margins ruled in gold, black, and blue (the same as No.40); one *sarlavḥ* on f.162b; 50 miniatures, all smaller than the text panels, and usually not so wide, and with stepped upper edges, but some protruding into the margins, usually without a formal frame; oriental cover, disbound.

Bibliography: IOL 1903, No.2775. Skelton 1958. ND, pp.58–63, col. repro. of two folios.

42 'Būstān'

COLOUR PLATE XIII

The Flower-garden of Saʿdī, a famous Persian work of moral tales, by the poet Muslīh ad-Dīn Saʿdī (*c.*585–690/1189–1291).

In addition to the Shirazi work associated with Mandu, there also has survived a copy of the *Būstān* of Saʿdī illustrated for Nāsir ad-Dīn Khaljī (1500–10) with 43 miniatures in a provincial version of the style of Herat.

The Ms. is a splendidly written copy, the scribe being named as Shāhsavār al-Kātib, although this seems more a title (master-scribe) than a name. The script is a large and elegant *Nastaʿlīq*, and both it and the good, creamy-brown paper resemble very closely the similar appearance of the *Miftāḥ al-Fuẓalā* (No.40). It is possible that Shāhsavār also copied the *Niʿmatnāma* text (No.41), but this is in *Naskhī* rather than *Nastaʿlīq*, although it does follow the same tradition of a very large style of script, which is probably unique to Mandu at this period.

The miniatures of the manuscript are in a style based on that of Herat, but, it must be clearly stated, are in no sense to be confused with the work produced in that city at this period.[1] Herat at the close of the 15th century under Sultan Husayn Bayqara had, in his principal court artist, Bihzad, the greatest painter Iran has ever produced, and his work and that of his immediate circle is renowned for its subtlety of colour and brilliance of composition. The miniatures of the *Būstān* share with this school the same general approach to composition, to figure types, and to colouring, favouring in the latter a cool palette, particularly blue, but are otherwise in a completely different category. The *Būstān* miniatures are of two sorts, the first of which, by far the smaller, may possibly be accepted as the work of an Iranian artist trained in the general Herati manner (such as ff.33a, 102b, 154a), but as for the rest, they reveal by the awkwardness of their compositions and placing of characters and the general harshness of the colours in their combinations that they are the work of an artist working in a totally foreign style, who even makes mistakes such as holding a tent over a king's head rather than a parasol (f.106b). He seems often unable to distinguish between the ground and background walls, so that characters float against an indeterminate pattern of either. We see the Ms. as the work of two artists, one possibly from Herat but more likely a better assimilator of an alien tradition than the other, obviously an Indian. The Herat tradition could have come to Mandu either through an artist or simply with a manuscript which served as a standard. The artists do not, it may be conceded, show any signs of other Indian styles, even contemporary Mandu ones, but practically every detail of their architectural decoration is different from what would be expected in an Iranian manuscript. Stone and brickwork are arranged in lovely patterns throughout, including *svastika* patterns, while the coloured tilework shows some striking combinations of brightly coloured floral arabesques over a black ground which we now know to be characteristic of Indian illumination from at least the late 14th century (see No.18). All of this surely reveals an Indian origin, and in one or two instances, such as the mosque-scene (f.137b) points specifically to features of Mandu architecture.[2] We need not hesitate then to accept this as Mandu work, especially since one of the paintings (f.190a) has now been discovered to bear the minute inscription 'Haji Mahmūd at Mandu'.[3] The artist's name is also known, as Ettinghausen pointed out, from the inscription on the *sarlavḥ* on f.1b, where it is clear that he was also the illuminator. As for the date, the inscription on the illuminated *shamsa* on f.1a tells us that the manuscript was prepared for Nāsir Shāh as reigning Sultan (1500–10), while on the colophon page there is an *ārzdīda* (inspection notice) dated 908/1502–3. The manuscript therefore may be securely dated to Mandu in the period 1500–3. A defaced note on f.1a records that it was presented (?) by Pazand Chand to Akbar at Ahmadnagar in 100–(?).[4]

National Museum, New Delhi, 48.6/4.

ff.229; 34 × 23·5cm; good creamy-brown paper; nine lines of large *Nastaʿlīq* in two columns in panels 25 × 16·5cm with margins ruled in gold and blue; headings in blue, gold, or red *Naskhī* across both columns; illuminated *shamsa*, with '*ex libris*' in white *Thuluth* on gold in an eight-lobed roundel, with 15th-century Shirazi-type illumination; one *sarlavḥ*; 43 miniatures, mostly about one third of the panel in size, and often L-shaped; dark-brown leather binding with medallion and corner-pieces stamped in gold, and plain doublures.

Bibliography: Ettinghausen 1959. MIC, pp.94–5, with col. repro. of f.154a.

[1]ND, p.9, where Khandalavala states that the Ms. was probably prepared in Herat as a present.

[2]Precise resemblance of painting to architecture is not to be expected at this period, but the appearance of the pillars and arches in this and in f.134a is highly reminiscent of Mandu architecture – see Marg, vol.XII, No.3, pp.18–19.

[3]I am indebted for this information to Dr Narendranath, Keeper of Manuscripts in the National Museum.

[4]This person is doubtless Chand Bibi, who defended Ahmadnagar against the Mughal armies in 1600. If the inscription is authentic, it raises intriguing questions of how the Ms. got from Mandu to Ahmadnagar. It may have been taken to Bijapur after the fall of Mandu to Akbar in 1562, and had some influence along with other Mandu Mss. in shaping the early Deccan style. Chand Bibi, daughter of Husayn Shāh of Ahmadnagar was married to the ruler of Bijapur, ʿAlī ʿĀdil Shāh I (1557–80), and on her return to her native country on her widowhood may have taken this manuscript with her.

43 'ʿAjāʾib aṣ-Ṣanāiʿ'

Illustrated on p.42.

A Persian translation of *Kitāb fī maʿrifat al-ḥiyal al-handasiyya* (Book of Knowledge of Ingenious Mechanical Devices) by Ibn ar-Razzāz al-Jazarī, an Arabic treatise on automata written for Nāsir ad-Dīn, the Artuqī King of Diyarbaka (in Mesopotamia) and completed between 1204 and 1206. The Persian translation is by Muhammad ibn Dāʾūd Shādiyābādī, who is now known to have been active at Mandu between 1468 (see No.40) and 1509, the date of this Ms., which is almost certainly the fair copy of the work. According to the preface, the translation was commissioned by Nāsir Shāh (Sultan of Mandu, 1500–10), although what was actually commissioned was a translation of another Arabic scientific work of the 9th century, the Kitāb al-*Ḥiyal* of the Banū Mūsà, of the 9th century. Shādiyābādī clearly believed that this was the work he was translating. The colophon states the copy was finished on Saʿbān 16, without stating the year, with a note beside it, by the translator, certifying the copy with the date 4 Shavvāl 914 (AD 1509).[1]

Manuscripts of al-Jazarī's work are usually illustrated with drawings of the various devices he describes, and this one is no exception. Early illustrated Mss. of this text come from Syria and Egypt, in particular two dispersed Mss. dated 1315 and 1354 respectively. These are illustrated in Mamluq style. 15th-century Mss. are copies of these, such as the Bodleian Ms. Graves 27, dated 891/1486. The illustrations in the Mandu Ms. are taken from a similar type of 15th century Ms. There are approximately 175 drawings, coloured mostly in vigorous reds, yellows, blues, and greens, adhering to the traditional diagrams, although with discrepancies from the best illustrated versions, indicating that the artist was copying from a defective manuscript or that he left out parts of the devices not realizing their importance. A small number have human figures from which stylistic judgements may be made. The human figures are of two main types, one a slender elegant figure, with long *jāma*, cummerbund, and small neat turbans, similar in fact to those of the *Niʿmatnāma*, though much less accomplished. The other is a much squatter figure, more crude, with a gown fastened up the front (*peshvaz*), and turbans which resemble those of certain Muslims represented in Jaina Mss. Occasionally one of the more elegant figures has the *peshvaz* or a small pointed cap instead of a turban. Of the four known illustrated manuscripts prepared for the Khaljī Sultans of Mandu, this must be the latest; it is completely distanced from the Shiraz and Herat influences seen in the other manuscripts (Nos.40–2). Architectural features of the buildings of Mandu, particularly the many-lobed windows and pools in the palace buildings (f.61b), occur occasionally in the miniatures.

British Library, London, Or.13718.

ff.191; 22 × 14·5cm; paper, thin, much wormholed; *Naskhī* script, 21 lines; illustrations; *sarlavḥ*, 19th century; modern binding.

Bibliography: Hill 1974. Coomaraswamy 1924. Chaghatai 1963.

[1] I am indebted to M. I. Waley for this information.

44 'Sharafnāma'

COLOUR PLATE XV

The first part of the *Iskandarnāma*, the Book of Alexander the Great, describing his victories, by the Persian poet Nizāmī (1140–1202). The author is regarded as the greatest of *mathnavī* writers, and spent most of his life in Ganjah, unattached to any court. Mandu, prior to the recent discovery and publication of this manuscript, was the only unimpeachable source of Sultanate painting, with manuscripts in styles related directly to those of contemporary Shiraz and Herat. This Ms. was copied in 938/1531–2 by Ahmad called Hamīd Khān for Nusrat Shāh Sultan of Bengal, and is in a style sufficiently distinct from possible Iranian sources to argue a considerable period of independent development in Bengal itself. The basic style is that of mid-15th-century Shiraz, with certain elements such as the rock formations on f.41b suggestive even of 14th-century Iranian painting. Of paintings from Muslim Bengal of earlier date, there is however no sign, and of the various hitherto unattributable Sultanate paintings, only one can now be attributed to this very distinctive style of Bengal.[1]

Distinctively Indian are the architectural details – cusped arches, brickwork alternating with polychrome tiles, terracotta tiles, *chattris*, projecting eaves with brackets, much of it featured in the surviving buildings of Gaur and Pandua. Other features of Sultanate painting are the predilection for people to stand in rows, the drawing of some of the horses, the strange round faces of the women with long hanging braids, and the depiction of their bosom. Unique to this manuscript are the sharply pointed caps round which the turban cloths are wound, which in one instance look as if they are meant to be Safavid baton turbans (f.53b). The highly charged colourful skies seem based on a certain Shirazi feature, but are here perhaps even hotter and more fanciful than their originals. There are certain non-Iranian features in the illumination – many pages have triangular panels of illumination on either side of obliquely written verses, in a style peculiar to itself. There is a double-page *ʿunvān* (ff.4b–5a) in fairly conventional format, though again with some original features – the white dots on the blue margins, the knotwork between the palmettes, etc. The colophon is enclosed in an ogival medallion with illumination of archaic appearance.

British Library, London, Or.13836.

ff.72; 31 × 20cm; polished paper; elegant *Naskhī*; 29 lines, in four columns in panels 23 × 14cm; margins ruled in gold and colours; one double-page *ʿunvān*; alternate openings sprinkled with gold; many pages with triangular panels of illumination round obliquely written lines; headings alternately in gold or blue *Naskhī* across two columns; nine miniatures all smaller than the text panels; colophon in ogival medallion; 19th-century binding.

Bibliography: IP, pp.135–52.

[1]Melikian-Chirvani 1969, fig.1.

45 'Candāyana'

COLOUR PLATE XVI

A poem in Avadhi or eastern Hindi by Maulana Dā'ūd (No.34).

Perhaps the most beautiful surviving manuscript of the Sultanate period is this copy of the *Candāyana* in the Prince of Wales Museum in Bombay, which came to them as a bound volume of 68 miniatures. Like all the *Candāyana* sets, the text is in *Naskhī* script on the verso, here arranged in 12 lines of red and black ink, each two-line couplet being in its own little margined panel, one red couplet having two black couplets side by side underneath it.

The paintings, all of them of course in the vertical format, can only be the product of a sophisticated Muslim court, whose artists had, at some previous stage, been exposed to considerable Shiraz influence, but who had long since passed the stage of imitation. Thus the high circular horizon, the decoration of the landscape with flowers, and domed architecture are basically all motifs taken from Iranian painting, but in fact they are all used in a different way. The artist was not happy with his high horizon, preferring to adopt the horizontal viewpoint, and to split his composition into two separate registers, rather than attempt to depict figures and action in the middleground. Landscape and architecture are decorated with a fantastic array of arabesque designs, while the domed architecture is often simply a layer across the top of the painting, as seen in the Berlin *Candāyana*, without structural support. Sometimes also he indulges in using architecture for pattern-making, as seen in the late 16th-century Mss. from Golconda (Nos.48–9). The colour range is wide, far wider than the hot colours of the *Caurapañcāśika* group, involving cool blues, greens, pinks and mauves, with lavish use of gold. The human figures are of the same basic type as the *Caurapañcāśika* style, but more subtly drawn and without angularity. The profile of both males and females is less square, with both forehead and chin being less prominent. Chandā and her attendants are usually so depicted, but sometimes her rival Mainā has a profile that recalls a similar one in the *Ni'matnāma* (No.41).

The marked development from a Shirazi base implies a *terminus post quem* of about 1500, and the presence of many of the characteristics of the style in the Cleveland Museum *Ṭūṭīnāma* gives us *c.*1565 as a *terminus ante quem*. Gaur is ruled out as a provenance, as we know what its style was like in this period (No.44), and of the others, only Mandu has yet been proved to have a court studio (Nos.40–3). There is in fact a most marked resemblance between certain features of the *Ni'matāma* from Mandu, and this *Candāyana*, in particular the presence in the former (on f.100b) of a lady with features the same as in this Ms., while there is a marked similarity in the rendition of some of the trees, particularly that with beautiful curving trunk and round or ellipsoid top[1], which occurs also in the Mandu *Kalpasūtra* of 1439. It is in fact not difficult to imagine these paintings as the product of the Mandu studio some decades after the *Ni'matnāma* had been produced. As noted in discussing the *Ni'matnāma* certain very distinctive colour effects and combinations link that Ms. with this *Candāyana* and then with the Deccani manuscripts of the latter part of the 16th century.

Prince of Wales Museum of Western India, Bombay, Acc.57.1/1–68.

ff.68; 27 × 21cm; paper; text in 12 lines on versos in alternate double-lines of red and black *Naskhī* within separately margined panels; 68 paintings on rectos (approx. 19 × 14cm) within margins ruled in gold and colours; originally bound, now mounted separately; some folios from this set now in other collections.[2]

Bibliography: ND, pp.94–9, figs. 156–75 and col. plate 24 (Jaunpur is the preferred provenance). Chandra 1976, pp. 48–9, plates 106–11. ('A north Indian provenance . . . perhaps for the Candāyana group' *i.e.* this and the Manchester *Candāyana*, No.46.)

[1]Compare ff.14b and 18a of the *Ni'matnāma*, reproduced in ND, fig.137, with fig.165 of the latter, one of the Bombay *Candāyana* folios.

[2]IP, p.17 (see references cited therein).

46 'Candāyana'

Illustrated on p.52.

The romance in Avadhi Hindi by Maulānā Dā'ūd (see No.34).

This heavily illustrated copy is lacking its beginning and end, and about one quarter of the text appears to be missing. Even so, the 318 surviving folios with 285 illustrations render it the most complete of the surviving versions of this romance. Like all the other versions of this text, the Ms. is in reality a picture book with explanatory text; only some 33 of the folios have text on both sides. The remainder have a full-size painting on the recto, and the text on the verso. The unillustrated passages of the text occur in places where the same picture would have to be many times repeated such as the *bājir*'s lengthy recital of Chandā's charms, or where Laurak gains access to Chandā's chamber and their love-making is described, although in the latter instance the artist has included two full-bloodedly erotic scenes.

The style of the illustrations links this Ms. very firmly with the incomplete Bombay *Candāyana* (No.45). The compositional structure is very similar, with a high, round horizon, or architectural feature across the top, with domes. Often the composition is divided into two registers. The colouring is very similar, with gold or gold and blue skies, sometimes with white cloud arabesque, and monochrome grounds of different hues, while the combinations of blues, reds, pinks, greens and yellows occur in both manuscripts. Neither artist is happy with the high horizon, and adapts it superficially to include his own preference for a horizontal viewpoint. Unable to adapt to the necessity of placing his figures within a landscape, the Manchester artist consistently has his figures standing on a lower band of architectural detail (such as a stepped pool) or landscape detail (a fairly solid band of green grass, strongly differentiated from the rest of the ground) or simply an unspecific band of colour.

The Manchester Ms. is lacking the elaborately beautiful arabesques which cover so much of the plain colours of the Bombay manuscript, while its artist has made much use of an elaborate double-storeyed architectural motif – a pillar supports an architrave with a projecting eave, which is supported by carved brackets with drooping boss. The upper storey usually has an elegant oriel window, through which the heroine is often seen, with tile decoration above and below. Of particular note are the developments in the human figure in the Manchester Ms.; the male figure with *kulāhdār* turban, short *jāma* with two hanging points in front, and tight *paijāma*, with curving moustache and darker-toned chin and jowls, is a somewhat more elegant version of the Bombay Laurak. The female on the other hand is decidedly an advance, her features having been regularized to conform more to the male type. She wears with her bodice and *oṛhnī* either the tight skirt with projecting *paṭkā* or a full-bottomed skirt that is seen in Indian painting for the first time in this Ms. The *oṛhnī* can stand out stiffly, or it can be draped elegantly over the head to fall over her side.

The Bombay and Manchester *Candāyanas* are sufficiently close for them to come from the same school but with some quarter-century difference in time between them. If the Bombay Ms. is close enough to the *Ni'matnāma* (No.41) to make Mandu a likely provenance, then the Manchester Ms. likewise must be from

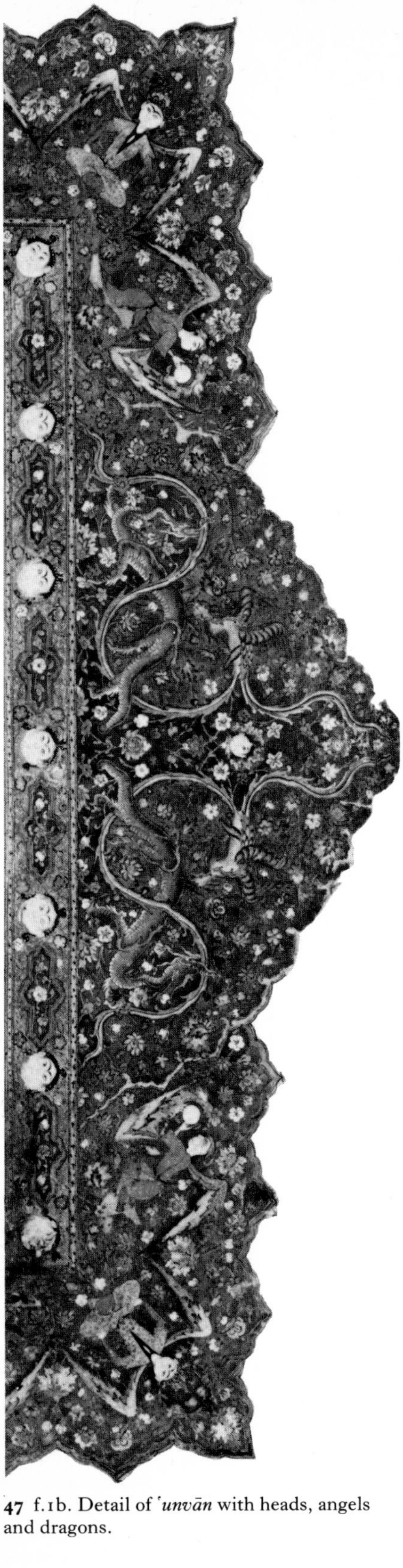

47 f.1b. Detail of *'unvān* with heads, angels and dragons.

Mandu, doubtless at a date closer to its final fall before the Mughals in 1562. It does not appear to have any recognizable effect on later Mss., whereas the Bombay *Candāyana* style is fully recognizable in the Cleveland *Ṭūṭīnāma*, a Ms. to be dated *c.*1560–5, at the beginning of Akbar's studio. The Manchester Ms. would thus be the last effort of a Sultanate court before being absorbed by the Mughals, and if this is Mandu, then it must be dated about 1560, and in the reign of Baz Bahādur.

John Rylands University Library of Manchester, Hindustani MS.1.

Provenance: Acquired for the Bibliotheca Lindesiana of the Earls of Crawford in 1866 from the collection of Nathaniel Bland; and then with the rest of that collection acquired for the Rylands Library in 1901.

ff.318 (numbered 1–326); 23·4 × 14·7cm; text panels light-brown paper 14·2 × 8·2cm, remargined in 19th-century oriental paper with foliation in Arabic script 1–326; nine lines of *Naskhī* in panels with margins ruled in gold, black, red and blue; text arranged in four compartments in two lines above and below, and five lines of verses on either side of a dividing column in the middle; text in black with names and significant lines in blue or red, a colourful effect like the Mandu Mss; 285 illustrations, same size as text panels, with some upper projections into margins; 19th-century oriental cover, European spine.

Bibliography: Khandalavala etc. 1962. Barrett and Gray 1963, p.69. ND, pp.99–103, with col. repro. of f.149a.

47 'Zakhīra-i Khwārizmshāhī'

A medical encyclopaedia in Persian, by Zain ad-Dīn Abū Ibrāhīm Ismā'īl al-Jurjānī (d.531/1136–7). The author lived in Khwārizm from 504/1110–1, and dedicated his encyclopaedia to its ruler Muhammad, son of Nūshtigīn, Khwārizmshāh.

This copy was made by Faqīr Bābā Mīrak of Herat in 980/1572, at Golconda. It has no illustrations, but bears beautiful illuminations in a purely Persian style, indicative of the strong metropolitan Persian artistic links with Golconda at this period when the other Deccani kingdoms were fast developing their own independent styles. The elaborate *'unvān* has the normal illuminated panels round the opening of the text, and then two separate borders, the first of cartouches separated by heads and then a much wider border of gold (interior) and blue (exterior), the divide between the two colours being of angels, and, in the *ansas* in the middle of the long side, of dragons. This would appear to be of Khorasani provenance. There are besides some 10 headpieces of similarly inventive designs, each different, of which one has an elaborate design of paeonies and another of simurghs.

Chester Beatty Library, Dublin, Ind. MS.30.

ff.604; 32·5 × 22·5cm; paper; 27 lines of *Nasta'līq* in panels 21·5 × 14cm; 1 *'unvān*; 10 *sarlavḥs*; bound in brown morocco.

Bibliography: Skelton 1973, fig.152.

48 'Sindbadnāma'

Illustrated on p.54.

Book of Sindbad, an anonymous Persian version of the tales of Sindbad. This extremely rare copy seems to exist in no other version, and is moreover remarkable for its miniatures.

It has been considered for some while that this undated Ms. whose style rests on that of Shiraz might ultimately be found a home in India. Now that more Mss. have been found with elements of the Safavid style but obviously Indian, it is possible to narrow the provenance. The Ms. is distinguished from contemporary Iranian work in various ways. The hand is a good but not elegant *Nasta'līq*, rather cramped, with thick strokes, a typical Indian hand. The illumination of opening medallion and *sarlavḥ* is remarkable only for the looseness of the arabesque work on the blue background. The 72 miniatures are in a style based on the Turkman school of Shiraz *c.*1500 with significant additions from the Safavid school, particularly that practised in Shiraz later in the 16th century.

Some of the paintings are particularly dense compositions of the type known from Golconda in the late 16th century, with very thick application of paint and busy, even fussy, detail. This is true in particular of many of the opening paintings, such as the double-page frontispiece of Solomon and the Queen of Sheba, with its crowded animals and people, and busy ground of Turkman vegetation. There are also some lovely passages of architectural decoration by this same artist, with brilliant tilework. Throughout, however, the basic figure drawing is exceptionally crude, with eyes and hands in particular very badly drawn. On occasion the artist forgets himself enough to draw a face in profile but gives it two eyes (f.154a). Costumes throughout are of the Deccani type, with long gowns opening down the front, and very often a looped girdle round the waist. The turban is very often the Safavid baton turban, and occasionally of the very earliest type as seen in the Uppsala University Library *Jamāl va Jalīl*.[1]

The most outstanding characteristic of the paintings, however, is the imaginative, indeed fantastic, use of architecture as decoration. Beginning quite soberly with large-scale architectural backgrounds, which are always entirely two-dimensional in the Iranian tradition, but with marked propensity for oriel windows supported on brackets protruding into the margins, and with imaginative use of tilework decoration to cover his surfaces, the artist progresses throughout the manuscript to a point where he is indulging in pattern-making with architectural blocks without any regard to the building he is depicting. Architraves and parapets are prolonged and twisted to enclose tilework and windows, domes become *sarlavḥs* or *ansas* (triangular marginal illuminations); thrones are subsumed into the pattern-making, their bottoms curving round to match their tops. Features such as these argue a style totally isolated from its traditions, an art practised in a provincial centre without any renewals from its roots, although this, of course, does not necessarily point to an Indian provenance. Specifically Indian, however, are the brackets and oriel windows, some of the costume details mentioned above, and some of the animal drawing in the frontispiece; combined with features such as the erased Qutb Shāh seal of Golconda on f.1a (an absolutely unmistakable shape but not readable), and Telugu captions throughout the manuscript, they point to a southern Indian provenance that can hardly be other than Golconda at this date.

The use of baton turbans at the Safavid court in Tabriz seems to have not lasted any longer than about 1560, so that there must have been direct influence from the Safavid style on Indian court styles in the first half of the 16th century. The Lalbhai *Khamsa* of Nizāmī is a product of such influence, in which paintings in a sub-Tabriz manner alternate with others in a provincial Iranian style and yet others in a Sultanate style.[2] The *Sindbadnāma* reveals influences from the Safavid style of Shiraz, from the earlier Turkman Shiraz style, and occasional details of even earlier provenance such as 14th-century rocks. A studio must have been set up in the first half of the 16th century with artists from Iran working with artists used to a Sultanate school and to the Turkman Shiraz style. The *Sindbadnāma* has assimilated these styles and the original direct imported influence has disappeared, which argues for a date *c.*1575. At this date Golconda was the only Indian court keeping to some semblance of the Iranian tradition; both Ahmadnagar and Bijapur had developed their own styles and there were no northern courts outside the Mughal one.

India Office Library, London, Persian MS.3214.

ff.166; 24·5 × 15cm; paper darkish-brown, occasional section on blue paper; text in *Nasta'līq* in two columns (some verses on bias) in 16 lines in panels 16·5 × 8cm with margins ruled in gold; *shamsa* on f.1a, lobed circular medallion; *sarlavḥ* on f.2b; 72 miniatures, mostly larger than the text areas, making much use of the margins; erased seals and inscriptions on f.1a; Telugu notes on early miniatures; red morocco cover with stamped medallion and corner-pieces.

Bibliography: IOL 1903, No.1236. Robinson 1951. Stchoukine 1959, p.137, and plates LXXVIII–IX, reproducing folios 120a and 36b.

[1]Zetterstéen and Lamm 1948.
[2]P. Chandra 1976, plates 97–105.

49 'Anvār-i Suhaylī'

Illustrated on p.54.

The Lights of Canopus, by Husayn Vā'iz al-Kāshifī who lived in Herat under Sultan Husayn Bayqara, where he died in 910/1504–5.

The work is a revision in more contemporary and artificial Persian style of Nasr Allāh's *Kalīla va Dimna*, a book of fables based ultimately via Arabic, Syriac and Pahlavi translations on the Sanskrit *Pañcatantra*. The fable is one of the earliest Indian literary forms, and the *Pañcatantra* (the Five Books) its earliest and most famous expression. Through the translations into the above languages, the stories spread ultimately to Europe in the Middle Ages.

This Ms. affords another example of the influence of Safavid Shiraz on the court style of Golconda. Here, however, there is no obvious pointer like the Telugu captions or erased Qutb Shāh seal of the *Sindbadnāma* (No.48), but instead there is a very close resemblance between the two manuscripts in the way they have taken the standard elements of Iranian composition and subjected them to a process of pattern-making without parallel in India. Again and again elements of the architecture such as brackets or architraves or domes are twisted out of their natural function to become elements of design – architraves are looped around on themselves to enclose illuminated cartouches, or domes are converted into *ansas*, or the frame of the painting bulges into the margin in a semi-circle, as if it were to enclose a panel of Koran illumination. Other resemblances to the *Sindbadnāma* include the trees – very tall date-palms extending into the upper margin (f.262a), looped up draperies such as curtains in doorways (f.327a), the same type of cavorting horses (f.124b), the elements of the architecture such as oriel windows supported by brackets in the margins, and utilization of the margins for people to stand in; specifically Indian are the occasional projecting eye and the well-drawn animals – especially in the episode of the elephants and hares (ff.196b and 199a), and of the monkeys leading the bears into the wilderness (ff.218b/219a). Also worthy of note are the enormous leaves covering the ground (f.207b), which are possibly derived from variants of the Turkman Shiraz style seen in the *Ni'matnāma*, as well as brilliantly hued clouds and skies in red, blue and gold, reminscent of the 1531 *Sharafnāma*. There is one appearance of a Safavid baton turban (f.303a), and one Deccani turban (f.114a). Like the *Sindbadnāma*, the *Anvār-i Suhaylī* starts off with a series of very densely composed and busy paintings like those in the *Kulliyāt* of Muhammad Qulī Qutb Shāh before suddenly simplifying its style and beginning its indulgence in pattern-making.

The original date in the colophon has been rewritten to read 990/1582. There is, however, nothing inherently implausible in this dating, knowing as we do the long-continued Shiraz influence in Golconda, before the emergence of the Golconda style proper in the court studio. Doubtless the modified Shiraz style went on being used in the city for longer. The original colophon could easily have been damaged in remargining and was rewritten.

Victoria and Albert Museum, London, I.S. 13-1962.

Provenance: Erskine of Torr Collection, Dunimarle Castle, Fife.

ff.441; 26·5 × 16cm; deep-brown paper with some blue sections; 18 lines of *Nasta'līq*, a rather cramped hand like No.48, in panels 15·5 × 9cm with gold-ruled margins; illuminated panel f.1a, medallion and corner pieces with field of green vegetation (!); illuminated margins in blue and gold round double-page frontispiece of hunting and court-scene (ff.1b/2a); *sarlavḥ* f.2b; chapter-headings in gold and blue; 126 paintings, mostly extending over margins; dark red European covers.

Bibliography: Robinson 1951, No.144. Stchoukine 1959 (repro. of ff.191b and 207b). [Both the above held this like the *Sindbadnāma* to be provincial Iranian; Robinson had changed his mind by 1967, and held them to be Indian – see Robinson 1967, p.113.]

50 'Nujūm al-'Ulūm'

The Stars of the Sciences, an anonymous work on astronomy, astrology and magic, followed by chapters on the horse, the elephant, and various kinds of weapons. The work appears to be unique, and no other manuscript has been found other

50 f.37b. The planet Jupiter with attendants. The two leaders are in the costume of Vijayanagar.

than an apparently 17th-century copy from this manuscript in the same collection (Ind. MS.54). The work is illustrated with 876 miniatures in an early Deccani style, and is dated three times to 978/1570. A note by a former owner records that the Ms. was once the property of Ibrāhīm ʿĀdil Shāh II of Bijapur (1580–1626).

The provenance of this Ms. is, of course, not certainly proved to be from Bijapur by this dubious inscription, and the fact that the other Ms. of the work also bears the same date of 978/1570 gives rise to the suspicion that both of them may be later copies from a third Ms. bearing this date authentically. However, the nature of the illustrations in this manuscript is such that to assume they were 17th-century or later would needlessly complicate the now generally accepted chronology of Deccani painting; the only corroborating piece of evidence for a later dating is the date of the *Javāhir al-Mūsiqāt* (No.51), which is assigned to the reign of Muhammad ʿĀdil Shāh of Bijapur (1626–56) in a later hand, but which contains miniatures in an archaic style linked very loosely to the miniatures of the *Nujūm al-ʿUlūm*. The argument, of course, is circular, but in support of an early dating we may call in evidence the *Tarīkh-i Husayn Shāhī* in Poona, which is datable to 1565–9 from Ahmadnagar.[1] The archaic draughtsmanship of the two 'Bijapuri' manuscripts here finds corroborating support.

The majority of the illustrations of the *Nujūm al-ʿUlūm* are of the signs of the Zodiac and their various degrees, organized nine to the page from ff.22b–52b, but there are some more representational subjects, such as the famous Throne of Prosperity on f.191a, or the procession of a king on f.37b, representing the planet Mushtarī or Jupiter. Both these may be linked to Vijayanagar, the Hindu kingdom of south India overthrown by the combined forces of the Muslim Sultans of the Deccan in 1565. The former depicting a ziggurat showing both sides in a schematic way is the great throne platform still visible among the Vijayanagar ruins.[2] The latter shows an old king or shaikh on horseback in procession, preceded by two men who are wearing the tall conical hats which are associated in the *Tarīkh-i Husayn Shāhī* illustrations with the forces of the Vijayanagar army (ff.43b, 44a).

The linear qualities of the drawing in the *Nujūm al-ʿUlūm* are echoed in the Ahmadnagar manuscript, although in the latter there is a starkness of decoration, without any of the sumptuous colour combinations and arabesques which are found throughout the Bijapur manuscript, and which are, we have argued, a legacy from Mandu. Common to both manuscripts is the costume of the tall elegant females, a sari draped round the lower body, and drawn up over the upper part and tied in a loop round the waist, although over the head in the Bijapur style, and just over the shoulders in the Ahmadnagar tradition. The ladies of the former wear their hair in a great bun on the back of the neck creating a bulge under the sari, in the southern fashion, but in the latter it hangs down behind in a pigtail in the northern manner. Male figures in both manuscripts in profile are sufficiently alike to need little comment. One difference between the two traditions is obvious. The Ahmadnagar manuscript, unquestionably of royal provenance, displays a style considerably removed from direct Iranian influence, with misunderstanding of conventions for horizons, architecture, awnings and so on, and with all the participants in profile; the whole approach of the Ms. is Indian, therefore, and the Iranian influence in the court studio would appear to have been filtered through earlier Mandu work. The Bijapur manuscript in contrast shows much more direct Iranian influence, in colouring, for example, with some figures in three-quarter profile, and it is this influence which becomes more dominant in the Bijapuri style in the 1591 *Pemnem* (No.52). Bijapur is lacking the sort of evidence we have for Golconda of direct Safavid influence at this period (see Nos.48–9), but there is apparently literary evidence that painting, probably in the Iranian manner, flourished at the court of ʿAlī ʿĀdil Shāh I (1555–80).[3] All in all, the evidence, such as it is, points to Bijapur as the provenance for this Ms., and the dubious inscription may be accepted as reliable.

Chester Beatty Library, Dublin,
Indian MS.2.

ff.348; 25·8 × 16cm; polished paper, deep cream; 21 lines of *Nastaʿlīq* in panels 17 × 9·5cm, with margins ruled in gold; three *sarlavḥs* of great delicacy; 876 paintings, from 3·7 × 3cm to whole page; rebound in a 16th-century Persian binding.

Bibliography: CB 1936, pp.2–4. Binyon 1927. AIP, No.805, plates 140–1. Barrett 1958, pp.8–9 (col. repro. of f.248b). Barrett and Gray 1963, pp.117–21 (col. repro. f.191a).

[1] Barrett 1958, plate 1; Barrett and Gray 1963, pp.115–7.
[2] Barrett and Gray 1963, p.120. See Elliot and Dowson vol.IV, pp.103–4.
[3] Barrett 1958, p.4.

51 'Javāhir al-Mūsiqāt-i Muhammadī'

Illustrated on p.53.

A work in Persian on Indian music and the mystical experiences brought on by listening to music, by Shaykh ʿAbd al-Karīm al-Jaunpūrī. There is a dedication on f.4a to Muhammad ʿĀdil Shāh of Bijapur (1626–56).

The work contains three sets of illustrations: eight representations of the *svaras*, or notes; 25 representations of *rāgas* and *rāgiṇīs*; and 27 hand-gestures and body-postures, including all 24 of Bharata's *hastābhinaya*. On the reverse of many of the pictures is a description in Dakhni Urdu in Arabic characters.

This little manuscript presents numerous puzzles. Nothing is known of the author, of his origin in Jaunpur, or of his (presumed) life in Bijapur. The dedication to Sultan Muhammad ʿĀdil Shāh ill-accords with the character of the illustrations, which seem more to be in tune with Deccani work of *c.*1570. At least three hands are to be distinguished in the writing, but all clues to the make-up of the Ms. have disappeared in rebinding, and there are numerous lacunae.

The Ms. is built round two sets of paintings. All the illustrations of the *svaras*, *rāgas* and *rāgiṇīs*, and the three body-postures are in an upright rectangular format without margin, with, on their reverse, a Dakhni inscription in a thin spidery hand akin to *Naskhī* which makes a point of separating all the letters, and sometimes the title of the subject depicted written on the painting itself. The 24 *hastābhinaya* on the other hand are virtually square in format and contained within a frame which continues upwards to include two lines of inscription in another hand, a thicker version of the first, which has also written two lines on the reverse. Both these hands are different from that of the main body of the Persian text, a rather scrawling, inelegant *Nastaʿlīq*. At some other time, yet another hand has inserted a folio, now f.4, in a cruder hand altogether, with a dedication to Sultan Muhammad ʿĀdil Shāh.

The pictures themselves are in a homogeneous style, of great simplicity and directness. Elongated figures, both male and female, are seen in strict profile against a monochrome ground, with no hint of landscape, but with the occasional tree or rock, and often under an arch. The men wear the long gown of the Deccan with cummerbund, the crossing fastened under both arms, and a small *pagrī*; the ladies are in bodice and sari, the latter draped round their shoulders and hanging in splendid folds, or in the case of the dancers demonstrating *hastābhinaya*, in bodice and *dhotī*, and wear their hair in a long braid, or again mostly for the dancers, tied up at the back of the neck and decorated with flowers. Their major items of jewellery are a heavy gold ring round the neck, and large circular ear-rings. All of these items of dress are to be found in early Deccani work associated with both courts of Ahmadnagar and Bijapur, but with the bias in favour of the latter. It is difficult however, to fit them into the known examples of Bijapuri work, the 1570 *Nujum al-ʿUlūm* (No.50), primitive in drawing but sumptuous in a way this Ms. is not, or the 1591 *Pemnem* (No.52), and they may in fact be even earlier than the 1570 Ms. At some subsequent date, probably in Muhammad ʿĀdil Shāh's reign, they were collected together to have a text written round them by ʿAbd al-Karīm al-Jaunpūrī, and at a later date still, the entire Ms. was dedicated to Muhammad ʿĀdil Shāh. It is, of course, possible that they are primitive because they were late derivatives from courtly Bijapuri art, but this seems unlikely in view of there being no comparable examples from the early 17th century in this style. In their colour schemes they display the typical early Deccani colour clashes of pinks and greens and purples and yellows.

British Library, London, Or.12857.

ff.214 (originally 281); 15·7 × 10cm; country paper; nine lines; one faded *sarlavḥ*; 48 miniatures, about 8·5 × 6·5cm, or 6 × 6cm; modern binding, on guards.

Bibliography: BM 1968, p.33; BL 1977, pp.1–2. Ebeling 1973, p.176, who unaccountably attributes the Ms. to Jaunpur 1626–56.

52 'Pemnem'

COLOUR PLATE XVII

The Toils of Love, a romance in Dakhni Urdu by Hasan Manjhū Khaljī, who assumed the poetical name of Hamsa (the Indian sacred goose), composed in Bijapur in 999/1590–91. The romance is framed in the usual manner of such stories, the hero prince being eventually united with his beloved princess after considerable suffering. Nothing is known of the author other than what he reveals in his introduction, in which he praises the city of Bijapur and its ruler Ibrāhīm ʿĀdil Shāh II (1580–1626). This appears to be the sole Ms. of this work.

It is unquestionably the finest and most beautiful Ms. to survive from the early Deccani studios, but presents some problems. It is difficult to reconcile the style of about half of the 34 paintings with the date of 1591 which was claimed by Barrett, as they seem more typical in their dead, clumsy way of archaistic Deccani painting of the mid-17th century. The finely drawn but dead *ʿunvān* is certainly untypical of the glittery Mss. associated with the Deccani courts, while the calligraphy is decidedly shaky. But Barrett's Hand A was worthy of being patronized by the king himself: his work gives the typical early Bijapuri richness of effect within a tightly disciplined framework, and is a development from within the school – it shows no evidence of contact with either Mughal or European influence, other than facial modelling which could in any case be a spontaneous development. The horizon is still the high Persian one, either rounded, or craggy, with castles perched on top in the Deccani fashion. He has no idea how to indicate spatial recession – on the two paintings showing significant events in the background (ff.75b and 197b), he simply lowers his craggy horizon and paints a procession of horses, elephants etc. outlined against the sky. At a slightly later date Mughal influence caused a significant opening out of the background, in the group of early 17th-century portraits for example. Among his most striking effects is his charming conceit of the heroine's portrait being stamped on the hero's heart.

Two other paintings (ff.89b and 138a) are given by Barrett to Hand A, but they seem untypical of his work. The faces of both males and females are much rounder than in Hand A, and the female body less attenuated; the ground is of gold strewn with flowering clumps, while the sky is plain blue streaked with clouds in white and red as opposed to A's double effect of gold below and blue with Chinese clouds above. They seem altogether more typical of Hand C, to whom we would also assign f.47a, which has the round face typical of his style, although on a dark green ground with gold sky. Hand C's other paintings are the wildest of all in his colour effects, his paint is smeared on thickly and he separates landscape and trees into component colours in the manner of the Impressionists. His f.70a is the most ambitious landscape in the Ms., with receding bands of colour built up to the horizon, but this is still the Safavid method of landscape building – the different colours do not indicate recession.

To turn from this body of work to that of Hand B is something of a shock, as his work is coarser and more pedestrian, and would normally be placed in the 17th-century archaistic period. However its presence here indicates how careful we must be in condemning work as late. Like that of Hand A it is derived from the style of the *Nujūm al-ʿUlūm*, and in its decorative grounds is considerably closer to it. We know nothing of 'popular Bijapuri' work of the 1590s which must have existed, and this artist may very well have been recruited from such a body of artists outside the court.

British Library, London, Add.16880.

Provenance: Book-plate of William Yule, 1805; presented by the sons of William Yule in 1847.

ff.239; 24·4 × 16cm; thin glazed paper, chain marks; eight or ten lines *Naskhī* in panels (17 × 9·5cm) ruled in gold and blue; 199 *dohas* in red, 1999 *caupais* in black ink; 34 paintings, by three hands; max. 17 × 12·5cm; *sarlavḥ*; modern binding.

Bibliography: BM 1899, pp.57–8. Barrett 1969.

CHAPTER III

The Imperial Library of the Great Mogul

In 1526 a young prince from Central Asia, Bābur, a descendant of both Tīmūr and Genghis Khān, defeated and killed the Sultan of Delhi, Ibrāhīm Lodī, at the battle of Panipat, and established the rule of his dynasty, generally called the Mughals, in India until 1857. Not that he or his descendants would have tolerated being called Mughals or Mongols, which was a term of abuse applied by their enemies emphasising the barbaric side of their ancestry. They rather saw themselves as the heirs of Tīmūr, the conqueror of half of Asia, including Delhi, and whose immediate descendants were some of the greatest patrons of art and letters and sciences the world has known.

Bābur, who inherited the minor princedom of Ferghana, was three times the master of Tīmūr's fabled capital Samarkand, before finally being driven out by the Uzbeks. He resolved to try his luck in India, restoring Hindustan to Timurid rule. A poet, scholar and man of letters, he has left us a *Dīvān* of poems in his native Turki, of which a manuscript exists with his own annotations on it, written in Agra in 1528–9 (in the Rampur State Library) and an autobiography, one of the greatest works of the genre in any language. He records in detail not only the events of his life but also his reactions above all to India, its people, its climate, its animal and plant life. This work translated into Persian was one of the most popular for illustration in the reign of his grandson Akbar. His reign was too brief to do more than establish his rule over the Lodī dominions of Delhi, the Panjab and the Jaunpur kingdom, from the Lodī capital at Agra. The only one of his manuscripts known to survive from his reign is his *Dīvān*, so it is impossible to know to what extent he patronized scribes and illuminators. That he was a collector of rare manuscripts is known for certain, for one of his and his descendants' most precious possessions was an illuminated *Shāhnāma* produced for Muhammad Jūqī in Herat about 1440, which passed with Bābur from Samarkand over the perilous mountains into India and which bears the seals of all his descendants up to Aurangzīb as well as the autograph inscriptions of Jahāngīr and Shāh Jahān. Bābur's brother Kāmrān also patronized the production of manuscripts – a solitary volume of Jāmī's *Yūsuf va Zulaykhā* survives commissioned by him probably in Kabul, with six miniatures in a poor version of the Bokhara style. There is no evidence that Bābur himself patronized painters, but with his turbulent life he would scarcely have been able to offer them the settled conditions necessary for the production of first-class work, especially since the court at Tabriz under Shāh Ismā'īl and his son Shāh Tahmāsp was attracting all the available talent from Iran and Central Asia.

Bābur's son Humāyūn was a much less forceful character who found himself unable to defend himself against the attacks of rival Muslim dynasties in India, and in 1540 he was driven from his throne by Shīr Shāh Sūr, an Afghan from Bihar. Humāyūn was devoted to books, and seems at times to have been more concerned with the loss of his library than of his kingdom. At a later period when he was struggling to regain the throne of Hindustan, his delight in regaining his temporarily mislaid portmanteau of books is recorded in his son's biography, the *Akbarnāma* (Nos.70–1). These must have contained his father's books as well as his

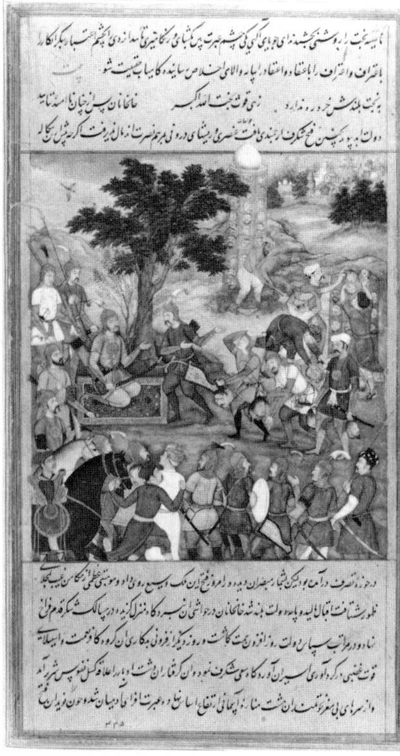

71 f.212b. Mun'in Khān has towers built of the heads of the vanquished Afghans of Bengal in 1575. By Manohar (No.71, p.93).

own, the library no doubt having been considerably enriched by his sojourn in Iran and Kabul. It was at Shāh Tahmāsp's court at Tabriz in 1544 that he was first exposed to the full panoply of the Iranian bibliographic tradition, where he doubtless saw the recently completed *Shāhnāma* and *Khamsa* of Nizāmī, the greatest masterpieces of Safavid manuscript production. Shāh Tahmāsp was becoming more orthodox as he grew older, and turned away from painting after 1544. His artists sought patrons elsewhere, and some responded to Humāyūn's invitation to join him in Kabul, which he had been able to regain in 1545. Two painters in particular took up his invitation, Mīr Sayyid ʿAlī, whose signed work is found in Shāh Tahmāsp's Nizāmī of 1539–43, and ʿAbd as-Samad, to whom work has been attributed in the *Shāhnāma* but about whose Iranian work much less is known. They and their fellow artists brought with them to Humāyūn's court, and then on to Delhi when he was able to regain his Indian dominions in 1555, the latest developments in the Iranian book tradition: elaborate and highly finished paintings by master artists; fine calligraphy; illumination in *shamsas*, *ʿunvāns*, *sarlavḥs* and other pieces scattered throughout the text, in profusion; sumptuously illuminated margins painted in gold with individual designs; bindings now sometimes painted and lacquered rather than simply in tooled and painted leather; and a burgeoning interest in portraiture and the assemblage of albums. The earliest work identifiable as being by these Safavid artists for Humāyūn is still in the pure Persian manner. This includes the fragmentary so-called *Princes of the House of Tīmūr*, a large painting on cloth originally intended probably as a record of Humāyūn and his court in Kabul. Humāyūn's return to Delhi was followed within a year by his death, through falling down the steep steps of his library, an octagonal, two-storeyed building still intact in the Purāna Qila (Old Fort) of Delhi, built by his rival Shīr Shāh Sūr. It was not until his son Akbar began to reorganize the royal studio and to impose on it his own standards and tastes that any movement away from the Safavid style becomes apparent.

Akbar was born in 1542 in the deserts of Sind when Humāyūn had been ousted from his throne, and while his father was in Tabriz, was already learning the hard art of survival in the house of his treacherous uncle Kāmrān Mirza in Kabul. Only 14 when he inherited the throne he was able quickly to crush all rebellions and to extend his dominions over all the independent kingdoms of northern and central India. A man of intense energy, he was intellectually interested in all that came his way, especially the religions of the majority of his subjects, Hinduism and Jainism, in Zoroastrianism, and in the Christianity which was conveyed to him through the Jesuits of Goa, who sent several missions to the imperial court, bringing with them European paintings and prints.

In 1556, the artistic state of India was a confused one. We have analysed above the various kinds of manuscript illustration practised in India in the first half of the 16th century – the schools of the Sultanate courts, attested from Bengal, Mandu and Golconda, but doubtless existing in other courts also, utilizing styles derived from metropolitan Iranian styles at greater or lesser remove; a much more Indianized school of Sultanate painting exemplified by the *Candāyana* manuscripts, possibly from Mandu; a Hindu school exemplified by the *Caurapañcāśika* group of manuscripts illustrating Sanskrit and Hindi texts, based at the Rajput courts; bourgeois schools derived from all three of

54 The prophet Elias rescuing Nūr ad-Dahr from the sea (No.54, p.85).

the above certainly practising in the Delhi–Agra area and probably elsewhere; Jaina painting, still practised in its strongholds in Gujarat and Rajasthan; and local schools in eastern and southern India about which little is as yet known. Shortly after his accession, Akbar decided on an immense expansion of the studio and turned mostly to the artists and workmen who were available, *i.e.* artists from all the above schools who flocked to Agra, the capital, from all over India. The evidence for this migration lies in the first known complete manuscript from Akbar's studio, the *Ṭūṭīnāma* (Tales of a Parrot) in the Cleveland Museum, in which examples of most of these styles are to be found. It is unlikely that the energetic Akbar would have allowed his Persian artists to sit about idle for years after his accession, so that the expansion of the studio can be dated to the late 1550s, as can the beginning of the *Ṭūṭīnāma*. It is to be regarded as a testing ground for different artists perhaps; but as its styles are all somewhat later than their parent styles, yet clearly cannot be regarded as being under much influence from the two Persian masters, it does in a way serve as a *terminus ante quem* for all of them. Much of it must have been finished before work began on Akbar's first huge and immensely important undertaking, the illustration of the *Ḥamzanāma*, a romance of the adventures of Hamza the Prophet's uncle (No.54), which probably commenced about 1562. The sources differ about the precise size of the undertaking, but it would seem to have been in 14 volumes each consisting of 100 paintings, and took 15 years to complete, so that it was finished by 1577. It was painted direct on to large sheets of cotton; originally five lines of text were written on the same side as the painting, leaving the verso blank, but the later paintings cover the entire surface, with the text written in large *Nastaʿlīq* on paper and mounted on the back of the cotton. The 100 leaves of each volume were then presumably bound up like album leaves, but no trace of their bindings has survived. Although scarcely more than 100 leaves have survived out of the whole gigantic enterprise, various stages in the development of the Mughal style can be distinguished. The decorative pattern-making of Iranian painting changes to a concern for naturalism, painting reality in depth, more realistic portraiture, all features that characterize the great period of Mughal painting under Akbar and Jahāngīr, even though the technical methods of achieving these ends, of modelling, of shading, of landscape recession, which were learnt from European paintings and prints over the last two decades of the century, had not yet been fully worked out. Apart from a few highly Persianized early paintings, which were doubtless drawn by the Persian masters, the rest of the pages are in a remarkably uniform style, immensely vigorous, very un-Persian that must have been hammered out in vigorous artistic discussion between the Persians and their erstwhile Indian pupils. The mid-1560s is the latest date this style can have been arrived at, as it appears in a manuscript dated 1568 (No.56).

The creation of the *Ḥamzanāma* demanded a huge expansion of the imperial studio from the few Iranian artists brought by Humāyūn from Kabul to many hundreds of artists and calligraphers, as well as the other craftsmen necessary for the production of books. Most of these artists could only come from the other regions of India; we know the origins of some of them from their names – the epithets Gujarati, Kashmiri, Lahori. About 70 per cent of the names we know of are Hindus, but it is not possible to sort out where they came from other than through their

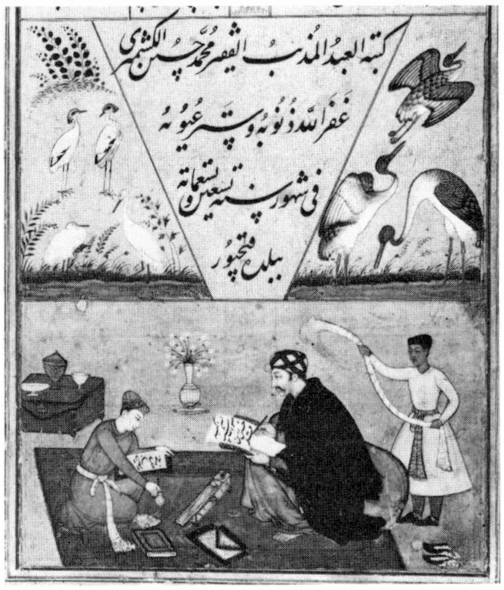

58 f.128. The scribe Muhammad Husayn Kashmīrī 'Golden-pen' and the painter Manohar. By Manohar (No.58, p.87).

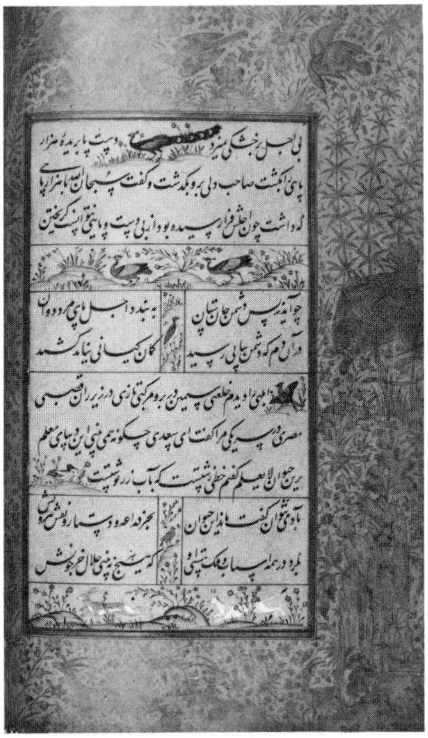

58 f.66b. A peacock and other creatures decorating the text. By Manohar (?) (No.58, p.87).

signed later work – Nānhā for instance is almost certainly an artist from the Deccan, and probably his nephew Bishndās also, while Mādhū Khurd (the Younger) may be pinpointed to Ahmadnagar, one of the three Deccani schools. A manuscript dated 1567 painted by Shahm (No.55) is in an entirely Bokharan style, while in the mid-1580s at least two artists arrived from Iran, Āqā Rizā and Farrukh Beg, bringing with them a renewed burst of Safavid influence especially favoured by Prince Salīm, Akbar's heir.

Mīr Sayyid ʿAlī was in charge of the studio for about half the production of the *Ḥamzanāma*. The method of work at first would have been for him to draw the picture and for the other artists to paint in the colours, until they had gained confidence in this new style. Both Akbar and Jahāngīr pay tribute at a later date to their artists' ability to copy anything, even the latest European work, so that no one could tell the difference. This is indeed a facility all Indian artists have and it was remarked on by the British in the late 18th century. It would not have been difficult for Indian artists to copy the Safavid style in the 1560s, so that they could produce paintings in it by themselves after initial training. Under Akbar's guidance, if not technical direction, the artists were trained to develop a style capable of illustrating in a realistic, naturalistic manner the great historical works of which he was so fond and which occupied his studio through most of the 1580s.

Few illustrated manuscripts other than the *Ḥamzanāma* were produced in the early period of the studio's work. A group of three manuscripts (Nos.55–7) dated between 1567 and 1570 occupy the middle of the *Ḥamzānama* period, along with the undated Zodiacal album in Rampur. This paucity must be due to the overwhelming priority of the production of the *Ḥamzanāma* which claimed the entire studio's attention. We know that six months was the average for the production of one of the highly finished but much smaller paintings of the later Akbar-period works, so that at least a year must be allotted to each of the *Ḥamzanāma* pages. For 1,400 paintings taking 15 years to complete, about 100 artists must have been employed on it. In the earlier period of course, progress must have been much slower, as the atelier was in process of being built up.

Abu'l Fazl, Akbar's court-historian, in his *Āʾin-i Akbarī* (The Institutes of Akbar) gives a short but valuable account of the *taṣvir-khāna*, the imperial studio. In *Āʾin* 34 he deals with the twin arts of calligraphy and painting, according in pious traditional fashion the primacy to the first, but as Pramod Chandra has pointed out actually giving primacy through his title to the painters. Among the calligraphers of Akbar's court, he praises above all Muhammad Husayn al-Kashmīrī, whom Akbar honoured with the title *Zarīn Qalam* (Golden-pen). His calligraphy may be seen in manuscripts datable between 1581 and 1604 (Nos.58, 64, 70, 71) and his portrait exists in the first of these. He died in 1611. Other calligraphers whom he singles out as being among the 'renowned calligraphists of the present age' include three others whose works have survived – Maulānā Daurī, whom Blochmann identifies as the poetic name of Sultān Bāyazīd, the scribe of the 1568 manuscript of Amīr Khusraw (No.56); ʿAbd ar-Rahīm, given the title *Ambarīn Qalam* (Amber-pen) by the Emperor, the scribe of the Dyson-Perrins Nizāmī of 1595 and the *Nafaḥāt al-Uns* of 1604 (Nos.65, 69), and whose portrait is in the former; and Mīr ʿAbdallāh, surnamed *Muskīn Qalam* (Musky-

62 f.84. The attack on Aush in 1498. By Shivdās (?) (No.62, p.89).

pen), a scribe in Sultān Salīm's entourage in Allahabad, and presumably earlier, who copied a *Dīvān* of Amīr Hasan Dihlavī in 1602 (No.72), and whose portrait we also possess at the end of this manuscript.

Abu'l Fazl goes on to discuss the imperial library and the Emperor's favourite books. Books were kept either within the harem or without, the former presumably being the most costly and treasured items, and each section carefully organized as to language and subject. Akbar was apparently illiterate, one of the most surprising things about one so brilliant and fond of books and philosophical enquiry, and enjoyed having his books read out to him in assembly every day, rewarding the readers with so much per page. Abu'l Fazl lists the favourite works which the Emperor never tired of hearing, including works on ethics and morality such as Nāsir ad-Dīn Tūsī's *Akhlāq-i Nāsirī* (of which an illustrated Akbar-period manuscript was discovered recently); the Persian classics; and works on history. Learned men were constantly translating from other languages into Persian. The memoirs of Akbar's grandfather Bābur were translated from Turki into Persian so as to be more readily understood by the courtiers (Nos.62–3), while a considerable number of Indian works in Sanskrit and Hindi were also translated – *Mahābhārata* (No.88), *Rāmāyaṇa, Harivaṃśa, Yogavāsiṣṭha* (No.68), the *Atharvaveda, Līlāvatī* (the mathematical work of Bhāskara) and various romances and tales. Akbar valued literature as a means of breaking down barriers between the men of different religions of his empire, for he considered prejudice was based on ignorance and incomprehension. He ordered copies of many of these works to be distributed to his courtiers.

As for painting, Abu'l Fazl tells us that Akbar was interested in this from his early youth both for study and entertainment. Jahāngīr in his Memoirs adds that Akbar was trained to paint by ʿAbd as-Samad. Each week the work done by every artist was set before him for his consideration, and rewards were given to the artist according to the excellence of the work. Much store was set by the quality of the materials, which the Emperor took pains to improve. Writing in the 1590s, Abu'l Fazl considered that the artists assembled at the court, of whom more than 100 were adjudged masters, were a match for Bihzād and for the Europeans. He singles out for special praise the two Safavid masters, Mīr Sayyid ʿAlī and ʿAbd as-Samad, although the former had left for Mecca in 1571–2, half way through the *Ḥamzanāma* project, stating that the work of both had been transformed by the Emperor's criticism. This is not idle flattery, but an honest appreciation that it was Akbar himself who had acted as the catalyst transmuting Safavid painting into Mughal. It is clear that Abu'l Fazl accords both Iranian masters, especially the former, the formal praise due to them as heads of the studio, but despite work being known from ʿAbd as-Samad's brush up to 1595 (No.65), he seems to have been moved into administrative posts from 1577. Akbar must have found his very Iranian style lacking in the qualities he valued most. Abu'l Fazl reserves his enthusiasm for two Hindu artists, Dashvant and especially Basāvan, both of whose attributed work is from the beginning in the style Akbar wanted his artists to achieve. He names another 13 artists as also famous masters, all but two of whom are Hindus. All of them, as well as 100 more artists, are known from the contemporary inscriptions on the margins of the manuscripts containing their work. When their paintings were presented to the Emperor every week, there

63 f.22b. Bābur visits the Hindu ascetics at Gura Kattri in 1519 (No.63, p.90).

were notes on the edges ascribing the work, and artists were paid and given handsome presents according to the reception which their work received; the notes were later usually covered up by the gilded margins. A more formal note was made on the outer margins by the court librarians, after the painting had taken its place in the manuscript. The practice of the artist actually signing the work found occasionally in the earlier period, as with Shahm in the 1567 *Gulistān* (No.55), was not favoured until under Jahāngīr, perhaps because few of the Akbari artists were competent pen-men. The ascription to artists by librarians' notes is attested from the Cleveland Museum *Ṭūṭīnāma* onwards, where occur the earliest attributions to Dashvant and Basāvan who must have been among the earliest artists to be recruited. Artists' sons seem to have followed in their father's footsteps – of three of Jahāngīr's master artists, Manohar, Abu'l Hasan and Bishndās, the first two were the sons of Basāvan and Āqā Rizā, and the last the nephew of Nānhā. The two sons of ʿAbd as-Samad, Muhammad Sharīf and Bihzād, were both painters, whose work is found in manuscripts of the 1580s. The former was Prince Salīm's friend from childhood, and in his reign he made him one of the grandees of the empire.

Several artists must have worked on each of the *Ḥamzanāma* paintings, but as all the surviving pages have been remargined, there are no attributions. At the conclusion of the project in 1577 (?), there was a large number of highly trained artists waiting for employment, and it was at this stage that they began work on a series of historical works that lasted throughout the next decade – the stories of Akbar's ancestors from Tīmūr (*Ta'rīkh-i Khāndān i Timūriyya*, in Bankipore), of his grandfather Bābur (Nos.62–3), and of his father's and his own reign, the *Akbarnāma* (Nos.70–1). At the same time, the Emperor commissioned Persian translations of the two great Hindu epics in Sanskrit, *Mahābhārata* and *Rāmāyaṇa*, and his artists worked on illustrated versions of them alongside the historical works. These manuscripts are on the grandest scale, with an average of 150 full-page paintings each. The scale of Akbar's studio can be appreciated by comparison with an Iranian one. No ruler of Iran before the unification of the country under Shāh Tahmāsp had the resources to include more than 30 or 40 large-scale paintings even in such a huge work as the *Shāhnāma*. Even Shāh Tahmāsp could only produce one lavishly illustrated manuscript in his long reign, whereas Akbar was having five done in a single decade. Of course the style was less highly finished and exquisite than Iranian work, and is at times only too obviously produced as in a production line, but the magnitude of the achievement is undeniable.

Akbar's artists were extending the techniques of manuscript painting at the same time as extending its range. In earlier manuscripts, whether Iranian or Sultanate, it was only occasionally that the margins were utilized, although examples date from the 14th century. Finials, trees or pavilions could project above the top margin, horses' hooves or landscape details could extend over the side margin, giving the effect of bursting out of the frame but not confined within another one. In the great Mughal manuscripts of the 1580s, however, the entire page is invariably utilized for the painting, the outer marginal rulings being nearly at the page's ends. This enlargement of the painted area to a size hitherto unknown for paper manuscripts creates a grandiose effect altogether fitting for these works. We can see the beginning of this process in the *Anvār-i Suhaylī* of 1570 (No.57).

The paintings in these manuscripts were usually produced by two or three artists, a master artist drawing the outlines and a lesser one applying the colour. The master would then finish it off. Occasionally a third artist who specialized in portraiture would do the faces. The names of those who drew the outlines are usually among the 17 master artists named by Abu'l Fazl.

In 1575 Akbar sent a mission to Goa specially to learn from the Portuguese, and to bring back paintings and prints for his artists to learn from and to copy. Techniques such as modelling and perspective were learnt in this way and included in the 1580s manuscripts.

Most of the historical works still tend to include large panels of text inside the painting, as the artists were still unsure of their recession techniques. Such panels hid awkward junctions very effectively. In the *Akbarnāma*, however, of *c.*1590, the text is usually reduced to a line or two, so that the double-page compositions in which this manuscript abounds are almost released from the subservience to the text appropriate for manuscript illustration. But this is not a simple matter of the earlier manuscripts having more text and the later less, as technical mastery in landscape and recession was attained throughout the studio. The *Ta'rīkh-i Alfī* of 1593, an historical work later than the *Akbarnāma*, has such large text panels proportionate to the paintings as to give the latter more the function of marginal illustrations. The same applies to as late a manuscript as the non-imperial *Razmnāma* of 1616. The biographical work of Jāmī, *Nafaḥāt al-Uns*, of 1605 (No.69), is treated in much the same way as the 1580s manuscripts, while the intervening poetical manuscripts tend to follow the examples of the *Akbarnāma*. The reasons may perhaps be sought in the nature of the texts themselves. Familiar texts such as the Persian poetic classics, or the events of recent history would scarcely have needed the text for the story of the illustration to be recognizable. Not so in more obscure historical periods, such as the 14th-century history of Tīmūr and above all in the early history of Islam in the *Ta'rīkh-i Alfī* and in the translations from Sanskrit. The arrangement of texts, the layout on the page, the choice of subjects for illustration – all these were planned in advance by the head of the studio doubtless including consultation with the Emperor himself. The colophon of the imperial *Razmnāma* tells us that the manuscript was organized by Sharīf, the son of ʿAbd as-Samad.

While these great co-operative projects were progressing, artists had an opportunity to produce individual paintings in smaller manuscripts. No dated work of this type has been found between the 1570 *Anvār-i Suhaylī* and the 1581 *Gulistān*, but the album of zodiacal and tilasm paintings in Rampur and the mutilated *Anvār-i Suhaylī* fragments in Bombay must have been done between these two dates, while the *Ṭūṭīnāma* in the Chester Beatty Library (No.60) and the *Dārābnāma* (No.59) belong to the end of this period. In these manuscripts it is clear that paintings were usually the responsibility of a single artist, and the result is considerable unevenness in the quality of the work. In the *Dārābnāma*, for example, a masterpiece by Basāvan jostles with some of the most garish and crude of all Akbar-period paintings. There has been speculation that this might reflect the change of capital from Fathpur Sikri to Lahore in 1585, when possibly new recruits were added to the studio from the locality, the epithet 'Lahori' being added to two names in the ascriptions on the *Dārābnāma*. There is good reason however to suppose that the *Dārābnāma* was begun before the move to Lahore, as the work of certain artists in it seems to predate work in the historical manuscripts. Nānhā for example is exposed as a Deccani artist of promise in the *Dārābnāma*, whereas in the manuscript of the history of Tīmūr, which appears to have been begun in the late 1570s on the evidence of its early pages, he contributes a double-page scene of great power and originality in the developed historical style. It is probable however that work was continued on all these undated manuscripts of the 1580s for a very long time indeed, perhaps for over a decade in the case of the Tīmūr manuscript in Bankipore.

Two poetical manuscripts have survived from the imperial studios of the 1580s, a *Dīvān* of Anvarī dated 1588 at Lahore, and an undated *Khamsa* of Nizāmī (No.61) now in the Keir Collection attributable to 1585–90 on grounds of style as well as the two-artist system of production. This latter system was apparently found unnecessary for the smaller-scale miniatures of the manuscripts of poetical and other literary works, and for the superb-quality manuscripts produced during the 1590s the system was abandoned. Instead, each miniature is the responsibility of one master, and finished to the highest degree. Such manuscripts are of thick, creamy paper, highly burnished, and contain illuminations of superb quality, in which Mughal illuminators or *naqqāsh* are seen to have finally diverged from their Iranian counterparts, through a heavier use of reds, oranges and other strong colours, an extreme fondness for floral arabesque, and in more daring shapes to their *ʿunvāns* and *sarlavḥs*. In the finest manuscripts as in the Nizāmī and *Bahāristān* of 1595 and the Amīr Khusraw of 1597 (Nos.64–6), all the margins are painted with landscape, figural and floral designs in gold. This kind of treatment is borrowed from Iran, where it reached perfection in Shāh Tahmāsp's Nizāmī of 1539–43, but quickly degenerated in both Iran and India into stereotyped designs applied using stencils. In manuscripts of high quality, however, all the margins are individually painted, although the themes tend to be repetitive and stock favourites – lions or tigers chasing or mauling deer is one of the most frequent. This type of work appears to have been done by artists at the beginning of their careers – two of Jahāngīr's great artists, Mansūr and Bālchand, worked on the illuminations and margins of Nos.64, 66 and 70. Finally the manuscript was bound in a luxurious cover – very few Mughal covers have survived, two of the finest being on the 1595 Nizāmī and the 1597 Amīr Khusraw, both painted and lacquered (Nos.65–6). There is no known leather binding which can safely be attributed to the period of Akbar, though one or two are known which may be Jahāngīri.

During the 1590s historical texts were not neglected. Akbar commissioned, in order to mark the one-thousandth anniversary of the *Hijra* a history of the past 1,000 years called the *Taʾrīkh-i Alfī* which was presented to him in 1593, a millennium (*alf*) after the flight of the Prophet from Mecca to Medina, the base of the Muslim calendar. This work is now dispersed and only fragments of it are known. The *Chingīznāma* (History of Genghis Khān) from Rashīd ad-Dīn's history *Jāmiʿ at-Tavārīkh*, now mostly in the Gulshan Palace, Tehran, was illustrated in 1597. After receiving the initial manuscript copy of ʿAbd ar-Rahīm's translation of Bābur's memoirs in 1589, Akbar ordered other copies to be made and distributed so that the work would be better known. Three other full-scale illustrated versions from the royal studio are known from between 1590 and 97 (Nos.62–3). Abu'l Fazl's *Akbarnāma* originally presented to the Emperor in 1590, was continued by the author up to his murder in 1601 by the partisans of Prince Salīm, and it may have been as a tribute to his dead friend that Akbar ordered another illustrated copy to be prepared. This, now divided between the British Library and the Chester Beatty Library (Nos.70–1), is incomplete, and bears only a date on one of the pictures equivalent to 1604. Work on it may have stopped on Akbar's death in the following year. Unlike the others in this group of historical manuscripts, the *Akbarnāma*'s paintings are mostly by two artists, a system apparently considered unnecessary for the others.

All the manuscripts of the 1590s are in the fully mature, eclectic Mughal style, in which all its elements, Iranian, Indian and European are now fully assimilated into a balanced, harmonious whole. In the manuscripts after 1600, however, is found a change of direction with a cooler palette in transparent blues and greens, while many paintings are in '*nīmqalam*' which are really drawings with washes of brown and highlighting in colours and gold. Perhaps it was the influence of European drawings and prints brought by the Jesuits and other visitors to Akbar, or drawings in the Persian manner from Isfahan, which set Mughal artists off along this path, in reaction against the richly coloured palette favoured hitherto.

In 1598 Akbar left Lahore, which had been the capital for 14 years, and returned to Agra, of course bringing the studio with him. The following year Salīm the heir to the throne left court without permission and took his studio with him to Allahabad where he remained until 1604. Salīm, who took the throne name Jahāngīr (World-Conqueror) on his accession in 1605, tells us in his Memoirs how great a connoisseur he was. He had an enquiring mind, which delighted in observation, and had his painters record things which pleased or intrigued him – animals, birds, flowers, curious happenings and so on. He tells us that the Iranian painter Āqā Rizā was in his employ from his entry into India some time before 1584, as was his son Abu'l Hasan born in the palace in that year. He strongly favoured the elegant, facile art of Iran at this time, perhaps in youthful, filial antagonism to his father's ideals in art. It is not known how many artists were in his studio, since of the three manuscripts known to have been produced at Allahabad for him (Nos.72, 74–5), only one (*Anvār-i Suhaylī*) has attributions to artists. Āqā Rizā and his son Abu'l Hasan were both with him, since the *Anvār-i Suhaylī* contains work by the former dated 1604 and dedicated to Shāh Salīm, the title he took in rebellion. Ghulām, another Iranian painter, is to be numbered among the Allahabad group on the basis of an inscription on a painting mentioning Shāh Salīm, and also Bishndās, whose work unmistakably appears in the *Rāj Kanvār* of 1603–4. Work on the *Anvār-i Suhaylī* was continued until 1610, so that it is impossible to determine which of the other painters did their work at Allahabad and which were present in the imperial studio at Agra when Jahāngīr took possession in 1605. Work done in Allahabad and in Akbar's studio at Agra after the return from Lahore in 1598 share very similar ideals, so that it is not possible to attribute to Salīm's taste alone the changes from the style at Lahore. Akbar in his last years shared Salīm's taste for portraiture and both of them were compiling albums at this time. Abu'l Fazl tells us that Akbar had the likenesses taken of all his chief nobles and the portraits bound up in albums. Only a few of these portraits appear to have survived. However some of Salīm's albums have survived intact – the Gulshan Album in the ex-imperial library in Tehran and another album in the Berlin Staatsbibliothek (No.78).

The practice of collecting pictures and specimens of calligraphy into albums or *muraqqa'* was already long established among Muslim bibliophiles by the end of the 16th century – Shāh Tahmāsp for example had a famous collection, now in the Topkapi Saray Museum in Istanbul. *Muraqqa'* were more than scrapbooks; they could exhibit a patron's taste to the most exquisite degree, far more so than a manuscript, since the subject of individual paintings was directly under his own control. It was usual to alternate facing pages of paintings with pages of calligraphy, apposite verses written by famous calligraphers especially for such collections, and illuminated with floral designs and arabesques. The paintings and calligraphic specimens were pasted on to thin card made up of many layers of paper, the margins decorated through the addition of arabesques, floral paintings, designs in gold or any number of other decorations. The finished mounts were then bound up into an album with leather or lacquered covers.

Jahāngīr's albums are at once the earliest and greatest Indian *muraqqa'* to have survived. Some of the earliest of all Mughal paintings are in the Gulshan Album, but it is unlikely that Salīm began putting his albums together much before 1599. Signed work in the Tehran volume is dated between 1599 and 1609, and in the Berlin volume between 1608 and 1618. The paintings of the Mughal school in the volumes are mostly portraits or genre scenes, animals and flowers, along with Persian and Deccani paintings, and European prints or Mughal versions of them. They are most remarkable however for the exquisite paintings in the margins. We have seen above at the imperial studio in Lahore how at least three of the luxurious manuscripts of the 1590s had their margins all decorated with paintings in gold. In all three there occur little vignettes of figures or animals in part or full colour, standing out from among the gold. Miraculously, the attributions of these little vignettes in the *Bahāristān* (No.64) have been preserved from the binder's knife – Khīm, Shivdās and Bālchand, the last named at the beginning of a glittering career under the Emperors Jahāngīr and Shāh Jahān. In the albums this concept is expanded so that fully-coloured or half-coloured portraits, of ascetics, courtiers, artists, Christian saints, float in front of the shimmering gold background. It is the Jahāngīri albums which develop this technique to the highest pitch of expressiveness, so that it is inextricably linked with his taste, but the same phenomenon also occurs in the first two pages of the 1604 *Akbarnāma* (No.70). Other great albums also are known from the first half of the 17th century associated with the other Mughal emperors and princes in which the marvellous freedom of the Jahāngīri border paintings can be seen slowly petrifying into stereotyped portrait figures or floral designs.

To artists so dependent on patronage, the change of ruler in 1605 brought great changes to their lives. Jahāngīr had no interest in the mass production of heavily illustrated manuscripts of inevitably uneven quality; for him perfection was what was required, which could necessarily only be achieved by the few. He was not particularly interested either in the idea of illustrating manuscripts, since his freedom

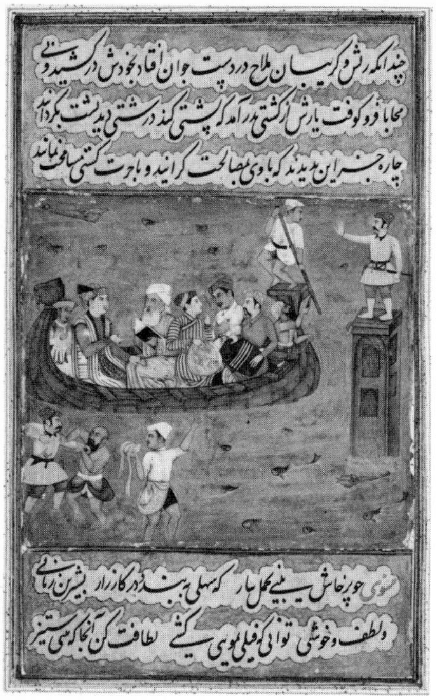

80 f.72. The ferryman abandons the objectionable young man in the middle of the river (No.80, p.98).

as a patron would necessarily be limited by another's choice, that of the author. His greatest artists – Abu'l Hasan, Mansūr, Govardhan, Bishndās, Bālchand, Bichitr etc. – had so perfected their technique towards the realism he expected, that they could perfectly implement his wishes. By commissioning individual paintings, whether of portraits, of animal and floral studies, of scenes from his life to illustrate his Memoirs, he was able to exercise complete freedom of patronage and show his individual taste for the rendition of the real world, echoing Prince Daniyal's earlier cry to poets to write of the world they knew in India, not the fanciful one of Iran (No.81). Thus, overwhelmed by the beauty of the spring-flowers of Kashmir, he ordered Mansūr to prepare an album full of them, or to take likenesses of rare creatures, such as a zebra and a turkey, which were presented to him. At the beginning of his reign however he still had some manuscript illustrations prepared – work on the *Anvār-i Suhaylī* seems to have continued until 1610, while a *Būstān*, *Gulistān* and *Kulliyat* of Saʿdī appear to have been commissioned about 1605. He also indulged in the age-old habit among Muslim patrons of tinkering with earlier manuscripts. Thus the artist Daulat added a self-portrait to the colophon-page of the 1595 Nizāmī (No.65), and seven unsigned paintings were added to the 1567 *Gulistān* (No.55). Govardhan, Nānhā, and Manohar added superb paintings to a *Khamsa* of the Turki poet Navāʾī, now in Windsor Castle (No.77), and nine paintings were added to a minute *Dīvān* of Hāfiz (No.76). Other Iranian manuscripts were subjected to a partial process of repainting, replacing the Mongoloid features of the Persian style with realistic Mughal ones, creating a very strange amalgam. Jahāngīr seems also to have started the habit among the Mughal emperors of inscribing manuscripts which he had just had brought to him from the library, and dating them. The dates occur throughout his reign; his successor Shāh Jahān contented himself with recording that they came into his possession on his accession in 1627.

Throughout the last decade of the 16th century and the first of the next, the two concepts of book-illustration which we have termed Iranian and Indian, had been battling in the Mughal studio for supremacy, and Jahāngīr's accession finally marked the victory of the Indian method. In most manuscripts of the 1590s, the lines of text allowed to intrude across a painting are very few, and in the *c.*1604 *Akbarnāma* these disappear entirely. Although text is found at top and bottom of paintings from this time on, the painting itself was released from subservience to the text, and its composition allowed to follow its own logic. It is in his reign too that the invariable Indian method of painting people in full profile triumphs in the Mughal school also.

Some of Jahāngīr's early manuscripts revert to the 14th-century manner of illustrating the text with horizontal paintings across the middle of the page, and this is continued by two of Shāh Jahān's (r.1627–58) earliest manuscripts commissioned in Agra in 1629–30, one of which he sent as a present to King Charles I (No.80). Shāh Jahān was far less interested than his father in painting, but appears to have maintained his father's academy. Numerous paintings from his reign are signed with the same names as occur on Jahāngīri paintings. His major productions include a few magnificent albums and an illustrated history of his reign (the *Pādshāhnāma*, now in the Royal Library, Windsor Castle, No.82) in which the Mughal style is displayed at its most sumptuous. Lacking any serious motivation in patronage of artists other than as glorification of himself and his achievements, Shāh Jahān's reign marks the culmination of Mughal painting as a serious art form but heralds no new developments. The interests which Jahāngīr instilled in his painters of representing the real and natural world and of cultivating their own artistic personalities as individuals, both previously unheard-of developments in a Muslim context, ruined them for manuscript illustration, an art which requires both imaginative efforts and a submergence of artistic personality which by this time were foreign to their work. Shāh Jahān's successor Aurangzīb (r.1658–1707) was a fundamentalist Muslim who reverted to the traditional condemnation of painting – under him the arts of the book suffered a lingering decline.

The great library of the Mughals with its reputed 24,000 manuscripts, many of them illuminated, was sacked by the Afghan Nādir Shāh in 1739 and many of its treasures carried off as booty to Iran. Little now survives to represent the achievements of the book-artists of the reigns of Akbar and Jahāngīr, but what does survive shows them to have been among the greatest in this field the world has seen.

53 f.119b. The opening of *Sūrat Maryam* (Chapter of Mary).

53 'Qur'ān'

The Holy Koran, unascribed in the text.

A note on f.246b in Persian states that the work was copied by Hibat Allāh al-Husaynī for the use of the Sultan, Lahore, 981/1573–4. There seems no reason to doubt this ascription, as the Ms. is unquestionably a product of the second half of the 16th century, and in quality good enough for a royal provenance. The Sultan of Lahore in 1573 was of course the Emperor Akbar.

The text is enclosed within gilded and coloured margins, and is written in different scripts, the first, middle and last of the 17 lines being in large *Muḥaqqaq*, alternately gold and blue, on a white ground, the intermediate shorter lines in a fine smaller *Naskhī* contained between illuminated upright panels. The *sūrah* headings are usually in gold in *Ruqā'* script on blue, with polychrome illumination, and the *bismillah* on a gold ground underneath. There are two double-pages of *'unvāns*, the first being a composite. The central two pages of illumination (ff.118b–119a) are around the beginning of the *Sūrat Maryam*. Other points worthy of note are that three of the folios (ff.2b, 3a and 246a) have margins decorated in peony arabesques in gold, and that the recto of every folio immediately above the text contains the impression of a small pear-shaped seal, all obliterated. It is the fondness for certain colours – pinks, orange, greens – which first distinguishes Mughal illumination from its Safavid counterpart before the actual content diverges, and this fondness is shown only occasionally in this Ms., indicating a comparatively early date.

British Library, London, Add.18497.

ff.246; 33×22cm; fine-quality polished paper; 17 lines in *Muḥaqqaq* and *Naskhī* scripts in panels ruled in gold and colours; the binding is of plain dark-brown morocco, with red doublures, with simple gold designs – at a later date cartouches were cut out on front and back, and flower and vase motifs impressed, presumably not in India.

Bibliography: BM 1871, No.808. BL 1976, p.80.

54 'Ḥamzanāma'

Illustrated on p.76.

The Romance of Amīr Hamza (see No.33).

Although this vast epic was not unknown in India, as it is one of the few surviving Sultanate manuscripts, it seems strange for the young Akbar to have chosen to have it illustrated on such a vast scale, as its theme of the slaughter of infidels is foreign to his tolerant nature. Perhaps it was the heroic exploits and deeds of derring-do which appealed to the youngster. However, we know from both Badā'unī's and Abu'l Fazl's accounts that work on it took 15 years, that it consisted of 1,400 paintings on large sheets of cloth bound in 14 (or 12) volumes, and that it was finished some time before 1582. Pramod Chandra has rigorously analysed all the literary evidence on the dating of the work and we follow him in assigning as early a date as possible to it, *c.*1562–77. Of the just over 100 surviving paintings, a few have five lines of text on blue and white paper pasted above and below the painting on the obverse, but the majority have full-size paintings on the obverse, and the text in 19 lines on paper pasted on the reverse. The attempt to integrate text and painting would be a Persian rather than an Indian concern, and indeed it may originally have been intended to have many fewer paintings and more text pages. This was quickly abandoned in favour of the Indian approach to illustrated manuscripts which was seen in all the *Candāyana* manuscripts (Nos.34, 45, 46) and *Bhāgavata Purāṇa* (No.36), of full-page illustrations with text on the reverse. Although manuscripts on paper on such a large scale are not unknown to the Iranian tradition (the dispersed early 16th-century *Fālnāma* is of similar size), while for a large Persian painting on cloth Akbar needed have looked no further than the so-called *Princes of the House of Tīmūr* painted probably in Kabul for his father, we follow Skelton in believing that it was the Indian practice of painting on large square pieces of cloth (*paṭa*) which finally determined the format of the manuscript. Many of the Hindu artists who flocked to the Mughal studio must have earned their living as painters of the *picchais* (cloth-paintings) which in later centuries are exemplified by the Nathdwara tradition but which must have been practised in all the Vaishnava centres of Braj and Mathura, the original home of the Nathdwara image, between Delhi and Agra. Totally unused to painting on paper, they would have taken to cloth as their natural medium.

Michael Rogers has recently drawn attention to the chaotic state of the text pasted on the reverse of the cloth, and firmly dismisses the idea of public recitation of the *Ḥamzanāma* text with the painting held up by the reciter, by showing that, at least for those in the British Museum, there is no necessary connection between text and painting. However, on one of the most beautiful and best preserved of the pages, Elias rescuing Nūr ad-Dahr, the painting is numbered 85 and the text 86, so that the text was meant to be read in conjunction with the facing painting. The paintings must then have been intended to be looked at in book format, and hence bound up. The surviving paintings are in a mixture of cloth and card frames, none of them probably original, but now cut down even further.

British Museum, London, 1925, 9-29,01.

Provenance: Gift of the Rev. Straton Campbell.

1 folio; 68 × 52cm; cloth, mounted in card frame, with margins painted in orange, white and blue; on obverse, painting 68 × 52cm, on reverse 19 lines of large *Nasta'līq* on gold-flecked creamy-brown paper, pasted on the cloth.

Bibliography: BM 1976, pp.24–8. Glück 1925. Grube 1969 (with locations of extant pages and bibliography). KC 1976, pp.236–7. Rogers 1980–81, pp.20–6.

55 'Gulistān'

COLOUR PLATE XIX

The Rose-garden, a collection of moral tales, one of the most famous works of Persian literature, by Muslīh ad-Dīn Sa'dī (*c*.585–690/1189–1291). Illustrated manuscripts of the work are extremely common, both from Iran and India (see Nos.58, 80, 138).

The Ms. was copied by Mīr 'Alī al-Husaynī at Bokhara in 975/1567–8 in elegant *Ta'līq*, and has six miniatures in a Bokhara-influenced style apparently contemporary with the text (four of which are signed by Shahm), and seven in a Mughal style of about 1600–10. An origin for the Bokharan paintings in the Mughal studio would seem to be indicated by the portrait of Akbar (f.30a) shown enthroned in young manhood (he was 24 in 1567), the Indian costume and features of many of the figures, the Indian style of architecture (arches with scallopped outlines), and the inscription on two of the paintings reading 'it was ordered in the days of the prosperity of the great king Jalāl ad-Dīn Muhammad Akbar, may Allah perpetuate his kingship and sovereignty'. Additionally a painting in the *Anvār-i Suhaylī* of 1570, of undoubted Mughal provenance, is in the very same style of Bokhara and almost certainly by Shahm himself (see No.57). The six paintings are all of larger size than the text panels, and in all but one case have no text included on them, so that there is no difficulty in supposing them to have been added to the Ms. on its arrival from Bokhara. It has been suggested by some scholars that the paintings as well as the manuscript were done in Bokhara itself, as a present intended for Akbar from the Shaybanid Sultan.[1] This explanation however presents historical difficulties. The years 1564–7 were those in which the Uzbek rebellion was at its height; the Sultan of Bokhara was the leader of all the Uzbeks as well as being the descendant of those who had driven Akbar's grandfather Bābur out of Transoxiana. It is unlikely therefore that Akbar would have been sent such a present at such a time. Nor is it apparent how Akbar's appearance would have been known in Bokhara, or the details of Mughal court costume, while the painting in the *Anvār-i Suhaylī* remains unexplained.

British Library, London, Or.5302.

ff.128; 34 × 22cm; paper; text in *Ta'līq* in double-columns on panels of gold-sprinkled light-beige paper 20 × 12cm, framed in dark-blue margins embellished with floral arabesques with outer margins of dark brown polished paper of the 19th century; brilliant *'unvān*; 13 miniatures almost full page; rebound in Persia in library of Fath 'Alī Shāh (1771–1834), with portraits of himself on both covers (now kept separately); modern binding.

Bibliography: BM 1968, p.44. BL 1977, p.147. BM 1976, pp.23–4. P. Chandra 1976, p.73, plates 37–8. Robinson 1967, pp.108–9.

[1] Shahm is known to have worked for Sultan 'Abd al-Azīz in Bokhara.

56 'Duval Rānī Khizr Khān'

COLOUR PLATE XX

The story of Duval Rānī and Khizr Khān, a Persian romantic poem by Amīr Khusraw. The poet was born in 1253 in Patiala, his father a Turkish officer and his mother an Indian. He was the greatest exponent of the so-called 'Indian' style in Persian poetry, and he composed also in Turki and Hindi. In his varied life he served many princes of India from Delhi to Bengal, as well as being a disciple of the great Chisti saint Nizamuddīn Auliyā, near whose tomb in Delhi he is buried. He died in 1324–5. In the poem Khizr Khān, the son of 'Alā ad-Dīn Khaljī (1296–1316), and Duval Rānī, the Princess of Gujarat, are in love from childhood, and eventually are united after separations; but Khizr Khān fell under his father's displeasure, and was incarcerated in Gwalior and there murdered by his brother along with Duval Rānī. The poet was asked by the prince to write of his love, and completed it after his murder.

The Ms. was copied in 976/1567 by Sultān Bāyazīd ibn Nizam. It is very much in the Bokharan tradition, and its illuminations and margins resemble closely its contemporary Ms. of the *Gulistān* (No.55). There is a brilliant opening *'unvān*, the illumination surrounding the text panels, while the stiff marginal frames are of blue or beige with gold marginal designs of arabesques, peonies, etc. Like the *Gulistān*, it may have been brought to Agra from Bokhara and had two miniatures added in Agra. The miniatures, which fill the whole page, are more Mughal in their character, and show that in 1567 the characteristic style of the *Ḥamzanāma* was already developed. In composition both owe something to Bokharan prototypes, such as those by Shahm in the *Gulistān*, but in details of colouring, landscape, human figures and architecture, they owe more to the *Ḥamzanāma* style, and demonstrate that that Ms. must have been begun some while before this date.

National Museum, New Delhi, L.53-2/7.

Provenance: ex-Kapurthala State Collection.

ff.157; 32 × 21cm; creamy-brown paper for text, with borders in blue or beige; 14 lines of *Ta'līq* in two columns in panels 19 × 9·5cm with margins ruled in gold and colours; headings in gold and black; *shamsa*, with seals, and *ārzdīdas* on f.1a; *'unvān* on ff.1b, 2a; marginal designs in gold; two full-page miniatures; oriental covers.

57 f.222. The impetuous king kills his favourite hawk unaware that it was warning him of a spring fouled by a dead dragon.

Bibliography: Chandra 1976, p.72 and plates 35–6. MIC, pp.96–7.

57 'Anvār-i Suhaylī'

The Lights of Canopus, by Husayn Vā'iz Kāshifī (see No.49).

This text was especially popular in the Mughal court, two imperial-quality manuscripts being prepared for Akbar and one for Jahāngīr. The earliest, this one, is dated 978/1570–1, and with the *Duval Rānī Khizr Khān* (No.56) is a key document for our understanding of the development of the *Ḥamzanāma* style, as they stand about midway in the 15 years that it took to complete that manuscript. Most of the 27 paintings are in a style to be expected from the artists of the *Ḥamzanāma*, the same characteristics of human and animal types, landscape and architecture. The typical *Ḥamzanāma* face with its round appearance and slightly pop-eyed expression, with the further eye of faces in three-quarter profile extending slightly beyond the curve of the face, is here in abundance. The possibilities of recession in landscape are not yet hinted at, as a wall of trees or rocks always closes off the middleground. However, in addition to this *Ḥamzanāma* type, there are two others. In one, of which there are two paintings, the style of Bokhara is immediately apparent, and there can be little doubt that the artist of the first painting is Shahm who painted the six Bokhara-style paintings in the *Gulistān* of 1567 (No.55). The six paintings of the *Gulistān* and the two of the *Duval Rānī Khizr Khān* are all full-page paintings without any text panels, and certainly in the latter manuscript the borders round the paintings are not the same as those round the text panels. If these paintings were all added, then their dates are not fixed at the colophon's dates of 1567 and 1568, but certainly the evidence of the *Anvār-i Suhaylī* suggests that they must have been added at about the same time. There is also in this manuscript a small group of paintings with the people in a slightly more refined version of the *Ḥamzanāma* style which links closely with those in the *Duval Rānī Khizr Khān*, for example the paintings of the king who killed his favourite hawk on f.222a and the king of Hindustan who had his elephants trample the perfidious Brahmans on f.320b.

The *Anvār-i Suhaylī* is the earliest Mughal manuscript available to us which shows the Mughal artists getting to grips with the problems of extending their paintings beyond the text panels, while trying to integrate both paintings and text fully into the overall design. There are several paintings in which the illustration is a simple rectangle within the text panel with a few lines of text above and below. The usual means of enlargement is to extend either of the lower panel's horizontal margins sideways, and the inner vertical margin upwards, into the border almost to the edge, and painting in most of the intervening border. This is quite usual form for the Mughal manuscripts of the 1580s but here we can see the process being worked out. The marginator had normally drawn his vertical margins round the text panels before the artist had started work, and these were simply overpainted. The main focus of the composition is often within the original area in the text panel, and the painting in the borders added perhaps as an afterthought simply extends the composition with minor detail, such as an outer courtyard to the side or roofs and a sky above. The earlier large paintings moreover show experimental variation – on folio 36a the painting includes the spine area of the border, as well as two other sides; on f.93b, the upper rulings of the text panel are retained even though there is no text; on ff.36a and 75a the upper areas including the sky of the border portion of the paintings are painted straight out to the edges of the page, with only the lower portions contained within an outer margin. These means of extending the space for painting worked out in this Ms. served the studio well for the next 20 or so years. Compared with later manuscripts, it is overmarginated to the detriment of the pictorial composition. Despite never having been remargined, none of the paintings is attributed. It is with the *Dārābnāma* (No.59) that this process began.

Library of the School of Oriental and African Studies, University of London, MS.10102.

Provenance: Gift of Miss Ousely, 1921.

ff.339; 33·5×21·5cm; paper, speckled brown, smooth and creamy; 19 lines in panels 21×11·5cm with margins ruled in blue, green and gold; one *sarlavḥ*, with *ansa* of broad, gold strapwork; 27 miniatures, unattributed, some within text panels, but most about two thirds of the page; border drawings of animals sketched in some folios; Indian 18th-century covers, rebacked.

Bibliography: AIP, No.636, f.181b in colour. Barrett and Gray 1963, pp.80–2, f.183b in colour. S.C. Welch 1978, plate 4. P. Chandra 1976, pp.72–4, plates 39–42.

58 'Gulistān'

Illustrated on p.77.

The Rose-garden of Sa'dī (see No.55), copied by Muhammad Husayn al-Kashmīrī Zarīn Qalam at Fathpur Sikri in 990/1581.

The text of the *Gulistān* is in an elegant *Ta'līq* in panels of gold-sprinkled biscuit coloured paper, each panel usually being divided up by gold double margins in various formats. Within the margins thus created are painted exquisitely detailed birds, about two thousand in all, together with occasional animals – rabbits, lynx, cheetahs, goats and the mythical simurgh and kilin. The Ms. was remargined at a later date – the outer margins are all in blue and covered with designs in two tones of gold – animals, birds, plants and landscapes, and abstract designs. On the colophon page is a self-portrait by the artist Manohar, son of Basāvan, and the calligrapher Muhammad Husayn.

The portrait shows a handsome man of about 40, smiling slightly and approvingly at the youthful painter Manohar who is concentrating on filling his pen. Manohar was presumably allowed the privilege of a self-portrait here on the basis of having done the work of illuminating the Ms.; the inscription simply says 'the work of Manohar' referring either to the portrait or to the whole book. Although there are several examples from the early Jahāngīri period of miniature birds being added to earlier manuscripts (see No.76), there is no reason to doubt that the birds in this *Gulistān* are contemporary with the Ms., as the layout of the text presupposes the inclusion of decoration in various places at the beginning of and in the middles of lines, as well as at the end.

It has been suggested that the colophon portrait, unique in Akbar-period Mss., might have been added in the early Jahāngīr period when several artists' portraits were painted (see Nos.65, 72),

Manohar, by then one of the great artists of the studio, having deliberately painted a portrait of himself as he was 25 years before; but this seems inherently unlikely, especially as the style of this scene seems very much work of the 1580s. It is easy to imagine the young Manohar, who was about 15 at the time, and son of the great painter Basāvan, being very much a favourite in the imperial studio and being allowed to paint this colophon page as a reward for what must have been an enormous amount of hard work on the birds and animals in the body of the text. Delicate and restrained at the beginning, towards the end of the volume they culminate in flocks of 20 large birds per page in vivid shades of green and blue.

Royal Asiatic Society, London,
Persian MS.258.

ff.130; 31 × 20cm; gold-sprinkled biscuit-coloured paper in panels with outer margins of blue paper with designs in gold; panels of text 22 × 13cm; 12 lines of *Ta'līq*; bird and animal portraits scattered through the text; colophon portrait of artist and scribe on f.128b; splendidly illuminated *sarlavḥ*; modern binding.

Bibliography: RAS 1892, No.258. AIP, p.143 and plate 121 [the colophon page, f.128a]. A. Welch 1979, No.76 and colour plate of the colophon page.

59 'Dārābnāma'

COLOUR PLATE XVIII

The story of Dārāb, son of Zāl, and the grandfather in the Islamic tradition of Alexander the Great, by Abu Ṭāhir Tarasūsī. It is based on episodes of the *Shāhnāma*, and expands greatly on the original stories by Firdausi.

This particular copy is one of the most enigmatic of Mughal manuscripts. It is only a fragment of the work (dealing with the story of Dārāb, and not going on to the story of his grandson, Iskandar, Alexander the Great, with which the work is mainly concerned), and lacks details of scribe and provenance. Its 157 paintings are mostly attributed, some to the most famous of Akbar's artists including those specially picked out by Abu'l Fazl – Basāvan, Kesu, Mādhū, Jagan, Mahesh, Tārā, and Sānvlah – while other famous artists who contributed to it include Nānhā, Miskīn and Dharmdās. It includes masterpieces of the mid-Akbari style, as well as amazingly crude and unsophisticated work. The variety of work represented in the Ms. both in the level of sophistication and degree of Mughalization displayed by different artists, as well as within the spread of work attributed to the same artists, argues that it was in production over a quite long span of time, and that it was probably used also as a trial Ms. for newly recruited artists. In some folios the appearance of the women is not far removed from that in the Cleveland Museum *Ṭūṭīnāma*, and datable to the 1570s. Nānhā has contributed a few paintings in this style. He has also contributed some of the most stylistically advanced paintings datable to the late 1580s, contemporary with his work in the Tīmūr Ms. in Patna (*e.g.* f.24a and 67a)[1]. Sānvlah contributes one painting in an early style but his work mostly covers a shorter time span towards the end of the Ms.'s production, most of it, like the lovely polo scene on f.11b[2] in a lightly coloured style, almost a tinted drawing. The famous painting by Basāvan (f.34a) with its virtuoso use of foreshortening[3] is no different in treatment from his study of the shaikh and the dervish in the Bodleian *Bahāristān* (No.64) and may be assigned to the early 1590s. An additional complication is the extremely crude work done by two artists, Ibrāhīm Lahorī (who is to be distinguished carefully from Ibrāhīm Kahār) and Kālū Lahorī. Both display a feeble line, crude and garish colouring, an elongation of their figures, and a decided tendency for the further eye in three-quarter profile to protrude into space. The similarity of their work and their common *nisbah* of Lahorī argues that the style was that practised in pre-Mughal Lahore, although no Sultanate manuscript is known in which it appears. It is possible that on the removal of the capital from Fathpur Sikri to Lahore in 1585 some local artists were recruited to swell the ranks of the studio. Neither is heard of again and they must have been dropped very quickly!

Another puzzle is the work attributed to some of those artists distinguished by Abu'l Fazl as the greatest in the studio – Mahesh, Jagan, Tārā, and Kesu. Their work is good, but not outstanding. On the other hand they all contributed very good paintings to the Jaipur *Razmnāma*, so that their work in the *Dārābnāma* must be attributed to a time some years before that Ms., which was begun in 1584. Miskīn was sufficiently advanced to be employed as a second artist on many of the *Razmnāma's* pages, and as a sole artist on the Tīmūr Ms., as was Dharmdās on the latter; both of their careers blossomed fully in the 1590s, and their work in the *Dārābnāma*, competent but not distinguished, must belong to its earliest layer of composition.

At least two of the artists in the *Dārābnāma* betray influences which argue that they came from the Deccan – these are Nānhā and Mādhū Khurd (Madhu the younger). Nānhā throughout his career hints at his origin, in his love of certain colour combinations, but here it is in his swinging robes as well. This is also seen in some of the work of Mādhū Khurd, particularly f.74a, where the influence is strong-enough to pinpoint his origin in Ahmadnagar.[4]

The Ms. is very incomplete, and breaks off abruptly. The numbers on the folios go up to 160, of which only 129 are present, while those on the paintings go up to 200, of which only 157 survive. The loss of the part of the text dealing with Alexander occurred at some time before it entered the royal library in Oudh, the vermilion stamps of which are impressed on the verso of the last folio. The earliest of these stamps appears to be dated 1244/1828–9.

British Library, London, Or.4615.

ff.129; 35·5 × 23cm; creamy-brown paper, unburnished; text in 25 lines of *Nasta'līq* in panels 23·5 × 14cm ruled in gold and colours; a fine *sarlavḥ*, much faded, with miniatures on both opening pages; 157 miniatures, mostly attributed (for list see BL 1977, pp.8–11) – the miniatures vary in size considerably, and are extended into the margins in all directions from the text panel, which is often divided in two by a portion of the miniature; only those near the beginning include all three margins, the largest measuring 34 × 19·5cm; many repairs; attributions in red in a large hand at foot of miniatures, some cut off in a rebinding; European covers.

Bibliography: BM 1895, p.241. BL 1977, pp.8–11. BM 1976, p.29. Barrett and Gray 1963, pp.84–6. S. Welch 1978, pp.48–51 (colour ills. of f.3b and 34a).

[1]Folio 67a actually is inscribed Kānhā not Nānhā. However, on examination of their work, it is clear that the two are identical, as the style is very individual. The artist's Hindu name must have included the word Jnāna, pronounced either Gyāna or Nyāna in northern India, for which the clerk noting the name could write either Gānhā (*gāf* always being written *kāf* by the Mughal scribes) or Nānhā.

[2]Reproduced by Binyon and Arnold 1921, plate VII.

[3]S. Welch 1978, plate 6.

[4]Losty 1982, plate 2; cf. the portrait of Burhān Nizam Shāh of Ahmadnagar reproduced by Barrett 1958, plate 5.

60 'Ṭūṭīnāma'

COLOUR PLATE XXII

The Tales of a Parrot, by Ziyā ad-Dīn Nakhshabī from Nakhshab in Central Asia, and who lived in Badā'un under the Khaljī and Tughluq dynasties of Delhi. The Tales of a Parrot is a Persian reworking of an earlier translation from the Sanskrit *Śukasaptati*, 70 Tales of a Parrot, one of the classics of Sanskrit prose, which is of early medieval date and exists in two separate versions. The amusing tales are told by a pet parrot to a lady whose husband is away, in order to prevent her from finding consolation elsewhere. The version by Nakhshabī is of 52 tales, some of them new substitutions, and was completed in 730/1329–30.

The earliest work completed in Akbar's studio was a copy of this work, now in the Cleveland Museum of Art. This second version in a more advanced and unified style was made about 1580. It is incomplete in its present state, and various miniatures are known from other collections in addition to the 103 in the Chester Beatty portion. As with the *Dārābnāma* (No.59), it appears to be in some ways an apprentice work, possibly trying out new artists, and in among the general run of somewhat crudely coloured and charming apprentice work, the hand of a master is suddenly apparent. The Ms. was however remargined at a rebinding and lacks all attributions to artists. The paintings mostly surround the text panels on three sides and occupy often the central portion, characteristics of the Mughal school first seen in the 1570 *Anvār-i Suhaylī* (No.57); often however, they are large-scale paintings without any text at all, and this would appear to be the first general appearance (excepting the gigantic *Ḥamzanāma*, No.54) in the Mughal studio of this trend, the gradual change from the Persian to the Indian concept of book illustration.

Chester Beatty Library, Dublin, Ind. MS.21.

Provenance: Acquired in 1836 by J.F. Allard, Generalissimo to Ranjit Singh, Maharaja of Lahore and passed to Baron F.S. Feuillet de Conches.

ff.143; 24·4 × 16·3cm; light, polished paper; 15 lines of *Nastaʿlīq* in panels about 14 × 8cm; verses within gold ruled margins in panels; remargined in 18th-century paper, with an additional blue line round panels; 103 paintings, some almost full page; 18th-century Indian lacquered binding.

Bibliography: AIP, p.142 (repro. of ff.14a and 38b). James 1981, No.47. Barrett and Gray 1963, pp.82–3, with col. repro. P. Chandra 1976, pp.60–1, figs.47–59. IP, p.4, for a leaf from this Ms. and references to others; the dispersal of the leaves would appear to have occurred at some time after the 18th-century remargining.

61 'Khamsa' of Nizāmī

COLOUR PLATE XXIII

The Five Poems of the Persian poet Nizāmī (see No.44). The poems are Nizāmī's five great *masnavīs*, often copied together. This exquisite little copy of the famous classic of Persian literature is the earlier of the two surviving copies prepared for Akbar (see also No.65), the later one being a sumptuous full-scale manuscript in the Lahore manner of 1595. The earlier manuscript was copied in Yazd in Iran by ʿAlī ibn Mubārak al-Fahrajī from 907/1502 to 912/1506. All traces of ownership earlier than the 20th century have vanished, so that there is no means of telling how it found its way from Yazd to the Mughal studio, but there in the late 1580s it had 35 miniatures painted in the spaces which had been left by the original scribe specifically for this purpose.

The Ms. has survived almost intact from this period, with numerous interesting notes on the borders which have mostly escaped the binder's knife, and from them, as Skelton points out, we can learn a great deal about how checks were kept on artists' work. A note at the foot of the miniature records the date and the number of days spent on the miniature, which was meant to be erased subsequently by the marginator. Further notes on the corner of the page or the side record the name(s) of the artist(s). The court librarian from these notes wrote the names of those responsible for the work in red below each painting, assigning it a number. This was done before the work went to the binder, who was supposed to trim the edges and remove the surplus notes, but this has not always happened here. Finally, some of the attributions in red have been erased and rewritten in black, which look as if they also belong to the Akbar period and are perfectly authentic. Perhaps because he was dealing with an already existing Ms., the marginator was not always able to do his work properly. The text panels already had margins ruled in gold and blue, the scribe originally envisaging paintings contained within his text panels, with script usually above and below. However, the more ambitious of the artists involved, Basāvan, Laʿl and Farrukh Beg, have extended their paintings around the text on two or three of the sides, removing some of the original margins in the process. The marginator has for the most part ignored these new edges, leaving them untidy, and confined his attention to the margins of some of the smaller miniatures.

The method of work revealed by the attributions is that of sharing, this being the only major non-historical work in which this Mughal characteristic of joint production is evident. This by itself indicates a date in the 1580s, when the work of producing the great historical and Hindu works was in full swing. The style is largely simple, fresh and vivid, without the grandeur of the 1590s Mss., but also without their rigidity. The presence in the Ms. of the work of Farrukh Beg indicates that it must be dated after his arrival in India from Iran in 1585, so that a date in the period 1585–90 seems most probable.

The subjects of the miniatures were already chosen by the original scribe in Yazd, who left blanks at the traditional places. Even so, many of the miniatures betray a knowledge of the traditional Iranian compositions for these subjects, which indicates that some of the artists must have had an Iranian model in front of them. This knowledge is to be expected in Farrukh Beg, but not in Hindu artists such as La'l, Mukund and Tārā.

The Keir Collection, Pontresina, Switzerland.

Provenance: collections of Lord Brabourne (1937) and A.C. Ardeshir.

ff.356; 16·2 × 10cm; paper, creamy-brown; 21 lines of *Nastaʿlīq* in four columns, in panels 10 × 5·7cm, within margins ruled in gold and blue; six *sarlavḥs* in gold and colours; 35 miniatures, all attributed (see KC 1976 for artists' names), some almost full page, others smaller than the text panels; 18th-century Indian binding.

Bibliography: KC 1976, pp.238–48, with repros. in colour and black and white. Ardeshir 1940. Sotheby, 10 July 1973, lot 7.

62 'Bāburnāma'

Illustrated on p.78.

The memoirs of the Emperor Bābur (1526–30), founder of the Mughal dynasty in India, composed originally in Chagatay Turki during Bābur's eventful life, from 1494 at the age of 12 till his death in 1530.

Bābur's grandson Akbar who spoke Turki as his mother-tongue had the work translated into Persian for his courtiers to be able to understand better this remarkable man. The translation is officially by ʿAbd ar-Rahīm Khānkhānān, although doubtless in fact the work was done by a team of scholars at his celebrated library. Four major illustrated versions of the Akbar period are known, whose interrelationships have been traced by Smart. The earliest is now held to be the dispersed Ms. represented mostly by folios in the Victoria and Albert Museum, the official version presented to Akbar in 1589 at the conclusion of the translation. Three other copies were produced in the 1590s – this one, in the British Library, about 1590; a slightly later one divided between the Walters Art Gallery, Baltimore and the Moscow State Museum of Eastern Cultures (No.63); and a third dated 1597–8 now in the National Museum in Delhi. Another in the Alwar Museum (No.108) with 20 paintings appears to be in part a Ms. of the 1590s with half its paintings and much of the text added about 1800. Smart has established the sequence of the Mss. through the iconography, the earliest following the text most minutely, the later ones being based on the earlier paintings with consequent dislocation of the text or miscomprehension of crucial details of the earlier paintings.

The British Library Ms. is nearest to the original and has fewest of this kind of faults. It is also the largest in scale, and many of the well-known Akbari artists worked on it – Farrukh Chela, Manohar, Nānhā, Shivdās, Tulsi, Sānvlah, Jagannāth, Narsingh, Mansūr. Fifty-four separate artists are named in the attributions, while five paintings lack any attribution. The trio of Basāvan, Miskīn, and La'l who contributed so heavily to the composition of the 1589 *Bāburnāma*, and to the earlier historical and Hindu manuscripts, are conspicuous by their absence, a fact which may lead us to the conclusion that they were too busily engaged with the composition of the *Akbarnāma* at this time to be spared, and thus confirming the date of *c.*1590. In the double-page compositions of this *Bāburnāma*, there is a certain uneasiness between the two halves which are almost invariably the work of two different artists, unlike the 1589 *Bāburnāma* and the *Akbarnāma* where the composition of both halves is the work of the one master artist. Although the general illustrative pattern of the 1589 manuscript is followed throughout, it is not slavishly copied; many of the paintings show slightly later or earlier moments in the same story, while in others a single-page painting is expanded to a double, or vice versa.

Ellen Smart has pointed out that the Ms. has suffered the removal of some of its paintings, in particular half of the double-page compositions. This probably happened about 1800, in the large scale 're-furbishment' of the imperial library; the gaps were cleverly concealed by cutting up the text on the other side of the folio (invariably double-sheets) and mounting it on the bias surrounded by added arabesques. The *'unvān* also belongs to this period, surrounding the original opening of the text, and the covers, which have since been removed.

British Library, London, Or.3714.

ff.528; 32 × 19cm; creamy-brown paper, original, with lighter coloured additions; 12 lines of large *Nasta'līq* in panels 20·5 × 10cm, with margins ruled in gold and colours; 143 miniatures mostly with attributions (see BL 1977, pp.122–5) and numbers running up to 183; 70 are full-page miniatures, the remainder smaller paintings of the flora and fauna described by Bābur; double-page *'unvān*, *c.*1800; many folios remargined and decorated at same time, with painted covers of the same date; now in modern binding, on guards.

Bibliography: BM 1895, p.51. BL 1977, pp.122–5. BM 1976, p.37. Suleiman 1970. Beveridge 1922. Smart 1977.

63 'Bāburnāma'

Illustrated on p.79.

The Persian translation by 'Abd ar-Rahīm Khānkhānān of the memoirs of the Emperor Bābur (see No.62).

This album with 31 miniatures is part of the third Akbar-period manuscript of the work, attributable to the years 1590–5, of which only the paintings have survived. The major part of it is in the State Museum of Eastern Cultures, Moscow. No attributions are left in the Baltimore volume, which was remargined in the 18th/19th century.

Walters Art Gallery, Baltimore, W.596.

ff.31; 32·2 and 21cm; paper, remargined; original text panels 17·2 × 9cm, with 12 lines of large *Nasta'līq*, with margins ruled in gold and colours; 31 paintings, mostly about 24·5 × 15·5cm; 19th-century oriental binding.

Bibliography: Smart 1977. Tyulaev 1960 (repro. of the Moscow portion).

64 'Bahāristān'

COLOUR PLATE XXIV

'The Garden of spring', a collection of didactic stories in prose and verse by the Persian poet Nūr ad-Dīn 'Abd ar-Rahmān Jāmī (817–98/1414–93), who lived in Herat under the Timurid rulers. This is one of the most famous of Persian classics, composed in imitation of the earlier *Gulistān* of Sa'dī (No.55).

The court of Akbar had left Fathpur Sikri in 1585 for Lahore in the north-west of the Empire, partly because of increased military activity against the Safavid ruler of Iran. The imperial studio must have been taken also, but dated evidence of work undertaken in Lahore is not common. This manuscript of the *Bahāristān* and the *Dīvān* of Anvari of 1588, are the most substantial pieces of evidence, since the colophons of both state that they were copied in Lahore. The *Bahāristān* was copied in the 39th regnal year of Akbar (1595) by the scribe Muhammad Husayn al-Kashmīrī Zarīn Qalam' (see also Nos.58, 70). There are six paintings in the manuscript, all but one attributed – by Basāvan, Miskīn, La'l, Mukund and Mādhū. All the margins are sumptuously decorated in designs of gold – hunting scenes, animals, birds, landscapes etc. – while 13 of the pages have coloured figures in them also, again mostly attributed – Bālchand, Shivdās, Khim, Akhlās and Husaynī are the artists. The *Bahāristān* is one of the 'luxury' manuscripts of the Persian classics produced for Akbar in the 1590s, exemplified also by the *Khamsas* of Nizāmī (No.65) and of Amīr Khusraw (No.66). All three have suffered somewhat – the *Bahāristān* is complete, apart from its binding, and does not appear to have been remargined at all. Its 67 folios are usually pale biscuit in tone, though some are darker, and others pale tones of green, pink or blue. A gold line about a centimetre from the edge of the page encloses the marginal decorations. The original binding has vanished, and it is now bound in red velvet with gilt appendages imitating stamped leather. A *shamsa* on the first page resembles those in the Nizāmī, and there are also inscriptions in the hands of Jahāngīr and Shāh Jahān.

Bodleian Library, Oxford, MS. Elliot 254.

ff.67; 28·5 × 17·5cm; biscuit-coloured paper, with a few folios in pastel colours; *Nasta'līq* script; 14 lines in panels ruled in colours and gold; six paintings; margins all decorated with gold designs, with some colours; one *shamsa*; one *sarlavḥ*; 19th-century red velvet binding with gilt appendages.

Bibliography: Bod. 1889, p.634. Bodleian 1953, plates 8–12, which show some of the marginal paintings.

65 'Khamsa' of Nizāmī

COLOUR PLATE XXI

The Five Poems of the Persian poet Nizāmī (see No.61).

The Nizāmī is one of the most perfect of the 'luxury' type of manuscript to have survived, even though it is now divided. The major part with 37 of the original 44 paintings is in the British Library, while a smaller section from two different parts of the text, with five paintings, is in the Walters Art Gallery in Baltimore. Two paintings have disappeared. Sections of the Ms. are missing from f.72 in *Khusrav va Shīrīn*, and from f.239 in the *Iskandarnāma*, where the catchwords have been erased to disguise the removals. Of the original 44 paintings, those numbered 12 and 27 to 32 are thus missing, of which Nos.12 and 29 to 32 are in Baltimore. All of these paintings are attributed to master artists of the imperial studio. The last and 45th painting, unnumbered, on the colophon page shows the scribe 'Abd ar-Rahīm Ambarīn Qalam, and the self-portrait of the artist Daulat, complete with apparatus for calligraphy and painting, and an inscription dedicated to Jahāngīr. This painting must therefore have been added after 1605, and appears to date from about 1610. Daulat is not among the artists who painted the 42 surviving miniatures, so it may be presumed he painted at least one of the two missing ones. Artists who contributed to the Ms. include 'Abd as-Samad, in his last-known dated work, Nānhā, La'l, Dharmdās, Sānvlah, and Miskīn.

The margins of this Ms. are all differently illuminated in various tones of gold, depicting principally animals and birds in landscapes – hunting, resting, running. Other pages have arabesque or geometric designs, usually so when surrounding the paintings. The sheer invention of these marginal designs is staggering; although the themes remain the same, the details are always different. A heavy outline in gold of one shade provides a shape to be filled with gold of different shades, always lines, never washed in, to produce modelling and shading. All these designs have suffered slightly in remargining. The folios have been trimmed and let into panels of paper of darker hue, and new outer margins in green and gold provided, as well as a slightly wrong wavy gold outer line. Originally they would have terminated most probably in a single gold line, as in the *Bahāristān*. The remargining, which must have been done in Europe at the turn of the century, has possibly caused us to lose the names of the artists who did these margins, information that is preserved in the *Bahāristān* and Amīr Khusraw's *Khamsa* (No.66). The illuminations are a joy for their brilliance and inventiveness. There are six headpieces of different shape (two of them signed by Khvāja Jān, see also No.66) progressively more inventive in content, culminating with the one on f.285b with two swooping simurghs. There are no less than eight glorious *shamsas*, again all different. Finally there are the covers, painted and lacquered. On the outsides in a central panel are designs in gold of simurghs, dragons and deer in a landscape; on the doublures are paintings of the Emperor Akbar receiving game after a hunt, and as a young man hunting. The doublures are slightly damaged, while the outer covers are in perfect condition; the probability is that they were reversed in a restoration. The covers of the *Khamsa* of Amīr Khusraw of 1597 have the figural subjects on the outside covers, and the fantastic designs as the doublures. At some stage ownership seals and inscriptions on the recto of the title-page have been defaced. A manuscript of this exceptional quality should have had imperial seals and inscriptions, and in fact the upper inscription is dated 102[–?]/161[1–9]; the lower one is too badly defaced to yield any information. A pear-shaped seal, of the same shape as that of Shāh Jahān and Aurangzīb, in the centre of the *shamsa* has been covered with gold, and a round seal near the upper inscription has been erased.

British Library, London, Or.12208.

Provenance: bequeathed by C.W. Dyson-Perrins.

ff.325; 30 × 19·5cm; light-brown polished paper; four columns of *Nasta'līq* script in panels 19·5 × 10·7cm with gold margins; outer margins with designs in gold 26·8 × 15·8cm laid into frames of darker brown with added margins in green, blue and gold; 38 paintings ascribed to artists (see BL 1977), varying in size; six *sarlavḥs* and eight *shamsas* in colours and gold; original lacquered bindings, restored at edges, black leather spine.

Bibliography: Martin 1912, plates 178–81. BM 1968, p.75. BL 1977, pp.142–3. BM 1976, p.57. Brown 1924, plates XVIII, XXXVI–VII, XL. T.J. Brown etc. 1961. Warner 1920. S. Welch 1960.

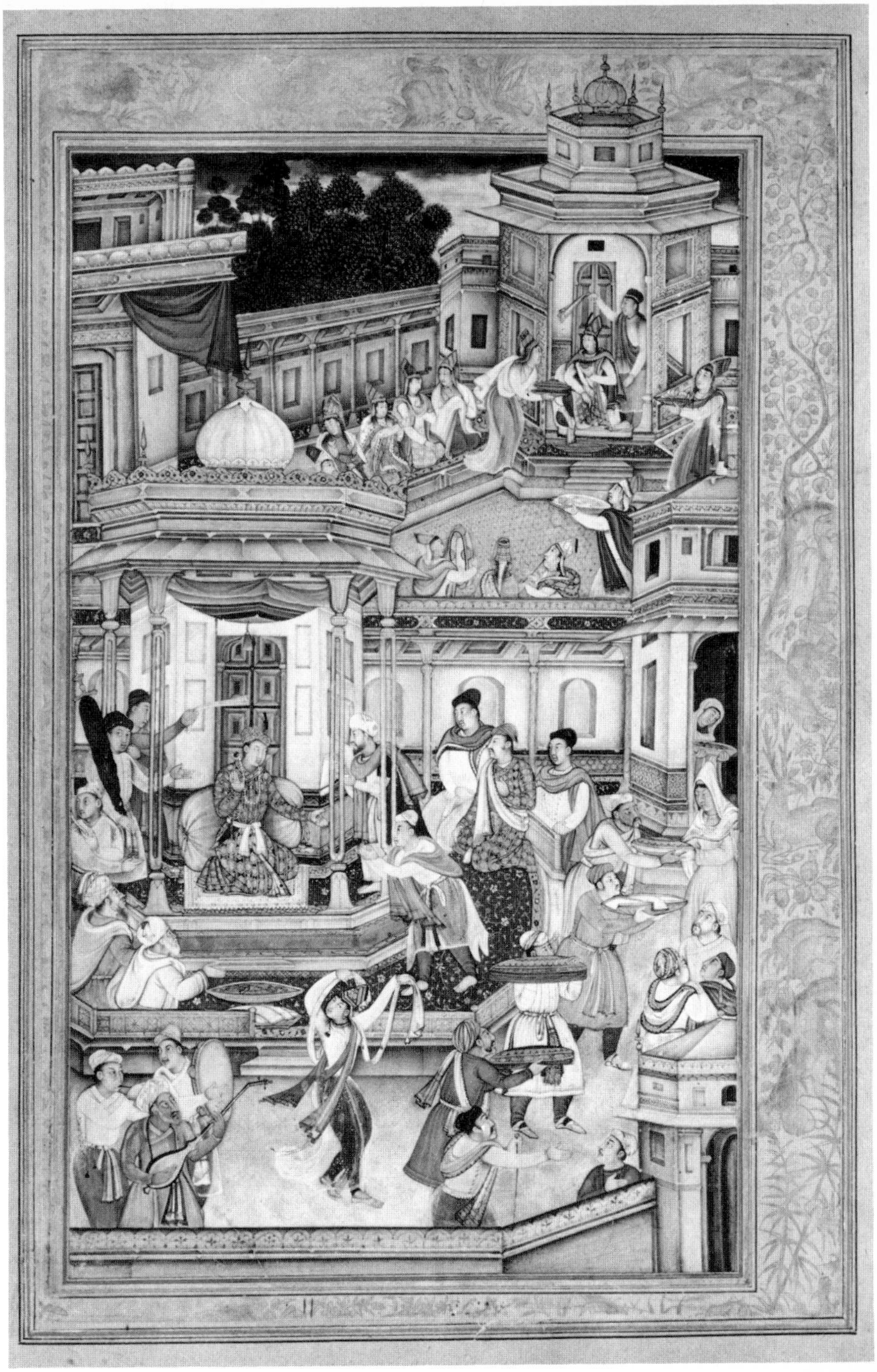

66 f.80. The quarreling Khusraw and Shīrīn hold separate celebrations. By 'Alī Qulī.

66 'Khamsa' of Amīr Khusraw Dihlavī

The quintet of *masnavī* poems composed in imitation of the quintet of Nizāmī by Amīr Khusraw of Delhi (see No.56)

This manuscript of the *Khamsa*, like its companion poetical manuscripts of the 1590s from Lahore, originally had painted and lacquered covers, superb illuminations, marginal paintings on all the folios, and highly finished miniatures. The *Khamsa* has preserved all of these features, but has lost some of its paintings and had the edges of some of the marginal paintings cut off in a rebinding. Many of the attributions have also been cut off. The calligrapher is Muhammad Husayn al-Kashmīrī Zarīn Qalam, who also copied the 1595 *Bahāristān* (No.64). It is a few years later than its companion *Khamsa* of Nizamī, being dated in the 42nd *Ilahi* year of Akbar (1597–8), and in it the scale of the paintings is somewhat more ambitious – landscapes are broader, with less dependence on panels of text to hide joins, while one (f.80a) has the most ambitious architectural layout of any Mughal painting. The marginal drawings, in addition to the drawings in two tones of gold seen in the Nizāmī, also have more highlights in colour, like the *Bahāristān* (No.64). Ettinghausen lists the artists responsible for the illuminations – Mansūr Naqqāsh, Husayn Naqqāsh, Khvāja Jān Shirāzī, and Lutf Allāh Muzahhib. The first of these painted the illumination of the *sarlavḥ* of the 1604 *Akbarnāma* (No.70) and of an undated opening page of a *Dīvān* of Anvarī[1], and also contributed paintings of animals to the second of the *Bāburnāma* manuscripts (No.62); he is the same person who went on to specialize in studies of flora and fauna whom Jahāngīr eulogises in his Memoirs. The second is possibly the same as the artist named Husaynī who contributed to the illumination of the 1595 *Bahāristān* (No.64). The artists responsible for the 21 paintings include La'l, Sānvlah, Manohar, 'Alī Qulī, Dharmdās, Narsingh, Jagannāth, Sūrdās, Miskīn and Farrukh. To them may be added the name of Basāvan who painted one of the eight paintings from this manuscript now in the Metropolitan Museum, New York – three of the other paintings are attributed to artists named in the Baltimore manuscript.

Walters Art Gallery, Baltimore, W.624.

ff.211; 28·4 × 19cm; highly polished, biscuit-coloured paper, with gold sprinkling in text panels; 21 lines of elegant *Nasta'līq* in four columns in panels 17·2 × 10cm with margins ruled in gold and colours, principally green; four illuminated *shamsas*; four *sarlavḥs*; every border illuminated with designs of animals and landscape in gold, with 17 pages with highlights in colour; outer border terminated by another margin in gold and colours, with a later, outer frame 24·7 × 16cm; 21 paintings (with an additional eight in New York), mostly full page; original painted and lacquered covers, 28·5 × 19cm with a tiger hunt and a mystic with a disciple in a cave on the upper cover, and a fight between angels and *dīvs* on the lower; doublures painted in black and gold designs and lacquered.

Bibliography: Ettinghausen 1961, plates 6 and 7 (col. repro. of f.208b and of one of the Metropolitan Museum pages, 13.228.26). Welch 1963, Nos.7 (colour repro. of upper cover) and 8 (two of the Metropolitan pages). Miner 1957 (repro. of lower cover, plate XXIIIa).

[1]Spink 1980, No.62.

67 'Kulliyāt' of Sa'dī

The complete works of the poet Sa'dī (see No.42).

This elegant manuscript dated 1011/1602 from the royal Mughal studio continues the tradition of sumptuous border decorations in gold found in manuscripts of the mid-1590s (Nos.64–6), although this time without any miniatures. All the borders are decorated with drawings in two tones of gold, of animals, hunting-scenes, landscapes and pavilions.

Government Museum, Alwar, MS.206.

ff.408; 31 × 18cm; polished paper; text in elegant *Nasta'līq* in panels with margins ruled in gold and colours; all borders painted in gold; some illuminations; Alwar binding by 'Abd ar-Rahmān (see Nos.108, 109, 138).

Bibliography: Alwar 1961, p.100.

68 'Jog-bāshisht'

COLOUR PLATE XXV

A Persian translation of the Sanskrit work *Yogavāsiṣṭhamahārāmāyaṇa*, the Great Story of Rāma and the Yoga-teaching of Vasishtha, a huge poetical work in which the sage Vasishtha instructs Rāma in Vedanta philosophy by means of long narratives demonstrating the illusoriness of physical reality. A much condensed Persian translation of the work was undertaken apparently at Akbar's command in 1006/1597–8.[1] The present copy with 41 illustrations was prepared in the 47th *Ilāhī* year, *i.e.* 1602, the name of the translator being given according to Arnold and Wilkinson as Farmulī, an inhabitant of Farmul, west of Kabul. No other details are known of this person.

The illustrations are very much in the new palette of the early 17th century, with cool and transparent tonalities, and simpler compositions, which likewise govern the miniatures in the 1605 *Nafaḥāt al-Uns* (No.69) done for Akbar in Agra and the three manuscripts (Nos.72, 74–5) done at the same period for Salīm in Allahabad. All five manuscripts are specifically concerned with mysticism or with Indian themes, so that it is perhaps not very surprising that a new style was evolved for them, contrasting forcibly with the elaborate historical and poetical manuscripts of the previous decade. There is no indication in the Ms. of whether it was done for Akbar or for Salīm. Most of the attributions have been cut off, leaving only two definite names Haribans and Kesu, whose other work at this period is unknown.

The cool palette and elegant compositions in this manuscript have the effect of etherealizing the subjects in a way altogether in accordance with the text, which sets out to demonstrate that the physical world is in fact an illusion. None of the figures is as firmly delineated in physical reality and volume as in the previous decade, and it is possible that here we are in fact witnessing the resurgence of the pre-Mughal artistic tradition of floating figures before a monochrome ground. The miniatures are either whole page, or are contained between the first and last lines of a text panel – no text is contained within them. By this time the guiding hand of the Persian masters had long been lifted, and we can see the resurgence of the old manner of doing things in works produced by artists trained in the imperial studio for non-imperial patrons, such as the 1598 *Razmnāma* (No.88). This is present even here in this undoubted imperial manuscript, which Shāh Jahān autographed after his accession. At the same time, however, as suggesting the illusinoriness of the characters, the artists here were making them the perfect embodiments of what they represented – the sages really do look holy and venerable, and the ladies as lovely as they are described in the text. The figures of Shiva and Pārvatī on f.230a paying obeisance to the sage Vasishtha are as charming a married couple as may be seen anywhere in Mughal painting, despite the attributes of his godhead in which Shiva appears.

Chester Beatty Library, Dublin, Ind. MS.5.

ff.323; 27 × 18·5cm; biscuit-coloured paper in text panels, remargined with a lighter-toned paper; 15 lines of elegant *Nasta'līq* in panels 19·7 × 10·8cm, with margins ruled in gold and red with an outer blue line; one *sarlavḥ*, in gold and colours; 41 miniatures, some full-page, others between the upper and lower lines of a text panel; autograph inscription of Shāh Jahān on f.1b, dated 1037/1628; numerous *ārzdīdāhs* of the reigns of Jahāngīr and Shāh Jahān; rebound in red oriental covers.

Bibliography: CB 1936, pp.21–5 (repro. of ff.41b, 128b, 178b, 230a). Wilkinson 1948. AIP, p.151. Barrett and Gray 1963, p.96 (col. repro. of f.73a).

[1]The translation is not mentioned by Abu'l Fazl in the *Ā'in-i Akbarī*, as among those undertaken at Akbar's command. Rizvi (1975, p.215), states that the translation is 'generally ascribed to Faizī', but Faizī of course died in 1004/1594–6. The British Library Ms. Add.5637 (BM 1876, p.61) states that the author, unnamed, made a new translation after Akbar had in 1006/1597–8 expressed a wish to procure a truer version than that found in the work of former translators. Little reliance, however, can be put on this statement, as this work is in fact an abridgement of the original Persian translation, and is only half the length of this illustrated version, which we may suppose to be the translation originally prepared for Akbar.

69 'Nafaḥāt al-Uns'

Breaths of Fellowship – notices of famous saints and Sufis, by the Persian poet Nūr ad-Dīn 'Abd ar-Rahmān Jāmī (1414–93). Jāmī was a Sufi himself, and wrote this work from 1476–9, being a modernized version brought up to date of two earlier works in Arabic. The main series of notices has 567 biographies of saints from the 2nd to the 8th centuries of the *Hijra*,

69 f.135b. The Sufi Abu'l Adyan praying on a bed of coals watched by Zoroastrians. By Daulut.

followed by smaller sequences on mystic poets and on female mystics.

This Ms. of the work was copied, so the colophon informs us, for the library of Akbar at Agra in the 49th regnal year (1605), by the scribe ʿAbd ar-Rahīm, known as 'Ambarīn Kalam' (Amber-pen) (see No.65). It is incomplete, having only 17 of the original complement of 30 paintings, some of which have found their way into the Chester Beatty Library, Dublin, while an additional six folios of text are also missing. Many of the artist's attributions have been cut off in rebindings, leaving us with only eight names – Hirānand, Narsingh, Daulat, Harārat (? – possibly Padarath), Bālchand, Mādhū, Khem Karan and Tārā. Most of these names appear in the contemporary *Akbarnāma* (Nos.70–1). Like the latter Ms. the *Nafaḥāt al-Uns* is in the 'new' style of the last years of Akbar's reign – cooler colours, less busy action, and a marked fondness for *nīmqalam*, with a highly burnished surface that imparts a glazed and hard look to some of the paintings. The most interesting paintings are by Daulat (f.135b), a fiery study in glowing purples and oranges of the saint Abu'l Adyan praying on coals; by Bālchand (f.226a), a lovely study of a group of Sufis at a party in his mature, soft manner; and an unattributed study in the new palette (f.142a) which shows an intimate domestic scene of a man, his wife and their child, which is a harbinger of the new concern for social realism that Jahāngīr was to bring to the studio. All that remains of the attribution on this lovely study is the quite clear syllable – kar –, which does not unfortunately point to any of the master artists of the period.[1] This like two other paintings has the puzzling inscription in a different hand, *aval*, meaning first, and possibly meaning the first painting in the Ms. of that artist's work. This does not seem to be a usage attested in other manuscripts. The Ms. has retained its original lacquered covers, now detached.

British Library, London, Or.1362.

ff.401 (of which ff.1–3 are later flyleaves with inscriptions); 27 × 14·5cm; biscuit-coloured, burnished, thick paper; 15 lines of elegant *Nastaʿlīq* in panels 18·5 × 8·5cm within margins ruled in gold and blue; space for a *sarlavḥ* left blank; 17 paintings (out of 30) in size 10·5 × 11cm to 24 × 12cm, the majority much larger than the text panels, which are in the narrow upright format seen also in the *Akbarnāma* (Nos.70–1), which however tends to keep the paintings within the bounds of the text panels; various later seals, mostly defaced; considerably damaged (including several of the paintings), many folios remargined, the whole now on guards in a modern binding; the original covers, damaged and detached, with panels showing painted flowers and trees in a landscape, and doublures of arabesques in bas-relief in leather.

Bibliography: BM 1879, p.350 (the scribe is ʿAbd ar-Rahīm, not ʿAbd al-Karīm). BL 1977, p.69 (add the names of the artists Harārat (Padārath?), f.150a, and Tārā, f.354b). Barrett and Gray 1963, pp.96–8 (f.142a reproduced in colour).

[1]Ashok Das in his study of the painter Bishndās (Chhavi 1971) refers to speculation that this painting is by Bishndās or Daulat. Neither name is justifiable on the grounds of the fragmentary attribution.

70–71 'Akbarnāma'

COLOUR PLATE XXX

and **71** illustrated on p.74.

The History of the Emperor Akbar (1556–1605), by Abu'l Fazl ibn Mubārak (1551–1602), is the official chronicle of Akbar's reign. The Emperor's friend and counseller, Abu'l Fazl, the brother of the Poet-Laureate, Faizī, carried the work up to 1590, when an illustrated copy was prepared, most of the surviving part of which is broken up and in the Victoria and Albert Museum. The work of writing the official history was continued, however, apparently up to 1602, the year of Abu'l Fazl's death, when Prince Salīm, jealous of the historian's influence over his father, had him murdered by the Bundela chief, Bīr Singh Dev. There has survived another imperial copy of the *Akbarnāma*, now divided mostly between the British Library (vol. 1) and the Chester Beatty Library (vol. 2 and part of vol. 3), which goes up to the year 1579. On the first folio, now hidden behind repairs, are two holograph library accession notices by the Emperors Jahāngīr and Shāh Jahān, dated 1028/1619 and 1037/1627–8. At the foot of the miniature on f.134b is a note giving the date 21st *Shaʿban* 1012/25th January 1604. From Jahāngīr's note, the calligrapher appears to have been Muhammad Husayn al-Kashmīrī Zarin Qalam ('Golden-pen'). There can be no doubt of the imperial stature of this and the Dublin volumes, and it is doubtless the copy commissioned at the termination of the *Akbarnāma* in 1602, the year of Abu'l Fazl's murder. As the colophon is lacking there can however be no certainty of this.

There is a marked difference in style between the two copies of the *Akbarnāma* – the rough-hewn, immediate style of the earlier has given way to the exquisite technique of the 17th century. Many of the paintings of this last historical manuscript of Akbar's reign are akin to the style of the manuscripts of the Persian classics illustrated in the intervening period in their exquisite finish and perfection of detail. There are, however, numerous paintings in the *nīmqalam* technique so prevalent in the early years of the new century. All the borders are replacements, but as the attributions below the miniatures and the border illuminations on the first two folios are on these borders, all of which are absolutely authentic, the whole manuscript must have been given new borders shortly after completion, but before 1619, the date of Jahāngīr's holograph on the front of the marginal portion of the first folio. This would in itself be most unusual, to remargin a Ms. so soon after its completion, unless for a specific decorative purpose which in this case was never completed. It is unlikely that this work would have been done just for the opportunity to illuminate the margins of the first two folios unless a more ambitious scheme had been contemplated. Unlike most of the marginal paintings of the two Jahāngīr albums datable between 1599 and 1618 (No.78), in which is continued the tradition of the 1590s manuscripts of painting figures mostly in gold with a subdued tonal range for the rest of the figure but with full colour for the face and other details, these pages in the *Akbarnāma* show figures fully painted against a golden landscape. The original illumination which these margins enclose is attributed to Mansūr in the columns between the text.[1] All the paintings of both surviving parts are contained within the textual margins, and some also include text within the same frames, which are remarkable for their tall, narrow format. Various paintings have notes in a minute hand, of which portions were erased in the ruling of margins and in the remargining.

British Library, London, Or.12988.

(70) ff.163; 40·5 × 27·5cm; creamy paper of dark hue; fine *Nastaʿlīq* script; 22 lines, in panels 23·5–24 × 12·5cm ruled in gold and colours; completely remargined; 39 surviving paintings out of 50, all with attributions (see BL 1977, pp.4–5); two opening pages with drawings in gold and colours round the *sarlavḥ*; remargined and rebound in Persia, with painted and lacquered Qajar covers, dated 1249/1833–4.

Chester Beatty Library, Dublin, Ind. MS.2.

(71) ff.268; 43 × 23cm; 22 lines of *Nastaʿlīq* script in panels ruled in colours and gold 24 × 13cm; completely remargined in lighter coloured paper; 61 paintings (all attributed, see CB 1936, pp.6–12), out of 110; two *sarlavḥs*; the covers of tooled and gilded leather signed by Muhammad Zamān ʿAbbāsi.

Bibliography: BL 1977, pp.4–5. BM 1978, p.52. CB 1936, pp.4–12. Martin 1912, plates 82–3, 209–10.

[1]This has just been pointed out by Hans-Caspar Graf von Bothner of the Universität des Saarlandes. Mansūr Naqqash (the illuminator) painted the *sarlavḥ* also in No.66.

72 'Dīvān' of Hasan Dihlavī

COLOUR PLATE XXVI

The collected shorter poems in Persian of Hasan of Delhi, a contemporary and friend of Amīr Khusraw (see No.56), who died in 1328.

This, like Nos.74 and 75, is one of a small group of manuscripts associated with Prince Salīm in his years of rebellion against his father, when he established a studio at his residence in Allahabad. It is dated Muhurram 1011/1602, and was copied at Allahabad by Mīr ʿAbdallāh Kātib Mushqīn Qalam ('Musky-pen'), one of the three Mughal calligraphers honoured with such soubriquets. It is in a large *Nastaʿlīq*, like the *Rājkunvār* of 1603 (No.74), but unlike the *Anvār-i Suhaylī* (No.75), which is in *Naskhī*. Mīr ʿAbdallāh is the subject of a portrait study on the final page (f.187a), surrounded by the implements of his art, which shows him to be an ascetic looking man of about 40 to 50.

The Ms. has 14 miniatures but without any attributions, in the new palette of the early 17th century. Two of them, like the paintings added to the Hāfiz Ms. (No.76) after he became Emperor, show Salīm himself, witnessing a polo game (f.40a) and hunting deer (f.109b). Of the painters who may now be associated with Salīm's studio – Āqā Rizā, Abu'l Hasan, Bishndās and Ghulām or Mīrzā Ghulām – only the latter's work may be identified in this Ms.[1]

Walters Art Gallery, Baltimore, W.650.

ff.187; 32 × 20·5cm; paper, biscuit-coloured; 14 lines of *Nastaʿlīq* in two columns, in panels 20 × 10·5cm with margins ruled in gold and colours; one *sarlavḥ*; 14 miniatures, usually larger than the text panels, about 20 × 12cm; original lacquered covers, 32 × 21cm, with interlacing floral bands on gold ground; red lacquered doublures.

Bibliography: Ettinghausen 1961, plate 8 (col. repro. of f.22b). Beach 1978, pp.33–40 (seven repros.)

[1]Beach 1978, p.34, who attributes five of the paintings to him.

73 'Dīvān' of Hāfiz

COLOUR PLATE XXVIII

The collected poems of the Persian poet Hāfiz of Shiraz (d.791/1389). Hāfiz of Shiraz ranks as the greatest of Persian lyricists, as well as one of the greatest of Sufi poets. The Mughal emperors were especially fond of the poet, and indeed Jahāngīr used a Ms. of Hāfiz's works for taking auguries, which still survives in the Khuda Baksh Library in Bankipore, a Persian Ms. which belonged to his grandfather Humāyūn, with notes in both their hands. There has survived one large imperial copy of the work in the Rampur State Library, and two pocket-size Mss. of Mughal provenance, both in the British Library.

The smaller of the two is this minute Ms. (the panels of text originally measuring 7·9 × 4·1cm) with 19 miniatures, all of the same size as the text panels. The flyleaf has the remains of two inscriptions, one of them the holograph of Shāh Jahān dated 1037/1627, recording the Ms. coming into his library on his accession, the other more fragmentary recording the possession of the Ms. in Allahabad. This last is unfortunately not the hand of Salīm the future Jahāngīr, so that this Ms. need not necessarily be joined with the manuscripts known to be productions of the Salīm studio in Allahabad. However, it could be a later librarian's note, and there is a strong likelihood that if it was in Allahabad, it was in Salīm's library there. Only one of the 19 paintings has an attribution – f.167a, attributed to Ustad Mādhū on a book in the painting itself. Mādhū's work is to be found in Akbari Mss. of the 1590s, as well as the 1604 *Akbarnāma* (Nos.70–1) and the 1604–10 *Anvār-i Suhaylī* (No.75), the latter begun for Salīm in Allahabad. The paintings have all suffered from a defacer, who did dreadful damage in many of the pictures.

British Library, London, Grenville XLI.

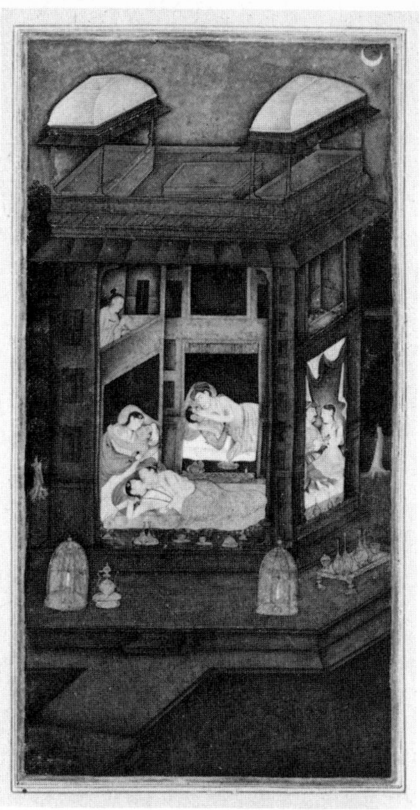

74 f.59b. The prince disguised as a mendicant in a bordello.

Provenance: Thos. Grenville Collection by 1824.

ff.258; 13 × 8cm; remargined in 18th century; original text panels and miniatures 7·9 × 4·1cm of creamy-brown paper; margins ruled in gold and crude blue and red lines; 10 lines of exquisite *Nastaʿlīq* script; one *sarlavḥ*; 19 miniatures; Iranian lacquered covers *c.*1800.

Bibliography: BM 1879, p.629. BL 1977, pp.58–9. BM 1976, p.59.

74 'Rāj Kunvār'

A romance in Persian, of dubious title (*'King's son'*), apparently anonymous, doubtless a translation of a Hindu story, concerning a prince who is obliged to disguise himself as a wandering mendicant and go through various fantastic adventures in order to win his beloved. The Ms. is dated 1012/1603–4, and was done at Allahabad. There can be no doubt that it was done there at Salīm's studio. The 51 paintings are closely linked stylistically with the non-Persianized paintings in Salīm's *Dīvān* of Hasan Dihlavī (No.72), and *Anvār-i Suhaylī* (No.75), in their palette and general simplicity of composition. Again, remargining has deprived us of the attribution to painters, but as Ashok Das has pointed out[1], four of them must be the work of Bishndās, as his style of portrayal of women is unmistakeable, and in the same early manner as the painting he contributed to Salīm's *Anvār-ī Suhaylī* (No.75). The paintings if full-page are wider but no higher than the text panels, and are often contained within the latter with a line or two of text above and below.

Chester Beatty Library, Dublin, Ind. MS.37.

ff.132; 29 × 17·5cm; light-brown polished paper; remargined with much lighter paper; 12 lines of elegant *Nasta'līq* in panels 19 × 10·5cm with margins ruled in gold; one *sarlavḥ* in gold and blue, with 18th-century additions of Hindu divinities; 51 paintings, often contained within text panels, but sometimes wider; modern covers of red silk.

Bibliography: Only a few pages have been published: Hayes 1963, plate 7.

[1]Das 1971, reproduces ff.69b and 106a; ff.15b and 122a he also attributes to Bishndās.

75 'Anvār-i Suhaylī'

COLOUR PLATE XXVII

The Lights of Canopus, by Husayn Vā'īz Kāshifī (see No.49).

Of the manuscripts produced for Salīm at Allahabad this is the only one which gives us any definite information about the artists he took with him, since it is signed and dated 1013/1604 on two of its paintings dedicated to Pādishāh Salīm by the artist Muhammad Rizā, who also contributed another four paintings. Jahāngīr in his memoirs boasts of how the famous Persian painter Āqā Rizā was his protégé from his entry into India, an event which took place some time prior to 1584, in which year was born Aqā Rizā's son Abu'l Hasan, who is known from an inscription on a youthful portrait of his dated 1009/1600 to have been born in the palace. Āqā Rizā is known to have worked at Allahabad for Salīm in designing the garden where his wife was buried in 1604. It may be assumed that the father took his son with him to Allahabad, as Abu'l Hasan contributed a stunning painting to this Ms. However, the colophon of the Ms. is dated 1019/1610–11, so that the remaining 29 paintings could have been contributed at any time between the two dates either in Allahabad or in the capital. Most of the paintings bear attributions; there is evidence that some of those named were in Allahabad with Salīm, such as Bishndās and Mīrzā Ghulām. The artist Bishndās painted a miniature in the Ms., illustrating the story of the Sultan of Baghdad who was infatuated with a Chinese slave-girl. Bishndās when very young contributed part of one painting to the dispersed 1589 *Bāburnāma*, a note on it saying that it was corrected by his uncle Nānhā. His next known attributed work occurs in this painting, by which time he had developed into a major artist. The presence of his portrait on the borders of the Jahāngīri album in Tehran done between 1605–8, indicates Jahāngīr's opinion of him as a major artist, and possibly gratitude for his going to Allahabad with him. It is remarkable for its faces, Bishndās's strongest point; he was considered by Jahāngīr to excel above all in portraiture, and was sent in 1613 to Iran to take the likeness of Shāh 'Abbās. His uncle Nānhā appears from his earlier work to be a painter of Deccani origin, and we are inclined to think that Bishndās learnt from him such Deccani traits as the attendant's fly-whisk, the long trailing scarf of the dancer, and the marvellously subtle colouring of muslin over orange and mauve, an effect beloved by Deccani painters. Very unusually for a Mughal Ms. of this period a double-page *'unvān* is included, further evidence of Jahāngīr's Iranian taste at this time.

An interesting feature of this Ms. is the long narrow format of its text panels, which may be compared to the contemporary *Akbarnāma* (Nos.70–71) and *Nafaḥāt al-Uns* (No.69). Sometimes the painters keep within the boundaries of the panels, at others they extend their work outwards into the margins. The somewhat clumsy remargining of the Ms. in the 18th century has reduced the impact of some of these latter paintings.

British Library, London, Add.18579.

ff.426; 24·5 × 15cm; pale-beige paper; *Naskhī* script, 19 lines in panels 15·5 × 7·2cm, with margins ruled in colours and gold; a splendid double-page *'unvān* in deep blue, gold and black, with polychrome floral arabesques; 36 attributed miniatures (see BL 1977); 18th-century remargining; covers blocked in gold, with doublures in red leather with stamped medallions and spandrels, gilded; edges of leaves stamped in gold patterns.

Bibliography: BM 1879, p.755. BL 1977, pp.62–3. BM 1976, p.59. Wilkinson 1929 [all paintings repro. in colour].

76 'Dīvān' of Hāfiz

COLOUR PLATE XXIX

The collected poems of Hāfiz (see No.73). This exquisite little manuscript of Hāfiz is now in two parts, the major part in the British Library (the bulk of the text plus eight miniatures), and the remainder with one miniature in the Chester Beatty Library in Dublin (Ind. MS.15). The Ms. is lacking a colophon, but is a product of the Mughal atelier, written in an exquisite *Nasta'līq*, and with every page decorated, like the 1581 *Gulistān* (No.58), with minutely detailed paintings of birds in the margins and spaces between the verses. They are smaller even than in the 1581 Ms., and are even greater triumphs of the miniaturist's art in their exquisite finish and perfect naturalism. The *shamsa* and *sarlavḥ* on each side of folio 1 are of undoubted Mughal provenance of the late Akbar period[1], and may be assigned to about the same period as the other little Hāfiz Ms., No.73, about 1600.

The miniatures, however, are somewhat later. Of the eight in the British Library portion, the first five are more or less connected to the text of the *Dīvān*, dealing with subjects such as dervishes, taverns, drinking parties and so on, as does the miniature in Dublin. The last three show the Emperor Jahāngīr. In the first he is playing polo with his sons Parvīz and Khurram, and Mīrzā Abu'l Hasan, Āsaf Khān, who in 1611 became his brother-in-law. In the next he is out hunting with a falcon in a landscape with attendants, unidentifiable, when stopped by an angel, a sequence which does have a justification in the text, which has the sentence – 'an angel has grasped his stirrup'. In the third he is shown seated in a pavilion with courtiers. Stchoukine has identified this scene as the presentation of jewels to his father by Prince Khurram (the future Shāh Jahān) at Urta near Kabul in 1607. This identification does not however explain the presence of the prostrating figure beside Khurram, and there is a strong likelihood that this may be Prince Karan of Mewar, and the subject the submission of the prince to Jahāngīr at Ajmer in 1614, as recorded in the Emperor's Memoirs. It is the work of one of the master artists of the atelier in its marvellous portraiture in a tiny compass.

The presence of Mīrzā Abu'l Hasan in the polo scene in such an intimate family game, strongly suggests that this was painted after he became the Emperor's brother-in-law through the marriage of his sister Nūr Jahān, an event which took place in 1611, while the following year his daughter Arjmand Bānū married Prince Khurram. Stchoukine has plausibly suggested Manohar as the artist of the polo scene, and Beach Bālchand for the lovely f.42a of a youth being enticed to a party. The scene with Jahāngīr and Khurram is the work of a brilliant portraitist who is definitely not Manohar, Bishndās or Bichitr, but may be Abu'l Hasan, of whose portrait work at this time little has survived, or Govardhan who painted a similar darbar scene now in the Rampur Library.[2] One is inclined to ascribe to Abu'l Hasan the marvellous dancing dervishes (f.66b). No artist is credited with the painting of the approximately 1,000 birds which decorate the Ms., but in their thin brushwork with delicately sketched in background they are consonant with the work of Mansur at this period.[3]

British Library, London, Or.7573.

ff.278; 14 × 9cm; text on biscuit-toned

paper; nine lines of exquisite *Nasta'līq* script in double columns in panels 7·1 × 4·1cm ruled in gold; the outer margins are of much later date, of a grey paper; one *shamsa*, one *sarlavḥ*, with prominent blues, greens, pinks, and purples; eight miniatures, added about 10 years after the Ms., about 8 × 5cm to 10·3 × 6·5cm, in spaces left blank, now under glass; text in modern binding, on guards.

Bibliography: BM 1968, p.53. BL 1977, p.60. Stchoukine 1931. Barrett and Gray 1963, pp.100–1, repro. of ff.42a and 66b in colour. CB 1936, pp.78–80, and plate 97, for the other part of this Ms., in 53 folios, with forged inscriptions and seals from another Ms. of Akbar's reign, and a different margin.

[1]Arnold and Wilkinson (CB 1936) seem to think the Chester Beatty part earlier than this, for no obvious reason, as the calligraphy and illumination is typically Mughal *c.*1600.

[2]P. Brown 1924, frontispiece.

[3]Basil Gray has pointed out two Mss. similarly decorated with birds at the Mughal court, a *Dīvān* of Shāhī in Paris and another Hāfiz in the Chester Beatty Library Dublin (P.150).

77 'Khamsa' of Mīr 'Alī Shīr Navā'ī

COLOUR PLATE XXXI

Five *masnavī* poems, written in imitation of, and on the same themes as, the *Khamsa* of Nizāmī, but in Chagatay or eastern Turkish, by the greatest poet in the language, Navā'ī (1440–1501). He was a friend from boyhood of Sultan Husayn Bayqara, the ruler of Herat (1468–1506) and patron of the greatest of Persian painters, Bihzād.

The text of this Ms. was written in the author's lifetime in 897/1492 in Herat by the great calligrapher Sultan 'Alī of Mashhad, and furnished with superb illuminations in the Herati style. It subsequently found its way to Bokhara, doubtless after the Uzbek sack of Herat in 1506, and it would appear that miniatures were added to it there, the spaces having been left blank originally. One of the miniatures has an inscription with a date 947/1540.

It is difficult to judge what the subject or compositions of these Bokhara paintings may have been; there are only six, all towards the beginning of the Ms. in the first poem. All, however, have been overpainted in the Mughal studio. On folio 1b is an inscription in the hand of Jahāngīr dated 1014/1605, stating that the Ms. 'one of my most treasured books' entered the royal library in the first year of the reign when 'the paintings were completed in my workshop'. This gives us the date of the repainting as 1605, and must have been one of the first tasks Jahāngīr set his artists after his accession. The names of the artists are recorded as: folio 5b – Nānhā and Manohar; f.6a – Narsingh; f.12b Dhanraj; f.20b – Govardhan; f.31a – Mohan; f.36b – Govardhan. Only the first of these is an original Mughal painting, a magnificent version after a European painting of the Last Judgement, Christ in Majesty above and the Resurrection of the Dead below. Needless to say it has nothing to do with the text. The other miniatures show mostly repainting of faces and landscape in the Mughal manner. Jahāngīr presumably considered the Bokharan paintings did not match up to the Herati illumination and calligraphy, and had them improved accordingly.

Royal Library, Windsor Castle, MS. A.8.

ff.308; 34 × 22·5cm; paper dark-biscuit in tone, gold flecked; 25 lines of *Nasta'līq* in four columns in panels 23·5 × 15cm with margins ruled in colours and gold; ff.1b/2a, superb Herati *'unvān*; six miniatures, about the same size as text panels; f.1a, Bokhara seal dated 947/1540 and seals of Shāh Jahān (1037/1627) and Aurangzīb; inscriptions of Jahāngīr (1014/1605) and Shāh Jahān (1037/1627); covers of brown leather with stamped medallions and margins.

Bibliography: Robinson 1951, No.65. BM 1976, p.63.

78 'Muraqqa'' of Jahāngīr

An album of paintings and calligraphic specimens, mounted in specially painted *hashīya* (borders) and assembled by the Emperor Jahāngīr (1605–27).

Two large collections of Jahāngīr album pages still survive: the earliest, the *Muraqqa' Gulshān*, in the Gulistan Palace Library, Tehran, contains work dated from 1599 to 1609, the second, this one, contains work dated from 1608 to 1618, while a number of separate pages are known from various collections with the remarkable borders for which the albums are famous.[1] The Gulshān Album is a much larger collection than the Berlin Album, but both exhibit the same type of work: Persian paintings, including ones attributed to Bihzād,[2] earlier Mughal paintings, including ones attributed to 'Abd as-Samad and of the Humāyūn period,[3] contemporary portraits of courtiers and royal personages, a few Deccani paintings, and European prints and paintings with Mughal versions and copies of them. The calligraphic specimens are dominated by the work of Mīr 'Alī (see No.55) with some pages by the even more famous Sultan 'Alī of Mashhad (d.1520).

Originally the albums were put together with painting facing painting and calligraphy facing calligraphy, and the borders painted accordingly, more subdued and with no figural representation round the paintings, but exuberant and with fully coloured figures round the calligraphy. So many pages have disappeared from the Berlin Album that little of this careful construction remains.

Jahāngīr had started to collect paintings into albums when still a prince. He states in his Memoirs how the Persian painter Āqā Rižā had worked for him since coming to India (some time before 1584) and his earliest identifiable work is in the Gulshān Album, although his earliest dated pages are the border paintings of 1599, which speak of Salīm as Shāh,[4] the title he took to himself in that year in rebellion against his father. In common with border paintings of the manuscripts of the 1590s (Nos.64–7), these are painted usually in heavier tones of gold with colour only for the faces and highlights. By contrast Daulat's border paintings in the same album[5], some of which are dated 1609, are in full colour, but there is no necessary chronological progression in this difference, more an artist's taste. None of the Berlin Album border paintings which are later is executed in full colour.

Bishndās is the only other artist whose work is signed in the Gulshān Album. In the Berlin Album, border paintings are signed by Bālchand, and Govardhan, while several of the portraits are either signed by, or attributed to (in the hand of Jahāngīr), Abu'l Hasan, Bishndās and Manohar. Bālchand is first known from his border paintings on folios 17a and 60b of the 1595 *Bahāristān* done for Akbar (No.64), while Govardhan and the other three artists are themselves the subject of penetrating portrait studies by Daulat on the margins of page 44 of the Gulshān Album.

The subject of these border paintings was anything that took the artist's fancy. Portraits however must have been executed on royal orders; this was a tradition that appealed to artists working on the Shāh Jahān albums, where full colour portraits in the borders often surround the main portrait painting. Other favourite sources of inspiration were animals and hunting scenes, probably worked up from sketches but with the artists still revelling in their immediacy and liveliness; European subjects, taken from the Flemish and German prints which so appealed to Jahāngīr; studies of usually unnamed shaikhs and holy men, courtiers, and ladies; workmen, including valuable studies of papermakers and burnishers, bookbinders and scribes and artists at work, all taken from the life in the imperial studies (fol. 18a of the Berlin Album); and copies of features of earlier paintings. One of the finest of the portraits is Daulat's copy of a portrait of the great poet Jāmī by Bihzād, on page 140 of the Gulshān Album. One of the finest pages in the Berlin Album shows Humāyūn in a tree-platform with a young prince, presumably Akbar, presenting a book; this is probably after the full painting by 'Abd as-Samad

78 f.24. Illuminated *hashīya* (border-decorations), including Humāyūn and the young Akbar in a tree. Calligraphy by Sultān ʿAlī al-Mashhadī.

79 f.52. A young prince playing polo watched by the dervish who dotes on him.

mounted in the Gulshān Album of Akbar presenting a painting to Humāyūn in a similar platform[6].

Staatsbibliothek Preussischer Kulturbesitz, Orientabteilung, Berlin, Libr. pict. A.117.

ff.25; 40 × 22cm; margins, creamy paper, sometimes tinted buff or pink, with decorations in gold and colours; central panels of calligraphy or paintings, of varying sizes.

Bibliography: Kühnel and Goetz 1926. Beach 1978, pp.43–59. Godard 1936.

[1] Beach 1978, pp.43–59.
[2] BWG, plate LXVII.
[3] BWG, plates CIV and CV.
[4] Godard 1936, pp.13–8.
[5] *ibid*, pp.18–33.
[6] BWG, plate CIVB.

79 'Būstān'

The Flower-garden of Saʿdī (see No.42) written in 655/1257, at the same time as the *Gulistān*. This Ms. of the *Būstān* is likewise a companion to the *Gulistān* (No.80), both of them being prepared in Agra for Shāh Jahān in 1629–30, and copied by the same calligrapher, Hakīm Rukn ad-Dīn Masʿud, called Hakīm Rukna. This person was a native of Kashan who was a poet at the court of Shah ʿAbbās, came to India in the time of Akbar and became one of the favourite poets at the court of Shāh Jahān. He then returned to his native country where he died at the advanced age of 105 lunar years either in 1057/1647 or 1066/1655–6. No other product of his penmanship seems to be known. Both manuscripts are in the same format, on a large scale, with very large calligraphy and small paintings in a horizontal format across the page, and wide borders, covered with gold designs in the case of the *Būstān*. This somewhat odd relationship between painting and text has an obvious predecessor in the *Gulistān* produced for Jahāngīr about 1605–10, of which only the small horizontal pictures survive.[1]

Jahāngīr had no desire to produce the heavily illustrated manuscripts so typical of his father's reign, and instead experimented with various formats to express his individual connoisseurship – compilation of *muraqqaʿs*, the addition of paintings to earlier manuscripts, and, in the instance of the *Gulistān*, the return to an earlier format of composition, the horizontal strip, almost universal in 14th-century Iranian manuscripts and very common still in the 15th. With the disappearance of the text of his *Gulistān*, it is not possible to say how it worked in that instance, but in Shāh Jahān's two manuscripts the effect is none too successful – the paintings are too small for the size of the manuscript, and the richness and heaviness of the pigments used ill accords with their status as book illustrations. They are still, however, on the whole exquisite little paintings, none of them unfortunately ascribed, but in the case of five by some of the best artists of the period. Pinder-Wilson has distinguished four hands in their production.

British Library, London, Add.27262.

Provenance: obtained by Sir John Malcolm in Kirmanshah in 1810 – acquired from his son in 1865.

ff.175; 38×25·5cm; paper; 12 lines of large *Nastaʿlīq* in double columns in panels 25×14·5cm, the text on ivory-toned paper in clouds on gold, framed in borders of various colours with gold arabesques; laid in margins of pink, blue, green, purple and yellow, all with drawings in gold of animals, birds, plants, etc; *sarlavḥ* on f.1b, with floral illumination around colophon on f.175a, and rectangular panels of illumination on this and the preceding page; 10 miniatures between 5·5×14·5 and 9·5×14·5cm; covers 19th century, painted and glazed, but with the damaged original lacquered covers laid down as doublures – the latter show a central medallion with pendants and cornerpieces of arabesques on gold, with animals and birds, real and imaginary, sporting in a landscape.

Bibliography: BM 1879, p.603. BL 1977, p.146. BM 1976, pp.80–1. Pinder-Wilson 1957.

[1]Beach 1978, pp.66–70.

80 'Gulistān'

Illustrated on p.84.

The Rose-garden of Saʿdī (see No.55).

The *Gulistān* accompanying No.79, is dated *Jumada I*, 1038 (Dec. 1628–Jan. 1629) at Agra. Both Mss. are written in the same very large hand, with wide margins. The *Gulistān*'s text is on white clouds on gold throughout, and has been remargined with wide borders of almost white paper, sprinkled with gold. There are nine miniatures in all, across the centre of the text panels, some of them being in a somewhat larger format than the *Būstān* miniatures, almost square. The effect is possibly even more unhappy than with the smaller miniatures. Imperial Mughal painting at this time was mostly involved with portraits, darbar scenes, and other paintings indicative of the power and glory of the Mughal *imperium*, or with natural-history paintings. The attempt to reduce the formal, static qualities of this type of painting into a true format of manuscript illustration was singularly unsuccessful, the grandeur of the former being turned to an unnatural stiffness.

Shāh Jahān himself must have felt that Mughal painting was now entirely unsuited to manuscript illustration, and had no more prepared other than the grand history of the reign (No.82), which is on the largest scale and in which the formal, hieratic qualities of the painting of his studio are seen to best advantage. He can hardly have cared very much for this *Gulistān*, since when the necessity arose to send a present to King Charles I of England, it was this Ms. which he selected and suitably inscribed on the reverse of the colophon page, in Wilkinson's translation: 'on the 17th of the month of Ṣafar

81 f.17. Prince Daniyal watches as the flames consume the *satī* and her dead lover.

of the year 11 [of the reign] corresponding to the year 1048 of the Hijrah, this exquisite *Golestān*, resembling the Garden of Eden, and in the writing of the Nādir of the time, Mawlānā Hakīm Roknā, I have sent as a gift to the glorious and exalted King of England. Written by Shibāb al-Dīn Muḥammad Shāh Jahān Pādishāh, son of Nūr al-Dīn Jahāngīr Pādishāh, son of Jalāl al-Dīn Akbar Pādishāh'. The date corresponds to AD 1638, and we do not know what occasion prompted the gift.

The Ms. remained in the royal library for nearly two centuries, when George IV sent it as a gift to the Shah of Persia, Fath ʿAlī Shāh, in 1827, having had it rebound in red velvet embroidered with the initials of George IV and a crown, and with the emblems of the kingdoms in the corners. Another inscription records, again in Wilkinson's translation: 'as ordered by his Majesty, Fatḥ ʿAlī Shāh, this Golestān, written in India, was brought as a gift by a special envoy from the glorious George, King of England, and has been placed . . . in the Royal Library among the special royal books. Written in Jumāda II, 1242 A.H. (*i.e.* January 1827)'. The Ms. subsequently (1259/1843) entered the library of Bahmān Mīrzā, elder son of the Crown Prince ʿAbbās Mīrzā, and presumably remained in his library until his death in 1884.

Chester Beatty Library, Dublin, Ind. MS.22.

ff.119; 35×26·5cm; paper, biscuit-coloured, entirely remargined with gold-sprinkled thick white paper; 12 lines of large *Nastaʿlīq*, in clouds on gold ground, in panels about 25×15cm with margins ruled in gold and colours; one *sarlavḥ*, with two birds; nine miniatures, all contained in text panels with text above and below; English binding of *c.*1825, covered in red velvet.

Bibliography: Wilkinson 1957.

81 'Sūz u Gudāz'

'Burning and Melting', the story of a Hindu princess who burnt herself on her husband's pyre in the reign of Akbar, a Persian *masnavī* by Muhammad Rizā Nauʿi of Khasbushan. The author went from Mashhad to India in the time of Akbar, and entered the service of ʿAbd ar-Rahīm Khān Khānān; he seems to have stayed at Burhanpur with his patron and Prince Daniyal, Akbar's younger son, at the time of the attack on Ahmadnagar in 1599–1600, and to have remained based there until his death in 1019/1610. Daniyal died in 1602 of acute alcoholism, but was the inspirer of Nauʿi's *Sūz u Gudāz*. The poet tells us in his introduction of how the prince told him how weary they were of the old heroes and heroines of Persian poetry – Khusraw and Shirin, Laila and Majnun – 'if we read at all, let it be what we have seen and beheld ourselves'. The story concerns a real hero and heroine, betrothed since birth, who were parted by the bridegroom's death on his way to the marriage. Not even Akbar could persuade the girl not to join her lover in the flames of his pyre, and he commanded his son Daniyal to convey her to the pyre as she wished, which she freely entered.

This lovely little Ms. is attributable to about 1630, with three miniatures and all its text panels laid in marbled paper of sombre hue, possibly contemporary with the text. We know little about marbling in India, although Cary Welch thinks it a speciality of Bijapur, to which he attributes two extraordinary 'drawings' in marbling[1]. The three miniatures showing the meeting of the lovers, Akbar's attempt to dissuade the girl from suttee, and the burning of the lovers on the pyre watched by Daniyal, are in a subdued *nīmqalam* style that heightens their pathos. The final scene is especially effective, the solidity of the onlookers contrasting with the faintness of the two figures in the pyre, already etherealised by their passion.

British Library, London, Or.2839.

ff.24; 21×11cm; paper; text in 15 lines of *Nastaʿlīq* in double columns on gold-sprinkled paper in panels 14·5×7·5cm with margins ruled in gold and colours, laid in borders of marbled paper, mostly slate-blue and ochre; one *sarlavḥ* of good quality; three miniatures of same size as panels; 18th-century European binding with Kissa Daniel engraved on it, which is also written on the flyleaf in an 18th-century hand. Seal in Persian of Archibald Swinton Rustam Jang Bahadur dated 1174/1760.

Bibliography: BM 1895, p.200. BL 1977, p.135. Dawud and Coomaraswamy 1912, with reproductions of the three miniatures.

[1]S.C. Welch 1976, pp.74–5.

82 'Pādshāhnāma'

COLOUR PLATE XXXII

The official History of the Emperor Shāh Jahān (1627–58), by ʿAbd al-Hamīd Lahorī. In 1635 Muhammad ʿAmīn Qazvīnī was entrusted by the Emperor Shāh Jahān with the task of writing the official history of the first ten years of the reign (1627–37), but beginning with the Emperor's birth. This was duly presented to the Emperor after a ten year delay in 1646[1]; it was given the title of *Pādshāhnāma*, the History of the Emperor, but he transferred the author to other duties and entrusted the official chronicling of the reign to ʿAbd al-Hamīd Lahorī, a pupil of Abu'l Fazl with instructions to rewrite Muhammad ʿAmīn's history of the first ten years in a much more flowery style.

It is not stated when precisely ʿAbd al-Hamīd was recalled from retirement in Patna to write the history, only that the Emperor was not entirely satisfied with Muhammad ʿAmīn's text and required something more akin to the bombastic panaegyric style of Abu'l Fazl's *Akbarnāma*, of which Lahorī was a master[2]. The inference must be that this was in 1646, when he had received Qazvīnī's version. ʿAbd al-Hamīd died in 1654–5, having completed only the first two decades of the reign and the work was completed up to the end of the third decade (1656–7) by his pupil Muhammad Wārith. The whole work must have been copied out immediately by the scribe Muhammad ʿAmīn of Masnhad[3], as this, the imperial presentation copy, is dated 1067/1656–7.

It is doubtful if the full manuscript with all its miniatures was ever completed. According to Beach, of the 44 miniatures in the volume, some 37 refer to events in the first ten years of the reign, and another four to events prior to Shāh Jahān's accession[4]; of these last, two are towards the beginning of the volume and the others inserted, apparently at random, towards the end. The remainder show him in old age, including a frontispiece portrait of him. None of the paintings within the Ms. actually bears a date of composition but three dated paintings out of about ten known pages which either were intended for the Ms. or else have been removed from it seem to refer to the date of composition being the actual date of the event. If this is the case, then most of the paintings in the volume can be dated at about the time of the event they depict; it was always intended that they be bound into the official history when it was completed. However, Shāh Jahān's dissatisfaction with Qazvīnī's long-delayed text may have dissuaded him from commissioning more pictorial records of events during the middle years of his reign, when he was in any case more concerned with architecture, in the building of new palaces in Delhi. No contemporary paintings are known of the buildings of Delhi or of the Tāj Mahāl, even though they form so large a part of the miniatures illustrating the numerous histories of Shāh Jahān prepared around 1800 (see Nos.107, 137). In any case the revolt of Aurangzīb put an end to his imperial patronage, and the Ms. was put together with what paintings were available.

The imperial copy of the *Pādshāhnāma* is the last of the great Mughal manuscripts, representing the culmination of many of the trends apparent in Mughal painting since 1600. The emphasis of the paintings, as of the text, is on formal occasions – darbars, battles, processions and other great state occasions, so that the

83 ff.19b, 20. Zafar Khān in Kashmir with poets and scholars while an artist takes their likenesses. By Bishndas (?).

paintings present a coldly formal appearance, in which the technique of portraiture is at its most brilliant, without any of the warmth or spontaneity which imbue Jahāngīri painting. These pages in the *Pādshāhnāma* along with some of the pages in the Shāh Jahān albums are technically the most brilliant of all Mughal paintings, building directly on the advancement in technique made possible by Jahāngīr. No longer is there even the slightest clash between the disparate European and Indian elements which can create such unintended tension to a European viewer, while some of the artists were now the masters of perspective and of a landscape technique of the greatest richness, as in the battle for Hooghly (f.117a) or Payāg's battle-scene[5] or the unattributed hunting-scene (f.165a)[6]. An artist such as ʿAbīd in his Death of Khān Jahān (f.93b) is the master of a technique of composition that has almost the feel of the European Baroque[7].

Gray has claimed that the Ms. was subject to two 'improvements' after 1657, once in the period after the death of Aurangzīb (1707) and again during its residence in Lucknow[8]. Only now is the full achievement of Shāh Jahān's artists being fully realised, so that there was understandable confusion in the earlier literature about this period. There was indeed a revival of Mughal painting after the death of Aurangzīb, but even though still brilliant in its draughtsmanship and painterly techniques (see No.106), it lacked the imagination to produce anything of the scale and power of these *Pādshāhnāma* pages. The Ms. itself was taken to Lucknow some time before 1776, as seals of that date belonging to Āsaf Jhā the Vazir of Oudh are found throughout the manuscript, and Gray's charge that paintings were added there is indeed a much more serious one. There is a variation in the quality of the work, particularly between certain facing pages, that suggests that some paintings have been removed and copies substituted, a well-known practice at the end of the 18th century. However, it has recently been claimed that all the paintings are in fact original, and the full publication of the Ms. with supporting evidence for this opinion is eagerly awaited.

Royal Library, Windsor Castle.

ff.239; 45·5 × 28·5cm; paper; original text panels, with 21 lines of *Nasta'līq*, 34·5 × 18·8cm, with margins ruled in gold and colours; all remounted in 18th-century frames with gold arabesque designs; opening *shamsa* of superb illuminative quality (f.1a); two pages of illumination around portraits of Tīmūr and of Shāh Jahān in old age (ff.1b, 2a); 44 paintings, with attributions to ten named artists, being Bālchand, Bichitr, Payāg, Murād, Rām Dās, Nola (Bola?), 'Abīd, Lālchand, Mīr Dast, and Daula, the paintings slightly less high than the text panels (with a few exceptions) and somewhat wider; splendid covers gilded with floral borders and central medallion, with doublures of gold on green with similar pattern, doubtless from Lucknow; the Ms. is still kept in the large silk wrapping cloth from the Lucknow library.

Bibliography: BM 1976, p.88. Beach 1978, pp.78–84 (for folios dispersed from the Ms. in particular). Gascoigne 1971, p.145 (col. repro. of f.50b by Bichitr) and p.149 (detail of f.194a by Payāg). AIP, pp.168–9 (repro. of f.117a). Barrett and Gray 1963, pp.112–4 (col. repro. of f.165a).

[1]Elliot and Dowson, vol. VII, p.1.
[2]*ibid*, p.3.
[3]Beach 1978, p.78.
[4]*ibid*, pp.28–9.
[5]Welch 1978, col. plate 33.
[6]Barrett and Gray 1963, p.113.
[7]Welch 1963, fig.4.
[8]Barrett and Gray 1963, pp.112–4.

83 'Masnavī' of Zafar Khān

Verses by Zafar Khān, son of Khvāja Abu'l Hasan, one of the chief nobles of the reign of Shāh Jahān, copied by the author in Lahore in 1073/1663. Zafar Khān was at various times Governor of Kabul, Kashmir and Sind, and was besides noted as a patron of letters, poets and artists. The most important poet patronized by Zafar Khān was Sā'ib of Tabriz, the inventor of the 'modern' style in Persian poetry, who visited him in Kabul, on his way to the court of Shāh Jahān, and again in Kashmir when he was made Governor in 1631–2. Zafar Khān remained Governor of Kashmir until 1639, and then again from 1641 until shortly before 1651, when he was appointed to the Governorship of Sind. At the beginning of Aurangzīb's reign in 1657 he was pensioned off and apparently retired to Lahore where he died either in 1663 or 1672 according to different sources.

This autograph copy of the *Masnavī* is finely illuminated only in part, and was not apparently finished. It has six double-page miniatures (of which one pair has been wrongly bound in separate parts), without any text at all on them, as well as marginal illuminations which peter out half way through the volume. The miniatures show scenes from the life of Zafar Khān, in three of which he is represented in darbar with Shāh Jahān, in the opening one represented on a terrace with river and city and plain beyond. The other five double-page paintings are all set in Kashmir, and the presence of Shāh Jahān in two of them doubtless records the occasion mentioned in the *Ma'āthīr al-Umarā* when Shāh Jahān visited Zafar Khān in Kashmir and inspected the garden he had laid out in Zafarabad[1]. This event took place in 1644. In the paintings Shāh Jahān is shown with Dārā Shikoh, and Zafar Khān and his brother, and other nobles, once on a platform near a waterfall in a beautifully laid out Mughal garden (ff.15b, 16a)[2], and once beside a large pool with arcading around it (ff.25b, 26a). The former garden might be that of Zafar Khān, but it seems more like the Nishat Bagh. The latter appears to be the Vernag garden, an octagonal pool surrounded by an arcade, a garden much loved by Jahāngīr.[3]

The other paintings show Zafar Khān in martial mood, reviewing troops (ff.11b, 12a)[4], and in more relaxed mood with poets and scholars. The ones most admired by him are listed in his autograph *Dīvān* now in the Khuda Baksh Library in Bankipore[5]. His biography in the *Ma'āthīr al-Umarā* further informs us that he had made an album with a selection of the poems of every poet who had been connected with him, written in their own handwriting, with the likeness of the poet painted on the reverse.[6] Some such scene appears to be going on in ff.19b, 20a, showing Zafar Khān and his brother in the company of poets and scholars in a highly decorated pavilion in Kashmir (through the open doorway can be seen a pyramidal-roofed Kashmiri building with the hills beyond). In the forefront sits an artist sketching a portrait, while among the poets one is engaged in writing on a piece of gold-sprinkled paper, a sure sign of an attempt at fine calligraphy, while many hold open books in their hands.

There seems little doubt that all these paintings were painted in the late 1640s to commemorate Zafar Khān's tour of duty in Kashmir, and were subsequently added to the *Masnavī*, with which they have little connection, on its completion in 1663. All of them are on a much thicker paper than the folios of text, with darker margins. The paintings are all by the one hand, a brilliant portraitist, whose studies of the poets in Zafar Khān's gathering are a joy in their range of vivid expression. Milo Beach has attributed them to Bishndās,[7] whose latest signed work is datable about 1620. We follow Beach in this attribution, as the idiosyncracies of the painter of the *Masnavī*'s miniatures, particularly his generalized facial types for women and attendants with their characteristic outline, and the sharpness of the observation of the portraits, recalls Bishndās's work. By the late 1640s he would have been in his 70s, the apparent age of the painter depicted on f.19b. It is now generally accepted that depictions of painters in the grand Jahāngīri and Shāh Jahāni paintings are in fact self-portraits of the artists, so that we may take this to be a self-portrait of Bishndās in old age.

Royal Asiatic Society, London,
MS. Persian 310.

ff.122; 25 × 14cm; thin paper; 15 lines of *Nasta'līq* in two columns on gold-sprinkled paper in panels ruled in gold; 15·5 × 7cm; margins decorated with stencilled gold flowers and plants up to f.44b with outlines drawn in up to folio 95, and the last 27 folios without any marginal decoration; *sarlavḥs* on ff.1b, 29b and 31b, with exquisitely minute flowers; margins on ff.29b, 30a and 31b, 32a in gold with fully painted flowers; headings in gold throughout in panels, on white clouds against blue etc. up to f.36a; triangular illuminated panels (f.21b, 22a, 24b, 25a, 27b, 28a); five double-page and two separate miniatures, the latter originally meant to be facing one another, but were misplaced (to ff.22b and 27a) when being pasted in presumably in 1663 – both have text panels on the other side which are in their rightful places according to the catchwords; all the paintings are larger than the text panels, the largest being 20·5 × 10·5cm (one half of the composition); reddish-brown oriental covers rebound in the European style.

Bibliography: RAS 1892, p.541. AIP, p.168. Pinder-Wilson 1957.

[1]Navāz Khān 1911–52, p.1017.
[2]Pinder-Wilson 1957, fig.15.
[3]Crowe 1972, p.51 (colour plate). Both painting and photograph show the pool swarming with fish.
[4]Pinder-Wilson 1957, figs.16 and 17.
[5]OPLB, vol.3, pp.117–20.
[6]Navāz Khān 1911–52, p.1019.
[7]Beach 1978, pp.110–11.

CHAPTER IV

Delhi and the Provinces, 1600–1850

85 f.182b. Tīmūr and his generals are lowered down a cliff-face during a battle in the Kaf Mountains in 1397 (No.85, p.122).

86 f.372. Alexander builds the wall against Gog and Magog. By Qāsim (No.86, p.122).

So far we have traced the development of the Mughal style at the imperial centres – Agra, Fathpur Sikri, Lahore, Agra and Delhi. But even though the imperial style was a rarified court product, it was nourished in its early days by streams of artists from all over India who aspired to make the grade in the studio, and in turn it contributed to the artistic life of India outside the imperial court. For many of those who joined were found eventually to be lacking the desired qualities and had to leave, but had picked up the basic elements of the style; while changes in taste and patronage at the court itself resulted in artists being laid off. Thus it is unlikely that during the 1590s Akbar would have retained the full complement of artists needed in the 1580s for the large series of historical manuscripts, while Jahāngīr on his accession must have drastically pruned the numbers of artists and other craftsmen in the imperial studio. Such artists had various alternatives. Some sought employment with other patrons, such as ʿAbd ar-Rahim Khānkhānān, one of the chief officials under Akbar and Jahāngīr, who maintained a flourishing bibliographic tradition in his own establishment. His huge library and munificence drew scholars from other parts of the Islamic world, but being more interested in scholarship than producing illustrated manuscripts, relatively few such manuscripts have survived associated with him. One such is an illustrated Persian version of the *Rāmāyaṇa* produced for him between 1589 and 1598, now in the Freer Gallery of Art, Washington, with various artists' names inscribed, none of them known from imperial manuscripts. Some of the names however appear in the *Shāhnāma* of 1616 (No.86), such as Qāsim and Kamāl, and it would appear that the Khānkhānān was its patron. Other illustrated manuscripts also are associated with him such as a *Khamsa* of Amīr Khusraw in Berlin (some time before 1617), and a *Panchganj* in Dublin (of about the same date). Two artists who worked on the *Rāmāyaṇa*, Qāsim and Mushfīq, also worked on these two later manuscripts, demonstrating that ʿAbd ar-Rahīm maintained a studio of artists over a period of some 30 years. It is unclear whether his studio was taken with him on his travels, when as a senior administrator he was put in charge of Gujarat or the Deccan. It is on the whole likely that it was, as we know of manuscripts produced for other noblemen in the provinces, one, the earliest such known, being dated 1583 from Hajipur (in Bihar), the patron being Akbar's foster brother Mīrzā Azīz Koka. Another manuscript of the *Anvār-i Suhaylī* without patron's name is dated Ahmadabad, 1600 (No.84) with paintings in the same style as a *Zafarnāma* of the same date (No.85); both must have been produced for a patron such as the Mughal Governor of Gujarat, who was in 1600 Mīrzā Azīz Koka. It is unlikely that Azīz Koka would have kept a permanent studio in employment, but it is quite possible that he found in Ahmadabad in 1600 the necessary talent for the work he wanted done, as ʿAbd ar-Rahīm had been three times Governor of the province of Gujarat and did apparently maintain his studio there.

Other artists would seem to have remained in the capital and possibly even in the imperial studio, but were now responsible for lesser-quality works. Akbar ordered copies of important works to be distributed among his nobles, such as the Persian translations of Bābur's Memoirs and the *Razmnāma*. Apart from the dispersed imperial copy of the *Bāburnāma*, three other versions are known from the 1590s for which an imperial provenance is likely, perhaps meant for members of the royal family, but there may have been other illustrated versions of lesser quality. Certainly an illustrated manuscript of the *Razmnāma* dated 1598 (No.88) is of a much less polished quality than contemporary imperial manuscripts, but it does have inscriptions attributing the paintings to artists who had worked on the grand manuscripts of the 1580s – Ibrāhīm Kahhar, Banvāri Khurd, Nārāyan, and others, but whose work is not found in the high-quality manuscripts of the 1590s which marked the end of the period of the mass-produced historical manuscripts.

87 f.273. A dragon and locusts (No.87, p.123).

88 f.17. The sacrificial horse is shown to the ladies of Krishna's harem. By Bhagvān (No.88, p.123).

The 1598 *Razmnāma* in fact is of two different worlds – it is still partly imperial, but in many of its paintings its style is the so-called Popular Mughal, that is paintings and manuscripts produced mostly in the capitals for patrons, apparently Hindus, unable to afford their own studios. These first appear from about 1600, the artists coming probably from the ranks of those who failed to make the grade in the imperial studio. Unlike Mughal painting done for noble patrons, which is still recognizably Mughal, even though in a simplified format, Popular Mughal painting has in many respects reverted to the type of compositions prevalent before the Mughal period – very simple compositions, the barest minimum of figures all in strict profile, simple pavilions by way of architecture, hardly any landscape other than stylized trees, no depth indicated by recessional techniques, no text panels breaking up the composition. It is in fact very similar to the emergent Rajput style which will be discussed in detail below. The lovely Manley *Rāgamālā* of *c.*1610 (No.89) develops out of this strand of the 1598 *Razmnāma*. The only name we can put to artists practising this style at the moment is that of Ustad Sālivāhana, who produced a dated document in Agra in 1610, and another in 1624 doubtless also in Agra. These, the *Rāgamālā* (No.89) and another in Berlin, a *Rasikapriyā* manuscript in Boston, and a *Rāmāyaṇa* in Delhi form a small group of highly accomplished work. A problem still to be solved is that the paucity of artists working for Jahāngīr is unmatched by a large amount of good work executed for other patrons.

Closely linked to the Hindu Popular Mughal work of the capitals is the work done for the Rajput princes who were such powerful figures in the reigns of Akbar and Jahāngīr. An inscription on a *Rāgamālā* from Chunar dated 1591 provides the earliest evidence that they too had studios. It states that the set was painted by three artists who had been trained in the imperial studio and that it was completed in 999/1591 at the fort of Chunar, near Benares. There is considerable disagreement as to the authenticity of the inscription, but universal agreement that the paintings are in the Rajput style associated with the court of Bundi in south-eastern Rajasthan, whose ruler had been given Chunar as a fief by Akbar in 1576. This lovely set is archaic in its treatment of figures, in the *Caurapañcāśika* tradition, but places them in three-dimensional architecture against a richly flowering and varied landscape. The genesis of the Bundi style then, if the inscription is genuine, would be the work of three painters, who, presumably, were trained in a pre-Mughal style, tried their luck at the Mughal studio and either left or were rejected, and worked instead for the Rao of Bundi at his fief in Chunar. From it were developed the other sets known from the Bundi studio in the early 17th century, produced either in Bundi or wherever the Rao was posted by the Emperors, such as a *Bhāgavata Purāṇa* now in the Kotah Museum of the early 17th century which is in a Popular Mughal style in terms of its treatment of landscape, people and architecture, and its high viewpoint. The treatment of architecture is three-dimensional, as it is in the 1591 *Rāgamālā* set. In both the upright format is used, the shape of the folios being that used in Mughal manuscripts, for the very first time in any Hindu text in the case of the *Rāgamālā*.

In contrast to this school of Rajput painting is that associated with Mewar in southern Rajasthan. Its ruling dynasty, the Sesodiya Rajputs, could trace its recorded history back to the foundation of Chitor in the 7th century, and as the head of the *Sūryavaṃśa* (Solar dynasty) back through the god Vishnu's avatar Rāma to the Sun itself. Under its mediaeval rulers the great rock fortress of Chitor was embellished with great temples and palaces, and its empire under Rānā Kumbha included Malwa and Gujarat. But in the 16th century, Chitor was twice captured and sacked, the second time by Akbar in 1568. However, the Rānās consistently refused to acknowledge Mughal sovereignty, and towards the end of Akbar's reign, Rānā Pratāp Singh and his son Amar Singh, driven by Akbar both from Chitor and the new capital Udaipur established by Udai Singh after 1568, were little more than bandit chieftains in the rugged hills of Mewar. The gentle arts of the court could not have been to the forefront of their minds, yet it is out of this precariously-existing Rajput household that comes the first fully authenticated document of what is usually termed Rajput or Rajasthani painting. This is a *Rāgamālā* series from Chawand, the temporary capital, dated 1605 and painted by an artist named Nāsir ad-Dīn (spelled Nusaratī in *Nāgarī*). It is a very simple set of paintings viewed from the traditional horizontal viewpoint, employing contrasting flat blocks of colour and two-dimensional architecture, against which are ranged human figures in stylized forms. It is obvious that this style is descended from the *Caurapañcāśika* group, and particularly from the *Gītagovinda* set (No.37) which employs numerous motifs common in 17th-century Mewar painting, and that it has not been touched by Akbari influence at all. The Chawand set is the natural outcome of the Mewar court's political and cultural dissociation from the imperial capital and its stylistic innovations, representing no more than the continuing vitality of the native Hindu artistic tradition.

The normalization of Mewar's political relations with the Mughals in 1614 under Amar Singh after the death of Akbar left open the way to cultural influences from the imperial court, especially as the heir-apparent Karan Singh's presence at court was required by the Emperor Jahāngīr. Yet Amar Singh and Karan Singh (1620–8) were extremely selective in their cultural borrowings; Goetz has rightly pointed out how old-fashioned in style are the palace buildings erected in this period, and they do in fact hark back to the great age of Mewar expansionism under Rānā Kumbha.

The reign of Jagat Singh (1628–52) marks the culmination of this phase of Mewar art. Relations with the Mughals were peaceful, due to the friendship established between Karan Singh and Prince Khurram, the future Shāh Jahān, while the former attended at the Mughal court as heir-apparent of Mewar. When Karan ascended the *gaḍḍi* in 1620, it was to Udaipur that Khurram came when in revolt against his father. Karan and his son must have absorbed influences at the Mughal court, but it became apparent in Udaipur in ideas rather than direct copying. The royal palace in Udaipur bears no resemblance to the Mughal palaces. In the field of painting it seems to have been Jagat Singh who came to the throne in 1628 at the age of twenty who established a court atelier of artists, perhaps under the direction of Sāhīb Dīn (Sahibadī in *Nāgarī*), for the majority of paintings of the reign are in the style of this artist (Nos.90, 92, 96). We know the name of only one other artist of this period, that of Manohar (No.91). The origins of these two artists are unknown. We may imagine that Sāhīb Dīn was trained by Nāsir ad-Dīn in Chawand and Udaipur, but Manohar's style is different, individual and fully formed at its first appearance. Sāhīb Dīn's work shows considerable advancement over the course of Jagat Singh's reign. In his *Rāgamālā* of 1628 he still uses the horizontal viewpoint for preference, and breaks his pictures into two registers rather than adopt a high viewpoint. Yet in the full-size paintings in manuscripts in *poṭhī* format of the *Bhāgavata Purāṇa* (No.90) and of the *Rāmāyaṇa* (Nos.92, 96), it is precisely this high viewpoint that he has adopted. He spaces his figures out in the foreground and middle distance, whether in landscape or architectural situations, and links them together by a broad sweep of rocks and trees or row of buildings at the back, with horizon and sky beyond. This technical innovation he can only have learnt from Mughal example. The other artists who contributed to the *Rāmāyaṇa* were less happy with the high horizon, being far less skilful in their compositions, and often break the scenes up into registers in the old-fashioned manner.

For the illustration of manuscripts on this large scale, Mewar artists evolved a fluent narrative technique that seems to have been experimented with in the *Bhāgavata Purāṇa* before work was properly started on the *Rāmāyaṇa*. Comparatively few of the former manuscript's paintings are on a large or ambitious scale, most of them being no more than half or a quarter of the page, with the figures set against simple plain grounds. For the *Rāmāyaṇa*, a much more ambitious undertaking, telling the history of the Rānā's chief ancestor, it was obviously of importance for the pictures to carry as much of the narrative as possible. Hence many of the paintings depict two or more episodes in the same story, which involves the repetition of the same characters. This is, of course, in direct contrast to the Mughal concept of illustrating manuscripts, which like the Iranian, chooses a precise episode for illustration and does not try to contain all the episodes of a story within the one frame. This Mewar method on the contrary is a continuation of the pre-Mughal tradition of Indian manuscript illustration, in which as in the 1516 *Āraṇyakaparvan* (No.38) or the dispersed *Bhāgavata Purāṇa* (No.36), the various events of a particular story are disposed on several registers, or contained within self-sufficient frames. This method of dividing up the painting is still seen occasionally in the Jagat Singh *Rāmāyaṇa*, particularly in the work of Manohar and his followers, but more subtle means are usually used to achieve this end – the use of architecture and landscape details in particular. Sometimes, however, no attempt whatsoever is made to try to separate events, and some of Sāhīb Dīn's most successful pages show the same characters repeatedly, as in the various farewell scenes leading up to Rāma's departure from Ayodhyā (No.92). In this artist's work in the *Yuddhakāṇḍa* (No.96), the detail is such that the narrative is continuous in pictorial terms, and this has the effect of rendering the text superfluous. The Indian artist was as we have seen never at home in the Iranian concept of book-illustration, which depends on a balance between text and pictures, with calligraphy and illumination keeping the visual interest alive until the next painting, but equally meant for a very literate person. For Indian illustrated manuscripts, on the other hand, in a much less literate society, the ability to read the text was never very important, as more often than not it was in a dead language incomprehensible to the patron. Hence the vogue for short texts to be illustrated verse by verse, in the pre-Mughal era, and here Sāhīb Dīn is paving the way for a reversion to this system but on a much greater scale (No.98).

The huge efforts made by the studio in Udaipur at the end of the reign of Jagat Singh (1628–52) seem to have temporarily exhausted it, and comparatively few paintings survive from the next fifty years. This may be because political conditions were unfavourable, as relations between the Rajput states and the Mughals deteriorated sharply under Aurangzīb, and constant warfare became the norm. By the time of Amar Singh II (1698–1710), however, there was a renewed burst of activity in painting, particularly of portraits, hunting scenes, festivals, and other court occasions, in which artists experimented with a *nīmqalam* style, combined with heavy stippling; while under his successor, Sangrām Singh II (1710–38), a huge new programme of manuscript illustrations was undertaken, of which a few products in the early years were of good quality.

The *Bālakāṇḍa* of 1712 (No.98) is illustrated with 201 paintings, of full size, and has 212 folios. This is in contrast to the 70:79 ratio of the Jagat Singh book, for the same text, in 1649 (No.91). To spin the text out over such a large body of paintings, the number of lines per folio has been drastically reduced. These illustrated manuscripts are now in fact picture books with explanatory text, reasserting the conception of Indian book-illustration first seen in the 15th century. Many huge sets of this sort still survive in the Udaipur Palace Museum: the *Bhagavadgītā* with a separate picture for each of its 710 verses, a *Mahābhārata* with over 4,000 paintings, and so on. The next step was a further reduction in importance of the text – a summary of the relevant verses from the *Rāmāyaṇa* or *Bhāgavata*, more often in Hindi than in Sanskrit; or a selection of verses rather than the whole text. This type of book illustration was especially popular in the Rajput courts of the Panjab Hills over the next century, mostly, ironically, in the 'Guler' and 'Kangra' styles of Pahari painting, which of all Rajput styles owe the most to Mughal influence, yet which have triumphantly reasserted the traditional Indian view of book-illustration over the Iranian conception exemplified most forcibly in their early works by the Mughals themselves.

We have dealt with Mewar manuscripts at some length because of the abundance of the available material and the fact that much of it is still in manuscript form. It was the fate of many other schools of Rajput painting for the great works to be broken up, so that many institutions throughout the world have various pages of this or that manuscript. Every major Rajput court and many of the minor *ṭhikānās* or fiefdoms had its own studio, whose main function was the production of portraits of the rulers, and was employed on illustrating smaller works such as the *Rāgamālā*, *Rasikapriyā* and so on. Few had the resources to attempt anything on a

100 f.3b. *Naṭa rāga*, a furious warrior (No.100, p.131).

larger scale. It is not part of our purpose here to examine all these different schools, as they all adopt a broadly similar approach to manuscript illustration. Stylistically they develop at different rates, and have high points at different times depending almost entirely on the patronage of the ruler. Those styles based largely on pre-Mughal or Popular Mughal styles, such as Mewar and Bundi, have their most important periods of manuscript production in the 17th century. Others such as Bikaner or Kishangarh scarcely seem established until late in the 17th century or the 18th century, as they depended largely on the employment of artists leaving Delhi during the reign of Aurangzīb or during the Afghan invasions. The vicissitudes which befell Delhi from 1739 caused successive waves of artists to leave for safer havens – the development of Rajput painting in the Panjab Hills in the 18th century is a progression away from a fierce, fiery-coloured Rajput style towards greater and greater Mughalization of palette and composition. Few of the Rajput studios of the plains bothered to produce illustrated manuscripts during the 18th century, concentrating instead on larger and sumptuous scenes of royal life, of festivals, processions and above all hunting. The influence of the sumptuous landscape tradition of the Mughals in the second half of the 17th century is here most apparent.

The format of Rajput manuscripts differs according to the text and the purpose. The format of the earliest, the Chawand *Rāgamālā* of 1605 is almost square, an indication perhaps of its descent from the *Rāgamālā* in the *Caurapañcāśika* group, which has two square paintings on each side of each folio. Other smaller sets of the early 17th century of texts such as *Rasikapriyā*, *Rāgamālās* and the *Nāyikabheda* are in the upright format seen also in Popular Mughal work (No.89), which is used throughout the 17th century (No.100). From the very earliest of them, the text of the verse is inscribed in black *Nāgarī* across the top of the painting against a ground, usually yellow, a development that occurs simultaneously in Popular Mughal manuscripts and in the Deccan with its *Rāgamālā* sets. The prototype of this sort of manuscript is of course the *Caurapañcāśika* group, conceived initially as sets of paintings illustrating a comparatively small number of verses. However, in Mewar and Malwa the landscape *poṭhī* format was retained for all the works on a grand scale, the *Rāmāyaṇa*, *Bhāgavata Purāṇa* (unlike the Bundi manuscript) and so on, with the texts written on the reverse of the paintings, and of course in the usual way on the unillustrated pages. This is true also of later illustrated manuscripts from Mewar in the 18th century which exist in great numbers, although many also have the text in panels above the painting, and in the large-scale works undertaken at the other Rajput courts, especially in the Panjab Hills. Among the latter, the *Bhāgavata Purāṇa* and *Rāmāyaṇa* were especially popular, although often the text used was a much shorter Hindi version or sometimes none at all. These manuscripts are the final embodiment of the Indian conception of book-illustration.

Other formats were also used from at least the mid-17th century in Rajasthan and elsewhere in northern India. Bound in a single section, they were first in landscape format (No.99) and then in vertical format (No.101). Illustrations could fill the entire page of the former, but in the latter there was a curious reversion to the small horizontal miniature across the page, as in the *Gulistān* and *Būstān* of Shāh Jahān (Nos.79, 80), going back ultimately to 14th-century Iranian paintings.

104 f.31. The rejected suitor is consoled by his friends (No.104, p.133).

105 f.154b. ʿAlī fighting miscellaneous *dīvs* and dragons (No.105, p.133).

Whereas it was only in royal studios that the larger-scale illustrated *poṭhī* manuscripts were produced, smaller and less ambitious manuscripts such as the single-section type or smaller-scale loose-leaf *poṭhīs* were produced for lesser nobles, chiefs and merchants throughout Rajasthan and Gujarat, some following the Popular Mughal tradition, others in frozen versions of earlier Jaina styles. These provincial styles of course are not those of the Rajput courts, which were the creations of individual artists of genius and patrons of aesthetic sensitivity. In these bourgeois productions, the style is a generalized Rajput one which follows the basic formulae of the more traditional court styles as to figural and landscape types, and invariably adopts the horizontal viewpoint.

Comparatively few illustrated manuscripts were produced for Muslim patrons in the north Indian provinces in the 17th century. Here the trend must have been the same as elsewhere, towards the production of isolated pictures. A *Rasikapriyā* from Gorakhpur dated 1077/1666 (No.104), which is in a Popular Mughal style, seems to be the earliest such example. The area along the Ganges between Jaunpur and Bengal produced illuminated manuscripts in the pre-Mughal period which have survived in small numbers, but which indicate that it supported flourishing schools of painters. While the Mughal court in the late 16th and 17th centuries was fostering a hot-house, eclectic style, in the provinces artists must have just gone on painting as they had always done, adopting new perspectives and techniques as they filtered through from the metropolitan centres. The 1591 Chunar *Rāgamālā* is the first evidence of this trend. The 1666 *Rasikapriyā* was produced for a local patron in a style which indicates that Rajput painting is a result of patronage rather than location, like the Chunar *Rāgamālā* itself.

In the north-west of the subcontinent from Kashmir down to Sind, there is considerable evidence for various provincial schools derived ultimately from Sultanate styles of the 15th century with various overlays of Mughal or Safavid styles. Such a one surfaces in Multan in 1686, in a *Khāvarnāma* (No.105) in which may be seen high circular horizons, plain gold grounds and 15th-century rock formations. Another finds expression in a slightly later *Shāhnāma* (No.125) produced at Rajauri in 1131/1719, one of the stages on the road to Kashmir via Sialkot. A princess of Rajauri was the wife of Aurangzīb and mother of Muʿazam Shāh, the future Emperor Bahādur Shāh (1707–12), and artists may have gone there from Delhi after 1680, when Aurangzīb left for the Deccan never to return. However, the style is not Mughal, but a fully developed local style, apparently an amalgam of Popular Mughal painting of the 17th century with a vigorous local style descended from a style of Sultanate painting of which we have as yet no knowledge. The manuscript is, however, a harbinger of the developed Kashmiri style of the late 18th century in its glittery appearance with gold and silver used in abundance, extremely fine polished paper, highly burnished pigments and general stylistic appearance, with composition in layers, hilly horizons, 'Deccani' colour combinations, and so on. A solitary manuscript from Thatta dated 1775 is the only evidence of a flourishing provincial idiom in Sind.

The only major centre for Persian manuscript production in the 17th century apart from Delhi was the Deccan, which during the course of the 17th century was attacked several times by the Mughals trying to incorporate the three independent Sultanates into their empire.

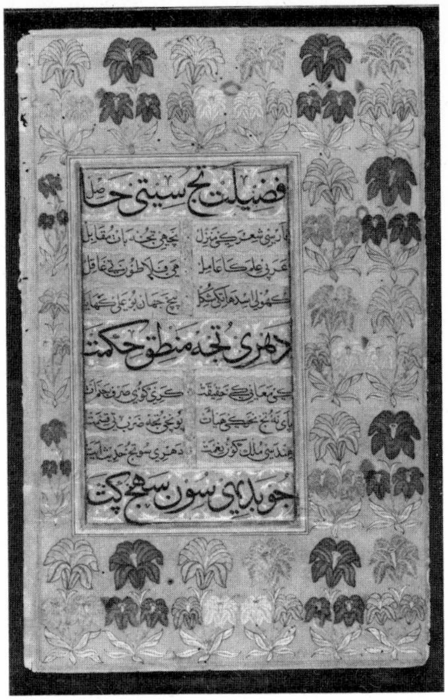

103 f.27b. Lilies, illuminated *hashīya* around text in large *Riqāʿ* and small *Naskhī* (No.103, p.132).

Ahmednagar fell in 1600, but continued resisting; Bijapur and Golconda survived as independent states until 1686 and 1687. Comparatively few first-rank illustrated manuscripts have survived from the Deccani kingdoms from this period. One of the most intriguing, although probably not of royal provenance, is the album of *Rāgamālā* and other paintings presented by Archbishop Laud to the Bodleian Library in 1639. The provenance of the *Rāgamālā* set has long been a subject of controversy, but there seems little doubt now that it is of Deccani origin. However, it is significantly different from paintings of the court Deccani styles, both in its directness of line and simplicity, and in the costumes, which are linked to the group of late 16th-century Deccani *Rāgamālā* paintings, associated apparently more with a Hindu than a Muslim tradition, in which the inscribed verses are in both *Nāgarī* and *Nastaʿlīq*. The paintings of the Laud *Rāgamālā* then would seem to be the product of a 'Popular Deccani' school. Just as patrons other than the Mughal Emperor and his immediate entourage were patronizing Mughal painters by the late 16th century, the same must have been happening in the cities of the Deccan also. The *Rāgamālā* is Hindu in feel, not Muslim, being related in structure and composition to 16th-century sets such as the *Caurapañcāśika* manuscript in which one or two people are disposed in front of a simple pavilion-like structure offset to one side. They may be dated to the period 1600–20.

The vigorous local styles of the early 17th-century Deccan kingdoms were quickly overlaid by an ever-more insistent Mughal style, so that by the time of their final fall the work produced there was really in a provincial Mughal idiom. However, the incessant wars provided ample opportunity for the intermingling of styles. The Mughal headquarters, Aurangabad, seems to have been a clearing post for the despatch of Deccani manuscripts and paintings, and, probably, artists to Rajasthan where their influence is felt in courts as far apart as Mewar (Nos.94–5) and Bikaner. At the time of the final collapse of Golconda in 1687, it was already producing work apparently for European consumption, for it was a great trading post for jewels and fabrics for export to Europe. Albums of the emperors and sultans of India were the favourite theme, typically the Mughal emperors from Bābur to Aurangzīb, followed by the ʿĀdil Shāhi and Qutb Shāhi rulers. The earliest of these albums are of small folios with the portrait in a painted oval frame, in imitation of the European miniatures which were popular in India in the 17th century. Slightly later in a more Mughal style were produced many similar albums, doubtless for the same market, with paintings in the usual vertical format.

In the arts of illumination of manuscripts they followed their own path, early abandoning such Iranian influences as appear in the medical encyclopedia of 1572 (No.51). As with Mughal illumination, the patterns diverge from standard Iranian ones and the colours follow an even more sumptuous and original path. In the *Qaṣīdah* (No.103) by the famous Dakhni poet Nusratī dedicated to ʿAbdallāh Qutb Shāh of Golconda (1626–72), every page is decorated with marginal designs in sumptuous gold and colours, alternating floral patterns with arabesque and geometric designs. Whereas Mughal marginal designs of the same date are never allowed to overwhelm the central panel of text or painting, impressing by the delicacy of their execution, in this Deccani manuscript the richness and sumptuousness of the illumination and the boldness of drawing of the flowers has quite the opposite effect.

106 f.29b. Prince Gauhar first sees his beloved Mālikā Zamānī who has been transformed into a gazelle (No.106, p.133).

111 Front cover. A prince hunting (No.111, p.135).

The lure of the capital as the one centre of artistic life in India gradually disappeared during the 17th century, as the number of artists employed in the imperial studio grew fewer and fewer. Shāh Jahān seems even to have dispensed with the services of some of Jahāngīr's greatest artists – Manohar seems to have taken service with Prince Dārā Shikoh, and Bishndās with Zafar Khān (No.83). Imperial patronage of painting was even less apparent under Aurangzīb, who had the Muslim fundamentalist's horror of the artist, and although some state portraits and fine scenes survive from his reign, from which it must be supposed that he did have the services of artists when required, there are no illustrated manuscripts which can be associated with him. Aurangzīb delighted in writing the Koran, and a considerable number are supposed to be in his hand.

Those paintings which can be confidently attributed to imperial patronage in the latter half of the 17th century exhibit no stylistic advance on the paintings of the *Pādshāhnāma* (No.82). The problems of landscape and perspective had finally been solved in this manuscript, and the solutions found are applied to great effect in some of the set pieces of hunting scenes of the Aurangzīb period. Otherwise an ever increasing rigidity is apparent.

The death of Aurangzīb in 1707 and the ensuing civil war marked the end of the internal stability of the Mughal empire. The reign of the weak Muhammad Shāh (1719–48) witnessed the collapse of central authority, the carving out of almost independent kingdoms by great nobles in the provinces, the sack of Delhi in 1739 by the Afghans under Nādir Shāh, and the rise of the Mahrattas as the most powerful force in India. In these conditions it would be idle to expect great art, but enough artists seemed to remain in imperial employ to be able to produce some very fine paintings and manuscripts, as in the *Kārnāma-iʿIshq* of 1735 (No.106), in which the formal and static art of the late 17th century is matched by an increasingly cold palette making much use of white, grey and green. European influence is also discernible in the work of some artists.

The collapse of central Mughal authority enabled powerful noblemen to establish independent states in the Deccan, Bengal and Oudh, paying nominal allegiance to Delhi. The flourishing and brilliant court of the Nawabs of Oudh at Faizabad and Lucknow in the reigns of Shujāʿad-Daulah (1754–75) and Āsaf ad-Daulah (1775–97) attracted *littérateurs* and artists escaping the wreck of Delhi, twice more sacked by the Afghans, and the maraudings of the Mahrattas and other bands of raiders who terrorized northern India in the later 18th century. In Oudh the Mughal style became even more sumptuous, with hotter colours, reds and oranges and purples and with a vast amount of gold set against cold whites and greys, giving an exotic effect of great splendour. The stock subjects are still the same as under Muhammad Shāh, although in Oudh, as in the other great provincial courts, *Rāgamālā* sets were perhaps the most favoured theme of all. Skies now tend to be full of multicoloured clouds, echoing the vivid hues of the garments worn by the nobles and ladies against cold architectural backdrops, with solemn and formal rows of flowers and sometimes of sombre trees. Faces are heavily modelled, with shadows marked.

The variety of the Mughal style which was practised in Hyderabad under the Nizāms descended from Āsaf Jāh owes something to earlier Deccani work, especially colour combinations, but is otherwise in a style

112 f.166b. Prince Kāmarūpa and his encampment (No.112, p.135).

113 f.391b. King Yudhishthira finds his uncle Vidura practising asceticisms (No.113, p.136).

similar to that practised in Lucknow. Archaistic work also abounds in the 18th century, as in a *Qiṣṣa Sayf al-Mulūk* in the British Library (Or.86), which appears to be a copy dated 1746 of a manuscript originally written in the reign of ʿAbdallāh Qutb Shāh (1626–72), while a *Khāvarnāma* in the India Office Library exemplifies the same trend. There also creeps into Hyderabad work of the later 18th century a considerable southern Hindu element; for example, Krishna is represented in a *Rasikapriyā* set with a tall south Indian crown. A variety of the Hyderabad style flourished in the Carnatic later in the 18th century.

The capital of the Mughal province of Bengal was shifted in 1704 from Dacca to Makhsudabad, a city on the banks of the Bhagirathi, by the Governor Murshīd Qulī Khān, who renamed it Murshidabad after himself. His successors from ʿAlīvardī Khān (1740–56) ruled as independent Nawabs like their counterparts in Oudh and the Deccan. ʿAlīvardī Khān maintained a studio at his capital for at least the last few years of his reign, and several coldly brilliant studies date from this period. Under Surāj ad-Daulah (1756–7), a pleasure-loving prince whose brief reign was cut short by Clive, and his successors to 1763, there was a brief flowering of another provincial Mughal style, again, like that of Oudh and Hyderabad, based on the formal language of the Muhammad Shāh period, but which in Murshidabad seems to have been influenced somewhat more heavily by European drawing and thus able to show some stylistic advance. Some of the paintings in the *Dastūr-i Himmat* (No.112) could not have been attempted without European influence. This manuscript and another, equally beautiful, in the Victoria Memorial Hall in Calcutta, a *Nal Daman*, demonstrate that in Murshidabad the royal studio did not just reproduce the stock subjects of the period but was concerned to illustrate manuscripts also, first-class examples of which are lacking from Lucknow and Hyderabad. By 1770, however, the role of Murshidabad as a great centre for the export trade had been lost to the British in Calcutta, to whom also was passing political power. Artistic patronage likewise became more diffused through other sections of Murshidabad society, and eventually even downriver to the great port on the Hooghly, some of whose officials, such as Sir Elijah Impey, the Chief Justice of Bengal from 1774–83, were great patrons on Indian painting, and it is probably to him that we owe the set of Murshidabad paintings in a manuscript of the *Razmnāma* (No.113).

In the twilight of the Mughal Empire when the Emperor was successively the puppet of the Afghans, the Rohillas, the Mahrattas and the British, and the glories of Shāh Jahān had long departed, the imperial studio in Delhi seems to have been particularly keen to produce illustrated manuscripts of his reign in sumptuous format, doubtless for presentation. Such manuscripts of one or other of the histories of Shāh Jahān are to be found in considerable numbers. It was also at this time that such albums and manuscripts of the earlier periods as remained in the imperial library were 'refurbished'. Some paintings from manuscripts were remounted in album pages with sumptuous border decorations, others from manuscripts and albums were removed and excellent copies inserted in their place. In some manuscripts such as the *Bāburnāma* (No.62), the removal of the painting was cleverly disguised by the rearrangement of the text and the addition of new marginal decoration, while another copy of the same text (No.108) had new paintings inserted. This kind of work was also being done in Lucknow,

109 Page from a Koran. After Hendley (No.109, p.135).

whither many of the Mughal artists had migrated with their working apparatus of sketches, designs and pounces, and where some of the great Mughal manuscripts also went. The *Pādshāhnāma* (No.82) was in the royal library of Lucknow in 1776, where it was extensively refurbished, and a good number of paintings probably removed. Whether any were substituted is as yet a debatable point, as there is considerable confusion over the Mughal style from the reign of Shāh Jahān onwards. There are features in absolutely authentic manuscripts such as the *Gulistān* and *Būstān* of 1628–9 (Nos.79–80) which appear to be of 18th-century date, but which it is absolutely impossible that they could be, as the *Gulistān* at least had left India for England by 1638.

In addition to the archaicizing work, the Delhi studio was turning out work in the latest Mughal style in these histories of Shāh Jahān (Nos.107, 137) and other texts, which have a sumptuous appearance but do not repay close inspection. Then the heavy modelling, dead colours and weaknesses of drawing are only too apparent. Presumably, first-class artists were employed on the archaicizing work leaving the second-rank artists to get on with this type of work. Many artists in Delhi in the early 19th century commanded a wide range of styles depending on the patron for a particular project. Ghulām ʿAlī Khān for example (Nos.135–6, 138), worked for the Emperors in the Mughal style and for James Skinner in the 'Company' style. The best traditional work of this period was done for a remarkable patron, Mahārao Rāja Vinay Singh of Alwar (1815–57), who maintained in his palace a flourishing studio for the production of manuscripts. As a patron he demanded the highest standards and invariably got them: standards of calligraphy, illumination and binding. One thing alone he could not command, artistic genius; the paintings in his manuscripts are excellent, far superior to the usual Delhi work, but the best artists had by now passed beyond the Mughal style. He employed Ghulām ʿAlī Khān, for example, to illustrate some of the paintings of the *Gulistān* of 1844–56, his most important manuscript (No.138), but this artist had twenty years earlier been working in a far more compelling manner for patrons such as James Skinner and John Fraser (Nos.135–6); new life could not be breathed into this outworn idiom. It was Ghulām ʿAlī Khān, however, who painted the last great work of the Mughal period, a portrait of the last Emperor, Bahādur Shāh II, bringing the insights of his Company manner to illuminate the pathos of the last descendant of Bābur, the Mughal conqueror of Hindustan.

While it is true that the influence of the Mughals was so pervasive that scarcely any region of India escaped being affected in its visual art forms, whether painting or architecture, nonetheless there were various areas on the fringes of the Mughal empire such as Orissa and Assam and the extreme south of India where this influence was only minimal and incidental, revealed more by details of costume or architecture than by any radical reappraisal of traditional methods in the light of new techniques. The whole of eastern India – Bihar, Bengal, Orissa and Assam – is one such area that may usefully be considered together.

The Pāla style of palm-leaf illumination, although destroyed in its monastic strongholds at the end of the 12th century, survived among families of artists into the 15th century (No.31), and its influence was still felt thereafter. Eastern India also responded to developments elsewhere; thus the two sets of covers of 1491 and 1499 (Nos.35, 33) reflect respectively a progressive tradition which was common to western and northern India during the 15th century, and an internal development within eastern India itself of progression towards extreme angularity. The school of painting at Gaur before 1531 (No.44) also incorporated significant eastern elements, as seen for example in the Bengali architecture, and in the fondness for depicting figures within architectural niches under many-cusped arches, a significant element of the Pāla style.

The next available documents from the region show various developments, as there is a gap of another century between them and the 1531 *Sharafnāma*. These come from Bengal, Orissa and Assam. The Bengal documents are more book covers (No.114) which perhaps show considerable influence from the Rajput/Popular Mughal style, although it is possible to explain them as the natural development from such examples as the 1491 Bihar covers. This style continues into the 18th century, but alongside it is a much more vigorous, more truly Bengali style associated with Midnapore in south-western Bengal exemplified by the manuscript of the *Rāmacaritamānasa* of Tulsi Dās in the Asutosh Museum, Calcutta, dated Midnapore, 1750, of which the *Simhāsanabattīsi* of 1775 in the British Library is a stylistic derivative. This employs a vigorous line, of an angularity directly descended from the 1499 covers from Vishnupur, especially in profile, with bold, primary colours against a plain ground, often under cusped arches. In Bengal the palm leaf was succeeded by paper in the 15th century, the paper employed being of a quite thick variety of no great refinement, one side of which was dyed with yellow orpiment containing arsenic to act as an insecticide. The *poṭhī* format was still employed up to the 18th century, the leaves sometimes being of considerable size. As happened in western India, the ratio of height to width was reduced to give a larger text area for writing. All the Bengal illustrated wooden covers were made for this type of manuscript. From the 18th century are found Bengal manuscripts of codex format, often sewn in a single section with card covered with cloth as bindings, of which the Midnapore manuscripts are good examples.

In Orissa the palm leaf continued in general use up to the 19th century, although paper manuscripts in codex format are found from a century earlier. All known palm-leaf manuscripts from Orissa are of comparatively late date and use the palmyra, on which the text is incised with a stylus in the southern Indian manner, and then inked. In Orissa there flourished from at least the 17th century a school of manuscript illustration in which the drawing like the text was incised onto the leaf. After the basic outline was drawn, it was filled in with more detailed drawing, in which degrees of light and dark were achieved by variations in the depth of incision. Solid areas were filled in by a most precise and delicate use of cross-hatching. In all cases the relationship between text and illustration is so close as to suggest that they are both the work of the same person.

The first examples of the style come from the late 17th century, and are apparently associated with the small state of Khurda. They exhibit a graceful and simple outline drawing combined with the most exquisite attention to detail where appropriate in architecture and textiles, against the severely plain ground of the leaf itself. Only in a certain sharpness of feature do they display the angularity traditionally associated with Orissan drawing. A *Gītagovinda* in this style is dated *c.*1690 (No.115), which has some colouring. An earlier date than this has been claimed for certain other fragments, particularly those in the Asutosh Museum, in which the drawing is spread over several sewn-together leaves, but in fact in style and technique they are indistinguishable from the 18th-century manuscripts, which usually are in an immensely ponderous style. The heaviness of limb which is present in the previous century's figures is now unrelieved by the lightness and grace of its line, while the contrast in the 17th-century style between areas of exquisitely detailed work and of blank background which gives it so much of its charm has been blurred by the inclusion of too much detail and the consequent lessening of empty space. The result is sometimes too fussy. In this century also colouring is more widely applied to some of the details, particularly figures, architecture and plants, which tends to offset the fussiness of detail in the best examples, such as the lovely manuscripts of the *Amaruśataka* in Bhubaneshwar and the *Rāsakrīḍa* in the British Library (No.117). In the 19th century when there appear many more such manuscripts, colour washes of reds or yellows are applied to the ground rather than to the figures with even greater loss of distinctiveness.

It would seem clear that there were several separate centres of manuscript production in Orissa, but it is not yet possible to distinguish them adequately. They are all united however by the continuous use of such ancient motifs as the positioning of figures under cusped arches or in pavilions. Even in the best-known of the paper-period manuscripts from Orissa, the dispersed 18th-century *Gītagovinda* which owes so much to a Rajput influence, doubtless brought in the train of one of the Rajput governors for the Mughals, this usage is found. The brilliance of colouring of this manuscript is very unlike the palm-leaf Orissan manuscripts, but the luxuriance of the vegetation and the fussiness of detail are very similar.

One of the earliest reliable historical references we have to Assam concerns its manuscript traditions. Bāna in his biography of the Emperor Harsha (r.606–646) tells us that King Bhāskaravarman of Kāmarūpa (Assam) sent as presents to Harsha various treasures including jewels, silks and 'volumes of fine writing with leaves made from aloe bark, and of the hue of the ripe pink cucumber'. This writing material is called *sāñcipāt*,and has been described above. Although no manuscripts of this early date have been recovered, we do have some from the 15th century (British Library Or.8905), now blackened with age, while the 17th- and 18th-century manuscripts fully merit Bāna's lovely description of the colour (Nos.120–2). Paper was also used for Assamese manuscripts, but of a peculiar kind. Known as *tulāpāt*, it is traditionally made from ginned and felted cotton.

The earliest reference to Assamese manuscript illustration occurs in the biography of the Vaishnava saint Shankaradeva (*c*.1449–1558) who is said to have painted on *tulāpāt* scenes from the celestial worlds, and also the picture of an elephant which he then stuck on to a wooden manuscript case and presented to his royal patron in Cooch Behar; Shankaradeva himself spent most of his life at the court of the king of Cooch Behar, having been driven out of Assam proper, and any paintings by him would be in a similar style. However no surviving manuscript with illustrations in the Assamese tradition is earlier than the mid-17th century. The manuscript on *tulāpāt* of a *Bhāgavata Purāṇa* in the Bali Sattra in Nowgong bears a date equivalent to AD 1539, but this is highly suspect as it is an added date, not part of the colophon. It, like the *Kīrtanaghoṣā* (No.119) in the same style, bears plentiful evidence of a 17th-century origin through the ubiquitous presence of the type of *pagrī* or turban associated with Popular Mughal and Rajput painting of this century, and which is seen in no Hindu or Jain manuscript of an earlier period. There is moreover not a single other example of the style dated from earlier than the latter part of the 17th century. The presence of this turban indicates a date for both the *Bhāgavata Purāṇa* and *Kīrtanaghoṣā* of slightly later than the recorded importation of artists into Assam under Pratāp Singh (1603–41). Many of these artists were from Cooch Behar, whose Rājas were of the same family as the Darrang Rājas of Assam, and which had come under Mughal rule early in the reign of Jahāngīr.

No artistic productions are known to originate definitely from Cooch Behar before the end of the 18th century, but that is not to say that they did not exist. The origin of the Assamese style must be sought in manuscripts and artists who must have journeyed up the Brahmaputra from Bengal, possibly under the Pālas, but more likely following the collapse of that dynasty and the establishment of Muslim rule in Bengal about 1200. We know that Buddhist monks fled to Nepal, where Buddhism was still prospering. What more likely than that Hindus would have fled to a neighbouring Hindu kingdom such as Assam, which remained free of Muslim domination for many centuries following the collapse of the Pālas? For this Assamese school is full of references to the Pāla style, *i.e.* the habit of showing all activities under lobed arches, extended in the case of these very wide leaves latitudinally across the page, and the representation of characters using *mudrās* to express themselves. The exquisite colours of Pāla miniatures have been succeeded however, as in many of the medieval schools, by a crude preponderance of blue and red which are universally used for the backgrounds, the red below the arches and blue above. There is of course a horizontal viewpoint. The line is crude, but immensely vigorous, displaying the strength of a developing rather than a declining style. All figures are in strict profile. Women wear wide skirts with a kind of scarf around their upper parts and without any covering for their hair which is tied in a bun at the nape. Men wear the *dhotī* and Popular Mughal turban. Trees are stylized monochrome ovals with the outline of branches and leaves sketched over them. Architectural elements are indicated by rudimentary outlines. The paintings of these manuscripts invariably share a page with the text which is usually in lines above the painting, although sometimes for special effect the text is in the centre of the folio as in the *Rāsamaṇḍala* where Krishna and the *gopīs* form their circle all around the text panel, and occasionally a smaller painting is added on top of the larger one, but to one side. Important passages have marginal illumination all around both text and painting, usually of a plain colour with yellow or white simple patterns on top. The total effect although crude in aesthetic terms is both charming and immensely effective at the level of religious art.

Although apparently such manuscripts were connected particularly with the Vaishnava *sattras* or monasteries of Assam, yet they were patronized and commissioned by the Ahom kings who followed Shaiva/Shakta Hinduism. Rudra Singh (1696–1714) for example commissioned a *Gītagovinda* manuscript and others were produced in the reign of his successor Sib Singh (1714–44) in this style, though it is noticeable that developments have occurred in the style in the meantime. Elements of landscape have been introduced, the function of the multi-cusped arch overhead has become much less clear and it is used for decoration. In one manuscript (the *Ānandalahirī* of about 1730) the curves have been ironed out into right angles.

It was when the Ahom kings began to commission illustrated manuscripts that most changes came over this monastic style. The Ahom kings were able to resist attempts by the early Mughals to add Assam to their empire, but in 1662 an expedition led by Mīr Jumla captured their capital Garhgaon and succeeding in making the Ahom king Jayadhvaja pay tribute to Delhi. The success was shortlived in imperialist terms, for the Ahoms were able to recover their position over the next 20 years, and Assam was finally lost to the Mughals by 1681. It is interesting to note that the Mughal commander at one time was Rāja Rām Singh of Amber; he was recalled in 1676 and doubtless brought with him the perfectly preserved group of Assamese manuscripts now in the royal library of Amber (Jaipur), These are on strawberry-pink leaves of *sāñcipāt*, with beautiful *pārśvacitra* or decorations on the edges of the leaves.

One of the results of the Mughal attempts to conquer Assam was its being opened up to outside influences, and there are references to artisans from outside Assam being brought there in the 16th and early 17th centuries. This included apparently under Mīr Jumla's occupation of Garhgaon the introduction of painters from Delhi, some of whom stayed there. Certainly it is at this time that the kings began to patronize painters to illustrate their manuscripts, and it was under Rudra Singh (1696–1714) that formal court dress in the Mughal style was introduced. It was however under the patronage of his son Sib Singh (1714–44) and his four successive queens that we first find considerable numbers of illustrated manuscripts of royal provenance, associated particularly with the flowering of Assamese literature that took place at the court led by Kavichandra Chakravarti, who composed the first Assamese translation of the Vaishnava *Brahmavaivarta Purāṇa* (No. 122) at the instigation of the first queen Ratnakānti, and of the *Ānandalahirī*, a Tantric work, at the instigation of the second, Phuleshvarī. This lady was an ardent persecutor of the Vaishnavas in Assam. Her death in 1731 was followed by the king's marriage to her cousin, a Vaishnava lady, Ambikā, for whom was compiled an impressive work on elephantology (*Hastividyārṇava*, No. 120) by Sukumāra Barkāth in 1734, and the *Dharma Purāṇa* by Kavichandra in 1736 (No. 121). There are several other manuscripts also surviving from this period. All of them display the same characteristics of being on a grand scale, with large sheets of aloe bark, lavishly illustrated and beautifully written, while often the portraits of kings and queens are added being shown receiving the manuscript from the author or scribe.

By the 1730s the Ahom court style differed considerably from the popular Assamese style of No. 119, although the latter was in continuous production up to the end of the 18th century. Whereas the popular school retained many of the characteristics of early eastern Indian painting, such as the presentation of all events and personages under elongated architectural motifs, and is remarkable chiefly perhaps for the immense physical vigour displayed by its protagonists, such characteristics were abandoned by the Ahom court painters in favour of a bland conformity to certain Mughal ideals. Important male figures now wear Mughal costume, and the ladies have exchanged their billowing skirts for a sari. Both sexes now wear shawls round their upper bodies. Modelling is sometimes attempted, and, quite often, faces are in three-quarter profile.

Occasionally now the viewpoint is raised so that trees can be shown in the middle distance. Very rarely is a horizon shown (there are one or two instances in the *Hastividyārṇava* of 1734) but more usual are a few clouds at the top of the flat green ground. All the cusped arches have disappeared, but are replaced often by a stepped interface between text and painting possibly derived from the rectangular upper features of the *Ānandalahirī* manuscript.

Like the Mughal school, the Ahom court style suddenly appears without any transitional stage, and may perhaps be put down to individual genius, whether of patron or artist. In fact three artists seem to have been responsible for most of the school's surviving production in Sib Singh's reign – Badha Ligirā, who painted the *Śankhacūḍavadha* of 1726, the *Dharmapurāṇa* of 1736 (No.121) and the *Bhāgavata Purāṇa* Book 6 of 1737, while two artists Dilbar and Dosāī were responsible for the *Hastividyārṇava* of 1734 (No.120). In the succeeding reigns there are very few surviving productions and none of royal provenance until the *Daraṅgarājavaṃśāvali* of 1791, a history of the kings of Darrang who were subordinate to the Ahom kings and related to the kings of Cooch Behar. It is noticeable that Bengali influence has increased in this manuscript considerably, especially in the architecture where the flat-roofed Ahom palaces have been replaced by curving roofs of Bengali provenance. This is taken to the furthest extreme in the last great royal Assamese manuscript, the *Brahmakhaṇḍa* of 1836 (No.122), commissioned by Purandara Singh, the last ruler of Assam (1818 and 1832–8). Although new elements in the 1836 manuscript include paintings of British officers and of sepoys in British uniforms, the style is still triumphantly Assamese, and bears no trace of Europeanisms in its technique. Indeed, the artist Durgārāma Betha has carried the rather desiccated Ahom court style to much greater heights of inventiveness, experimenting freely with landscape and architecture. The ground is covered with tufts of flowers or shrubs growing out of little hillocks, while mountainous terrain is represented in one of the most charming landscape stylizations ever seen even in India, hillocks in rows behind one another all of different colours, with animals and birds playing hide-and-seek among them, and flowers and trees crowning their summits. Everywhere are birds and insects, sometimes dominating the composition. The manuscript marks the end of the independent style of Assam, since with Purandara Singh's dethronement in 1838, there was no significant patron left.

Southern India, the southern part of the Deccan plateau and the coastal plains down to Cape Comorin, although subject to periodic raids and conquest by the Muslim rulers of the north, developed along her own lines in comparative freedom. No amount of cross-fertilization of cultures could induce her to abandon her traditional, austere approach to the palm leaf, in striking contrast to the lavish paintings on temple and palace walls. There is not a single painted palm-leaf manuscript later than the Digambara Jaina manuscripts of Moodabidri of *c.*1112, whose style seems related to the fragmentary frescoes found on the earlier Badami caves of northern Karnataka. Not a single illustrated manuscript is associated with the great kingdom of Vijayanagar (1336–1565), where we know painting flourished in fresco form. Even the art of incising drawings on palm leaves which flourished in Orissa had no discernible influence further south. The huge palm-leaf manuscript libraries of

Trivandrum, Tanjore, Mysore and Madras can only muster between them two solitary folios showing this art, of 19th-century date. Nor is it possible to point to more than a few wooden manuscript covers decorated in any way. The Telugus were slightly less austere than the Tamils, and there are a few interesting covers decorated with ivory, either in the form of ivory inlaid in wood (No.123) or complete sheets of ivory pegged to wooden cores and incised.

The establishment of schools of manuscript illustration on paper in the Muslim courts of the northern Deccan in the later 16th century seems to have had little effect on Hindu manuscript production for about a century. The use of paper was slowly spreading southwards during the 16th century through the Mahratta country, and it is late in the following century that the increasingly politically important Mahratta courts began to patronize painting. The most flourishing school of Mahratta manuscript production was, however, at their court in Tanjore. Venkajī, half-brother to Shivājī, the fiercest antagonist of the Mughals in the Deccan, and a general in the service of the ʿĀdil Shāhs of Bijapur, drove out the last of the Nāyak rulers of Tanjore and established himself on the throne in 1676. Sahājī II, his successor, was a patron of art and literature, but few, if any, paintings have survived from this period. Surviving examples of Tanjore manuscript painting from the mid-18th century are highly distinctive, and are fully formed. The origin of the style is to be found in Vijayanagar art of the 16th century, of which survive only frescoes at Lepakshi and a few other places, but which must have been widespread over most of southern India. The collapse of the empire in 1565 heralded the desiccation and ossification of the style into a highly stylised art of icon painting, with heavily modelled and elaborately jewelled, crowned and gilded figures of the deity. Under the patronage of the Mahratta kings of Tanjore some of the 18th-century manuscripts, such as the earliest *Aśvaśāstra* and *Gajaśāstra* manuscripts, now in the Saraswati Mahal Library in Tanjore, display a leavening of this heavy style with elements, particularly colouring, of Deccani painting, transmuted intact from the 17th century. These delightful manuscripts on the origin, classification and care of horses and elephants, inhabit a world of colour and fantasy. Suddenly, under the cultured Sarabhoji II (1797–1833), a bibliophile in the European tradition, who reorganized the palace library, had thousands of manuscripts collected and copied, and collected books in English and French from the presses of London and Paris, this style was exposed to a disastrous European influence, resulting in a coarsening and a lowering of standards through an attempt to conform to wretched European ideas of modelling and landscape.

The earliest Tanjore manuscripts are in a large, upright bound format, but more usual from the time of Sarabhoji on is a reversion to the *poṭhī* format on a large scale, with the text in a central panel within wide margins running from edge to edge and crossing over each other. These margins could then be decorated with floral and arabesque motifs, often derived in the 19th century from European rather than Indian inspiration. Miniatures, if added, would be within the central panel (No.124). This type of *poṭhī* complete with marginal decorations was a model for the production of the early lithographic presses of Bombay, which kept to the traditional format for the production of Hindu texts such as the epics and *Purāṇas*.

In the Deccan itself a similar Mahratta style seems to have been practised in the late 18th century in Nagpur, and a flourishing southern school, allied to that of Tanjore, in Mysore. Under the patronage of the Mysore Rājas, lavishly gilded manuscripts in Kannada of the *Rāmāyaṇa* and similar texts were prepared in the 19th century.

Throughout the centuries in which Muslim and Hindu book-production had continued side by side, there had been scarcely any *rapprochement* between the two until the 18th century. In Kashmir, the traditional format of birch bark had been changed to accommodate the bark sheets being sewn and bound, and in Rajasthan we begin to find paper manuscripts being sewn, even if as yet only in a single section, from the mid-17th century. Yet is was not until Hindu patrons demanded from their scribes and illuminators, as well as their painters, the standards which Muslim patrons expected as of right, that Hindu manuscripts approached in quality those of Persian manuscripts. For no matter how much critical attention they paid to the paintings in their manuscripts, Hindu patrons had very low standards of expectation from their scribes. Even so important work as the Mewar *Rāmāyaṇa* of 1649–53 (Nos.91–7) is written in a thoroughly careless manner, with mistakes painted out in yellow rather than the whole page being rewritten. Until, in fact, Hindus were willing to treat calligraphy as a serious art, no improvements along these lines could be expected. It was in Kashmir that standards were first established in this field.

The Kashmiri style of painting has an obscure origin not yet properly fathomed. It is found only in 18th- and 19th-century manuscripts, and is there fully formed. The paintings are always on a small scale, enclosed by the text, with simple compositions, often a group of people in front of a pavilion to left or right, set in a landscape. Recession in the landscape is attempted by drawing various horizons across it, each of the sections being differently coloured, and usually with purple rocks on top of each horizon. In Persian manuscripts, humans tend to wear antique Persian dress rather than contemporary costume, with the high Chagatay headdress and long gown for women and long, front-opening gowns (*peshvaz*) for men. The architecture is usually a simple pavilion in contemporary style with a canopy stretched from it. There is a marked fondness for very bright reds and oranges for items of dress, liberally covered with gold, with greens, browns and purples in the landscape. The horizon is often dotted with tall firs, the sky beyond being slate-blue.

Comparatively few of these manuscripts bear dates or provenances, but for the latter the place mentioned is 'in Kashmir', *i.e.* the vale of Kashmir around Srinagar. The manuscript of the *Shāhnāma* (No.125) from Rajauri offers perhaps some evidence as to the origin of the style, as many of the characteristic traits of the Kashmiri style are present therein already. This we have seen is the product of the influence of Delhi artists on some unknown local style. Rajauri is on the normal Mughal route from the Panjab up to the vale of Kashmir. Going further back in time and further down onto the plains, there is in a private collection in London a manuscript in Panjabi of the *Aśvamedhaparvan* of the *Mahābhārata* dated 1749/1692, which bears numerous illustrations in two styles, the earlier being a provincial Mughal style of the late 17th century, the other a Kashmiri style of a century later. In the earlier style it exhibits numerous features, like the Rajauri manuscript, which are later incorporated into the Kashmiri style, particularly the landscape (which is very hilly, so hence probably from near the mountains) and architectural elements. Here in this Hindu manuscript, however, the people wear normal contemporary dress. The absence of any Hindu manuscript from Kashmir of a narrative kind (rather than the ubiquitous collections of *stotras*, *Pañcaratna* etc.) makes comparison difficult, but obvious resemblances between the *Aśvamedhaparvan* and the Kashmiri Sanskrit anthology (No.126) are the use of spandrels to close off the top two corners, and the headgear worn by pundits and Brahmans, a cloth bag that covers the hair on top of the head and encloses it at the back also. In the latter manuscript the few lay male figures all wear the short *jāma* and turban of Popular Mughal work of the 17th century.

It would seem then that the style of Kashmir is based at least partly on a late 17th-century provincial style from the northern Panjab which spread up into the northern-most hills via such places as Rajauri, and in Kashmir may have influenced an already existing style about which we know nothing as yet. There is every likelihood that a Sultanate style was in existence in Kashmir based on 15th-century Shiraz work, which would account for the format of the Persian manuscripts illustrated in the valley – very archaic in layout, with their small paintings enclosed in the text. This gradual diffusion of artistic styles to Kashmir via both artists and the physical travels of manuscripts (the *Aśvamedhaparvan* travelled to Kashmir where it was added to) is in contrast to the way styles developed in the hill states east of the Sutlej. Being ruled by Hindu chiefs favouring a 'Rajput' style of art, developing within their own traditions as there was no style in neighbouring territories sufficiently in tune for them to be influenced by, they were suddenly exposed to a full blast of Mughal influence of the Muhammad Shāh period by artists fleeing Delhi during the disasters of the 18th century.

It has scarcely been necessary in this discussion of Kashmiri painting to distinguish between Muslim and Hindu styles, for here in Kashmir there occurred in the 18th century a spontaneous synthesis, in which Hindu manuscript illumination came closest to Muslim. They adopted the same format as Muslim manuscripts, the bound volume, with the text, beautifully written by Kashmiri scribes in an elegant *Nāgarī* within gilded and coloured margins in a central panel, on fine paper, with border decorations of floral subjects around miniatures, and in one manuscript at least (No.126), uniquely, an attempt at the *hashīyas* illuminated in gold as in Mughal manuscripts. The typical Kashmiri illumination of *sarlavḥ* and *ʿunvān*, broad bands in gold, blue and pink providing the ground for arabesques and flowers, a style based on a certain strand of Mughal illuminations found as early as the 1570 *Anvār-i Suhaylī* (No.57), is found as the frontispiece to Hindu and Muslim manuscripts alike. The elegance of the *Nāgarī* script found in fine-quality Kashmiri manuscripts is unique in India; only Jaipur manuscripts can compare with it, but here the scribes were often Kashmiri anyway. They revived the ancient practice of writing with gold and silver ink on blue or black paper (No.11), a characteristic of Nepalese manuscripts but not seen in Indian manuscripts before. They even were prepared to bind their manuscripts in leather – although this does not appear on illuminated manuscripts, it does on birch-bark manuscripts bound in codex form. In the mid-18th century they had adopted the vertical format of Persian manuscripts (as in No.126), with the text parallel to the short side of the folio; however, by the end of the century they had reverted generally for their *guṭkas* (small bound volumes) to writing parallel to the long side, and binding along that edge. The boards were sometimes painted and lacquered, but more usually covered in cloth, as in Jaipur, embroidered with silk or gold or silver wire (Nos.128–9).

The Mahārājas of Jaipur from Jai Singh II (1700–43), the famous astronomer and builder of the city of Jaipur, began to commission new first-class work for their already well-stocked *poṭhīkhāna*, and to bring the standards prevailing in Kashmir to the plains. A lovely manuscript of the *Sarasarasagrantha* dated 1794/1737, is perhaps the earliest example of this trend, apparently commissioned by Jai Singh when in Agra. It is in both Persian and Hindi, the former in elegant *Nastaʿlīq* on gold-sprinkled paper in central panels, the latter in equally elegant *Nāgarī* in side panels on the bias in white clouds against gold, decorated with flowers, with triangular panels of illumination and thirty-three paintings. Succeeding manuscripts done at Jaipur or commissioned from Kashmiri scribes continue this trend. It seems to have been partly occasioned by a desire of Hindu patrons to have manuscripts of the Hindu sacred texts as beautiful and elegant as copies of the Koran, and the number of texts finely illuminated in this way is small, principally the *Bhagavadgītā* with its associated smaller texts (No.129), the *Devīmāhātmya*, and some Shaiva *stotras*, while the *Gītagovinda* (No.128), though more a poetic than religious text, was also so treated.

These texts as well as the *Bhāgavata Purāṇa* and a few others were also written in minute script on long paper scrolls and handsomely illuminated. This kind of work appears to have been done at various centres in northern India – Jaipur, Alwar, Benares and perhaps some others – which makes use of Persian features such as the *sarlavḥ* to begin the scroll, and largely borrows the early 19th-century Delhi style for the miniatures (No.130). These features were generally diffused throughout northern India in the early 19th century, so that many Hindi and Sanskrit texts are automatically enclosed within margins ruled in gold and colours and bound up in codex form.

130 Vasudeva arranges the transfer of the babies; Nanda carries the infant Krishna across the Jumna; and Krishna suckles to death the demoness Pūtanā (No.130, p.145).

84 'Anvār-i Suhaylī'

The Lights of Canopus, by Husayn Vāʿiz Kāshifī (see No.49).

Two sub-imperial manuscripts of this popular text are known. This one is dated 1009/1600–01 at Ahmadabad, the capital of the province of Gujarat, copied by one Taymur Humus for an unnamed patron, the other undated, of about 1610.[1] Mīrzā Azīz Koka, Akbar's foster-brother, was the Governor of Gujarat in 1600, and may have commissioned this Ms. in Ahmadabad. When in Hajipur in Bihar in 1583, he had similarly commissioned an illustrated copy of an astronomical text[2]. Ahmadabad was the seat of government of the *subah* of Gujarat, one of the most prosperous in the Empire – it was given in turn to Azīz Koka and ʿAbd ar-Rahīm Khānkhānān, while Prince Murād held it from 1593 till his death in 1599. The two former were both patrons of art, while Murād would have had access to his father's studio. There is no evidence of an indigenous Popular Mughal school in Ahmadabad unlike Agra, and therefore artists would have been attached to the suites of the great nobles from the capital rather than working in the city itself.

The 43 miniatures in this Ms. are stylistically in two groups. The first, much the larger, is a simplified version of the Mughal style, in bright colours with on the whole little subtlety of colouring. Prominent in this group are Persian effects of intertwining trees and flowering shrubs in serpentine shape, as well as on occasion a total disregard of the naturalistic rendition of spatial relationships built up laboriously in the Mughal studio since the *Ḥamzanāma* years. He uses a simplified landscape style, of plain grounds filled with flowers, with abrupt colour changes to signify recession, and lumpish, ill-defined rocks of variegated colour. Our artist may be regarded perhaps as one initially trained in a non-Mughal idiom, who sought patronage at the imperial court, was perhaps trained by an Iranian such as Āqā Rizā, but was then dismissed in the 1590s to seek his living from other patrons. Other work is known from his hand (see No.85).

84 f.31b. Ghanīm carries the stone-lion up the mountain. By the same artist as 85.

A small group of paintings in this Ms. is by an artist much more attuned to the latest style of the Mughal court. His technique is much more complex, allowing subtle effects of colouring on the ground, where he uses stippling, while his animals are subtly drawn and modelled, as distinct from the charming but linear animals of the other artist.

The paintings in this Ms. vary considerably in size and shape, some being retained within the oblong format of the text panels, others protruding into the margins in various ways. The total effect is somewhat undisciplined, as compared with a royal Ms. of the time. The calligraphy is a good *Taʿlīq*, but rather compressed.

British Library, London, Or.6317.

ff.207; 30×19·5cm; paper, creamy-brown, unburnished; 21 lines *Taʿlīq* script in panels 20×11·5cm, with margins ruled in lines of gold, blue, brown, and green; one *sarlavḥ* in colours and gold, with gold floral decoration round the colophon; various seals and inscriptions on the recto of the first page have been overpasted; 43 paintings of varied sizes; modern binding.

Bibliography: BM 1968, p.45. BL 1977, pp.63–4. BM 1976, p.58. Pinder-Wilson 1969.

[1]British Library, Or.13942.
[2]IP, pp.19–23.

85 'Zafarnāma'

Illustrated on p.102.

The Book of Victories of Sharaf ad-Dīn ʿAlī Yazdī, the history of Tīmūr, the ancestor of the Mughals, was compiled from the records kept by the conqueror's secretaries and turned into elegant prose by the author at the command of Tīmūr's grandson Ibrāhīm Sultān in Shiraz in 828/1425.

The earliest illustrated Indian Ms. of this text appears to be this Ms., executed in a sub-imperial style in 1009/1600–01. The scribe is unnamed; he has a most elegant *Taʿlīq* hand. There are seven miniatures, all full-page. The Ms. is linked in its format and painterly style with the *Anvār-i Suhaylī* Ms. of the same year (No.84). The scribe is different, but the margins of the text panels are in exactly the same uncommon combination of gold, blue, brown and green, and the paper is the same.[1] At least two hands can be distinguished in the paintings, the majority by the artist who contributed most of the paintings in the *Anvār-i Suhaylī*. Details of architecture, sky, the tiling of the floor are identical in some of the paintings, while the human type of this *Zafarnama* artist conforms very closely to that in the other Ms. Both show very clearly on occasion a non-Mughal approach to composition, where a mountainous terrain provides an opportunity for dividing the composition into upper and lower halves with separate activities in each. Rock formations with their lumpy outlines and two-colour effects are identical. The similarities are so obvious that the *Zafarnāma* of 1600 may be assigned to the same atelier as the *Anvār-i Suhaylī*, which we have seen to be most likely that of the Governor of Ahmadabad, Mīrzā Azīz Koka.

British Library, London, Or.1052.

ff.333; 31×20·5cm; paper, creamy-brown, unburnished; 21 lines of *Taʿlīq* script in panels 20×11·5cm with ruled margins in gold, blue, brown and green; one *sarlavḥ*; seven paintings, unascribed, full page within the same type of ruled margins; modern binding.

Bibliography: BM 1879, p.176. BL 1977, p.154. Wilkinson 1934.

[1]An otherwise undated and unascribed Koran in the British Library (Or.13803) has this same combination of marginal colouration, and may be attributed to the same manuscript studio. In addition, the *Razmnāma* of 1605, published briefly in Chaghatai 1943–4, plates 2–6A, and now vanished, appears to be from this same studio, and written by the calligrapher of the *Zafarnāma*. Chaghatai's list of contributing artists is unfortunately too confused to be of use here.

86 'Shāhnāma'

Illustrated on p.102.

The epic history of the Persian kings by Firdausī (see No.22).

This Ms. bears the inscription that it was given by his late majesty Jahāngīr in the 8th year of the reign (1022/1613) to Ilāhvirdī Chela, and that the latter gave it to his brother Khvāja Muhammad Rashīd. Ilāhvirdī Chela is known as a courtier who rose high in the service of Jahāngīr and Shāh Jahān, and there is no reason to doubt the inscription. However one of the miniatures (f.274a) bears the date 1025/1616.[1] There are 89 miniatures, most with attributions to artists in a neat hand in black ink on the pictures themselves, in a manner never seen in an imperial painting.

The style of the miniatures is unusually stiff and stilted, being cramped into a part of a quite small text panel. A closer examination reveals that the Mughal paintings are in fact overpaintings, and that the paintings of an earlier manuscript have been Mughalized. A set of Persian paintings lies underneath, of probable 15th-century date, judging by the appearance of the manuscript whose main features the Mughal artists have kept, but altered in details of faces, costumes and particularly landscape and buildings. Underneath the monochrome landscape of Mughal paint may be seen when suitably lit the flowering and fruiting vegetation beloved of Persian landscape. Flaking paint in places reveals a different composition or colour beneath. Only occasionally however is any area of text covered up, as in f.372a, building the wall against Gog and Magog, where the upper quarter of the picture is painted over a few lines of text originally written on the bias. The artists named are, principally, Qāsim, Kamāl, Shamāl, Banvāri and Bhagvati. Qāsim and Kamāl are known as artists who worked on the *Rāmāyaṇa* done for ʿAbd ar-Rahīm Khānkhānān from 1589–98; various Banvāris are known – this one could be the same as the Banvāri Khurd (the younger) who worked on the non-imperial 1598 *Razmnāma* (No.88). Qāsim worked also on the Khānkhānān's MS. of the *Khamsa* of Amīr Khusraw now in Berlin, before 1617, so it would seem that the *Shāhnāma* ought to be attributed to his studio also.

However, this neat solution is belied by the evidence of the dated painting, which year, 1616, is apparently after the presentation of the manuscript in 1613. The inference is that Ilāhvirdī Chela had the original Persian manuscript repainted in the Mughal style; although this practice was usual with Jahāngīr, it would be a doubtful, even dangerous, course for a courtier to do the same to an imperial present. This would also involve Ilāhverdī Chela having access to a studio whose artists worked habitually for the Khānkhānān. We are surely justified in concluding that the author of the inscription was right in his facts but mistaken as to the precise date.

Banvāri's style is characteristically sub-imperial Mughal, *i.e.* the imperial style much simplified. Qāsim, Kamāl and Shamāl on the other hand betray a much more Iranian style, related to that of Qazvin. Qāsim's work in the Amīr Khusraw Ms. in Berlin is in any case in an idiom still basically Iranian, but with Mughal overtones. The Khānkhānān would seem to have recruited some of his artists direct from Iran, but obviously had, in deference to the Emperors' taste, to instruct them to Mughalize their work, which was probably done through the medium of such artists as Banvāri.

British Library, London, Add.5600.

Provenance: ex-N. Halhed Collection; acquired in 1795.

ff.585; 31·5 × 20cm; original panels of text (16·5 × 10cm) of ivory paper with 25 lines of *Nastaʿlīq* in four columns within margins ruled in gold and colours; headings in *Thuluth* in panels; set in a darker and thinner 18th-century paper with elaborate pink markers and painting protectors; *ʿunvān* around opening of preface (a version of the old pre-Baisunghur preface) and one *sarlavḥ* beginning the text proper both probably Indian; 89 miniatures, all overpaintings, mostly occupying part of a text panel (for list of artists see BL 1977); early 17th-century Indian covers, with flap, of boards with scenes of a lion fighting a buffalo and other animals and birds in a landscape painted in gold on black and lacquered, slightly damaged, with fine doublures of red morocco of flowers and birds in gold on red, laid into an 18th-century frame of leather painted black and tooled in gold, with a leather spine of alternate buff and black panels tooled in gold; the original flap connector, or possibly spine, of plain black leather with stamped medallions in gold, was set in black leather and reused.

Bibliography: BM 1879 p.536. BL 1977 pp.41–2.

[1]This hitherto unnoticed date was recently discovered by Mr J. Seyller.

87 ʻʿAjā-ʾib al-Makhlūqātʼ

Illustrated on p.103.

'The Wonders of Creation', an anonymous Persian translation from the Arabic of Zakariyā ibn Muhammad al-Qazvīnī (d.682/1283), a work recounting the inhabitants of heaven and earth, the constellations, mythical creatures, animals and plants.

This work was extremely popular both in Persia and India, and was often lavishly illustrated with hundreds of drawings. Normally these drawings follow the iconography of the manuscript being copied, and it took a bold innovator to vary the items selected for illustration or even to alter their style. The earliest illustrated Indian copies appear to date from the early 17th century, although a now vanished one was prepared in Bijapur in 1547.[1] No imperial Mughal copy is as yet known,[2] but many in Popular Mughal style. This particular copy abandons the colouring of the miniatures in favour of a bold style of drawing, and filling in with gold. The results are particularly happy in the animal sections, each one being drawn true to life. The artist was much less good at drawing the human figure, but on their evidence a date of about 1620 may be assigned to the Ms.; he begins by giving Indian features and clothing to the people, but then repents his rashness and reverts to the standard format based ultimately on an Arab style of the 13th century.

British Library, London, Add.7706.

Provenance: ex-Claudius James Rich collection; acquired in 1825. Rich presumably acquired the Ms. in India before he was appointed Resident in Baghdad in 1808.

ff.286; 30 × 18cm; creamy paper; 21 lines of good *Nastaʿlīq* in panels 19·5 × 10·2cm with margins ruled in gold and blue; 279 miniatures, mostly drawings with gold infill (the opening ones of the constellations against a blue sky filled with flowers!); the first two folios later replacements decorated with *ʿunvān* and marginal illumination in the style of Oudh *c.*1800–20; the final folio is a later replacement dated 1051/1641, with a spurious conclusion according to Rieu – it is on 18th-century European paper; dark-blue leather cover with sunk gold medallions; red doublures.

Bibliography: BM 1879, p.463. BL 1977, pp.78–81.

[1]BM 1879, p.995.

[2]The pages of Mughal animal and plant drawings noted in CB 1936, pp.26–7 as being from this text are now generally thought to be from the natural history section of the *Bāburnāma*.

88 'Razmnāma'

Illustrated on p.103.

The Book of Wars is the Persian translation of the Sanskrit epic *Mahābhārata*, which was commissioned by Akbar in 1582 from Nakīb Khān. The literal translation produced by him, the historian Badāʾunī and others with the help of learned Brahmans, was then turned into elegant prose by Abu'l Fazl's brother, the poet Faizī. The work was apparently finished by 1586 when Abu'l Fazl wrote his preface to the translation. The imperial presentation copy is now in the Jaipur royal collection[1]. Badāʾunī also states that the order was given that further copies should be made for the Amīrs, in furtherance of Akbar's policy of increasing understanding between Muslims and Hindus. Of these other copies, the only illustrated ones are dispersed Mss. dated 1598 and 1616, and a now vanished one dated 1605[2].

The bulk of this Ms. was dispersed in a sale in 1921, but it seems to have had originally at least 200 paintings. The colophon of Canto 17 bears the date 1007/1598, but no details of scribe or patron are anywhere given. Of the 24 paintings in the British Library's section of the Ms., 11 of the artists named are known to have been in the imperial atelier, and contributed work to the *Dārābnāma* (No.59) and *Bāburnāma* (No.62). Their work here however is rarely of imperial calibre, and it must be assumed that they had left the court studio or were allowed to take on work from other patrons.

The 1598 *Razmnāma* exhibits three kinds of work. Principally, it is the standard Mughal painting of the period but simplified to a greater or lesser degree. Rarer is another kind of work, seemingly a throwback to the Cleveland Museum *Ṭūṭīnāma*, in which pre-Mughal characteristics are included, and which constitutes a link between the pre-Mughal schools and the Popular Mughal tradition of the Manley (No.89) and Berlin *Rāgamālās*. Folio 17a in this manuscript by Bhagvān illustrates this linkage perfectly, while f.13b by Bhavāni shows the emergent Rajput characteristic of using architecture to fill background space without regard to structural principles. Also rare is a more progressive style in *nīm-qalam*, in which colours are sparingly applied in pale washes, highlighted in gold. The painting in which Rāma's servant overhears the quarrel in the *dhobī*'s household (f.48a of Or.12076) painted by Dā'ūd[3], the brother of the great artist Daulat, is one of the earliest specimens of this style, which proved extremely popular in the early decades of the next century. Artists who worked on this *Razmnāma* include Kamāl and Banvāri, who both worked for the Khānkhānān, in Kamāl's case both before and after this manuscript. It is probable therefore that it was commissioned by the Khānkhānān.

British Library, London, Or.12076.

ff.138; 30×19cm; beige paper; small *Naskhī* hand, 27 lines in panels 20×10·5cm with margins ruled in gold; some replacement folios, many marginal repairs; 24 paintings of varying sizes, attributed (for artists see BL 1977); another major portion is in the Baroda Museum; one small *sarlavḥ*; modern binding.

Bibliography: BM 1968, p.37. BL 1977, p.134 (repro. f.76a). BM 1976, p.55. Meredith Owens and Pinder-Wilson 1956. Sotheby 25 Oct. 1921, lots 203–79. AIP, No.654. Chaghatai 1943–4.

[1]Published in full in Hendley 1883–5.
[2]Published briefly in Chaghatai 1943–4.
[3]Reproduced by Meredith Owens and Pinder-Wilson, plate XIX.

89 'Rāgamālā'

COLOUR PLATE XXXV

The Garland of the Rāgas, an album of paintings meant to be pictorial representations of a *rāga* or *rāgiṇī*, the modes of Indian music, arranged into families, each *rāga* being personified as male with five wives or *rāgiṇīs*, and in the more elaborate systems with *rāgaputras* or sons also. First of all apparently a literary conceit, each mode was described in a verse in Sanskrit, and later in Hindi. From at least the 15th century, the verses were made the subject of paintings. It does not appear to have been a theme which appealed to the taste of the Great Mughals, but it would certainly have done to the Rajput nobles of the Mughal court, for one of whom possibly this set in a Popular Mughal style would have been made.

The set is almost complete, having 34 of the paintings of a set of 36, with verses in Sanskrit inscribed at the top. The text followed is of unknown authorship, first appears about 1500–50, and is according to Ebeling the main source of the Rajasthani tradition of *Rāgamālā* verses.[1] The compositions are usually very simple with an extremely simplified Mughal landscape – green with sometimes a rocky horizon, sometimes only a merging into the sky, the lower part of which is pink, merging above into white and then slate blue. Architecture and dress conform to Popular Mughal type, while the female is a slight advance in elegance on those first seen in the 1598 *Razmnāma*, wearing the skirt, short bodice, *paṭkā* and transparent *orhnī* draped over her head, and round her skirt – the back of her head is still often slightly pointed, and she is still liberally adorned with pompoms. There are perfunctory attempts at modelling. The especial glories of this set however are the marvellously sympathetic depiction of birds and animals, and the beautifully stylized trees, which make no attempt at a Mughal naturalistic depiction but instead are in a fully formed Rajput idiom, a stylized pattern of brightly coloured leaves over a darker ground. Its date must be about 1610, and Agra is the only definitely known centre for this work, although an attempt has recently been made by Cran to pinpoint a Bundelkhandi origin for it.

Some time before 1774 it almost certainly entered the library of the Rohilla chieftain Hāfiz Rahmat, since it was acquired by one William Watson 'in the Rhohillah Campaign, in the year 1774' (see No.111). Watson had it bound up, in no particular order, and interleaved, so that he could write notes on the subjects of the paintings, entirely fanciful, as he himself admits. Apparently before 1774, it was the subject of two separate foliations in Arabic characters, neither of them corresponding to the clearly labelled *Nāgarī* enumeration nor indeed to its reversal, and during one of which the names of the *rāgas* were written, correctly, in *Nasta'līq*, probably in the library of Hāfiz Rahmat. These were cropped in binding. In 1815 it was given to Mary Watson by her father.

British Museum, London, 1973, 9–17.

Provenance: ex-W.B. Manley Collection, acquired in the 1930s; acquired in 1973.

ff.57; 26×17·2cm; brownish paper; text in two lines of *Nāgarī*, with *Nasta'līq* inscriptions; English descriptions and notes opposite each painting; 34 paintings, in frames ruled in black, green, white and blue, about 20·5×14·5cm; many repairs to the borders; European binding.

Bibliography: Ashton 1950, No.401, painting 17. Ebeling 1973, pp.161–2. Cran 1980.

[1]Ebeling 1973, pp.118–28.

90 'Bhāgavata Purāṇa'

COLOUR PLATES XXXIII, XXXIV

The Legends of Krishna (see No.36).

This incomplete manuscript (Cantos 8–9 and 11–12) of the *Purāṇa* was copied in Udaipur by the scribe Jasvant in 1705/1648, and is heavily illustrated in the Mewar style. The artist is named at the foot of two of the miniatures as Sāhīb Dīn (f.5b of Canto 8, and f.24b of Canto 9), who flourished in Udaipur between 1628 and 1653, his greatest work occurring in the *Rāmāyaṇa* of 1649–53 (Nos.92, 96). It is difficult to believe that all of the work in this *Purāṇa* is from his hand, as much of it is on an extremely simple level, with the exception of certain key passages such as the *Gajendramohana* episode (the Elephant's deliverance) which begins the eighth canto. The tenth canto, the most important in the *Purāṇa*, is missing, and it is possible that a few scattered and damaged pages in other collections, of a much more ambitious type, were originally Sāhīb Dīn's work in this manuscript. Some ten paintings at the end of Canto 11 are in the style of Manohar, whom we meet in the first book of the *Rāmāyaṇa* of 1649 (No.91).

Bhandarkar Oriental Research Institute, Poona, No.61/1907–15.

ff.84, 65, 131, 43; 21·5×39cm; country paper; *tripāṭhī* format, various lines of *Nāgarī* across centre with commentary (of Shrīdhara) above and below; between red margins; 129 paintings, 88 full-page, ten half- and 31 quarter-page, within red and yellow borders; unbound, without covers.

Bibliography: Gode 1938. Khandalawala 1951, repro. f.5b of Canto 8.

91–97 'Rāmāyaṇa' of Jagat Singh of Mewar

The story of Rāma, the Sanskrit epic attributed to the sage Vālmīki, in 20,000 verses. The story of Rāma's banishment with his wife Sītā and brother Lakshmana due to the wiles of a wicked stepmother, their life together in the forest, Sītā's abduction by Rāvana the demon king of Lankā, the befriending of Rāma by the monkeys and bears of the forest and their

91 Mithila is besieged by Sītā's disappointed suitors. By Manohar.

assault on Rāvana's stronghold, the rescue of Sītā and their triumphant return home, all of this is an extremely ancient story which must have assumed a bardic shape by 500 BC. The epic grew to its present size over the next millennium, during which the hero Rāma was identified with the seventh incarnation of Vishnu. Nonetheless the *Rāmāyaṇa* is the most moving and universally loved of all Indian stories, telling as it does a story of human grief and human emotion, despite its divine garb.

Rāma, who lived on earth as a human being, had of course an ancestry and descendants, and the Hindu genealogists traced his ancestry back to the Sun. The Solar Rajputs, whose principal representatives were the Sesodiyas of Mewar (Udaipur), therefore included Rāma as the chief of their ancestors, and treated the *Rāmāyaṇa* as a family history rather like the history of Tīmūr to the Mughals.

By the middle of the 17th century, the studio at Udaipur was sufficiently large to embark on the production of a heavily illustrated *poṭhī* manuscript of the *Rāmāyaṇa* on the largest scale, with about 400 paintings, which fill the entire page. Mahātmā Hīrānanda wrote the various books between 1649 and 1653, the last two books being completed after the death of Jagat Singh in October 1652 and accession of Rāj Singh. They were all copied in Udaipur, and the colophons mention the reigning monarch, but only one of them, the *Ayodhyākāṇḍa*, specifically mentions that it was prepared for Jagat Singh. However, in view of the total dependence of Rajput painting on patronage, it is inconceivable that all the books were not prepared for the royal library.

Karan Singh and Jagat Singh were familiar with the habits of the Mughals; they knew of their vast library, stocked with illustrated versions of the histories of their ancestors, Tīmūr, Bābur and Akbar, and perhaps they knew of the *Ḥamzanāma*, the first great Mughal undertaking, with its 1,400 paintings. We know that the architecture of Udaipur, the palace buildings and, especially, the Jagadīsha temple built by Jagat Singh, deliberately recall the great period of Mewar architecture at Chitor. It is not surprising then that the *Rāmāyaṇa* should have been the text selected for this grandiose treatment for it concerns the great hero of the Solar race, Rāma the ancestor of the Rāṇā of Udaipur, the present head of the *Sūryavaṃśa*, and it may be seen as a Hindu reaction to, and imitation of, the ancestor-glorifying traditions of the Mughals.

Despite the immense pains that went into the making of this manuscript, the art of calligraphy was not considered important enough for the scribe to throw away a sheet with a mistake and start it again; instead there are innumerable passages simply scrubbed out with yellow paint. The scribe Mahātamā Hīrānanda belonged to the Jaina scribal tradition, and he follows the normal western *Nāgarī* traditions – beginning the text with the Jaina diagram, leaving a central diamond pattern without letters in the middle of the page usually, but not invariably, on all folios without illustrations, sometimes leaving five such patterns at beginning or end of a book (he abandons the practice by the time he reaches the *Yuddhakāṇḍa*), the partial inclusion of red medallions in the centre and margins of the versos of opening folios (up to f.9b in the *Ayodhyākāṇḍa*), and so on.

It is apparent from the wide variation in the number of lines per page throughout each book, that the paintings must have been produced before the text was written. Some episodes have a painting per folio for ten or more folios together, and then there may occur an uninterrupted sequence of text. In the former instance there may only be nine lines per side, rising to 22 in the latter. The subjects of the text and paintings coincide generally throughout the manuscript.

If all the paintings were produced first, then the dates in the colophons must be taken very generally as the concluding date of the writing of the text, and we may freely speculate on the number of years needed for the entire work. There are about 150 large paintings in Sāhīb Dīn's style. We know that a Mughal painting in the Akbar period could take six months for an artist working alone. Even though the Udaipur paintings are less complex technically, it would be unsafe to allow less than two or three months for one painting. This must presuppose the existence of a quite large studio, if the Ms. was to be completed in a reasonable time. How long depends on the as yet totally unknown number of junior artists working in the studio. If there were five or six master artists drawing the compositions and the major figures, there were probably twice this number assisting with the solid areas of paint and so on. Even so, with two or three junior artists assisting him, Sāhīb Dīn would have taken at least ten years. There is considerable stylistic advancement from the 1628 *Rāgamālā* to the first paintings of the *Ayodhyākāṇḍa*, so that it would be reasonable to assume the project began in the late 1630s. Further advance has been made in the *Yuddhakāṇḍa*. Similar calculations apply for the other artists involved.

91 'Bālakāṇḍa' of the 'Rāmāyaṇa'

The first book (Book of Childhood) of the *Rāmāyaṇa*, like the last, is one of the latest parts of the epic, and concerns the circumstances leading to the birth of Rāma and his brothers, and the marriage of Rāma to Sītā.

The *Bālakāṇḍa* of the Jagat Singh *Rāmāyaṇa* was completed in Udaipur in 1706/1649 by Mahātmā Hīrānanda, and painted by Manohar. There were originally 79 folios in all, most of them with paintings on one side and text on the other, of which 20 are in the Prince of Wales Museum, Bombay, two in the Baroda Museum[1], and about 55 in the Sir Cowasji Jehangir collection in Bombay[2]. The book was commissioned by Ācārya Jasvant, who must be the court librarian, or the administrator of the studio. He is probably the same person as the scribe of the 1648 *Bhāgavata Purāṇa* (No.90).

Manohar is an artist all of whose work occurs in the middle years of the 17th century. The *Bālakāṇḍa* is his only signed piece of work, but two other books in the *Rāmāyaṇa* (*Āraṇyakāṇḍa*, and *Uttarakāṇḍa*, Nos.93, 97) are in his general style, and he also produced other smaller sets about this time[3]. His only known work datable before this *Rāmāyaṇa* is a small group of ten paintings at the end of the 11th book of the *Bhāgavata* (No.90)[4] completed the previous year. His work, which is in a different manner from the normal Mewar style of the first half of the 17th century, has no discernible influence on later work, and represents an at present inexplicable phenomenon in Mewar painting. His conventions for the human figure, for architecture, horses and chariots, landscape and vegetation, are all different from those of Sāhīb Dīn's school, while his palette is much harsher, employing garish reds and oranges on occasion as well as a high degree of burnishing. Manohar is a good artist, but is lacking in many of the skills which distinguish Sāhīb Dīn's work. He has little sense of dramatic composition, and is often content to divide up the various episodes of a story within fairly obvious framing devices. When he does juxtapose the same characters side by side, as with the meeting with Parashurāma or Rāmas's breaking of Siva's bow, the effect is faintly although unintentionally comic. Only in the very occasional painting such as the siege of Mithilā do all his considerable gifts come together in a satisfying and unitary way.

Prince of Wales Museum of Western India, Bombay, 54.1/1–20.

ff.20 (out of 79); 23×39·5cm; paper; about 15 lines of *Nāgarī* between margins ruled in red, text area about 15×33cm; each folio painted on recto, with borders of red and yellow with text on reverse; unbound.

Bibliography: Moti Chandra 1955–57. Moti Chandra 1957, plate 2 (folio 33a in colour). Moti Chandra 1971, plate VI (folio 76a in colour).

[1]Numbered P G 5a. 64a–b. See Gangoly 1961, pp.83–4 (with illustrations).
[2]Khandalawala and Chandra 1965, No.76 (just one painting illustrated). The precise number of folios in the Jehangir collection has never been stated.
[3]See Moti Chandra 1971.
[4]I am indebted to Shridhar Andhare for pointing this out to me.

92 f.70. Rāma and the exiles begin their life in the forest.

92 'Ayodhyākāṇḍa' of the 'Rāmāyaṇa'

The second book of the epic *Rāmāyaṇa*, dealing with the life of Rāma and Sītā in Ayodhyā, their exile brought about by Rāma's stepmother, and the beginning of their life in the forest.

This book was completed in Udaipur in 1707/1650, the scribe being Hīrānanda and the commissioner Jasvant. It was prepared specifically for Mahārāna Jagat Singh's inspection, the only one of these volumes to say so. There are 68 paintings illustrating this volume, although this time no artist is named. There can be no doubt, however, that they are in the hand of Sāhīb Dīn, whose attributed work is known from the *Rāgamālā* of 1628[1], the *Gītagovinda* of 1629[2], the *Bhāgavata Purāṇa* of 1648 (No.90), the *Yuddhakāṇḍa* of the *Rāmāyaṇa* of 1653 (No.96), and the *Sukarakṣetramāhātmya* of 1655[3]. Unascribed but in his style is the *Kavipriyā* in the Udaipur Palace Museum. Apart from the first two, this work all dates from the middle years of the 17th century, and from its sheer bulk argues the existence of a flourishing studio system in Udaipur. Even where Sāhīb Dīn's name is specifically mentioned in the colophon, as in the *Yuddhakāṇḍa*, it is inconceivable that he alone could have produced such a large body of work unaided in less than a decade; while in reality he was engaged on other projects as well.

The *Ayodhyākāṇḍa* then is the work of the Sāhīb Dīn studio; with the master perhaps sketching the compositions but leaving most of the colouring to other artists. The paintings are of a very high standard, although not the summit of this artist's achievement, which occurs in the *Yuddhakāṇḍa*. However, certain sequences, such as the paintings leading up to the departure of Rāma into exile, have an overwhelming impact when viewed together that argue the hand of the master himself. Sāhīb Dīn's style is normally one in which fairly small groups of people are juxtaposed and balanced against one another or against landscape or architecture. Only occasionally does he indulge in a grand design. There is a slow build-up of tension through the association of groups in each picture and then through the viewing of the paintings in sequence. Some of the artist's greatest effects are achieved in this way, as in the sequence beginning with Kaikeyī's dream through the announcing of Rāma's exile, the scenes of lamentation, the disposal of his property, the scenes of farewell to his mother and Dasharatha, all pictures built up detail by detail, small groups of people juxtaposed against one another. However, the sequence culminates in a farewell scene organized on a grand scale, without repetition of characters, in which Rāma is accompanied into exile by the people of Ayodhyā with Dasharatha supported by his wives making a tragic gesture of farewell.

It is his ability to handle crowds that distinguishes Sāhīb Dīn from other Rajput painters of the 17th century, and indicates that he must at some stage have worked in the Popular Mughal tradition. The crowds he draws are precisely that, and not the serried rows favoured by Manohar. All of Sāhīb Dīn's work in this late period indicates long experience in painting from the high viewpoint, in contrast to his 1628 *Rāgamālā*. It may possibly be that some time between 1628 and his next dated work in 1648, he was in Agra gaining experience of the Mughal tradition of painting – this might account for the absence of datable material throughout the 1630s.

British Library, London, Add.15296(1).

Provenance: Royal Library in Udaipur till about 1820; given by Mahārāna Bhīm Singh of Udaipur (1778–1828) to Colonel James Tod and by him presented to the Duke of Sussex, son of George III. Acquired at the sale of the Sussex collection in 1844.

ff.129; 21×38·5cm; thin brown paper; 9–22 lines of *Nāgarī* with colophons, *daṇḍas*, etc., in red between margins with three red vertical lines and two horizontal ones above and below; text area 14×26–18×32cm; 68 paintings (17–18×35cm) within red and yellow borders, which usually extend to the edge of the page, but sometimes not; no covers originally, but now the folios are all framed in stout European paper and bound up (together with the *Kiṣkindhākāṇḍa*) in a handsome European binding prepared for the Duke of Sussex, the covers measuring 32×49cm.

Bibliography: BM 1902, pp.30–32. Losty 1978. Losty 1982, plate 13 (f.56a reproduced in colour). Barrett and Gray 1963, p.139, col. repro. of f.71a. Thompson 1980, pp.18–29 (col. repro. of folios 14a, 24a, 34a, 56a, 66a, 112a).

[1]Khandalavala etc. 1960, No.29.
[2]Andrew Topsfield is to publish this set in Chhavi vol.II.
[3]Referred to often in the literature, but now missing from the libraries of Udaipur.

93 'Āranyakāṇḍa' of the 'Rāmāyaṇa'

The Book of the Forest, the third book of the *Rāmāyaṇa*, which describes the life of the exiles in the forest and the abduction of Sītā by Rāvana, the demon-king of Lankā.

This volume was again commissioned by Jasvant, written by Hīrānanda and completed in 1708/1651 while Mahārāna Jagat Singh was reigning victoriously in Chittor in Mewar. This emotive usage of the old capital is not meant to imply either that Jagat Singh was living in Chittor, or that the manuscript was copied there. A similar usage in the colophon of the *Kiṣkindhākāṇḍa* (No.94) goes on to say that the work was in fact copied in Udaipur.

There are 36 paintings in the *Āranyakāṇḍa* in a style that is the same as that of Manohar, but possibly not actually by him. The paintings are at a consistently good level for this style, remarkably even in quality. They lack any of the ambitious compositions of the *Bālakāṇḍa*, the set pieces with the repetition of the chief characters; instead the artist is content to use standard divisions of architecture or landscape features to divide up the separate scenes of the composition, a river bank or a line of stones to divide his upper register from the lower one. These simple devices are remarkably successful. The palette is slightly more restricted than Manohar's and is far from the virulent palette noted by Barrett[1] as in the same hand as the *Uttarakāṇḍa* (No.97).

Rajasthan Oriental Research Institute, Udaipur.

Provenance: Royal Library, Udaipur.

ff.72; 23×39·5cm; paper, 9–15 lines of *Nāgarī* between margins ruled in red; 36 paintings, within red and yellow borders; unbound.

Bibliography: Brunel 1981, plates 12 and 13.

[1]Barrett and Gray 1963, p.138.

94 'Kiṣkindhākāṇḍa' of the 'Rāmāyaṇa'

The Book of Kiṣkindhā, the forest in which Rāma, searching for the abducted Sītā, encounters the monkeys and bears of the forest, intervenes in the quarrels of the monkey king and his brother, and persuades them to help in his search for Sītā.

This volume was completed in Udaipur by the same scribe Hīrānanda in 1710/1653, after the death of Jagat Singh which occurred towards the end of 1652. The new ruler, Rāj Singh, is mentioned in the colophon as ruling over Chittor in Mewar, and now a new commissioner is named, Vyāsa Jayadevajī. The new ruler seems to have put in a new head of the library. This is the latest of the six books of the *Rāmāyaṇa* with colophons, being finished some nine months after Jagat Singh's death. However, it is not likely the volume was an afterthought commissioned by Rāj Singh; it is intimately connected with the other volumes and must have been planned by Jagat Singh along with the others. There are however occasional pieces of evidence that the volume has not been properly finished – the absence of the passages usually written in red (the chapter colophons and the *daṇḍa* or punctuation marks), and of the double-lines above and below the text, while the paintings are not all in a uniform style.

93 Rāvana sends the golden deer to lure Rāma and Lakshmana away from Sītā.

The 34 paintings are for the most part in a totally different style from the work associated with the names of Sāhīb Dīn and Manohar and their schools. The artist employs a much broader brush with much less fine detail; figures are much larger; the composition usually depicts a single dramatic moment rather than a sequence of several events; the palette is different, purples, yellows and browns being very prominent, while the artist is particularly fond of a very dark ground against which to set his figures, as opposed to the red favoured by Sāhīb Dīn; the high horizon is often made of craggy peaks, and above it the blue sky is streaked with white clouds; and he often uses modelling. He starts his composition from the point of view of representing a dramatic happening, so that the key event is usually in the centre of a page. The total effect of this style is splendidly barbaric, as perhaps befits the subject-matter of the book. Rāma and Lakshmana are virtually the only humans to appear, the other characters being monkeys and other animals. It is difficult therefore to make valid stylistic judgements on the basis of physical appearance, while the deliberately barbaric architecture is not susceptible of comparison. Nonetheless, it is clear that the unnamed artist had a training in a Deccani style, as may be judged from his favourite colour schemes, details of trees and so on.[1] However considerable unevenness argues an atelier of artists rather than a single individual doing all the work.

A mixed Mewar–Deccan school first surfaces in a Ms. dated 1650 written in Aurangabad in the northern Deccan, one of the headquarters for the Mughal attack on the Deccani kingdoms of Bijapur and Golconda.[2] The Ms. was copied for a prince of one of the fiefdoms (*ṭhikānās*) owing allegiance to Udaipur. The Rajput chiefs were constantly in the Deccan engaged in the Mughal wars, and had plenty of opportunities to send home to Rajasthan Deccani artists and paintings. Indeed it is only by positing such an event for some Mewar nobles can the paintings of the *Kiṣkindhākāṇḍa* be accounted for. There are numerous resemblances to the 'Aurangabad' manuscript in details of architecture, landscape, plants, carpets, and so on. Of the 34 paintings, 30 are in this style; but of the remainder three are in a contemporary style akin to Manohar's, and one appears to be a later addition in a weak 18th-century Mewar style. Some text pages also appear on a different paper and in a different larger hand. The evidence suggests that the *Kiṣkindhākāṇḍa* was not in fact finished in 1653.

British Library, London, Add.15296(2).

Provenance: As No.92.

94 f.86. Hanumān passes through the demonic Surathā who obstructs his flight across the ocean.

ff.88; 23×39cm; thin brown paper, with some whiter folios, apparently later; 11–21 lines of *Nāgarī* with headings etc. in red, but some omitted entirely, between margins in three red lines; sometimes double red lines top and bottom; text area 13×28–19×33cm; 34 paintings, 22×38cm, within plain red or yellow borders with a thin white line; the three in the Manohar style have the usual red and yellow borders; bound in the same covers as *Ayodhyākāṇḍa* (No.92).

Bibliography: BM 1902, pp.30–32. Losty 1978, fig.2. Losty 1982 (f.14a in colour).

[1]See Welch 1973, No.75, from the pre-1600 Deccan *Rāgamālā*, set, for a very precise parallel in the rendering of trees.

[2]Doshi 1972. She identifies various other paintings which would appear to belong to this school, including those previously assigned to a 'Nagaur' school by S.C. Welch.

95 'Sundarakāṇḍa' of the 'Rāmāyaṇa'

The Beautiful Book, the fifth book of the *Rāmāyaṇa*, in which, with the aid of Hanuman and the monkeys, Rāma discovers that Sītā has been abducted by Rāvana, and her rescue is planned.

It is not clear whether the fifth book of the Jagat Singh *Rāmāyaṇa* was ever actually completed, or indeed begun, as no surviving Ms. has a relevant colophon. However, this volume of 18 pictures from a Ms. of the *Sundarakāṇḍa* may possibly represent some at least of Jagat Singh's *Sundarakāṇḍa*. Of the six books with colophons, that of the *Kiṣkindhā* is the latest, and it bears considerable evidence of not having been properly finished. The *Sundarakāṇḍa* might have been begun even later, but was allowed to lapse incomplete.

The 18 paintings of the *Sundarakāṇḍa* album are in a style that is basically a continuation of the *Kiṣkindhākāṇḍa* style, but since, in contrast to the latter book, there is a considerable amount of human representation, it is easier to see the album as an example of the mixed Mewar–Deccan style first seen in the 'Aurangabad' manuscript of 1650[1]. There are direct resemblances between the human figures in both in the characteristic shape of the head, while the long *jāma* of the Deccan (as opposed to the Mughal three-quarter length one) seen in the Aurangabad Ms. also occurs on the person of Vibhīshana in the *Sundarakāṇḍa*. There is also self-evident resemblance between the folios in which Rāma and Lakshmana are present, with their very individual garb and hair styles, and their appearance in the *Kiṣkindhākāṇḍa*,[2] while the very individualistic trees are common to both. Again there is considerable unevenness of quality between the paintings, arguing a number of hands. There seems little difficulty therefore in accepting this album as of the Mewar school, and of roughly comparable date to the Jagat Singh volumes, although probably slightly later than the main body of work, *i.e.* it is assignable to the early Rāj Singh period, 1652–65. The layout of the text is mostly very similar to the other volumes of the Jagat Singh set, with some variations which are also found in the other volumes, of size and margination, particularly in the *Kiṣkindhākāṇḍa*. However, the text shows many signs of never having been finished; like the *Kiṣkindhākāṇḍa* it is lacking in the red punctuation marks. The final folio, numbered originally 141, does in fact conclude the text of the *Kāṇḍa* in the northern recension of the epic which the Ms. follows. Only the first letter of the word *iti* (thus), the beginning of the colophon statement, has been written,

95 f.12b. The monkeys get drunk on the honey in Sugrīva's grove despite its guardian's remonstrations.

despite there being room for some more lines.

The text of the *Sundarakāṇḍa* is somewhat longer than that of the *Kiṣkindhākāṇḍa*, which in No.94 occupies 89 folios with 34 paintings. If this Ms. of the *Sundarakāṇḍa* had been finished (and there seems every reason to believe that the text portion at least was completely written, even if not properly finished off), then covering as it does 141 folios, there would have been very many more paintings, probably as many as a 100 in all, the rest of which have so far escaped discovery.

India Office Library, London, Skt. MS.3621.

ff.18 (out of 141); 24 × 39cm (ff.1 and 2, 24 × 37·5 and 24 × 36cm); paper; 14–18 lines of *Nāgarī* between margins ruled in three red lines, with some folios having double red lines at top and bottom of text, and with red lines at extreme edge of pages; 18 paintings on rectos, with text on versos; modern binding.

Bibliography: IOL 1935, No.6561. IOL 1981, No.509 [all 18 folios illustrated, ff.3 and 9 in colour]. Losty 1978, p.8. Thompson 1980, pp.43 and 47 (col. repro. of ff.13 and 3).

[1]Doshi 1972.
[2]Compares figs.2 and 3 in Losty 1978.

96 'Yuddhakāṇḍa' of the 'Rāmāyaṇa'

COLOUR PLATE XXXVII

The Book of the Battle, the sixth book of the *Rāmāyaṇa*. Rāma and his allies, the monkeys and bears, launch the attack on Lankā, Rāvana's citadel. After an immense battle, Rāma slays Rāvana in single combat, and returns with Sītā in triumph to Ayodhyā.

This book was finished in 1709/1652, two months before Jagat Singh's death,[1] again copied by Hīrānanda in Udaipur. No commissioner is named in the Ms.; however the colophon ends with the statement that Sāhībadī (*i.e.* Sāhīb ad-Dīn) painted the pictures, of which there are 88. In contrast to the attributions to Sāhīb Dīn in the 1648 *Bhāgavata Purāṇa* (No.90), which are in the form of notes underneath two pictures, the inference being that he was responsible for those alone, other artists painting the other paintings, here in the *Yuddhakāṇḍa* is the statement that he was responsible for them all, and it is by these works of his full maturity that Sāhīb Dīn must be judged as an artist. His complex compositional technique in building up his structure through the use of small groups is here tested to the full in scenes such as the attack on Lankā, which is a triumph of a sort never before seen in Rajput painting. The schematic view of the city, which the Rajput, indeed native Indian, viewpoint insisted on showing in full from above, is surrounded by a struggling mass of demons, monkeys, elephants and horses, rendered in a manner reminiscent of an Akbar-period historical painting.[2] And this level of achievement is maintained throughout the volume. Not all are as complex of course, but there is a continuous tension from picture to picture, that is something very new in Indian book-illustrations.

British Library, London, Add.15297(1).

Provenance: as No.92.

ff.206; 23 × 39cm; smooth brown paper; 9–19 lines of *Nāgarī* with colophons, *daṇḍas* etc. in red between margins ruled in three red lines, with two red lines at top and bottom; text area 15·5 × 29–18 × 32cm; 88 paintings within red and yellow borders, unbound originally, but now in European binding like No.92.

Bibliography: BM 1902, pp.30–32. Losty 1978. Losty 1982 (col. repro. of f.27a). Thompson 1980, pp.50–63 (col. repro. of ff.27a, 34a, 100a, 162a, 166a, 194a, and 203a).

[1]The widely quoted date of death of Jagat Singh, 10 April 1652, which occurs in Tod and later publications, seems mistaken on the evidence of this colophon, which is dated Saturday, *badi 6 Bhādrapada*, 1709, which falls in August, 1652, when Jagat Singh was still reigning according to the colophon. He actually died in October, 1652.
[2]See Thompson p.51 for colour reproduction.

97 'Uttarakāṇḍa' of the 'Rāmāyaṇa'

The Last Book of the epic, much of it being a later addition recounting the origin of Rāvana and explaining much that was unclear in the earlier books, and Rāma's enforced repudiation of Sītā, the birth of their sons, and eventual reconciliation.

This book was completed in 1710/1653, in Udaipur, in Rāj Singh's reign, by Hīrānanda, the Ms. being commissioned, like the *Kiṣkindhākāṇḍa*, by Vyāsa Jayadeva. It is the most heavily illustrated of the six completed books, with 92 paintings, in a virulent palette which has called down Douglas Barrett's wrath[1]. In the last few paintings the quality of the draughtsmanship deteriorates rapidly. One suspects that the artist thought that with a new, perhaps uninterested, ruler, if he did not finish it quickly, he would not be able to do so at all. However, the majority of the paintings are in a competent and decorative hand, in the tradition of Manohar, but again almost certainly not by him. The palette indeed rules this out, with its heavy use of bright pinks and purples. The *Rāgamālā* from Mewar *c.*1650 in the National Museum, New Delhi, is probably by this artist[2].

British Library, London, Add.15297(2).

Provenance: as No.92.

ff.114 (numbered 1–112, with two folios unnumbered having just paintings on one side and no text); 23 × 39cm; light-brown paper; several pages of text have blank rectos; 7–24 lines of *Nāgarī*, occasional diamond patterns in centre; headings, colophons etc. in red; between margins ruled in three red lines, lacking all upper and lower lines; text area 11·5 × 28–19 × 32·5cm; 92 paintings, within yellow and red borders, generally with blank paper surrounds, size of paintings 21 × 31–21·5 × 35cm; unbound originally, now in European binding.

Bibliography: BM 1902, pp.30–32.

[1]Barrett and Gray 1963, p.138.
[2]Pramod Chandra 1957.

97 f.70. Rāma and Sītā enjoy their last untroubled moments together.

98 f.210. The wedding night of Rāma and Sītā and his brothers and her cousins.

98 'Bālakāṇḍa' of the 'Rāmāyaṇa'

The first book of the Sanskrit epic (see No.91).

This huge copy of the *Bālakāṇḍa* copied in Udaipur in 1769/1712 is one of the better products of the early Sangrām Singh II (1710–38) period. In style it is consciously archaic as it makes no attempt to use the landscape techniques seen in contemporary Udaipur court painting, but conforms to Sāhīb Dīn's landscape style. However there have been some developments since the mid-17th century. The size of the figures relative to that of the page has been increased, a trend first brought to Mewar painting by the artist of the *Kiṣkindhākāṇḍa* (No.94), whose love of dark backgrounds has also filtered through into this new style. A new feature is the use of a great deal of white, in architecture, grounds and other quite large areas, an innovation in the Amar Singh paintings, and altogether a much lighter, colder palette than in the Jagat Singh period.[1] Most noticeable however is a sharpness of line and a heaviness of modelling which, together with the coldness of the palette, impart a hardness to the paintings.

British Library, London, Add.15295.

Provenance: as No.92.

ff.212; 21·5×38cm; paper; mostly 2–6, occasionally 15 or 16, lines of *Nāgarī* within margins ruled in red; 201 paintings, in red and yellow frames; unbound originally, now inlaid in frames and between handsome European covers.

Bibliography: BM 1902, pp.31–2. Thompson 1980, pp.6–17 (col. repro. of folios 57a, 58a, 72a, 80a, 183a, 199a).

[1]Topsfield 1980, p.10, for a discussion of this period of Mewar paintings.

99 'Madhumālatīvārtā'

The story of Madhumālatī, by the Rajasthani poet Caturbhuj Dās, in a miscellany with four other Rajasthani poems.

The works were copied between 1829–32/1772–5, by Bhat Harirāma at Madhakaragarh, for Luhār Dhanajī. These names are not known from other sources. There are 88 illustrations, the majority (53) illustrating the *Madhumālatīvārtā*, with the rest divided between the next three items; there are besides some 32 outline drawings, 11 of them apparently doodlings between two of the texts, involving elephants, horses and camels. The paintings are in the style of south-eastern Rajasthan, of Mewar, but Madhakargarh has so far eluded precise identification.

The paintings are by three different artists, the first of whom has contributed the first 63 in the first two texts in a simplified Mewar idiom, in a bright palette of pinks and reds. The second artist who contributed the 23 paintings in the third text, has a much darker palette favouring browns and yellows. The third artist has contributed just two paintings at the beginning of the fourth poem, but in the style more of Bundi than of Mewar. These two paintings are in fact on separate pieces of paper which have been stuck into the manuscript. The remainder of the fourth poem contains 21 sketch-drawings likewise on separate paper and stuck in.

The Ms. is sewn in a single section, with 235 very wide sheets of paper, which have been folded in two and sewn. Stiff card protects the central pages from the friction of the cord, while 16 sheets at the bottom of the pile have been left blank to protect the text pages from the binding. The latter is a piece of leather, with two extra pieces sewn on at the back to make up the width. To protect the text, the cover protrudes slightly at top and bottom, and is bent round in a flap to cover the bulge in the front caused by all the sheets being the same size.

British Library, London, Or.13682.

ff.470 in all with numerous blanks, ff.411 with text or painting; each folio (*i.e.* half-sheet) 12×13cm; paper; 11–12 lines of *Nāgarī*, between margins ruled with two red lines, text area 9×8·5cm; outer edge of each page marked with a red line; headings, colophons, *daṇḍas* etc. in red; 88 paintings of varying sizes, many full page, others within the margins and of varying height; 32 sketches in red; leather cover, with flap, 41cm wide in all, and 14cm high.

Bibliography: Unpublished.

99 ff.219b, 220. A prince and his horse at the centre of a Ms. sewn in a single section.

100 'Rāgamālā'

Illustrated on p.107.

A set of paintings with descriptive Hindi verses illustrative of the musical modes of Indian music. The text used is an anonymous Hindi set of 36 quatrains in *caupaī* form, which according to Ebeling first appears about 1700 in Malwa and Bundelkhand.[1]

There are numerous sets of this type known, all closely related to one another, suggesting a flourishing studio.[2] The main features of the style are small, elegant figures, somewhat elongated, dwarfed by a three-storeyed architectural backdrop behind, all in white. There are only two known colophons, however, the one without provenance dated 1824/1767, the other dated 1822/1765 from Ranthambhor, the latter with the same kind of architecture but with human figures drawn in a more folky way. The set is obviously a provincial version of the style of a metropolitan centre. The great fortress of Ranthambhor, the guardian of Rajasthan, was at this period on the south-east frontier of the Amber/Jaipur state, having been wrested from the Mughals in the late 17th century, and it has been suggested that these *Rāgamālā* sets are actually from Jaipur *c.*1750[3]. However, no similar Jaipuri work of the period is known.

British Library, London, Or.2821.

ff.34 (out of 36); 30 × 21cm; card with red borders; text and painting in frame of silver, red and white, 25 × 18cm, with text of 5–6 lines *Nāgarī* in black on yellow in panel above, about 4 × 18cm, with paintings (about 21 × 18cm) protruding into it; on modern guards, in a 19th-century binding of red leather with stamped medallions etc. in gold.

Bibliography: BM 1899, Hindi, p.62. Gangoly 1935 (reproductions of 27 paintings). Ebeling 1973, pp.190–1. Prakash 1960 (col. repro. of a very similar set).

[1]Ebeling 1973, pp.142–6.
[2]*ibid.*, pp.94–100, and 190–1.
[3]Andhare 1972.

101 'Hitopadeśa'

COLOUR PLATE XXXVI

The Book of Good Counsel, an ancient book of Indian fables, in an anonymous Rajasthani version. The *Hitopadeśa* is a set of fables in four books, told by a sage to a king's sons to teach them wisdom and polity, and is a recast, arranged towards the end of the first millennium AD, by one Nārāyana, of the much earlier *Pañcatantra*, the Five Books. It is this latter work which was translated into Pahlavi, Syriac, Arabic and the languages of Europe, under the title of Kalila and Dimnah, the names of the two jackals who narrate the frame story of Book I (Karataka and Damantaka in the Sanskrit original). The Arabic version of ʿAbd Allāh ibn al-Muqaffaʿ of *c.*AD 750 formed the basis of Nasr Allāh's Persian version of *c.*1145. This was extensively rewritten in a more elaborate style by Husayn Vāʿiz Kāshifī under the title of *Anvār-i Suhaylī* (the Lights of Canopus) and this version returned to India in the 16th century where it proved very popular. Numerous Indian illustrated manuscripts of the *Anvār-i Suhaylī* survive from 1570 onwards (see Nos.49, 57, 75, 84). The original Sanskrit versions, *Pañcatantra* and its offshoot *Hitopadeśa*, are much less frequently found in illustrated versions.

This Rajasthani version was copied in *Nāgarī* script by the Brahman Ciramjī Rājarāma from Banhatā (near Tonk) in 1818/1761–2 at the behest of Kanvar Jasvant Singh, son of Rao Rāja Sardar Singh of Uniara (r.1740–77). Jasvant Singh in 1762 was still a boy; he is depicted as such with his father Sardar Singh in two formal court portraits at the end of the volume, where he appears to be about 12 to 14 years old. He is also depicted with his father in an earlier manuscript dated 1759 of the *Bhāgavata Purāṇa* in the Uniara State Collection where he appears to be about 10, but in this case the manuscript was commissioned by his father[1]. It is doubtless a charming gesture on his father's part that the young prince should have been allowed the use of the royal studio for the production of this book of animal fables, which is couched in the form of moral and political instruction for young princes.

There are 132 illustrations, mostly disposed in horizontal bands across the middle of the page; the artist is named in the colophon as Dhano from Bundi. The miniatures are in a charming style typical of Uniara painting, which at this stage is an offshoot of the Bundi style. Dhano's work reveals him not as a great master but as a competent journeyman, occasionally inspired, particularly in the illustrations to the animal stories. His illustration to the beginning of the frame story of Book II, for example, shows his adroit welding together of animal principals with a charming landscape, here populated by monkeys (f.28b).

The format is of sheets of country paper, only slightly burnished, folded and sewn with a thick cord in a single section. Limp covers were also sewn on at the same time, a flexible layer of papers pasted together, here covered with dark-brown leather with blind tooling in a rough pattern. Leather is but rarely employed in Hindu manuscripts, but was used not infrequently on 18th-century manuscripts from Rajasthani courts in imitation of Persian manuscripts. Here the similarity is continued by the use of a flap (*jihvā* or tongue), which is usually left resting on the top cover, rather than under it as in a Muslim binding.

British Library, London, Or.13934.

ff.78; country paper; 34 × 24·5cm; 24 lines of *Nāgarī* between margins painted in yellow; text area 28 × 18cm; 130 paintings, in horizontal format across centre of page, about 18 × 8·5–13cm; with two full-page court portraits; sewn in single section; thin card binding covered with brown leather with flap, blind tooled, sewn with rest of Ms.

Bibliography: BL 1979–80, p.23 (colour repro. of f.16a).

[1]Beach 1974, fig.48.

102 f.7. *Vibhāsā rāgiṇī*, two lovers awakened at dawn.

102 The Laud 'Rāgamālā'

An album of Indian paintings and of calligraphic panels, presented by Archbishop Laud to the Bodleian Library, Oxford, in 1639. All its contents and its binding are thus earlier than this date, but how it found its way into the Laud collection is unknown. The album consists of 30 paintings, of which 18 form a distinct set, part of a *Rāgamālā* cycle, with inscriptions in a heavy *Nastaʿlīq* hand identifying the *rāga* on each painting, which are of Deccani origin, *c.*1600–20. The other 12 paintings are of various sizes and subjects – birds, portraits, etc. – and are mostly in a provincial or popular Mughal style. All the paintings and calligraphy are mounted in frames of various coloured papers and set in mounts of different colours, usually plain. Some of the calligraphy is on marbled paper of great beauty; some of the borders are of paper with gold designs, while others appear to have been decorated in a process akin to the Batik technique with animals and birds in soft outlines in natural colour on a ground of soft pink. The album is of the greatest importance for various reasons. Its early date, as proven by its 1639 entry into the Bodleian, makes it one of the earliest specimens of Indian art to reach Europe. Unlike other albums of this date, it reflects the taste not of the Emperor or members of his family but of a provincial nobleman or aesthete. Its simplicity renders it a charming survival of the times, and provides valuable evidence that patrons other than the grandest in the land were discerning collectors who were able to put together the same sort of *muraqqaʿ* as their grander compatriots.

Bodleian Library, Oxford, MS. Laud. Or.149.

ff.65, numbered 1–67, with three omitted (21–3) and two counted twice (5); album leaves measure 37·5×24·5cm; 30 paintings, and 100 specimens of calligraphy; the 18 *Rāgamālā* paintings measure 15×10·5cm; contemporary binding of dark-brown morocco with stamped medallions, pendants and corner pieces, and plain doublures, with flap.

Bibliography: Bod. 1889, No.1900. Stooke and Khandalavala 1953.

103 'Qaṣīdah' of Nusratī

Illustrated on p.109.

A panegyric in Dakhni Urdu in praise of ʿAbdallāh Qutb Shāh of Golconda (1626–72) by Mulla Nusratī, copied by ʿAlī ibn Naqī al-Husaynī Damghānī.

Nusratī was the favourite poet of ʿAlī ʿĀdil Shāh II of Bijapur (1656–72) for whom he composed numerous works in Dakhni Urdu, including an account of his reign, the *ʿAlīnāma*. This poem, however, is in praise of the Sultan of Golconda, so that we must suppose it to have been composed perhaps as a royal present from Bijapur to Golconda; it is unlikely to have originated from Golconda itself, as although Golconda is renowned for its sumptuous illumination during the 17th century, it does tend to follow a basically Iranian format.

The text is written in large *Riqāʿ* and smaller *Naskhī* in a central panel, while the margins are illuminated alternately with arabesque or geometric patterns and large stylized plants. The plants are not the delicately naturalistic ones to be seen in Mughal album borders, but massively drawn and painted stylized flowers scarcely identifiable, and sombrely coloured with gold outlining; the effect like that of the arabesque pages is rich and overpowering. A similar effect is achieved by what little Bijapuri painting from the 17th century remains on site, as in the wall paintings of the Ashraf Mahal and the decorations of the *mihrāb* in the Jāmī Masjid. This latter is recalled by the other pages of illumination, where rich colours clash, pinks and chocolates and mauve, and in their sombre tones overwhelm even the massive use of gold.

The Ms. opens with two facing *shamsas* with twelve lobes, with twining gold arabesques between which the panels are filled in in the beloved Deccani colour combinations (ff.5b, 6a). The *sarlavḥ* on f.6b is unusual for its use of massive peonies in pink, brown, purple and blue. Every portion of this opening is decorated with gold colours in a rich diamond patterning, a lavish effect found on other pages including the colophon pages in rich pinks and browns.

British Library, London, Or.13533.

ff.33 (text ff.5b–29b); 28·5 × 15cm; paper, pale biscuit; panels of text (15·75 × 9·5cm) in nine lines, lines 1, 5 and 9 in large *Riqā'* with small *Naskhī* in two columns in between, set in clouds against gold and with gold arabesques; two opening poly-lobed *shamsas*, and a *sarlavḥ*; all margins richly illuminated; 19th-century binding, removed; the folios are kept under glass.

Bibliography: BM 1976, p.95, where the Ms. is attributed to Golconda.

104 'Rasikapriyā'

Illustrated on p.108.

The Hindi treatise of Keshavadāsa on the erotic sentiment in poetical composition and the classification of heroes and heroines of poetry. The work was completed in 1591 at the court of the Rāja of Orccha.

The manuscript was copied in Gorakhpur for Muhammad Nāsir called Abu'l Fazl, son of Shaikh Dā'ūd Ghorī in 1077/1666, in the *Nasta'līq* script and is illustrated with 24 paintings in a Popular Mughal style. The work was done for a Muslim patron, and so needed to be in a style derived from the Mughal, but as the artist was apparently a Hindu he combined with it characteristics that are associated with Rajput painting – the flat treatment of architecture, the drawing of the figures, and so on. The female type, which is tall and slender with a small head, and small eyes, wears a bodice and skirt with a non-transparent *oṛhnī* wrapped round the skirt and up round the head, and resembles the 'Malwa' type of about 1680. It is not a style that can at present be associated with a particular school. Although the large town of Gorakhpur in eastern Uttar Pradesh is not known as a centre of painting, there is no reason to suppose that this manuscript could not have been done there, as other places of the same name in India are in no more promising locations.

We know nothing about its patron, as he is not included in the standard biographical dictionaries of the period, so that he is probably a local man of no great fame. The work done for him in this Ms. is less dependent on Popular Mughal sources and has developed along lines, particularly in the lofty architecture, which are seen in the so-called 'Central Indian' group of *Rāgamālās* and which are now generally attributed to Amber/Jaipur (No.100). The existence of this type of architecture in painting dated as early as 1666 may occasion a reassessment of this attribution.

Christ's College, Cambridge, MS. Dd.5.9.

Provenance: Presented by John Hutton in 1862.

ff.79; 27 × 18·6cm; paper; 15 lines of *Nasta'līq* in panels 18·5 × 11cm, with margins ruled in gold and colours; 24 miniatures, almost full-page; cover of plain red morocco with stamped medallion, corner pieces and infill panels with arabesques and inscriptions.

Bibliography: Cambridge 1922. Moti Chandra and Gupta 1965.

105 'Khāvarnāma'

Illustrated on p.108.

A Persian poem in epic metre by Maulānā Muhammad ibn Husam ad-Dīn, known as ibn Husam (d.875/1470–71). It relates the fantastic adventures of 'Alī, the Prophet's son-in-law, with his companions, and his battles against various heathen kings principally the Shāh-i Khāvarān, whence the title of the work, and dragons and demons.

This Ms. of the work was copied by the scribe Mūlchand Multānī in 1097/1686, with 156 miniatures by the artist, 'Abd al-Hakīm Multānī. It is laid out on a grand scale, with pictures befitting its heroic subject-matter, in a style of marked peculiarity for the period. There can be little doubt that the Ms. was produced in the city of Multan in the Panjab – both scribe and artist are Multanis, and there is a close architectural resemblance between the buildings of that city, particularly the tombs of the Suhrawardi Shaikhs, and those depicted in the Ms. These famous domed octagonal tombs made of brick and covered with polychrome tilework, recur again and again in the paintings.

The paintings reveal numerous archaic features, indicating the existence of a vigorous pre-Mughal style in this area which Mughal painting did little to change. Examples are the high circular horizons, plain gold grounds, and the rock formations, all of them derived ultimately from 15th-century Persian painting via some Sultanate school. The artist also had a knowledge of antique Persian dress, of Mongol headgear, and of the Chaghtai headdress worn by high-born Mughal ladies; his tents are of the archaic circular type with domed tops and his boats have high prow and stern with animal heads, both features of Akbari manuscripts. His men are usually dressed in long gowns with bulbous turbans (with some Safavid baton turbans) with a small tail on top and a piece hanging down the back, although some wear contemporary costume; women usually wear long gowns with sometimes a shorter tunic over the top, with a girdle with very long ends which they like to wave about, or sometimes a long scarf wrapped around the body. His palette is a brilliant one of primary colours and his draughtsmanship is crude, but these features are redeemed by an immense vitality and originality that is very rare among late 17th- and 18th-century manuscripts done for provincial Muslim patrons. The lavish use of gold and silver (the latter still mostly untarnished) creates an effect of the greatest richness.

The patron for whom this was done is unknown, the original name having been replaced by one Kamāl ad-Dīn Khān at a later date. A pair of splendid painted and lacquered covers depicting hunting and animal scenes, probably from the Deccan, were added to the Ms. about 1760, at which time the edges of the leaves were also decorated with floral patterns. It seems to have found its way into the library of Tipū Sultān at Seringapatam, whence it was removed after the fall of that city to Arthur Wellesley in 1799.

At least two other lavishly illustrated Mss. of this text in the same style survive, one in the India Office Library (Ethe 897), and the other in the Buhar Library in Calcutta (Catalogue No.328). Neither is dated or signed, but they are obviously from the same school as Add.19766, and appear to be slightly inferior copies from this Ms.

British Library, London, Add.19766.

ff.362; 35 × 27cm; creamy paper, burnished; *Nasta'līq* script in four columns between margins decorated in gold; text panels 24 × 16·75cm with margins in gold and colours, two *'unvāns* in gold and colours with floral arabesques; 157 paintings, mostly T-shaped, about 23cm wide, occasionally utilizing the upper and lower margins as well; covers depicting animals and hunting scenes, surrounded by margins with aquatic animals in basket-pattern water, painted and lacquered; original leather spine decorated with floral arabesques, continued round edges of leaves – doublures of red leather with painted medallion and margin.

Bibliography: BM 1879, p.642. BL 1977, pp.64–7. Titley 1979, fig.11 (f.81a in colour).

106 'Kārnāma-i 'Ishq'

Illustrated on p.110.

The Book of Affairs of Love, a romance in Persian, by Rāi Ānand Rām, called Mukhlis. The author was a Hindu, the son of Rāja Mardī Rām, a Khatrī of Lahore; in 1132/1719–20 he obtained an official position as Vākīl of Itimad ad-Daula Qamar ad-Dīn Khān, the Vizier of Muhammad Shāh (1719–48), with the title of Rāi Rāyān, but afterwards retired from office. He died in Delhi in 1164/1750–1. He wrote several works in Persian and Urdu, including a *Dīvān* of poems and a history of the invasion of Nādir Shāh, in 1739, of which he was an eye-witness.[1] His

Kārnāma-i ʿIshq, which seems hitherto to have escaped literary notice, is a romantic fairy-story of the type beloved of Indian writers, in which a young prince, Gauhar, becomes enamoured of a lady who has been changed into a gazelle, and after encounters with fairies and surviving numerous perilous adventures, he is eventually united with her in her original form. The work was composed in 1731 and dedicated to the Emperor Muhammad Shāh, and this Ms. appears to be the dedication copy. It was copied by one Harko Laʿl in 1148/1735 but a note on the flyleaf signed by the author and dated 1151/1738–9 records that the artist Govardhan took five years to complete the miniatures. This artist appears to have been one of the leaders of the Mughal school at the period, with both attributed work and work in his style now known.[2] There are 37 miniatures, of which the first is a double-portrait of the Emperor Muhammad Shāh with his vizier Qamar ad-Dīn (f.7b), while the remainder illustrate the text. They are splendid examples of the best Delhi style of the period, which is usually found in isolated court scenes rather than in manuscripts.[3] Govardhan's work has the sureness of technique of the best 17th-century work, but a hardness of line and an icy stiffness and formality that is divorced from the much softer technique of the previous century. The cool palette of greys and greens combined with splashes of brilliant colour is typical of the Muhammad Shāh style.

India Office Library, London, Johnson Album 38.

Provenance: Richard Johnson Collection, acquired in 1807.

ff.123; 39·5 × 25cm; fine creamy paper; 13 lines of *Nastaʿlīq* in panels 22 × 13cm with margins ruled in gold; fine *sarlavḥ*, very tall, mostly gold with floral arabesques; 37 miniatures, some full-page, but usually size of text panels; Indian covers.

Bibliography: IOL 1981, p.313.

[1]BM 1876, p.997; Garcin de Tassy 1870–1, p.376; Elliot and Dowson, VIII, p.76.
[2]IOL 1981, pp.109–111.
[3]See for example Welch 1978, plate 39.

107 ff.689b, 690. Shāh Jahān on the Peacock Throne being offered pearls during an entertainment.

107 'Pādshāhnāma'

The History of the Emperor (Shāh Jahān) by Muhammad ʿAmīn Qazvīnī (see No.82).

In 1815, the 'King of Delhi', *i.e.* Akbar II, presented to J.T. Roberdean, acting judge and magistrate of Allahabad, two volumes containing the history of Shāh Jahān, the first being the work of Muhammad ʿAmīn on the first ten years, the second[1] being that of Muhammad Salīh Kanbū from the 11th year of the reign to the death of the deposed Emperor (see No.137). They are splendidly illuminated in the style of Delhi about 1800.

No attempt was made in these or similar Mss. to match the scale and number of illustrations in the *Pādshāhnāma* of 1657 (No.82) – there are 44 in the Windsor Ms. and at least 11 more in other collections, all of them of superb quality, whereas the later Mss. have a maximum of 30 paintings of much smaller scale and achievement.[2] They give the impression of being worked to a rigid formula and it may be assumed they were. Numerous paintings in the different manuscripts are of the same scenes, including in particular paintings of the great architectural monuments built by Shāh Jahān – the Tāj Mahāl, the Red Fort in Delhi and its white marble buildings, the Delhi Jāmī Masjid etc. Whatever was the original of this stereotype, it does not appear to be the imperial Ms., which contains no scene precisely similar to these, nor does it contain any paintings of the architecture of Shāh Jahān's reign. By 1776 it had in any case left Delhi for Lucknow. The conclusion is inescapable that they were all produced as presents for the Europeans, who were fascinated by the pomp and state of the former Mughals and by their buildings, which in the early 19th century were being widely painted by both British and Indian artists. The later Mss. of this type even have figures of Europeans admiring the buildings (No.137).

British Library, London, Add.20734.

Provenance: Earl of Munster Collection, acquired 1855.

ff.445; 39·5 × 23cm; creamy paper; 15 lines *Nastaʿlīq* in panels 26·5 × 14·5cm, with margins ruled in gold and colours; one *ʿunvān*; four single-page and five double-page miniatures, of about same size as text panels, all with border illuminations; sumptuous 19th-century European binding.

Bibliography: BM 1879, p.259. BL 1977, p.125.

[1]British Library Add. 20735.
[2]The paintings in a Ms. of the *Pādshāhnāma* in the Khuda Baksh Library have been published in full – see OPLB 1920.

108 'Bāburnāma'

Memoirs of Bābur (see No.62).

This manuscript would appear to be a composite, made up around the remnants of a manuscript of this text of the 1590s. The Persian translation used is that of ʿAbd ar-Rahīm Khānkhānān, which was not completed until 1589. The clearly expressed date of this manuscript, 937/1530, the year of Bābur's death, must therefore be a deliberate forgery, as is the addition of a page of imperial Mughal seals at the beginning including one of Humāyūn's dated 934/1527. However, some of the remaining 19 paintings as well as part of the text are original, the rest of the text being written by the scribe ʿAlī al-Kātib in imitation of the usual large *Nastaʿlīq* found in *Bāburnāma* Mss.

The original Mughal paintings are not very distinguished examples of the 1590s, whereas a few of the added paintings are splendid examples of Delhi work about 1800, including a wonderfully anachronistic one of Bābur in 1526 visiting the sights of Delhi including the tomb of Nizammudīn, which is shown to be the splendid marble affair erected by Shāh Jahān in the mid-17th century! After its arrival in Alwar, the manuscript was remargined throughout with marbled paper borders in greens, browns and blues, and finely rebound by ʿAbd ar-Rahmān.

Government Museum, Alwar.

ff.458; 31 × 20cm; paper of text panels light beige, and gold sprinkled; 12 lines of large *Nastaʿlīq* in panels *c.*20 × 13cm with margins ruled in gold and colours; borders all of marbled paper, 19th century; 19 miniatures; double-page *ʿunvān*, with panels of illumination in text at end, all *c.*1800; Alwar binding, covers stamped and gilded, doublures red leather with stamped gold medallions.

Bibliography: Alwar 1961, p.98. MIC, pp.95–6.

109 'Qurʾān'

Illustrated on p.112.

The Holy Koran.

This unascribed manuscript was purchased by Mahārāja Rao Vinay Singh of Alwar (1815–57) from a passing Muslim for the sum of Rs3,000 and a dress of honour, and is one of the most sumptuous of all 19th-century copies of the Koran. Every page bears the most elaborate border decorations in alternate dark and light blue panels within gold arabesques. The place of production is not noted but was probably Delhi. The Ms. was bound in Alwar by ʿAbd ar-Rahmān.

Government Museum, Alwar, MS.784.

ff.472; 30 × 18cm; paper; 12 lines of *Naskhī*, dark blue with white shading, on gold, surrounded by arabesques within panels with broad gold margins; sublinear Persian translation in red *Nastaʿlīq*; chapter headings in light-blue *Thuluth* repeated at top of each text panel; commentary written in minute letters diagonally around main text panel; outer wide border of illumination on every page; covers stamped and painted in gold and blue with marginal cartouches.

Bibliography: Hendley 1888, plate LXXI. Alwar 1961, pp.97–8.

110 f.4. *Śrī rāga*, the hero walking with his beloved. By Bahādur Singh.

110 'Rāgamālā'

Six paintings mounted in an album depicting *rāgas* and *rāgiṇīs*, with descriptive verses in *Braj-bhāṣā* Hindi by Pyāre Rangalāla, who is possibly to be identified with the court poet of the same name of Surajmall of Bharatpur, who flourished about 1754.

The verses of the six *rāgas* are somewhat different in conception from other *Rāgamālā* sets, and hence needed a different iconography for the paintings. All six of the paintings are attributed, to Sītal Dās, Girdhāri Laʿl, and Bahādur Singh, in neat *Nastaʿlīq* at the bottom of the pictures. Another Persian inscription in the top margin identifies the *rāga* subjects, which are of course identified in the Hindi verses. The paintings are conceived as a single unit with their elaborately decorated margins, instead of being laid into a mount as was usually the case.

The work of all three artists is in the standard Lucknow manner of the late 18th century, and probably dates from about 1780. Bahādur Singh seems the most animated of the three in this by then somewhat lifeless school.

These six paintings, and another two in the Bodleian Library (in Album Or.b.2), are all that remain of a highly-finished set, of which the complete preliminary drawings are in the India Office Library (Johnson Album 44), probably commissioned by Richard Johnson in Lucknow in 1780–82.[1] Sītal Dās did work for Johnson in these years[2] and Bahādur Singh is a well-known artist of the period.

British Library, London, Add.21934.

Provenance: ex-Dr Solander's collection; acquired from I.R. Isaac in 1857.

ff.6; 25 × 17cm; paper; text in black *Nāgarī* on a gold ground in four lines in panels 5 × 13cm above the paintings; surrounded by gold margins with floral decoration; bound in a European-style album.

Bibliography: BM 1899, Hindi, 95. Gangoly 1934–5, who reproduces all six pages.

[1] IOL 1981, No.351.
[2] *ibid.*, p.136.

111 Album of Hāfiz Rahmat Khān

Illustrated on p.110.

An album of paintings and calligraphy assembled probably in the third quarter of the 18th century, perhaps in Lucknow, but more likely in the library of the Rohilla chief Hāfiz Rahmat Khān, from whose library in Bareilly it was taken, according to a note on the flyleaf, after the attack on the Rohillas by the forces of the East India Company and the Nawab of Oudh in 1774.

The 31 paintings are mostly of the Lucknow style *c.*1750–70, with examples of earlier Mughal work, as well as two fine Lucknow copies of a Mughal painting of the early Akbar period showing Humāyūn in a camp, and of Akbar in darbar about 1600. The covers are splendid examples of Lucknow work of the 1760s, boards painted with hunting scenes in a fairy landscape in gold, and lacquered.

British Museum, London, 1974,6-17,010 (formerly Add.22470).

ff.32; 38 × 28cm; stiffened paper; 31 paintings and 33 calligraphic specimens mounted in frames; pasteboard covers, painted and lacquered.

Bibliography: BM 1876, p.785. BL 1977, p.16.

112 'Dastūr-i Himmat'

Illustrated on p.111.

The Model of Resolution, a poetical version of the story of Kāmarūpa and Kāmalatā, written in 1685 by Muhammad Murād, who named it after his patron, Himmat Khān Mīr ʿĪsā, one of Aurangzīb's officials, who died in Ajmer in 1681.

The story concerns a prince of Oudh, Kāmarūpa, and a princess of Serendip (Ceylon), Kāmalatā, who simultaneously dream of each other and fall passionately in love. Kāmarūpa sets out to find his beloved, and after many adventures including shipwreck, finds Ceylon and his princess, who chooses him as her husband in a *svayaṃvara* organized by her father.

The Ms. is undated, but on the evidence of its illustrations can be assigned to Murshidabad about 1760. There are 209 in all, of which 23 are full-page. Many

114 Inside cover. Dancing devotees of Krishna.

of them are of ambitious scope for this period of manuscript-illustration with compositions in depth. Palace scenes with activities in foreground and background, viewed from the traditional aerial viewpoint, and with fairly rigid lines of perspective, are a feature of individual paintings of the period but are rarely seen in manuscripts. Also of great interest are some ambitious attempts at foreshortening, as when an army of horsemen is viewed head on from above, and depictions of ships and shipwreck.

The Ms. is of the richest appearance, with every page decorated lavishly with gold and brilliant colouring. The appearance of Prince Kāmarūpa might be taken as a flattering portrait of Sirāj ad-Daula (1756–7) whose beauty was famed throughout Bengal.[1] The attendant figures, however, have a tendency towards dumpiness which appears to be a stylistic trait of a slightly later period, *c.*1760. However, we need not hesitate to regard the Ms. as a royal Murshidabad creation of *c.*1755–65.

Chester Beatty Library, Dublin, Ind. MS.12.

ff.197; 33 × 20·3cm; paper, pale-cream in colour; 17 lines of *Nastaʿlīq* in two columns in panels 25·5 × 12cm with margins ruled in gold and colours; text in white clouds against gold; one *sarlavḥ*; 209 miniatures, of which 23 are full-page, and the others smaller than the text panels, while some are tailpieces with animals and plants; original covers of papier-mâché, painted and lacquered, with lattice design filled with flowers.

Bibliography: CB 1936, pp.63–71.

[1]Skelton 1956.

113 'Razmnāma'

Illustrated on p.111.

The Book of Wars, the Persian translation by Nakīb Khān and others, of the Sanskrit epic *Mahābhārata* (see No.88).

Akbar's desire that the mutual understanding he hoped for between Muslims and Hindus could be brought about by their knowing each other's sacred books did not alas come to fruition in the intolerance practiced by his successors. However, the chief monument to Akbar's hopes, the *Razmnāma*, was still often copied in the next two centuries, though seldom illustrated. This copy is in three uniform volumes, and is dated Moradabad 1175–7/1761–3. It was copied for one Rae Bahādur Singh, by Muhammad Khān, an Afghan Shirvānī from Thatta, and has 134 illustrations all painted on card with floral margins and bound in. They are numbered in large Roman numerals.

Moradabad lies 100 miles east of Delhi and was founded about 1625 and named after Murād Baksh, one of the sons of Shāh Jahān. From 1740 it was part of the Rohilla dominions, under the control of the Rohilla chief Hāfiz Rahmat, who kept a well-stocked library in Bareilly. However, Moradabad is not known as a centre of painting.

By 1775, the volumes had found their way into the collection of Sir Elijah Impey in Calcutta, whose Persian seal with this date is found on the volumes. This strongly suggests that like No.111 they were in Hāfiz Rahmat's library at the time of the attack on the Rohillas in 1774 by the combined forces of the East India Company and Shūjaʿ ad-Daula, Nawab of Oudh. Impey was a patron of artists working in the Murshidabad style as well as of Company artists in Calcutta. The style of these illustrations strongly suggests that Impey had Murshidabad artists prepare a set and then had them bound in. They are mostly undistinguished work of the period about 1780, when court patronage was largely dead and artists were glad of any work they could get, but towards the end a much more competent painter has contributed work of great loveliness, distinguished particularly by the prominence given to trees in compositions, whether singly or in lovely groups. Late Murshidabad work utilizes various Hindu stylizations for architecture and landscape, in a way foreign to the Lucknow school, although this is not surprising in a work like the *Razmnāma*, where the subjects of the paintings are based on earlier models. A striking feature of the Ms. is the return to a landscape format for many of the pictures, first seen among Persian manuscripts in Akbar's copy of the *Razmnāma* prepared 200 years previously, in which the book has to be turned through 90 degrees to look at the picture. This of course was the traditional shape of Hindu manuscript paintings of Akbar's time; its re-emergence here suggests an as yet unknown tradition of *Razmnāma* illustration going back directly to the archetype.

British Library, London, Add.5638–40.

Provenance: Elijah Impey, then N.B. Halhed, from whom they were purchased in 1795–6.

ff.413, 371, and 440; 40 × 25cm; good glazed paper; 22 lines large *Nastaʿlīq* in panels 30·5 × 14cm with margins ruled in red and black; 134 paintings on paper, laid in frames of heavily painted card and bound in European covers.

Bibliography: BM 1879, pp.57–8. BL 1977, pp.130–34.

114 Pair of manuscript covers

The text of the Ms. which these covers enclosed is not known, but is said to have

116 f.2b. Krishna lifts Mount Govardhan.

117 f.13. The *gopīs* (cowgirls) ask the trees and shrubs where Krishna has gone.

been dated equivalent to 1647, and was found, like No.32, at Vishnupur in south-western Bengal.

The covers are painted on their exteriors with medallions containing flower and leaf patterns on a ground of flowers. The interiors show on one cover a scene of Krishna approaching a grieving Rādhā, with four female attendants and two deer. On the other is a scene of two young men and an older one dancing to the music of drum and cymbals, obviously devotees of Krishna dancing in his worship. The text of the manuscript must have been a devotional Krishna text, probably the *Gītagovinda*. By this date the angularity of the 1499 covers has given way to a much smoother line and a more varied rhythm, capable of considerable expressiveness. It is quite possible that this change is due to natural development within the style without any necessity to postulate Mughal influence. The ground is still red and the viewpoint from the horizontal, without any landscape or horizon.

British Museum, 1955, 10-8,06.
Victoria and Albert Museum, I.S.103-1955.

Provenance: found in Bankura District; J.C. French Collection.

Two wooden covers, bevelled edges; 15×41cm; painted on upper and lower sides.

Bibliography: AB, No.49, col. repro. of V & A cover.

115 'Gītagovinda'

The Song of the Cowherd by Jayadeva (see No.37), with the commentary of Nārāyanadāsa.

This manuscript is one of the few finely illustrated examples of Orissan work with a date and full details of provenance. It was written and illustrated during the 39th *aṅka* of Mukundadeva of Khurda, *c.*1690, by Dhananjaya, who very probably also illustrated the *Rādhākṛṣṇakeli* (No.116) in the same style. Unlike this latter manuscript, however, it includes many passages of colour, of red, yellow, blue and green applied mostly to clothes, and sometimes to figures. Krishna is sometimes yellow, sometimes green.

Most scenes take place under stepped pyramidal roofs, supported by pillars either square or rounded, but often with conceits such as faces or diamonds between the ornate base and capital. Both men and women wear their hair in tight chignons on top of the head, or sometimes loose in a pigtail. Krishna often wears a jaunty little hat. They both wear the *dhotī*, and the females have an *oṛhnī* wrapped round their upper half, which is inclined to stand out stiffly. Occasionally gentlemen in mid-17th century Mughal costume make an appearance.

Orissa State Museum, Bhubaneshwar, Ext.166.

ff.81; 4×29·5cm; palmyra leaves; text in one or two lines in centre with commentary above and below, in incised Oriya script; most folios with incised drawings on both sides; wooden covers with bevelled edges, inlaid with ivory.

Bibliography: Unpublished.

116 'Rādhākṛṣṇakeli'

The Sport of Rādhā and Krishna, a poem in simple Oriya verse composed by Kārttika in the 17th century, based on the *Gītagovinda* of Jayadeva. It describes Krishna's boyhood and exploits, and then the first meeting in public of Rādhā and Krishna, the arrangements Rādhā makes to fulfil her desires via a go-between, and the eventual union of the two lovers. It is full of pastoral illusions to the river, the flowers and trees, the moon and the birds, all the standard motifs of Indian love poetry.

This lovely little manuscript of this rare work is fully illustrated with incised drawings in the Orissan style; it is undated, but must belong to the earliest group of surviving illustrated manuscripts of Orissa, and is probably the work of Dhananjaya, the illustrator of the *Gītagovinda* (No.115) *c.*1690. His work is of the greatest elegance, with a lovely contrast between the extremely detailed drawing of figures and architecture, and the blank leaf behind.

British Library, London, Or.11612.

ff.20; 4·5×24cm; palmyra leaves; Oriya script, 11 lines between margins with incised decorations; most folios with incised illustrations; covers lacking.

Bibliography: Losty 1980 (most folios reproduced).

117 The 'Rāsakrīḍa' from the 'Bhāgavata Purāṇa'

The tenth canto of this *Purāṇa* dedicated to Krishna/Vishnu (see No.36) was the one most frequently copied, both in Sanskrit and in its vernacular translations, and from it the episode of the *Rāsakrīḍa*, the Play of Love, is the most famous. In it the Lord Krishna satisfies the desires of the *gopīs* (cowgirls) of Brindaban in a mystical, communal union, which later commentators regarded as a symbol of the soul's longing for, and eventual union with, God.

In Orissa this text and others in Sanskrit or Oriya which stress the erotic nature of the encounter between Krishna and the *gopīs* were particularly popular. This Ms. of the *Rāsakrīḍa* section is probably of early 18th-century date, and is in the mainstream of Orissa illustration at this time, with immensely ponderous limbs and sharply pointed features, although despite the heaviness of the style the effect is still of considerable gracefulness. The sparing use of colour on some of

118 f.23. The vision of Akrūra, who sees Krishna and Balarāma in their divine forms in the waters of the Jumna, worshipped by the gods.

119 f.67b. The *gopīs* in the forest.

the folios creates a most charming effect, as in the episode where the *gopīs* ask the trees of the forest where Krishna has disappeared to (ff.12b, 13a), each of the trees named in the text being carefully differentiated. It was probably intended originally to be decorated throughout with colour. There are several unfinished folios in which the outline only is drawn, which may be compared with their finished counterparts.

British Library, London, Or.11689.

ff.27; 4·5×37cm; palmyra leaves; Sanskrit in Oriya script; various lines per side (up to 16), text in centre with commentary of Shrīdhara above and below, between margins with geometric and arabesque decoration; most folios with incised drawings, three with colour; plain bevelled wooden covers.

Bibliography: Losty 1980 (most folios reproduced, four in colour). Barrett and Gray 1963, pp.74–5 (f.1b illustrated in colour).

118 The 'Akrūra Upākhyāna' from the 'Bhāgavata Purāṇa'

The tenth canto of the *Bhāgavata Purāṇa* after describing the *Rāsakrīḍa* (No.117) deals with the wicked plots of Lord Krishna's uncle Kamsa to entice Him to Mathura to kill Him. He sends the good Akrūra to persuade Krishna to come to Mathura to fight his champion wrestler, which Krishna laughingly agrees to do. On the way back to Mathura they stop at the river Jumna and Krishna allows Akrūra a vision of Himself and His brother Balarāma in Their divine forms respectively as the four-armed Vishnu, Divine Preserver of the Universe, and the cosmic serpent, the 1,000-hooded, 1,000-headed Ananta.

This 18th-century manuscript from Orissa is in a rather unusual style – the draughtsmanship is superior to that of the *Rāsakrīḍa* (No.117) and is indeed probably somewhat earlier, as it lacks the fussiness of excessive detail displayed by that manuscript. It is, however, in a tradition of even greater angularity and distortion of the human figure compared with other Orissan styles, with narrow waist and immensely wide shoulders and breasts and a human profile which displays a sharpened nose and chin and receding forehead. The ladies wear their hair in a great bun at the back of the neck, which may indicate a survival in Orissa of elements of the Vijayanagar and Deccani styles, so perhaps an origin in the southern portion of Orissa might be indicated for this style, although the angularity seems also related to the Vishnupur style of Bengal. The Ms. is much damaged but displays a singular elegance and charm in its drawing, rising at the end to a not unworthy representation, despite its tiny scale, of the cosmic vision experienced by Akrūra in the waters of the Jumna.

British Library, London, Or.13719.

ff.28; 4×22·5cm; palmyra leaves; 3–8 lines between margins with geometric and arabesque decorations; most folios with incised drawings; bevelled wooden boards, with floral designs in interiors and traces of paint on exteriors.

Bibliography: Losty 1980.

119 'Kīrtanaghoṣā'

A cycle of poems in Assamese in praise of Krishna by Shankaradeva (*c.*1449–1558),

120 f.115. The young elephant is to be made fearless by matching it against buffalos. By Dilbar and Dosāī.

121 f.3b. King Sib Singh and his Queen, Ambikā, with their son the Tipam Rāja. By Badha Ligirā.

which is one of the classics of Assamese literature by one of its greatest poets and religious mystics.

The Ms. has suffered some depredations and now consists of 179 double-leaves of paper (originally there were 204) of the *tulāpāt* variety, each leaf being folded in two lengthwise and lightly stitched along the fold. Chain and wire marks are very prominent. Only the recto of each half-sheet was utilized for the text. There are 351 paintings in all in the popular style of Assamese painting, *i.e.* that practised from at least the 17th-century in the Vaishnava *sattras* or monasteries in Assam. Its style is very close to the *Bhāgavata* Ms. in the Bali Sattra Nowgong which bears the doubtful date of 1539[1]. Doubtless both manuscripts were produced in such a *sattra* about 1650.

British Library, London, Or.13086.

ff.179; 17×40cm; *tulāpāt* paper; 16 lines Assamese text, 13×32cm; important passages (*Gajendramokṣa*, *Rāsakrīḍa*, etc.) with coloured margins; 351 paintings, usually underneath some of the lines of text; foliation on verso left margin preceded by *śrī*; plain wooden boards 18×48cm; no stringholes.

Bibliography: Marrison 1969.

[1]Datta Barua 1949.

120 'Hastividyārṇava'

The Ocean of Knowledge on Elephants, a treatise in Assamese on everything to do with elephants – their varieties, functions, modes of keeping and training them, their illnesses and remedies, etc. It was written by Sukumār Barkāth for the Ahom King Sib Singh and his queen Ambikā in 1656/1734. Goswami states that it was written for the benefit of the *Hati Barua*, the Keeper of the Royal Elephants, but nothing is known of the author.

The manuscript was written in a large and elegant Assamese hand on 193 folios of *sāñci* bark, coloured yellow, of which 135 still survive. Most of the leaves are illustrated with gaily painted pictures of elephants in their numerous varieties and functions, with their keepers and other attendants. Numerous pictures show the royal function of elephants, with King Sib Singh riding one, or watching from his palace windows with his queen beside him. The colophon implies that the author also wrote out this work, and gives the name of the two artists responsible, Dilbar and Dosāī, who depict themselves receiving the manuscript from the author for illustration. Their names do not re-occur on any other manuscript.

The *Hastividyārṇava* is perhaps the loveliest of the group of manuscripts in the Ahom court style associated with Sib Singh and his queens, and is decidedly livelier than the others of the group. The two artists hardly stray beyond the normal limitations of the style – monochrome grounds, horizontal viewpoint – but their realistic subject-matter enables them to give us glimpses of daily life in 18th-century Assam.

Department of Historical and Antiquarian Studies, Gauhati.

Provenance: Collection of Mohidhar Burhagohain, grandson of Purnananda Burhagohain (see No.122).

ff.135 (out of 193); 17×66cm; *sāñci* bark, coloured yellow; ten lines of Assamese script; central stringhole, with floral decorations around it; 95 folios with illustrations.

Bibliography: DCAM 1930, pp.65–7. Choudhury 1976 (facsimile edition).

121 'Dharma Purāṇa'

The 'Book of Right Conduct' an Assamese Vaishnava metrical text of Hindu doctrine and religious practice by Kavichandra Dvija, the court poet of King Sib Singh (1714–44) composed in 1736 at the command of the king and his queen Ambikā. This is the royal presentation manuscript, written on 174 leaves of *sāñcipāt*, coloured pink.

King Sib Singh (or Sivasimha) and his second queen Phuleshvarī who died in 1731 being Shaiva-Shākta Hindus were persecutors of the Vaishnavas. However, the king married his late queen's cousin who was a Vaishnava, and this lady, Ambikā Devī, softened the king's attitude. This manuscript marks the reconciliation between the court and the Vaishnavas, for the opening paintings show the king accepting the royal copy of this work. These scenes are the most interesting in the whole volume, for there are also portraits of Queen Ambikā with her young son, the Tipam Rāja, while the work ends with the King and Queen being carried in state in their royal palanquins. These Assamese royal portraits are unique in India, for there was no purdah in Assam, and Ambikā's portrait must be based on her real appearance. Other portraits of her for example in the *Hastividyārṇava* (No.120) merely show her looking out of a window, but here are two full-length portraits of her. She was a highly cultivated lady who patronized men of letters and artists, constructed public works, and wielded real power in the kingdom. Her description as *Rāja-paṭeśvarī* in the labels which accompany all the pictures, or Mistress of the King's Diadem, has misled Barnett into thinking this to be a portrait of the Goddess of Sovereignty, whereas it actually refers to Ambikā as Queen-regnant, which she, like Phuleshvarī, was. Sib Singh was so under the influence of astrologers, who predicted in 1722 that his reign would shortly come to an end, that he declared first Phuleshvarī and then in 1731, Ambikā, to be the Bara Rāja or Chief King. The royal portraits are on the second and third folios and the last, showing them with their young son the Tipam Rāja, who is on one occasion dressed in full Mughal costume.

On the last folio the royal pair are carried in separate palanquins in a procession led by elephants, both of them with royal umbrellas and large circular chowries designating their equal royal status, and on the reverse the royal couple and their child seated in state are shown receiving the completed Ms. which is on a pedestal table showing the original painted sides and with a cord wrapped around it. The presenter of the Ms. is named as one Badha who in the colophon is called the beautifier of the manuscript; under his full name, Badha Ligirā, he is known as the painter of the *Śaṅkhacūḍavadha* and *Bhāgavata* Book VI.[1] He must be the senior artist responsible for the overall plan of the Ms. and the five royal portraits, while other junior artists did the rest of the work. The majority of the paintings are on a lower artistic level than the royal portraits, although they yield many charming and most interesting studies of daily life and ritual in Assam in the 18th century.

British Library, London, Or.11386.

ff.174 (originally 179); 17×58cm; leaves of *sāñcipāt*; 12 lines of Assamese in panels 11×47cm; the text and paintings have been applied straight on to the bark without a ground, while the margins have been heavily sprinkled with pinkish-red pigment; remains of *pārśvacitra* on sides; foliation is on the verso left margins, each number preceded by *śrī*; approx. 350 paintings in all; covers of rough *sāñcipāt*, the lower one with a large drawing of an elephant; central stringholes throughout with floral ornamentation.

Bibliography: Barnett 1933.

[1]Das Gupta 1972, p.14.

122 'Brahmavaivarta Purāṇa'

COLOUR PLATE XXXVIII

The *Brahmakhaṇḍa*, the Book of Creation, the first of the four books comprising this least studied of *Purāṇas* in an Assamese translation by Durgāchārya, grandson of Āgamāchārya. The *Brahmavaivarta* is a late medieval document, in which whatever early material it might have contained was thoroughly reworked by the followers of the Vaishnava sect of Nimbārka, which makes Krishna the Supreme Brahman and Rādhā his eternal consort during the periods of creation, when both sport with the *gopīs* and *gopas* in Goloka, the Cow-world, a divine Brindaban high above the heavens of the other gods.

The *Purāṇa* was especially popular in Assam and was translated at least four times into Assamese, the first time by the great poet Kavichandra Chakravartī for Ratnakānti, first wife of King Sib Singh. This translation by Durgāchārya is apparently unknown outside this Ms., nor is anything known of the author. His grandfather Āgamācharya flourished during the reign of Rājeshvara Singh (1751–69). This Ms. is dated Saka 1758/1836, and was copied by Jādurāma Chāṅgakākatī (*Kākatī* being a professional scribe at the Ahom court). The approximately 400 paintings are by Durgārāma Betha. The first eight folios of the Ms. are occupied with a royal genealogy, with pictures of the personages named, which traces the descent of the Ahom King Purandara Singh from Rudra Singh (r.1696–1714). Purandara Singh was the unhappy victim of the collapse of Ahom authority at the end of the 18th century, in the civil anarchy which raged in Assam. This precipitated a Burmese occupation of the Brahmaputra valley (1816) and a subsequent invasion by the forces of the East India Company in the resultant Anglo–Burmese war of 1824–6. He came to the throne at about the age of ten in 1818; he was married to the daughter of the powerful Pūrnānanda the Burha Gohain or chief minister, who was largely responsible for upholding Ahom rule during the reign of his predecessors, but died in 1816. Purandara was ousted almost at once from the throne by the adherents of the Burmese party. It was not until 1832 that he was restored to any part of his ancestral dominions, when the British returned Upper Assam (the Sibsagar and Lakhimpur Districts) to him and Jorhat was made his capital, but he was deposed in 1838, allegedly on grounds of misrule.

This Ms. of the *Brahmakhaṇḍa* was commissioned by Purandara Singh and his wife, the daughter of the former Chief Minister the Burha Gohain, here called *Rājamantrī*. She is accorded extra special praise in the panegyric, being likened to the goddesses Sarasvatī, Lakshmī and Gaurī. An oddity is that the original name of the lady who is described as the daughter of Pūrnānanda the Burha Gohain has been completely erased, and a new name, Kamalā, written over the erasure. This lady might be Kamalapriyā, the wife of Purandara Singh's grandson Kandarpeshvar Singh.

The Ms. represents the last great flowering of Assamese manuscript illustration, and is laid out on the grandest scale. The paintings by Durgārāma Betha vary the illustration of the text with scenes of contemporary life in Assam, with paintings of king and queen in procession or out hunting, as well as with a most valuable series of portraits showing Purandara Singh's descent from Rudra Singh (1696–1714), who is depicted on f.4a; his third son Rājeshvara Singh (1751–69) is on f.4b; his son Sarujana Gohain (f.4b); his son Nirbhaya Singh (f.5a); and his son Brajnātha Singh (f.5b), whom Pūrnānanda the Burha Gohain invited to be king in 1818 to overthrow Candrakānta Singh and the Burmese party. Brajnāth was however ineligible to sit on the throne owing to having been mutilated, and his young son Purandara Singh was made king, and is pictured on f.6a with his wife. They are shown again in the next three paintings, while on f.8a are shown portraits of Pūrnānanda the Burha Gohain and his son Rucinātha who succeeded to his position.

The manuscript consists of 210 large leaves of *sāñcipāt*, with yellow arsenic applied to act as ground and insecticide. The text is written in a large and beautiful

123 Outer cover. Rāma and attendants with mythical birds.

124 f.112b. King Dasharatha with Rāma and Sītā (left) and their departure from Ayodhyā.

hand by Jādurāma Chāṅgakākatī in only 12 lines per page, where, unusually, faint ruled lines were first drawn. Most folios have illustrations on both sides of the leaf, varying in size between small panels and the full width of the script. Where text meets painting the border is staggered, giving a stepped appearance to many of the paintings.

The residence of King Purandara was in Jorhat, but the Ms. appears to have been made in Debgaon (Devagrama in the colophon), which is on the border between Purandara's kingdom of Upper Assam and the British district of Nowgong.

British Library, London, Or.11387.

ff.210; 24·5×64·5cm; *sāñcipāt* leaves; 12 lines of Assamese script in panels 13·5×49·5cm; about 400 paintings of varying sizes with the last few folios not being finished; strengthened bark covers.

Bibliography: Barnett 1933. Losty 1980, p.25 (col. repro. of ff.3a and 142b).

123 Manuscript cover

A wooden cover inlaid with designs in ivory depicting Rāma enthroned with attendants in the centre, and a large fabulous bird on each side, apparently based on the simurgh, surrounded by *mārvārī* leaves. The work is of the 17th century, probably from the Andhra country in southern India.

British Museum, London, 1971, 3-2, 2.

124 'Rāmāyaṇa'

A translation of Vālmīki's Sanskrit epic (see Nos.91–7) into Marathi *ovī* metre, made by Mādhavasvāmi in 1693 under the patronage of the Maratha Rāja Sahājī II of Tanjore (1684–1711). The translator was a Vaishnava *bhakta*, the grandson of Eknāth of Pandharpur, who founded a *math* at Tiruvendur in the Tanjore district. Mādhava also translated the *Mahābhārata*, *Bhāgavata Purāṇa*, and *Yogavāsiṣṭha* into Marathi.

Sarabhojī, the Rāja of Tanjore (1797–1833), had many copies made of the *Aśvaśāstra* and *Gajaśāstra* manuscripts with his own Marathi translations from the Sanskrit, which continue the vertical and bound format of their predecessors. More usual however was a loose-leaf *poṭhī* format for illustrated manuscripts, with the text contained within a frame, and the decorated margins crossing over one another.[1] This *Rāmāyaṇa* is such a manuscript, each of the 220 *prasaṅgas* or chapters into which the text is divided having these frames round its opening, decorated with arabesques or fruits or flowers displaying considerable European influence. Also at the beginning of the individual *Kāṇḍas* is a pair of paintings within these frames, showing the elaborately gilded but dead style to which Tanjore painting had been reduced by the middle of the 19th century, the date of this manuscript.

British Library, London, Or.13535.

ff.1,050; 16×35cm; European paper, watermarked between 1845 and 1855; 11 lines of *Nāgarī* script with red *daṇḍas*, colophons, etc., between margins ruled in red in two double lines, 26cm apart; opening pages of chapters with marginal decorations; 14 paintings, about 5×8cm; unbound originally, now bound up in separate volumes.

Bibliography: Unpublished.

[1]Appasamy 1980.

125 'Shāhnāma'

The Book of Kings, by Firdausī (see No.22).

The Ms. is of the second half of the *Shāhnāma* from the accession of Lahrasp, and was copied by Kalīl Allāh called *Haft-kalamī* (seven-penned) at Rājūr in 1131/1719. There are 97 miniatures, many of them whole page, in a most interesting provincial style that has hitherto not been possible to pinpoint. The three colophons are most difficult to decipher, but yield the information that the Ms. was copied for one Mahant Ajagat Singh Jīv, the Vizier during the reign of Rāja Azmat

Allāh Khān. The date is corroborated by the mention in the first colophon of Emperor Farrukhsiyar as reigning in Delhi (1713–19) and in the last of Emperor Rafiʿ ad-Darajat, who reigned for a few months in 1719.

There are many places named Rājūr in India, most of them in the northern Deccan. However the place that seems most suitable as a provenance is Rajauri also called Rampur, now in the state of Jammu and Kashmir, which is on the road to Srinagar from Sialkot via the Pir Panjal pass. Its early history is obscure, although often mentioned in the Kashmiri chronicle, the *Rājataraṅginī*; its rulers apparently became Muslims about 1500, but interestingly kept the Hindu title of Rāja. Akbar and Jahāngīr always used this route up to Kashmir and stayed at Rajauri. A passage in Jahāngīr's Memoirs, in which he calls the place Rajaur, refers to the rulers' title of Rāja and how Hindu and Muslim customs had become mixed there. The ruler in 1719 was Rāja Azmat Allāh Khān, who reigned from 1703 to 1760, according to the royal records[1]. Only three years old at his accession, the throne was seized by his uncle Rafiʿ Allāh Khān and the boy fled to Delhi, to the Rajauri princess Rahmat un-Nisa, one of the wives of Aurangzīb, and mother of Muʿazam Shāh, the future Emperor Bahādur Shāh (r.1707–12). When somewhat older, the boy returned to Rajaur and apparently reigned until about 1760. These Rajauri records are inaccurate (the Rajauri princess was probably dead by 1691), but the main outline seems correct. Corroborating evidence that the Rajaur of the Ms.'s colophon is this little state in Kashmir is furnished by another Ms. of a *Shāhnāma* imitation dated 1090/1679, now in a private collection in London, done at Rājūr in the reign of Rājā Inayat Allāh Khān with paintings in the same style as the 1719 manuscript. In the Rajauri family records, Rāja Azmat Allāh Khān's grandfather was Rāja Inayat Allāh Khān who reigned *c.*1648 to 1676. The paintings of this Ms. must have been added *c.*1720, as they are in precisely the same style as the 1719 *Shāhnāma*.

This style is one of great richness achieved by lavish use of gold and silver and good-quality pigments; the paintings are by an artist of originality, without many models to follow for his compositions. The style on occasion has a Deccani feel about it – female costumes, occasional Deccani turbans, favourite Deccani colour combinations of greens and purples, blues and pinks, the sky painted in bands of gold and blue, occasional composition in layers – but it is noteworthy that many of these are also in Kashmiri painting. The artist has made a conscious attempt to indicate the Iranian origin of the text, to judge from the

125 f.103b. Alexander and Roshanak, daughter of Darius.

126 f.277. Illuminated border (*hashīya*) round the *Bhagavadgītā*.

frequent appearance of Iranian turbans; male costume is invariably the Iranian *peshvaz*, although in other respects it resembles 17th-century Indian costume, *i.e.* the gown is three-quarter length and tied at the waist by a cummerbund with short *paṭkā*.

Landscape is normally a flat green, olive or brown ground dotted with regularly disposed tufts of grass, and ending in a hilly high horizon from which protrude trees or buildings or people. Rocks are frequently depicted in vivid shades of blue and purple, brown and orange, but rarely terminating the landscape or protruding above the horizon. Water is silver or silver-green in old-fashioned basket-pattern and whorls. The architectural details seem basically mid-17th century – there is an occasional Bengali roof and pillars of the Jahāngīri type. Much of his idiom conforms to the Popular Mughal tradition, while some of it goes back through the Sultanate tradition to a 15th-century Persian origin. In one painting a Chinese scroll-cloud drifts across the landscape. In many instances, the powerful Indian instinct for spatial organization according to higher criteria than mere naturalism has combined with the more fantastic elements in the *Shāhnāma* story to produce paintings of the greatest originality as in the scene of Iskandar and Israfil talking to the birds (f.125a), while there are some scenes of great loveliness, as in the traditionally Indian court scene of f.104a, Alexander with Darius's daughter.

British Library, London, Add.18804.

ff.358; 36 × 24cm; highly polished paper; four columns of *Nasta'līq* script, in panels 23 × 14cm, with margins ruled in gold and colours; two *sarlavḥs*; 97 paintings from full-page to horizontal strip in size; original leather binding with flap, with central sunk medallions and pendants, and frame of cartouches etc., and doublures of blue leather painted with gold rosettes.

Bibliography: BM 1876, p.538. BL 1977, pp.46–7.

[1]Hutchison and Vogel 1925.

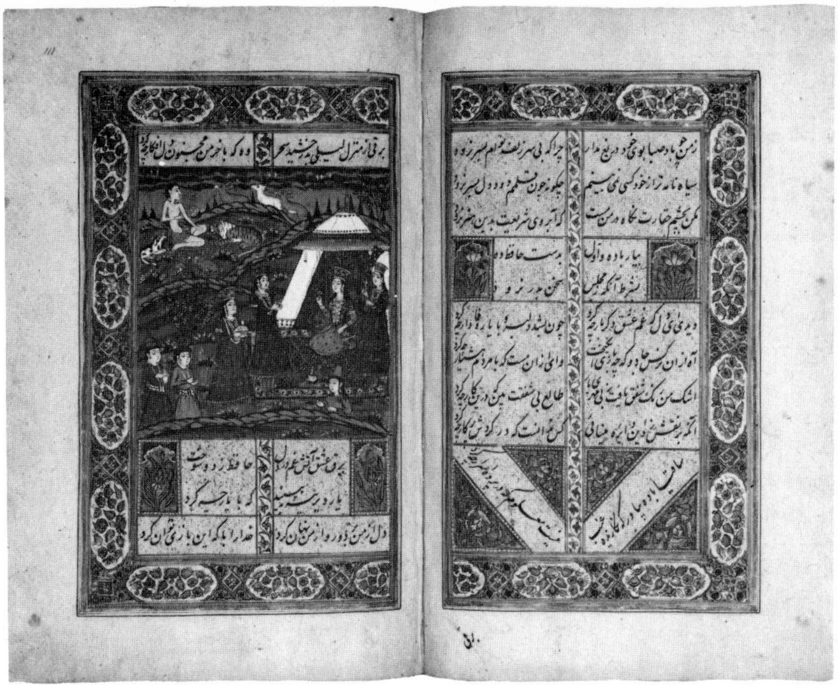

127 f.111. Laylā in her tent and Majnūn with the wild beasts.

126 Collection of Sanskrit Devotional Texts

A collection of Hindu texts, the *Bhagavadgītā*, *Devīmāhātmya*, and many other ritual and devotional texts. There are several hands involved in the writing of the texts, the script being the *Śāradā* hand of Kashmir, probably of the mid-18th century. The Ms. is important however for its illuminations, which were only partly completed, but which represent an attempted synthesis of the Hindu and Muslim manuscript traditions.

There are 27 miniatures in the Kashmiri style by two different hands, one of which, the finer, seems closely derived from the hand of the painter of the *Aśvamedhaparvan* of 1694; he attempts ambitious landscapes with varied buildings, with spandrels occupying the top corners of his pictures, while his male lay-figures wear Popular Mughal dress of the 17th century, and his Brahmans cover their hair with bag-like headgear, all features seen in the 1694 Ms. Elaborate floral frames surround his paintings, of the type seen in the *Pañcaratna* from Jaipur of 1772 (No.129), but which appear to be of earlier date in Kashmir. The other hand seems derived from the first one, still keeping the spandrels, for example, but in a somewhat simplified and later style with less elaborate borders. There are also two 'carpet pages' of illumination, one apparently of the *Pārijāta* or wish-fulfilling Tree of Heaven of Hindu mythology, all in gold and colours, the other of the famous Kashmiri whorl, the origin of the Paisley pattern. All of these pages have been introduced into the manuscript, as none has text on the reverse, and are on slightly different papers, differing actually among themselves.

In addition to the miniatures, there are 28 pages (ff.276a–285b, ff.583a–586b) in which appear marginal illuminations of flowers and animals and birds in elaborate arabesques in two tones of gold in the Mughal fashion, around the Sanskrit text, which is here written on alternate bands of gold-covered, and gold-sprinkled white, paper, while many other pages were prepared for illumination in this fashion but were never completed.

The Ms. appears to have been in course of production over a period of time. The marginal illumination is intimately connected with one of the paintings of the earlier artist, so that these may all be assigned to the first period of the manuscript's production about 1725–50. It was left incomplete, judging from the prepared but not illuminated state of some of the pages, and also had not enough paintings in it – the *Bhagavadgītā* contains only two paintings by the earlier artist, the chariot of Arjuna and Krishna between the armies, and the Fish avatar of Vishnu. At about 1775 the other paintings were added, including repeats of the same two *Bhagavadgītā* pages. The Paisley whorl on f.340a was probably added even later.

British Library, London, Or.11835.

Provenance: Bequeathed by P.C. Manuk and Miss G. M. Coles through the National Art-Collections Fund, 1948.

ff.608 (602–608 being flyleaves with notes); 20·5 × 14cm; thin, burnished paper; 14 lines of *Śāradā* script in panels 13 × 8cm with margins ruled in gold and colours; 14 folios with decorated gold margins; 29 full pages of illumination and miniatures; modern binding.

Bibliography: Unpublished.

127 'Dīvān' of Hāfiz

The collected poems of the Persian poet Hāfiz (see No.73).

Fine-quality Persian manuscripts from Kashmir in the 18th century exhibit some of the richest illuminations ever attempted in India. In addition to the normal *sarlavḥ* and *'unvāns*, every page may have a fully illuminated border of floral decoration, and scattered throughout the text can be little illuminated rectangles and triangles, quite apart from the numerous miniatures themselves. The paper is of the thinnest, finest quality, burnished and gold-sprinkled, a speciality of Kashmir, for it is found nowhere else at this time, while the covers are often painted and lacquered, or finely patterned in leather. Kashmir was famous for its paper through-

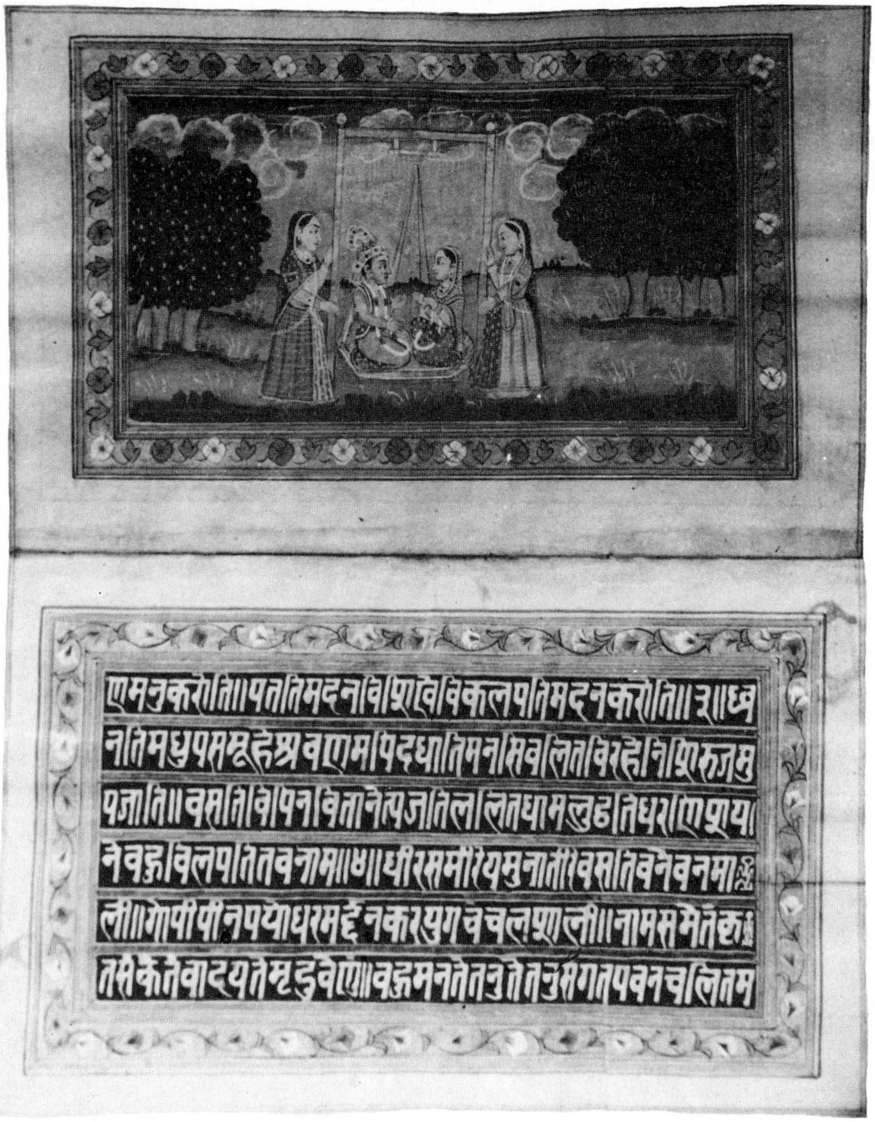

128 ff.17b, 18. *Hindola rāga*, the melody of this section of the *Gītagovinda*.

out the east at this time.[1] All these qualities are displayed by this copy of the *Dīvān* of Hāfiz, a superbly glittery manuscript which exhibits Kashmiri illumination at its best. Of course as a work of art it is not up to the highest standards, seeking to compensate for the lack of high quality miniatures by over-indulgence in other forms of illumination. Every page has a wide border around the text of flowers and stylized leaves in a star pattern in gold and colours. Occasionally these are varied to include cartouches with different floral arrangements. More flowers in rectangular or triangular panels are sprinkled throughout the text. The 112 miniatures are fairly elaborate compositions without the deadness and uniformity which affects Kashmiri work in the next century. The *ʿunvān* (ff.13b–14a) has the broad gold and blue bands typical of Kashmiri illumination in the border around the normal arrangement of panels around the opening of the text and displays a characteristic Kashmiri element – the two side *ansas* are echoed by ones at top and bottom in the middle, split between the two pages. A final gold bookplate is in the shape of the Kashmir tree of life seen in No.126, with a date of 1211/1796–7 at its base, and the name Yūsuf, without any other information. This would seem to be the date of the Ms., and the name of the illuminator, who was perhaps also the artist. A very similar Ms. of Hāfiz in the State Public Library, Leningrad, bears this same date of 1211/1796–7.[2]

British Library, London, Add.7763.

Provenance: Collection of Claudius James Rich, acquired in India before 1808; purchased in 1825.

ff.404; 22 × 14cm; thin, highly polished paper; 12 lines of good *Nastaʿlīq* in two columns on gold-sprinkled panels 13·5 × 8cm; panels of floral illumination throughout text; text panels with gold and green ruled margins with border one cm wide of floral illumination with outer ruled margins of gold and colours; one *ʿunvān*; two *sarlavḥ*; one gold bookplate; 112 miniatures, occupying about one-third of the text panels; covers with central panel stamped and gilded and red leather margins painted in gold with stamped and gilded cartouches; red doublures painted in gold; rebound in Europe with new spine.

Bibliography: BM 1879, p.630. BL 1977, pp.56–8.

[1]Forster 1798, vol.II, p.19.
[2]Adamova and Greck 1976, p.73, with colour repros.

128 'Gītagovinda'

The Song of the Cowherd, by Jayadeva (see No.37).

The text was copied in 1850/1794 by the scribe Mahtāb Rāya in Kashmir, in white *Nāgarī* on a black ground, with borders of gold illuminated with simple floral arabesques. Like several other such manuscripts in the Jaipur royal library, after acquisition (in this case through Mārphat Rāya Ratnalāl, Minister of Mahārāja Pratap Singh in 1852/1796) it was embellished with miniatures, 21 folios being inserted with paintings on the versos, and bound up. The miniatures' subjects include the *rāgas* to which the *Gītagovinda* is sung. Mahtāb Rāya was a well-known scribe in the later 18th century who also was employed by William Jones and Charles Wilkins in Calcutta, where he copied several manuscripts for each of these scholars, now mostly in the Bodleian and India Office Libraries respectively. He was more than a simple copyist, as many of the Wilkins' Mss. involve re-arrangements of the text at the latter's request. His clear and elegant style is typical of the Kashmiri scribes' work at this period, although paradoxically he does not appear to have been a Kashmiri – in one of the Wilkins Mss.[1] he says he comes from the south (*dakṣiṇadeśa*). Some of his Calcutta work is dated to between 1787 and 1790, and he appears to have moved on first to Benares[2] and then to Kashmir. Other work by him is to be found in the Jaipur royal library, including another *Gītagovinda* copied in the same year (1794) also in Kashmir, in an extremely large style of *Nagarī*, and similarly embellished with inserted miniatures.[3]

Maharaja Man Singh Museum, Jaipur, MS AG 2172.

ff.33, with 21 extra illustrated leaves; 9·5 × 17cm; polished white paper; six lines of white *Nāgarī* on black ground (7 × 14·5cm) within gold margins with polychrome arabesque; 21 miniatures, same size as text panels with gilded borders with floral decorations; binding of boards along long edge covered in *misru* cloth, *i.e.* white cloth embroidered with

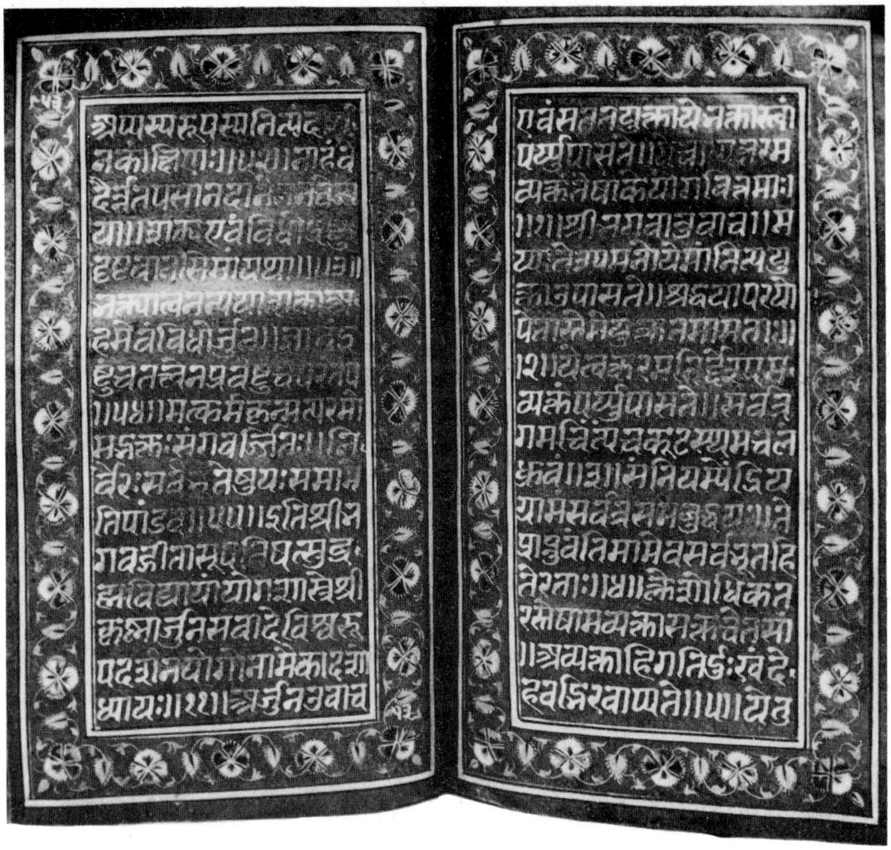

129 f.54. The *Bhagavadgītā* illuminated.

four lines of red stylized flowers; with flap (*jihvā*) with scalloped edge.

Bibliography: Jaipur 1971, pp.51–2.

[1]IOL, Skt. MS.2816.
[2]IOL, Skt. MS.2803.
[3]Jaipur 1971.

129 'Pañcaratna'

The Five Jewels from the *Mahābhārata*. This group of five Sanskrit texts is of the *Bhagavadgīta*, and four lesser hymns and didactic passages from the epic. They were often copied in the late 18th century.

The *guṭka* format, a Hindu Ms. in upright format and bound, was brought to perfection in the late 18th century, above all in the Jaipur royal library. For the first time manuscripts of Hindu texts were being produced which vied with contemporary Muslim manuscripts in the perfection of their paper, calligraphy, illumination and binding. Typical is this elegant Ms. of the *Pañcaratna* from the Jaipur collection dated 1828/1772, copied in an extremely fine *Nāgarī* in gold ink by the scribe Ghāsi Mahātmā for Mahārāja Prithvi Singh of Jaipur (1767–78). All the folios are of dark-blue paper, against which the gold of the ink glows satisfyingly. Around each text panel is a polychrome border, with floral geometric decoration, different in every opening.

Maharaja Man Singh Museum, Jaipur, MS No.25

ff.130; 21·25 × 12cm; dark-blue paper; 17 lines of gold *Nāgarī* in panels 16·5 × 7·5cm, with wide borders of polychrome floral and geometric designs; covers of *zari* (dark-red velvet) embroidered with silver and blue thread, forming peony flowers in lozenges in central rectangular panels on front and back, with similar flowers in border, and on flap.

Bibliography: Jaipur 1971, pp.28–9.

130 'Bhāgavata Purāṇa'

Illustrated on p.121.

The Book of the Lord (see No.36). During the 18th century, the Hindu sacred texts were frequently copied in minute script and illuminated on long rolls of thin, highly burnished paper, the most frequently occurring being the *Bhāgavata Purāṇa*, *Bhagavadgītā* and *Devīmāhātmya*. Some of the earliest appear to be from Kashmir[1] of the early 18th century and it may have been a fashion started in imitation of the long strips of birch-bark which were not infrequently made into rolled manuscripts as amulets. Another possible source is the Middle Eastern tradition of rolled-up copies of the Koran in minute script kept as amulets within cases. Certainly the minuteness of the writing employed points to this source, and also the type of illumination. However, whereas the Koran could be copied onto a relatively small roll of paper, a text like the *Bhāgavata Purāṇa* could require, as in this instance, a roll nearly 20 metres in length.

Very rarely do any of these Mss. boast of a colophon, and those that do are usually out of the normal style, as the copy of the *Adhyātmarāmāyaṇa* in the Bodleian, copied by Ghāsīrāma Kāshmīra in Benares in the early 19th century[2]. More usually the style is similar to this one, a more or less indeterminate style common to much 19th-century work in northern India. From the large number of them presently in the Alwar Museum, the royal studio in Alwar under Vinay Singh (1815–57) seems to have been a centre for their production, and Jaipur also must have been a centre for such work. The lavish illumination and attention to detail of this one betoken a rich patron. A series of eight-lobed cartouches at the beginning first introduce the great gods of Hinduism – the sacred syllable Om, Ganesh, Brahmā, Vishnu and Shiva, and then twelve scenes from the life of Krishna, before the text proper begins. The twelve *skandhas* are separated by twelve (the tenth canto is in two parts) paintings in cartouches containing subjects from the *Purāṇa* itself, and there are 55 smaller paintings in roundels within the text of Krishna, sages, princes, and other personages. Borders illuminated in gold with a floral creeper run the length of the roll on either side of the text, and the spandrels round the cartouches are similarly illuminated. The very opening of the roll before the first picture is the equivalent of a *sarlavḥ*, a rectangular illumination with a W-shaped top and finials, in which peony arabesques are conspicuous.

The illustrations are in the Hindu equivalent of the Delhi style, with heavily modelled features and luxuriantly coloured landscapes. Two artists are involved, the style of the opening series of 17 paintings being much lighter than the remainder.

British Library, London, Add.16624.

Provenance: Purchased at Wilks Sale in 1847.

Scroll format; 19·8m × 11–11·5cm; very thin burnished paper; minute *Nāgarī* script; five lines to the cm, 8cm wide between broad borders gilded and with floral creepers; opening *skandha* within cartouches of alternating sizes, with polychrome illumination in spandrels; 17 miniatures in eight-lobed cartouches at opening, and another 12 between the *skandhas*; 56 smaller miniatures in roundels scattered throughout text at regular intervals (apart from last two *skandhas*).

Bibliography: BM 1902, p.34.

[1]*e.g.* the damaged British Library MS. Add.26419.
[2]Bodleian MS. Sansk. e.13.

CHAPTER V

European Influence on the Manuscript Tradition

Europeans had been visiting India regularly since the 16th century, with the discovery of the sea route round southern Africa. The Portuguese were firmly established in Goa, which was part of Bijapuri territory, and the Sultans of Bijapur valued the trading links this presence afforded them with the outside world. They sent presents to Akbar in Agra, including European paintings and prints, and for many years Jesuits were present at court. European art greatly intrigued Akbar and his son and considerably influenced the development of the Mughal style, as we have seen. Other Europeans came to trade and as ambassadors – Roe, Manucci, Bernier. Some must have collected paintings and manuscripts – the Laud *Rāgamālā* (No.102) must have been brought back to England by one of these early embassies. Not until later in the century do we have evidence of European patronage of painting – the albums of Emperors and Sultans of which Golconda made a speciality for dealing with Europeans, particularly the Dutch, until well into the 18th century. Although Europeans may have commissioned these albums of portraits, they had no influence on their style which is purely Golconda work.

It was not until Europeans established themselves in the political system of India during the process of the dismemberment of the Mughal empire that their patronage had any serious impact on the various Indian styles. The British East India Company was officially established in political control of Bengal from 1765, and had representatives and agents at many of the Indian courts, as well as a full bureaucratic establishment in Calcutta. The French were denied any serious political role in India as a consequence of the Treaty of Paris in 1763 which ended the Seven Years War, but many Frenchmen were still resident in India. Some were content simply to collect. Men like Richard Johnson and Antoine Polier, both of whose Indian careers took them to Hyderabad and Lucknow, the latter especially being a dispersal point for the royal Mughal collections, assembled *muraqqaʿ* in the way Indian collectors did, having their paintings and calligraphic specimens mounted in frames and bound up (No.131). They both also collected manuscripts, in the various languages used in India (No.106). One of Polier's great achievements was his commissioning a complete set of manuscripts of the Vedas which he was able to obtain only with the greatest difficulty from scribes in Jaipur with the aid of Mahārāja Pratap Singh, and on his return to Europe in 1789 made haste to deposit them in the British Museum for the benefit of scholarship. His most important *muraqqaʿ*, which is probably the album visible on the table in John Zoffany's portrait of Polier with his friends painted in 1786 or 87, contains notable examples of Mughal, Deccani and Lucknow painting.

Others like Elijah Impey, the Lord Chief Justice of Bengal, and his wife, both collected and commissioned examples of Murshidabad painting (No.113), but also commissioned artists to draw things that they wanted and in the way they wanted. Despite being in the East, the governing classes in Calcutta lived much as they did in England and wanted paintings of their houses, their horses, their dogs and their wives, and in a style to which they were accustomed. The Indian artist, who had so radically changed his style to suit Mughal taste in the 16th century, now changed it once more in the 18th to accommodate English sensibilities. For every patron like the Impeys who appreciated his own paintings and persuaded him to essay natural-history drawings, having divined the Indian artist's passion for minute attention to detail and intuitive sympathy with the natural world, there were a hundred who wanted paintings only according to the latest received opinion in London on what constituted correct perspective and the correct manner of rendering the 'picturesque'. The Indian artist, ever eager to please his patron, obliged by churning out in station after station, as British influence spread throughout India, albums of stock themes: the Emperors and princes of India, select views of Calcutta or of Agra and Delhi, above all traders and occupations, the 'native' types, as mementoes for the memsahib when she returned to England. They often have a certain charm, but the monotony of these sets is finally repellent. The style is termed Company, after the East India Company's officials who patronized the artists.

Numerous artists went out from England to India to try their luck among the expatriates and also the Indian princes. John Zoffany was the most distinguished artist who visited India, and the Daniels, Thomas and William, did fine work there. But it was the more run-of-the-mill artists who had the greatest influence in shaping the Indian artist's new style. Tilly Kettle, for example, visited Lucknow in the 1770s and painted portraits of Shujaʿ ad-Daula with his sons, which were imitated by various Lucknow artists and became the standard prototypes for the Nawab's portrait. From this period on, there is a consistent Europeanizing trend in Lucknow painting first found in the work of Mīr Kalān Khān. The Lucknow rulers were gripped by a fervent love of things European in the first half of the 19th century. Tilly Kettle and Zoffany in the 1780s were succeeded by a string of British painters including the Daniels, all of them finding favour at court. Robert Home and George Beechey were successively court painters to all the Nawabs (created Kings by George IV in 1819) from Ghāzi ad-Dīn Haidar (1814–27) to Wājid ʿAlī Shāh (1847–56), and the palace of Lucknow was built in European style, hung with European oils and decorated in European taste (No.133). The Kings held banquets in the European fashion for British visitors, and there are paintings in the India Office Library of different Nawabs entertaining successive Governors-General – Moira, Bentinck and Hardinge.

132 f.89b. The fairies tell Tāj al-Mulūk at a bathing-pool that his beloved Bakāvalī is in a temple in Ceylon (No.132, p.151).

Lucknow was one of the few courts which still maintained a manuscript studio during this period, and the Nawab's taste for European art greatly affected the manuscript style. In the 1780s, an important stream of Lucknow painting was a water-colour style with figures all in three-quarter profile (after Tilly Kettle's portrait of Nawab Shujaʿ ad-Daula), with heavy modelling and shadows (always falling to the right), with still occasionally brilliant colouring, but set in a drab, washed out, flat landscape with tiny distant hills dotted with trees under a pale wash of blue for a sky, of a type apparently invented by Mihr Chand in the 1760s. Polier patronized this sort of artist, with a commission for a set of Hindu deities (No.131). For the next half century this style dominated Lucknow painting, although stronger colours were usually employed. In manuscripts such as the *Gulzār-i Nasīm* (No.132) and *Nizām ʿIshqnāma*

134 f.30b. Shiva with his wife Pārvatī and mount, the bull Nandī (No.134, p.151).

135 f.134b. The blind musician Miyān Himmat Khān Kalāvant. By Ghulām ʿAlī Khān (?) (No.135, p.152).

(No.133), may be seen the extent of Lucknow's surrender to European taste, in the palaces and their decorations, the chandeliers and the oil-paintings, and in the Europeanized features of the participants in the story, some of whom, the fairies in the former manuscript dated 1839, have hair styles reminiscent of the young Queen Victoria. In the more ambitious *Nizām ʿIshqnāma* of 1849–50 the Europeanized surroundings dominate the participants, the young Wājid ʿAlī Shāh himself and the bevy of beauties who constantly attended him. The annexation of Oudh by the East India Company in 1856 put an abrupt halt to the development of the style, but we get a last echo of it in a de luxe edition of the exiled king's letters to his queens in Lucknow, now in the British Library (Or.5288). The border illumination is a riotous fantasy on the theme of mermaids who are the supporters of the royal crown in the arms of Oudh, and the only miniature, which shows the king enthroned in his court, seems a travesty of the admittedly heavy style of the Oudh court in its blurred and furry outline and muddy paint.

Upcountry from Calcutta, other British officials, civilian and military, found time from their duties to investigate India through its manuscript tradition. As Sanskrit was a sealed book to all but a few Europeans, they found it convenient to work through the medium of Persian, still the official language of India. Charles Boddam, the District Judge in Chapra in Bihar, translated into English the popular Sanskrit text *Adhyātma Rāmāyaṇa*, via a Persian translation made by a pundit at the Benares Sanskrit College and had it illustrated by local artists (No.134), while another Benares pundit made a succint account in Persian of the castes and sects of the Hindus for John Glyn, the Registrar of Benares, a copy of which the scholar H.H. Wilson had illustrated and on which he based his published account of what was one of the most fascinating aspects of life in India for early visitors.

One of the most important Indian manuscripts of the early 19th century is concerned with this subject. The *Tasrīḥ al-Aqvām* by James Skinner is a work in Persian dealing with the castes, tribes and sects of the Panjab (No.135). Skinner was half Indian, the son of a Rajput mother, who was the founder of the famous regiment of Skinner's Horse, his 'yellow-boys', so-called from their uniforms, based at Hansi Cantonment in the Panjab. He is the author of this as well as another Persian work on the reigning families in the Panjab and Rajasthan (No.136). Both are heavily illustrated with paintings in the Delhi 'Company' style practised by Ghulām ʿAlī Khān and others in the first half of the 19th century, which was the most successful of all the mixed styles of the period, combining European naturalism in the human figure with a certain Indian stylization and smoothness of articulation. Work in this style done for Skinner and his friend John Fraser is one of the high points of 19th-century Indian painting. Ghulām ʿAlī Khān was one of the last great Mughal painters, and worked both for the Mahārāja of Alwar (see No.138) and Bahādur Shāh II. Other Delhi artists at this period continued working in the dead, traditional style of the Histories of Shāh Jahān, with minor concessions to Europeans, such as British officers disporting on the terrace of the Tāj Mahāl in a bosky landscape from the Home Counties (No.137), or produced the albums of views of the great monuments of Delhi and Agra which abound from this date, and in which the Indian passion for minuteness of detail reaches perhaps its

136 f.8b. Rānā Javān Singh of Udaipur. By Ghulām ʿAlī Khān (?) (No.136, p.152).

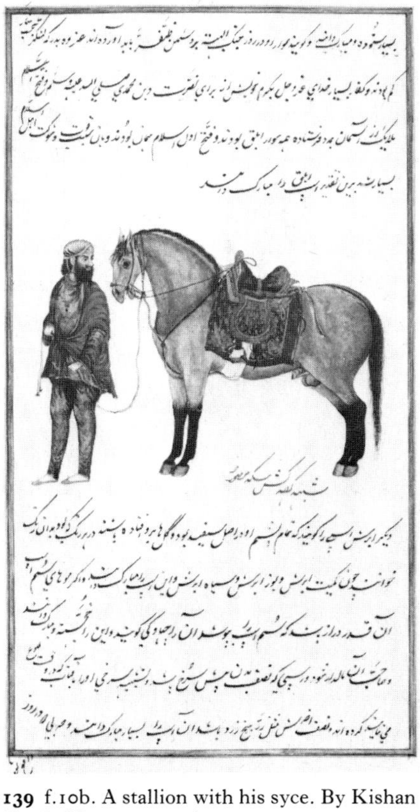

139 f.10b. A stallion with his syce. By Kishan Singh (No.139, p.154).

greatest height in attempting to render every semi-precious stone in the fabric of these bejewelled buildings.

None of the manuscripts we have been discussing so far could be claimed to have made any noteworthy advance in terms of book production. Fine-quality manuscripts produced for Indian patrons had reached their final form, Persian and Hindu manuscripts now having arrived at a near identity. Niceties as to the precise illustration of the text, the balance between calligraphy and illustration, were now no longer considered, since the Indian conception of an illustrated manuscript as being a set of paintings with accompanying text had finally triumphed even in Persian manuscripts. The pictures were painted as self-sufficient entities and inserted into the manuscript at the appropriate places, with maybe a line of description above or below, but separate.

The most successful fusion in this period of European and Hindu ideas on book-production is found in a Benares manuscript of the 1830s (No.140), ostensibly a horoscope in Sanskrit of Prince Navnihal Singh, grandson of Mahārāja Ranjit Singh, the Lion of the Panjab. It is lavishly illustrated with miniatures, in the Benares 'Company' style, of the signs of the Zodiac, lunar mansions and so on, while every page bears decoration, much of it of European inspiraton, in floral designs and geometric patterns around the text panels and astronomical tables.

Looking at the whole of this period from the late 18th century when Europeans first came to exercise a decisive impact on the nature and pattern of patronage, it is obvious that there was a rapid decline in standards wherever there was too sudden an exposure to European taste. Indian painting had been nurtured for centuries by discriminating patrons, who exercised decisive influence on the choice of subjects, the style and presentation. The art with which we have been concerned is primarily one of manuscript illustration, and its strengths and weaknesses are derived peculiarly from this background. By the late 18th century this tradition, whose history we have traced for 800 years, seemed to be inevitably coming to an end, for the Indian patron no longer wanted illustrated manuscripts or small pictures for mounting into albums. Where royal patronage was still active, in Rajasthan and Lucknow for example, it was larger paintings which were required, of festivities or hunts or great occasions of state, perhaps as a reaction against the sense of dwindling power which the rulers felt. The sudden intrusion of foreign patrons, commissioning mostly minor work but on a large scale, offered security to artists who anyway seemed about to lose their livelihood, and it is not to be wondered at that they seized what opportunities were available. But it was only a few artists who were able to take advantage of new horizons to add a significant new phase to Indian painting. For the majority, suddenly exposed to European taste, the result is an unhappy amalgam; subtle Indian stylizations arrived at by centuries of experimentation were distorted into approximations to a naturalism that had no meaning to the artists, while the medium changed from the pure, opaque gouache, to a softer technique with pale washes of water-colour combined with muddied admixtures of Chinese white. Perhaps they would have surmounted these distortions, given time, as the at first overwhelming Safavid influence in the 16th century had been absorbed and transmuted into something truly Indian. But the collapse of native patronage was the death-blow to the various schools, for without it there was no living for the artists, while British patronage itself

131 f.7. A Hindu shrine – the Goddess slays the Buffalo-demon, with Ganesh and Kubera in attendance.

disappeared with the introduction of the camera, which so admirably captured the outward forms of Indian life and civilization. As for the manuscript tradition itself, though not dependent on British patronage, it was nonetheless a victim of the interest of a few men like William Jones, N.B. Halhed, Charles Wilkins and Henry Colebrooke, who were the earliest western scholars to study systematically the languages and literatures of India, and to interpret them properly. It was Jones who first published the relationship of Sanskrit to Greek and Latin, and his translation of Kālidāsa's dramatic masterpiece, the *Śākuntala*, was admired throughout Europe, not least by Goethe. Such scholars as these naturally collected manuscripts, being concerned to gather together the basic literature of India, and used the printing-press in Calcutta as the means of printing and hence widely disseminating India's ancient learning. A slow trickle of works in Bengali, Persian and Sanskrit towards the end of the 18th century was succeeded in the new century by a flood of editions of the Indian and Persian classics from presses throughout India. In such conditions the need to have works laboriously copied by hand disappeared, and the manuscript tradition itself had by the middle of the 19th century all but come to an end.

131 Album of paintings of Hindu divinities

A set of 64 paintings bound in two volumes, of the Hindu gods, the incarnations of Vishnu, and of minor divinities and the planets.

The 64 paintings, 32 in each volume, are bound up in pairs facing each other, with decorated margins of two dark-blue frames with gold and silver-leaf designs separated by a wider frame of flowers in arabesque. The paintings are in a Lucknow style of the late 18th century, when Lucknow artists had already been considerably influenced both by European art directly and by 'Company' artists who worked for the British.

Notes on the flyleaves state the volumes were part of the Beckford sale at Sotheby's but mistakenly cite the Van Braam collection as the provenance for Beckford. On May 6th to 9th, 1817, Mr Sotheby sold '... a portion of the library of William Beckford Esq of Fonthill, comprising ... original Chinese and Hindu Drawings, from the Collections of Van Braam, Bradshaw and Polier ...', of which lot 329 was 'Two volumes comprising upwards of 60 miniatures, finely executed, representing the system of Indian Mythology; ... with an explanation in the hand writing of Col. Polier',[1] *i.e.* the two volumes under discussion, which were sold to White for the huge sum of £267.15s. Comparison of the handwriting of these notes with that of Polier's letter to Sir Joseph Banks giving his Vedic manuscripts to the British Museum in 1789[2] confirms Sotheby's catalogue entry. Beckford acquired manuscripts from Col. Antoine Polier following his murder in Avignon in 1794.

It is not clear what hand if any Polier had in the formation of this Lucknow style, which was employed also in sets of portraits of the Mughal Emperors and the Nawabs of Oudh, and sets of tradesmen and castes, the standard preoccupations of the 'Company' painters under British patronage, but he approved of it sufficiently to commission these two volumes of Hindu divinities, a subject much closer to his sphere of interests than the standard sets. It also appealed very much to British tastes to judge by the large sum paid for these albums in 1817 being among the first sets of Hindu paintings to come on to the European market, at a time when old master drawings could be purchased for a few guineas. The albums must therefore date 1780–89, when Polier left Lucknow to return to Europe.

The oddity of the albums' peculiar, washed-out Lucknow style is re-echoed by the presentation of the divinities and the attempt to rationalize the apparent eccentricities of Hindu mythology – the Goddess's multiple arms are reduced to wings behind her back and the mounts of Ganesh and Kubera, the rat and the peacock, are increased in size so as not to appear too diminutive when compared with their riders.

British Library, London, Or.4769–70.

ff.64 (32 in each volume); painting on paper, 21·5 × 15cm, mounted on card, 34·5 × 26cm; water-colour heightened with gold; inscriptions in *Nasta'līq*; European covers of red leather with fly-leaves watermarked 1868; five folios of English description at front of volume 1.

Bibliography: BM 1899, Hindi, 97.

[1]Sotheby, May 1817.

[2]British Library Add.5346–56, BM 1902, p.1.

132 'Gulzār-i Nasīm'

Illustrated on p.147.

The Rose-garden of Nasīm. The romance of Tāj al-Mulk and Bakāvalī, a *masnavī* in Urdu by Dayashankara Kaula called Nasīm (1811–43) composed in 1254/1838–9, is based ultimately on the Persian version of this famous tale by ʿIzzat Allāh Bangālī, who translated the original Hindi in 1134/1722 under the title *Gul-i Bakāvalī*, 'The Rose of Bakāvalī'. Nasīm was a Kashmiri who settled in Lucknow, and was a learned interpreter of Hindu law, as well as a famous Urdu poet.[1]

This illustrated version of the work appears to be a presentation copy of the work dated in the year of its completion. There are 44 miniatures in the European-influenced style of Lucknow of the first half of the 19th century. In the miniatures of this Ms., the people frequently have European features and even hair styles (the nude angels with looped Victorian hairdos of f.89b), many of the buildings are in European style (the hall of f.19a), and are hung with European chandeliers. Trees and landscapes are in European style. The king on f.4a wears the royal crown of Oudh[2] and may indeed be a portrait of the contemporary monarch, Muhammad ʿAlī Shāh (1837–42), while the fish emblem of Oudh appear above a gateway on f.29a.

British Library, London, Or.13755.

ff.110; 20·5 × 13cm; paper, various shades of green, yellow, pink and buff; text panels 15 × 8cm; margins ruled in gold and colours; text in two columns in elegant *Nastaʿlīq*; 44 miniatures of same size as text panels; *sarlavḥ* (f.1b) of gold and ultramarine sprinkled with flowers; marginal gold floral arabesques ff.1b and 2a; red leather binding tooled in gold, with photographs of nautches mounted on both flyleaves.

Bibliography: Sotheby, 23 November 1976, lot 366 (illustration of f.19a), where the Ms. is attributed to Delhi.

[1]Garcin de Tassy 1870–1, pp.414–8.
[2]IOL 1972, plates 54–6.

133 picture 80. Sultān ʿĀlam and his beauties in 1262/1846, in the palace at Lucknow.

133 'Nizām ʿIshqnāma'

A King's Book of Love, a collection of poems in Persian and Urdu, apparently by Wājid ʿAlī Shāh, King of Oudh (1847–56), with 118 paintings illustrating his life. He is referred to throughout under his poetical name Sultān ʿĀlam. The king was a famous poet and musician, and published various *dīvāns* and *masnavīs* under his poetical names of Sultān ʿĀlam and Akhtar. The Ms. is dated 1266/1849–50, and the paintings all bear dates between 1250 and 1265/1834–49, the earliest illustrating the birth of a prince, presumably Sultān ʿĀlam himself, although Wājid ʿAlī Shāh was actually born some while before this. We are perhaps meant to take the pictures to represent the ideal life of a king, with lovely ladies to care for him far from affairs of state. The paintings are in the highly Europeanized style of Oudh in the mid-19th century, set in the king's European palace in Lucknow. It was removed from the royal library after the annexation in 1856; a letter tipped in speaks of it illustrating the 'Customs of the Court of Oudh', hence its usual title.

Royal Library, Windsor Castle.

ff. unnumbered (about 350); 44 × 27cm; paper; two columns of *Nastaʿlīq* script in panels 24 × 14·5cm; 118 paintings of same height but slightly wider than the text; leather cover blocked in gold, with blocked silver doublures.

Bibliography: Garcin de Tassy 1870–1, pp.181–4. AIP, No.626 (wrongly dated to 1826). IOL 1972, p.157 (wrongly attributed to the reign of Ghāzi ad-Dīn Haidar).

134 'Adhyātmarāmāyaṇa'

Illustrated on p.148.

The *Rāmāyaṇa* of the Supreme Self, from the Sanskrit *Brahmāṇḍapurāṇa*. A work of Vedantic synthesis like the *Yogavāsiṣtha*, it expounds the Vedanta philosophy in terms of the story of Rāma.

This is in fact an English translation of this extremely popular work, whose purpose was the introduction of the complex philosophy of non-duality to the ordinary Hindu in terms he could understand. The translation is by Charles Boddam, who from 1793–1811 was the District Judge and Magistrate at Chapra in Bihar, some 30 miles upstream from Patna, but on the north bank. He translated it from the Persian version made by Ānand Gyān, a pundit of the Benares Sanskrit College. The work was finished in 1804 and two fair copies were made, both copiously illustrated with paintings by local artists under the direction of some pundits.[1]

Although the school of artists working for British patrons in Patna is well-documented, little is known of the artists working at Chapra, who perhaps migrated there in the late 18th century from Patna. The artists of the two copies of the *Adhyātma Rāmāyaṇa* generally employ a weak water-colour, but some of the purely iconographical studies opening the work are in a stronger idiom.

India Office Library, London, MSS. Eur. C.215.

Two volumes, ff.347, 330; 26·5 × 19cm; European paper, watermarked 1803; 21 lines of copperplate; 111 paintings in wide black frames, some of them in horizontal format, 22 × 17cm; European bindings.

Bibliography: IOL 1972, pp.126–32.

[1]The other is IOL MSS. Eur.C.116, 1–2.

135 'Tasrīḥ al-Aqvām'

Illustrated on p.148.

A work in Persian, by Col. James Skinner[1] (1778–1841) containing notices of the castes, tribes and sects of the Panjab.

The work is in three sections, of which the first, by far the shortest, deals with the house of Tīmūr, from whom the Mughals descended, and is unillustrated; the second section, the bulk of the work, deals with the Hindu castes and sects; the third, with a few Muslim families and tribes, beginning with the Kings of Oudh.

Dated 1825, and copied in a large fair *Nasta'līq*, the work is now illustrated with 110 portraits, out of the original 122. The missing illustrations are scattered throughout the Ms. All of the portraits appear to be studies from life, with a few religious sufficiently famous to have their names inscribed in a neat *Nasta'līq* on the paintings themselves.

The medium of the paintings is water-colour with some gold heightening. They are on paper pasted on card and bound in, and they vary somewhat in size; a few have been extended to fit the format, somewhat clumsily it must be said, as the colours do not match too well. This is true of two of the superb annotated portraits, which were doubtless in Skinner's possession before 1825 and incorporated into the album. At least five hands may be distinguished. One of them, a superb portraitist, appears to have done all the annotated portraits, mostly ascetics whose wisdom or holiness or forcefulness jumps out from the page. The artist has found a most attractive means for the depiction of the human body, modelled yet smoothly fluent, with an attractive, free landscape style. His portraits of ascetics are in this vein, and contrast with the more formal portrait of the famous musician Miyān Himmat Khān on f.134b set against grey wall and white ground, as well as other studies of various castes of workers (tailor, cloth-printer, artist, etc.) and sect members. All of these are attributable to the same artist, whose work appears in the Fraser Album[2] and the Skinner Album[3] and is probably Ghulām 'Alī Khān. Although much of his work in this Ms. is less highly finished, it is characterized by a remarkable intentness on the work in hand, a new phenomenon in Indian art, exemplified best perhaps by a marvellous study of an ear-picker cleaning his bored client's ear (f.276b). Something over half of the paintings may be attributed to him.

A second hand in the *Tasrīḥ al-Aqvām* is distinguished by a deliberate elongation of the human figure, with small heads and immensely long legs, and was responsible for some powerful studies of warriors. This work corresponds to a well-defined group of paintings in the Fraser Album where this elongation is particularly noticeable, as well as a delight in loops of drapery[4], on which basis another few paintings in the *Tasrīḥ al-Aqvām* may be attributed to him. Three other hands may be distinguished in this Ms. for the rest of the work, two of whom contributed a very small number of good-quality paintings, one of them in a style and colouring close to No.136. The third who did the remainder is a much more pedestrian artist both for his figures and background, whether landscape or architectural.[5]

British Library, London, Add.27255.

Provenance: Ms. dedicated to General Sir John Malcolm; acquired from his son in 1865.

ff.462; 31·5 × 22cm; thick, creamy paper; nine lines of *Nasta'līq* in panels 18 × 11cm with margins ruled in gold and colours; one double-page *'unvān*; 110 paintings, of varying sizes between 24 × 17 and 18 × 11·5cm, on paper pasted on card and bound in; original binding of dark-brown leather painted with gold designs, plain red doublures with ruled gold frames.

Bibliography: BM 1879, pp.65–7. BL 1977, pp.155–7.

[1]M. Archer, 1960.
[2]Sotheby 7–8 July 1980, illustrated lots 4, 5, 15 and 31, also Sotheby New York, 9 December 1980.
[3]IOL 1972, No.169.
[4]Sotheby, *op. cit.*, illustrated lots 21–5 and 42–5.
[5]Another illustrated copy of this text passed through London recently, see Christie, 23 April 1981, with the scribe named as Muhammad Baksh.

136 'Tazkīrat al-'Umarā'

Illustrated on p.149.

Historical notices of princely families of Rajputana and the Panjab, written in Persian by Col. James Skinner, some time before 1830. The work is in four parts called *Ṭabaḳah*. The first part is on the Rajput families, in four chapters, on the families respectively of Udaipur (head of all the Rajputs); of Jodhpur and their relatives in Kishangarh and Bikaner; of Jaipur and their 15 feudatory chiefs; and of Rewari and Sonipat. The second part is on 12 Sikh families of the Panjab, beginning with Ranjit Singh of Lahore. The third part deals with four Muslim princely families – Farrukhnagar, Dujana, Rania and Bahawalpur. The fourth part contains a description of Haryana, in the south-eastern Panjab, and its chief towns of Hissar and Hansi, in the latter of which Col. Skinner was based with his irregular cavalry regiment, Skinner's Horse. With the exception of the first four Rajput families and of the Bahawalpur house, all the families noted were in the vicinity of Hansi.

This copy is dated 10 June 1830 and is illustrated with 37 portraits of the current heads of the princely houses, as well as a fine portrait of Col. Skinner himself opposite a dedication to General Sir John Malcolm (1769–1833) (ff.4a and 3b). This, like No.135, has the paintings pasted on card and bound in. All the portraits are in water-colour heightened with gold, and though unsigned, some are in the style of Ghulām 'Alī Khān.

Apart from the fine portrait of Skinner himself on f.4a,[1] the most successful work attributable to Ghulām 'Alī is perhaps that of the forceful Javān Singh, Mahārāna of Udaipur (1828–38) on f.8b, seated on a pile of blue cushions smoking a hookah, while a handsome young attendant waves a chowrie over him. The glowing colours of this and the other portraits, though required by precedent, are untypical of Ghulām 'Alī who preferred at this date a much cooler and subdued palette for his best work. Another hand which may be distinguished is that of an artist who revelled in a deliberate elongation of the human figure, whose work is also in No.135 and the Fraser Album. Most of the portraits are in the Company style, but a few are in traditional Indian style standing in full profile holding a flower or a sword. These must be copies of state portraits from the court concerned, rather than taken from the life, presumably those who were either dead or whom Skinner never met. At the great meeting at Rooper in October 1831[2] between the Governor-General Lord Bentinck and Ranjit Singh of Lahore, most of the trans-Sutlej chiefs would have been present in Ranjit's suite and portraits could be taken. The cis-Sutlej chiefs were of course Skinner's neighbours. And a similar meeting at Ajmer in 1832 would have provided opportunity to take the portraits of the Rajput chiefs. It is possible therefore that the portraits were not added to the volume until 1832, and were probably collected by Skinner over a period of years.[3]

British Library, London, Add.27254.

Provenance: Dedicated to Sir John Malcolm; acquired in 1865.

137 ff.611b, 612. Shāh Jahān in procession, and his tomb the Tāj Mahāl, being visited by a group of British officers, while angels shower gold on it.

ff.289; 30×21cm; thick creamy paper; nine lines of large *Nasta'līq* in panels 18×11cm with margins ruled in gold and colours; elaborate *'unvān*; 37 paintings, mostly 20×13cm, in water-colour heightened with gold; contemporary binding, dark-brown, painted with gold designs; arabesques in gold and colours on folio edges.

Bibliography: BM 1879, pp.302–3. BL 1977, p.157.

[1]Skinner wrote to Ghulam 'Alī Khān in 1834 ordering a portrait, describing him as 'the counterpart of Mani and Bihzad'. See M. and W.G. Archer 1955, p.67.

[2]Fraser 1851, pp.205–18.

[3]Another illustrated version of this text is in the Chester Beatty Library, Dublin (Ind. MS.33) dedicated to J. Watkins, and an unillustrated version in the British Library (Add.24051), all in the same hand; this suggests that the illustrations were inserted at the appropriate place into certain copies and not in others.

137 ''Amal-i Salīh'

The history of Shāh Jahān by Muhammad Salīh Kanbū. The author was an important calligrapher at the time of Shāh Jahān and son of the famous earlier calligrapher Mīr 'Abdallāh Mushkīn Qalam (see No.72). The work is one of the many unofficial histories of the reign.

By about 1830, the probable date of this Ms. of the *'Amal-i Salīh*, the Delhi Mughal style was incorporating Europeanisms, including perspective. About 1820–30 the paintings of the architectural glories of Delhi and Agra done by Indian artists for the British had passed through the stage of strict architectural drawings, and now incorporated landscapes and figures, giving them a more romantic aura in keeping with the times.[1] In this Ms., all the architectural drawings now incorporate these elements, and figures of British army officers may be seen on the terrace of the Tāj Mahāl, which is seen at the end of a bosky vista, in striking contrast to the more traditional portrait of Shāh Jahān on horseback opposite.

British Library, London, Or.2157.

ff.920; 39·5×24·5cm; creamy paper; 15

138 The scribe Āghā Mīrzā presents the finished Ms. to Rāja Vinay Singh. After Hendley.

lines *Nastaʿlīq* in panels 26·5 × 14cm with margins in gold and colours; two *ʿunvāns*; 11 double-page and 6 single-page miniatures of same size approx. as text panels; contemporary covers of blocked gold panels of arabesque, with doublures of red morocco with stamped and gilded medallion.

Bibliography: BM 1879, p.1,069. BL 1977, p.128.

[1]Archer 1972, pp.166–71.

138 'Gulistān'

The Rose-garden of Saʿdī (see No.55).

Mahārao Rāja Vinay Singh of Alwar (1815–57) was one of the last of the great patrons of manuscript illustration. He enticed to his court painters, calligraphers, illuminators and book binders, mostly from Delhi, including such artists as Ghulām ʿAlī Khān. His copy of the *Gulistān* is said to have taken 12 years to complete, and is the most famous manuscript he had produced for him, spending it is said a lakh of rupees. In addition to the 17 miniatures by Ghulām ʿAlī Khān and Baladev, each page has illuminated borders as well as exquisite little square panels of illumination within the text itself, containing arabesques or miniatures of birds or animals. This work was done by Nātha Shāh Panjābī and ʿAbd ar-Rahmān. The calligraphy in large *Nastaʿlīq* is by Āghā Mīrzā of Delhi, and the binding of finely painted leather by ʿAbd ar-Rahmān, who bound many of the finest manuscripts in the Alwar Library.

Government Museum, Alwar.

ff.287; 34·5 × 18cm; paper; eight lines of large *Nastaʿlīq* in panels ruled in gold and colours; all margins with gold designs, and medallions in gold and colours throughout text; 17 miniatures, within the text panels; covers with designs stamped from blocks, and painted and gilded; edges painted with floral border.

Bibliography: Hendley 1888, plates LXIV–LXX. Alwar 1961, p.97.

139 'Sālhūtār'

Illustrated on p.149.

A treatise on farriery, translated into Persian from the original Sanskrit work, *Śālihotra*, under the direction of Khvāja ʿAbd Allāh, called ʿAbd Allāh Khān Bahādur Fīrūz Jang, a nobleman of the Mughal court in the reigns of Jahāngīr and Shāh Jahān. The Sanskrit text itself is a work of uncertain date attributed to the sage Shālihotra, and deals with the classification of horses (on basis of colour), their care and their ailments.

This Ms. of the Persian translation was copied in 1268/1851–2 apparently at Kapurthala in the Panjab. The 17 paintings of stallions are by the Sikh artist Kishan Singh from Kapurthala who describes himself as a servant of Mahārāja Randhir Singh.[1] Obviously Randhir Singh of Kapurthala (r.1852–70), is here referred to. Archer notes that in 1864, Kishan Singh exhibited an album of water-colours at the Lahore exhibition, and work by other artists for Randhir Singh indicates a quite flourishing school.[2] The paintings are all of different coloured stallions being held by their Sikh syces or grooms, except for the final painting after the colophon on f.42a which shows a mad stallion savaging its grooms, a nice touch by the artist who was obviously bored by painting so many sedate horses. The main section of the paintings corresponds to the description of the different colours of horses and their properties at the beginning of the work. Kishan Singh's style indicates that he was trained as a Company school artist presumably either in Delhi or in Hansi where Colonel Skinner kept artists in his employ. The paintings are all included as it were in the text, there being no formal frame between text and illustrations which are with one exception set against the same white ground as the script, creating a less formal impression than other Mss. of this date.

British Library, London, Or.6704.

ff.42; 32 × 20cm; *Nastaʿlīq* script; 15 lines within gold ruled frames 26·2 × 14·5cm; headings, keywords etc. in red; red morocco cover, gilt-tooled frames.

Bibliography: BM 1968, p.30. BL 1977, p.2, plates 2 and 3.

[1]Griffin and Massy 1910, vol.2, pp.415–24, for a brief account of the Kapurthala state.
[2]Archer 1966, p.61; and Randhawa 1971.

140 'Sarvasiddhāntattvacūḍāmaṇi'

The Crest-jewel of the Essence of all Systems of Astronomy, a comparison in Sanskrit of the astronomical systems of Europe, Islam and India, by Durgāshankara Pāthaka of Benares. The point of departure for this treatise is apparently the horoscope (*janmapatra*) of Prince Navnihal Singh, grandson of Ranjit Singh, Mahārāja of the Panjab (1780–1839), and this is the presentation manuscript, lavishly illuminated.

According to Sudhākara,[1] the author was the son of Shivalāla Pāthaka, was born in 1787, and lived in Benares where he became a well-known astronomer. This Ms. was apparently commissioned by Kharrak Singh when he ascended the throne in Lahore following the death of Ranjit Singh in 1839. Durgāshankara went to Lahore to deliver it, but was driven out by the enmity of Navnihal Singh and returned to Benares only with much difficulty. Kharrak Singh, who was apparently of weak mind, died in 1840, and his son immediately afterwards – he was killed by falling masonry when returning from his father's funeral.

The Ms. does not entirely bear out Sudhākara's account. Navnihal is nowhere mentioned, but there are several folios missing near the opening. At the beginning are portraits of Guru Nānak, Guru Gobind Singh, a missing but captioned portrait of Ranjit Singh and then a portrait of a boy of about 10 or 12, with a halo, and a woman, presumably his mother (f.25a). This must be Navnihal Singh and his mother, Rānī Chand Kaur. Since the boy is at most 12 years old, while Navnihal was 18 on his grandfather's death in 1839, the painting must have been done about 1833. A *terminus post quem* is provided by a dated watermark of 1833 in at least one of the folios, while Ranjit Singh is spoken of as still living. The main part of the Ms. must therefore have been completed between 1833 and 1839, the date of the colophon and the completion of the work. The text also pays considerable tribute to Laihnā Singh[2], and to his father Desā Singh. This is the famous Sardar Laihnā Singh Majithia,[3] one of the chief Sikh nobles, the confidant of Ranjit Singh, Governor of the Hill States and of the Golden Temple in Amritsar. He was also a man of science and interested in astronomy and engineering. It seems likely however that Durgāshankara would not have met him before 1839, when he visited Lahore, and was befriended by Laihnā Singh when escaping from Navnihal Singh's anger. There appears to be a portrait of him at the end of the manuscript (f.291a), in which

140 ff.56b, 57. A star-map according to the Hindu system.

he is seated with a boy of about 10, perhaps his son Dayāl Singh, and a pundit, obviously discussing astronomical matters from the number of instruments scattered about; the pundit must be the author, who is also seen in another painting using a table-mounted telescope, watched by his nephew Jatāshankara (f.29a). These portraits and the verses eulogizing the Majithia, were perhaps added after the author's return to Benares, while the details about Navnihal Singh were probably removed. All the formal portraits at the beginning are in traditional gouache, while those of Laihnā Singh and of the author with his nephew are in water-colour. There is no reason why they should have been put in the Ms. before 1839.

Apart from the portraits, the Ms. contains full-page paintings of representations of the signs of the Zodiac (with some missing), of the constellations according to Indian and European conceptions, of the traditional cosmography of the Hindus centred on Mount Meru as well as many smaller paintings of the planets, lunar mansions, etc. All these latter are more sketchily painted in water-colours, and by artists who were familiar with the work of both Lucknow and Chapra artists of the early 19th century. The folios are tinted in pastel shades, and every page bears decoration, much of it of European inspiration, floral designs, geometric patterns etc. Even the many astronomical tables are beautifully laid out and decorated. The illuminator was an extremely skilful artist who must have had access to European pattern books, and seen pictures of early Victorian angels which he has used to charming effect several times, surmounting their curls with raffishly decorated turbans. The brilliant Zodiac plans are also his work.

British Library, London, Or.5259.

ff.293 (numbered 1–304, the missing folios being mostly portraits at the beginning and five of the signs of the Zodiac); 18 × 22cm; paper, of European manufacture, watermarked 1833, tinted beige, pink, green, yellow and blue; 13 lines of *Nāgarī* script in panels 15 × 11cm with margins ruled in gold and colours; 70 miniatures, many full-frame or full-page, 16 astronomical charts; most pages decorated with floral designs; original cover of green velvet with spangle and silver-wire decoration, with red velvet doublure, let into a green leather frame and spine in a European re-binding.

Bibliography: BM 1902, p.208. Pattie 1980, fig.6, the Hindu star-map repro. in colour.

[1]Sudhākara 1892.
[2]Sudhākara calls this personage the Rāja of Kotah, so clearly did not have access to all the facts.
[3]Griffin and Massy 1910.

Select Bibliography

All books published in London unless otherwise noted

Abbreviations

AB	*The Arts of Bengal*, Whitechapel Art Gallery, 1980
AI	*Arts of Islam*, 1976
AIP	*The Art of India and Pakistan*, ed. L. Ashton, 1950
Alwar 1961	*Catalogue & guide to Government Museum, Alwar, Part I*, Jaipur, 1961
AO	*Ars Orientalis*, Ann Arbor
BAAB	*Bulletin of the American Academy of Benares*, Benares
BBSM	*Bulletin of the Baroda State Museum & Picture Gallery*, Baroda
BL 1976	*The Qur'ān*, by Martin Lings and Yasin Hamid Safadi, 1976
BL 1977	*Miniatures from Persian manuscripts : a catalogue and subject index of paintings from Persia, India and Turkey in the British Library and British Museum*, by Norah M. Titley, 1977
BL 1979–80	*British Library Annual Report 1979–80*, 1980
BL 1980–81	*British Library Annual Report 1980–81*, 1981
BM 1846, 1871	*Catalogus codicum manuscriptorum orientalium qui in Museo Britannico asservantur. Pars secunda, codices arabicos amplectens*, 1846, 1871
BM 1879	*Catalogue of the Persian manuscripts in the British Museum*, by Charles Rieu, 1879–83
BM 1895	*Supplement to the Catalogue of the Persian manuscripts in the British Museum*, by Charles Rieu, 1895
BM 1899	*Catalogue of the Hindi, Panjabi and Hindustani manuscripts in the library of the British Museum*, by J.F. Blumhardt, 1899
BM 1902	*Catalogue of the Sanskrit manuscripts in the British Museum*, by Cecil Bendall, 1902
BM 1905	*Catalogue of the Marathi, Gujarati, Bengali, Assamese, Oriya, Pushtu and Sindhi manuscripts in the library of the British Museum*, by J.F. Blumhardt, 1905
BM 1968	*Handlist of Persian manuscripts 1895–1966*, by G.M. Meredith-Owens, 1968
BM 1976	*Paintings from the Muslim courts of India*, 1976
BMQ	*British Museum Quarterly*
Bod 1889	*Catalogue of the Persian, Turkish, Hindûstânî, and Pushtû manuscripts in the Bodleian Library*, by E. Sachau and H. Ethé, *Part I, the Persian Manuscripts*, Oxford, 1889
Bod 1905	*Catalogue of Sanskrit manuscripts in the Bodleian Library, vol.II*, by Moritz Winternitz and Arthur Berriedale Keith, Oxford, 1905
Bombay 1930	*Descriptive catalogue of Sanskrit and Prakrit manuscripts in the library of the Bombay Branch of the Royal Asiatic Society*, by H.D. Velankar, Bombay, 1925–30
BPWM	*Bulletin of the Prince of Wales Museum*, Bombay
BWG	*Persian miniature painting*, by L. Binyon, J.V.S. Wilkinson, and B. Gray, Oxford, 1933
Cambridge 1922	*A supplementary handlist of the Muhammadan manuscripts in the libraries of the University and Colleges of Cambridge*, by E.G. Browne, Cambridge, 1922
CB 1936	*The library of A. Chester Beatty : a catalogue of the Indian miniatures*, by Sir Thomas W. Arnold, edited by J.V.S. Wilkinson, 1936
Chhavi	*Golden Jubilee volume of the Bharat Kala Bhavan*, Benares, 1971
Christie	Sale catalogues of books, oriental miniatures and manuscripts, various dates
CUL 1883	*Catalogue of the Buddhist Sanskrit manuscripts in the University Library, Cambridge*, by Cecil Bendall, Cambridge, 1883
DCAM	*Descriptive catalogue of Assamese manuscripts*, by H. Goswami, Calcutta, 1930
ICMAA	*Inde, cinq mille ans d'art*, Paris, 1978

IIH	*Illuminierte islamische Handschriften*, by I. Stchoukine, *et al.*, Wiesbaden, 1971
IOL 1903	*Catalogue of the Persian manuscripts in the library of the India Office*, by H. Ethé, Oxford, 1903
IOL 1935	*Catalogue of the Sanskrit and Prakrit manuscripts in the library of the India Office*, vol.II, by A.B. Keith, Oxford, 1935
IOL 1972	*Company drawings in the India Office Library*, by Mildred Archer, 1972
IOL 1981	*Indian miniatures in the India Office Library*, [by] Toby Falk and Mildred Archer, 1981
IP	*Indian painting, Mughal, Rajput and a Sultanate manuscript*, [by Toby Falk, Ellen Smart, and Robert Skelton], 1978
JAA	*Jaina art and architecture*, ed. A. Ghosh, Delhi, 1975
Jaipur 1971	*Catalogue of manuscripts in the Maharaja of Jaipur Museum*, by G.N. Bahura, Jaipur, 1971
JAS	*Journal of the Asiatic Society*, Calcutta
JISOA	*Journal of the Indian Society of Oriental Art*, Calcutta
JRAS	*Journal of the Royal Asiatic Society*
Keir 1976	*The Keir Collection : Islamic painting and the arts of the book*, by B.W. Robinson, E.J. Grube, G.M. Meredith-Owens, and R.W. Skelton, 1976
LK	*Lalit Kalā*, New Delhi
MIC	*Manuscripts from Indian collections*, New Delhi, 1964
ND	*New documents of Indian painting – a reappraisal*, by K. Khandalavala and Moti Chandra, Bombay, 1969
OA	*Oriental Art*
OPLB	*Catalogue of the Arabic and Persian manuscripts in the Oriental Public Library*, prepared by Maulavi Abdul Muqtadir, Bankipore, 1908–42
OPLB 1920	*Descriptive list of photographic reproductions of illustrations from three Persian manuscripts in the Oriental Public Library at Bankipore*, by Wali ad Din Khuda Bakhsh, [Patna, 1920]
PIL	*Paintings from Islamic lands*, ed. R. Pinder-Wilson, Oxford, 1969
RAS 1876	'Catalogue of Buddhist Sanskrit manuscripts in the possession of the Royal Asiatic Society (Hodgson Collection)', in *JRAS*, vol.8, 1876, pp.1–52
RAS 1892	'Catalogue of the Arabic, Persian, Hindustani and Turkish manuscripts in the library of the Royal Asiatic Society', in *JRAS*, vol.24, London, 1892
Sotheby	Sale catalogues of books, oriental miniatures and manuscripts, various dates
Spink 1980	*Islamic art from India*, Spink & Son, 1980
UH	*Urdu Handschriften*, [von] S.M.H. Zaidi, Wiesbaden, 1973

Abdul Aziz, Sh. *The imperial library of the Mughuls*, Lahore, 1967

Abu'l Fazl *The Ain i Akbari*, translated by H. Blochmann, Calcutta, 1873–1910

Abu'l Fazl *The Akbarnāma* . . . translated by H. Beveridge, Calcutta, 1903–39

Adamova, A., and T. Greck *Miniatures from Kashmirian manuscripts*, Leningrad, 1976

Andhare, S. 'A dated Amber Rāgamālā and the problem of provenance of the 18th century Jaipuri paintings', in *LK*, no.15, 1972, pp.47–51

Appasamy, J. *Thanjavur painting of the Maratha period*, Delhi, 1980

Archer, M. 'The two worlds of Colonel Skinner', in *History Today*, London, 1960, pp.608–15

Archer, M. *India and British portraiture, 1770–1825*, 1979

Archer, M. and W.G. *Indian painting for the British*, 1955

Archer, W.G. *Central Indian painting*, 1958

Archer, W.G. *Indian miniatures*, 1960

Archer, W.G. *Painting of the Sikhs*, 1966

Ardeshir, A.C. 'Mughal miniature painting', in *Roopalekha*, vol.1, New Delhi, 1940

Arnold, *Sir* T., and A. Grohmann *The Islamic book*, 1929

Bābur *The Babur-nāma in English*, by A.S. Beveridge, 1922

Bahura, G.N. *The literary heritage of the rulers of Amber and Jaipur*, Jaipur, 1975

Bāna *The Harṣa-carita*. Translated by E.B. Cowell and F.W. Thomas, 1897

Banerjee, P. 'A manuscript dated in the regnal year 53 of Rāmapāla', in *Indo-Asian Culture*, vol.18, no. 1, New Delhi, 1969, pp.61–3

Banerjee, P. 'An illustrated Astasahasrika Prajnāpāramitā manuscript in the collection of the National Museum', in *LK*, no.16, 1974, pp.33–6
Barnett, L.D. 'Two illustrated Assamese manuscripts', in *BMQ*, vol.VIII, 1933, pp.10–12
Barrett, D. *Painting of the Deccan, XVI – XVII century*, 1958
Barrett, D. 'Some unpublished Deccan miniatures', in *LK*, no.7, 1960, pp.9–13
Barrett, D. 'Painting at Bijapur', in *PIL*, 1969, pp.142–59
Barrett, D., and B. Gray *Painting of India*, Geneva, 1963
Beach, M.C. *Rajput painting at Bundi and Kotah*, Ascona, 1974
Beach, M.C. *The Grand Mogul*, Williamstown, 1978
Bhuyan, S.K. *Tungkhungia Buranji, or a history of Assam, 1681–1826, an old Assamese chronicle*, translated by S.K. Bhuyan, Calcutta, 1933
al-Bīrūnī *Alberuni's India, an English edition*, by E. Sachau, 1910
Bhattacharya, B. 'Twenty-two Buddhist miniatures from Bengal (11th century AD), in *BBSM*, vol. 1, 1944, pp.17–36
Bhattacharyya, B. *The Indian Buddhist iconography*, 2nd ed., Calcutta, 1958
Binyon, L. 'Relation between Rajput and Moghul painting – a new document', in *Rupam*, no.29, Calcutta, 1929, pp.4–5
Binyon, L., and T.W. Arnold *The court-painters of the Grand Moguls*, 1921
Bodleian Library *Mughal miniatures of the earlier periods*, Bodleian Library Picture Book, no.9, Oxford, 1953
Brough, J. *The Gāndhārī Dharmapada*, 1962
Brown, P. *Indian painting under the Mughals*, Oxford, 1924
Brown, T.J., G.M. Meredith-Owens, and D.H. Turner 'Manuscripts from the Dyson-Perrins Collection', in *BMQ*, vol.XXIII, 1961, pp.27–38
Brown, W. Norman *The story of Kālaka*, Washington, 1933
Brown, W. Norman *A descriptive and illustrated catalogue of miniature paintings of the Jaina Kalpasūtra*, Washington, 1934
Brown, W. Norman 'A Jain manuscript from Gujarat illustrated in Early Western Indian and Persian styles', in *Ars Islamica*, vol.IV, Ann Arbor, 1937
Brown, W. Norman *Manuscript illustrations of the Uttarādhyayana Sūtra*, Newhaven, 1941
Brunel, Francis *Splendour of Indian miniatures*, Boulogne, 1981
Bühler, G. *Indian palaeography*, Calcutta, 1959
Burnell, A.C. *Elements of south Indian palaeography, revised edition*, reprinted Varanasi, 1968
Chaghatai, M.A. 'The illustrated edition of the Razm nama . . . at Akbar's court', in *Bulletin of the Deccan College Research Institute*, vol.V, Poona, 1943–44, pp.281–329
Chaghatai, M.A. *Painting during the Sultanate period*, Lahore, 1963
Chandra, Moti *The technique of Mughal painting*, Lucknow, 1949
Chandra, Moti *Jain miniature painting from western India*, Ahmedabad, 1949
Chandra, Moti 'Paintings from an illustrated version of the Rāmāyaṇa painted at Udaipur in AD 1649', in *BPWM*, no.5, Bombay, 1955–7, pp.33–49
Chandra, Moti *Mewar painting in the 17th century*, Delhi, 1957
Chandra, Moti *Mewar painting*, Delhi, 1971
Chandra, Moti 'A pair of painted wooden covers of the Kāraṇḍavyūha manuscript dated AD 1455 from eastern India', in *Chhavi*, 1971, pp.240–2
Chandra, Moti, and P.L. Gupta 'An illustrated manuscript of the Rasikapriya', in *BPWM*, no. 8, 1965, pp.18–21
Chandra, Moti, and U.P. Shah *New documents of Jaina painting*, Bombay, 1975
Chandra, Pramod 'A Ragamala set of the Mewar school in the National Museum of India', in *LK*, nos.3–4, 1957
Chandra, Pramod 'Notes on Mandu Kalpasutra of AD 1439', in *Marg*, vol.XII, no. 3, Bombay, 1959, pp.51–4
Chandra, Pramod 'Ustad Salivahana and the development of Popular Mughal art', in *LK*, no. 8, 1960
Chandra, Pramod 'A unique Kālakācāryakathā MS. in the style of the Mandu Kalpasūtra of AD 1439', in *BAAB*, vol.1, 1967, pp.1–10
Chandra, Pramod *Ṭūṭī-nāma . . . Commentarium*, Graz, 1976
Chaudhary, R. *The university of Vikramasīla*, Patna, 1975
Choudhury, P.C. *Hastividyārṇava*, ed. by P.C. Choudhury, Gauhati, 1976
Chowdhury, A.M. *Dynastic history of Bengal*, Dacca, 1967
Conze, E. 'Remarks on a Pala MS. in the Bodleian Library', in *OA*, vol.1, 1948, pp.9–12
Coomaraswamy, A.K. *The treatise of Ibn al-Jazari on Automata*, Boston, 1924
Cran, R. 'The Manley Rāgamālā', in *British Museum Yearbook*, 1980
Crowe, Sylvia, et al. *The gardens of Mughal India*, London, 1972

Das, A.K. 'Bishndās', in *Chhavi*, 1971, pp.183–91
Das Gupta, R. *Eastern Indian manuscript painting*, Bombay, 1972
Datta-Barua, H.N. *Citra-Bhāgavata*, Nalbari, 1949
Dawud, Mirza Y., and A.K. Coomaraswamy *Burning and melting, being the Sūz u Gudāz of Muhammad Ṛiza Nauʿi*, 1912
Digby, S. 'The literary evidence for painting in the Delhi Sultanate', in *BAAB*, vol.1, 1967, pp.47–58
Diskalkar, D.B. *Materials used for Indian epigraphical records*, Poona, 1979
Doshi, Saryu 'Twelfth century illustrated manuscripts from Mūdbidri', in *BPWM*, no.8, 1965, pp.29–36
Doshi, Saryu 'An illustrated manuscript from Aurangabad dated AD 1650', in *LK*, no.15, 1972, pp.19–28

Ebeling, K. *Ragamala painting*, Basle, 1973
Elliot, H.M., and J. Dowson *The history of India as told by its own historians*, 8 vols., 1867–77
Ettinghausen, R. 'The Bustan manuscript of Sultan Nasir-Shah Khalji', in *Marg*, vol.12, Bombay, 1959, pp.40–3
Ettinghausen, R. *Paintings of the Emperors and Sultans of India in American Collections*, New Delhi, 1961
Ettinghausen, R., and I. Fraad 'Sultanate painting in Persian style', in *Chhavi*, 1971, pp.48–66

Forster, G. *A journey from Bengal to England through . . . Kashmir*, 1798
Foucher, A. *Étude sur l'iconographie bouddhique de l'Inde*, Paris, 1900
Fraser, J. Baillie *Military memoir of Lieut. Col. James Skinner*, 1851
French, J.C. 'The land of the wrestlers', in *Indian Art and Letters*, vol.1, 1927

Gait, *Sir* E. *A history of Assam*, Calcutta, 1926
Gangoly, O.C. *Rāgas & Rāgiṇīs*, Calcutta, 1934–5
Gangoly, O.C. *Critical catalogue of miniature paintings in the Baroda Museum*, Baroda, 1961
Garcin de Tassy, J. *Histoire de la litterature hindouie et hindoustanie*, 2nd. ed., Paris, 1870–71
Gascoigne, Bamber *The Great Moghuls*, 1971
Ghosh, D.P. 'An illustrated Rāmāyaṇa manuscript of Tulsīdās and paṭs from Bengal', in *JISOA*, vol.XIII, 1945, pp.130–9
Ghosh, D.P. 'Eastern school of medieval Indian painting', in *Chhavi*, 1971, pp.91–103
Glück, H. *Die indischen Miniaturen des Hamzae Romanes*, Vienna, 1925
Godard, Y. 'Les marges du Murakkaʿ Gulshan', in *Athar-é Irān*, vol.I, Haarlem, 1936, pp.11–33
Gode, P.K. 'The Bhāgavata Purāṇa–an illustrated manuscript copied in AD 1648', in *New Indian Antiquary*, vol.I, Bombay, 1938, pp.249–53

Goetz, H. 'The first golden-age of Udaipur', in *AO*, vol.II, 1957
Goetz, H. 'Two illustrated Persian manuscripts from Kashmir', in *Arts Asiatiques*, vol.IX, Paris, 1963, pp.61–72
Griffin, L.H., and C.F. Massy *Chiefs and families of note in the Punjab, rev. ed.*, Lahore, 1910
Grube, E.J. *Islamic painting from the 11th to the 18th century in the collection of Hans P. Kraus*, New York, 1969

Ḥamzanāma *Ḥamza-nāma, vollständige Wiedergabe der bekannten Blätter der Handschrift aus den Beständen aller erreichbaren Sammlungen*, Graz, 1974–[in progress]
Hayes, R.J. *The Chester Beatty Library*, Dublin, 1963
Hendley, T.H. *Memorials of the Jeypore exhibition, 1883, vol.IV, the Razm Namah*, 1883–5
Hendley, T.H. *Ulwar and its art treasures*, 1888
Hickmann, R., and V. Enderlein *Indische Albumblätter, Miniaturen und Kalligraphien aus der Zeit der Moghul-Kaiser*, Leipzig, 1979
Hill, Donald R. *The book of ingenious mechanical devices*, Dordrecht/Boston, 1974
Hiuen-Tsiang, *Buddhist records of the western world*, trans. S. Beal, 1883
Hoernle, A.F.R. 'An epigraphical note on palm-leaf, paper and birch-bark', in *JAS*, vol.LXIX, 1901, pp.93–134
Hutchison, J., and J. Ph. Vogel 'The history of Rajauri state', in *Journal of the Panjab Historical Society*, vol.IX, Lahore, 1925, pp.131–60

Jahāngīr *The Tūzuk-i-Jahāngīrī, or Memoirs of Jahāngīr*, translated by A. Rogers, edited by H. Beveridge, 1909–14
James, David *Islamic masterpieces of the Chester Beatty Library*, 1981
Joshi, K.B. *Paper making (as a cottage industry) with appendix 'Migration of paper from China to India A.D. 105–1500'*, by P.K. Gode, Wardha, 1944

Kalhana *Kalhaṇa's Rājataraṅginī, a chronicle of the Kings of Kashmir*, translated by M.A. Stein, 1900
Kaye, G.R. *The Bakhshālī manuscript: a study in medieval mathematics*, Calcutta, 1927–33
Khandalavala, K. 'Leaves from Rajasthan', in *Marg*, vol.IV, Bombay, 1951
Khandalavala, K. 'A "Gita Govinda" series in the Prince of Wales Museum', in *BPWM*, no.4, 1953–4, pp.1–18
Khandalavala, K. 'The Mṛigāvat of Bharat Kala Bhavan', in *Chhavi*, 1971, pp.19–36
Khandalavala, K., and Moti Chandra 'An illustrated Kalpasūtra painted at Jaunpur in AD 1465', in *LK*, no.12, 1962, pp.9–15
Khandalavala, K., and Moti Chandra *An illustrated* Āranyaka Parvan *in the Asiatic Society of Bombay*, Bombay, 1974
Khandalavala, K., and Moti Chandra 'A consideration of an illustrated MS. from Maṇḍapadurga (Mandu) dated 1439 AD', in *LK*, no.6, 1959, pp.8–29
Khandalavala, K., and Moti Chandra *Miniatures and sculptures from the collection of the late Sir Cowasji Jehangir, Bart*, Bombay, 1965
Khandalavala, K., and Moti Chandra 'An early Akbari illustrated manuscript of Tilasm and Zodiac', in *LK*, no.14, 1969, pp.9–20
Khandalavala, K., Moti Chandra and Pramod Chandra *Miniature paintings from the Sri Motichand Khajanchi Collection*, Delhi, 1960
Khandalavala, K., *et al.* 'A new document of Indian painting', in *LK*, no.10, 1962, pp.45–54
Kirfel, W. *Kosmographie der Inder*, Bonn, 1920
Kraemer, J. *Persische Miniaturen und ihr Umkreis. Buch- und Schriftkunst arabischer, persischer, türkischer und indischer Handschriften aus dem Besitz der früheren Preussischen Staats- und der Tübinger Universitätsbibliothek*, Tübingen, 1956
Krishnadas, Rai 'An illustrated Avadhī MS. of Laur-Chandā', in *LK*, nos.1–2, 1955–6, pp.66–71
Kühnel, E., and H. Goetz *Indian bookpainting from Jahangir's Album in the State Library in Berlin*, 1926

Levi, S. 'Note sur les manuscrits provenant de Bamiyan (Afghanistan) et de Gilgit (Cachemire)', in *Journal Asiatique*, tome CCXX, Paris, 1932, pp.1–45
Lewis, B. *The world of Islam*, 1976
Lewis, C. 'An illustrated Sanskrit manuscript', in *BMQ*, vol.XXIV, 1959–60, pp.25–7
Losty, J.P. 'Some illustrated Jaina manuscripts', in *British Library Journal*, vol.I, London, 1975, pp.145–62
Losty, J.P. 'A pair of illustrated binding-boards from Bihar of 1491–2, in *OA*, vol.XXIII, 1977, pp.190–9
Losty, J.P. 'The Jagat Singh *Vālmīki-Rāmāyaṇa* manuscript from Udaipur', in *Bulletin of the International Association of the Vrindaban Research Institute*, no.4, 1978, pp.3–14
Losty, J.P. *Krishna, a Hindu vision of God: scenes from the life of Krishna illustrated in Orissan and other eastern Indian manuscripts in the British Library*, 1980
Losty, J.P. *Masterpieces of Indian painting in the British Library*, New Delhi, 1982

Mallmann, M.-T. de 'À propos d'un MS. illustré du XIe S.', in *OA*, vol.XI, 1965, pp.224–34
Mallmann, M.-T. de *Introduction à l'iconographie du tântrisme bouddhique*, Paris, 1975
Marek, J., and H. Knížková *The Jenghiz Khān miniatures from the court of Akbar the Great*, 1963
Marrison, G.E. 'Kīrtana-ghoṣā – an illustrated Assamese manuscript', in *BMQ*, vol.XXXIII, 1969, pp.108–10
Martin, F.R. *The miniature paintings and painters of Persia, India and Turkey*, 1912
McCrindle, J.W. *Ancient India as described in classical literature*, 1901
Melikian-Chirvani, A.S. 'L'école de Shiraz et les origines de la miniature moghole', in *PIL*, 1969, pp.124–41
Meredith-Owens, G.M. *Persian miniature painting*, 1965
Meredith-Owens, G.M., and R. Pinder-Wilson 'A Persian translation of the Mahabharata', in *BMQ*, vol.XX, 1956
Miner, D. *The history of bookbinding 525–1950 A.D.*, Baltimore, 1957
Minorsky, V. *Calligraphers and painters – a treatise by Qāḍī Aḥmad*, Washington, 1959
Mookerjee, M. 'Two illustrated manuscripts in the Asutosh Museum of Indian Art, Calcutta', in *JISOA*, no.15, 1947

Naik, C.R. *'Abdur-Rahīm Khān-i-Khānān and his literary circle*, Ahmadabad, 1966
Nakhshabī, Ziyā ad-Dīn *Ṭūṭīnāma* [facsimile edition of the Mughal MS. in the Cleveland Museum], Graz, 1976
Navāz Khān, Shāh *The Maāthir-ul-Umarā: being biographies of the Muhammadan and Hindu officers of the Timurid sovereigns of India ... 2nd. ed.*, translated by H. Beveridge and Baini Prashad, Calcutta, 1911–52
Nawab, S.M. *The oldest Rajasthani paintings from Jain bhandars*, Ahmadabad, 1959

Pal, P. 'A new document of Indian painting', in *JRAS*, 1965
Pal, P. 'Evidence of Buddhist painting in eastern India in the 15th century', in *JAS*, 1966, pp.267–70
Pal, P. *The arts of Nepal ... sculpture*, Leiden/Köln, 1974
Pal, P. *Nepal: where the gods are young*, New York, 1975
Pal, P. *The arts of Nepal ... painting*, Leiden/Köln, 1978
Pattie, T.S. *Astrology*, 1980

Pinder-Wilson, R. 'Three illustrated manuscripts of the Mughal period', in *AO*, vol.II, 1957, pp.413–22
Pinder-Wilson, R. 'An illustrated Mughal MS. from Ahmadabad', in *PIL*, 1969, pp.160–71
Prakash, S. *Ragaragini miniatures from the Central Museum*, Jaipur, 1960
Punyavijaya, Muni, and U.P. Shah 'Some painted wooden book-covers from western India', in *JISOA*, special number, 1966, pp.34–42

Rājashekara *La Kāvyamīmāṃsā de Rājaśekhara*, traduite par N. Stchoupak et L. Renou, Paris, 1946
Randhawa, M.S. 'Two Panjabi artists of the nineteenth century, Kehar Singh and Kapur Singh', in *Chhavi*, 1971, pp.67–9
Rhys-Davids, T.W. *Buddhist India*, 1903
Rizvi, S.A.A. *Religious and intellectual history of the Muslims in Akbar's reign*, Delhi, 1975
Robinson, B.W. *Catalogue of a loan exhibition of Persian miniature paintings from British collections*, 1951
Robinson, B.W. *Persian miniature paintings from collections in the British Isles*, 1967
Rogers, M. *Princely paintings from Mughal India*, British Museum, 1980–81
Rosenfield, J. 'The arts of Buddhist India in the Boston Museum', in *Bulletin of the Museum of Fine Arts, Boston*, vol.LXIII, Boston, 1965, pp.130–67

Safadi, Y.H. *Islamic calligraphy*, 1978
Sankalia, H.D. *The university of Nalanda*, Delhi, 1972
Saraswati, S.K. 'East Indian manuscript painting', in *Chhavi*, 1971, pp.243–62
Saraswati, S.K. 'Rare architectural types in manuscript illustrations', in *Bangladesh Lalit Kala*, vol.I, Dacca, 1975
Saraswati, S.K. *Architecture of Bengal, Book I, Ancient phase*, Calcutta, 1976
Saraswati, S.K. *Tantrayana art – an album*, Calcutta, 1977
Scott, A. 'Laboratory notes: stains in silhouette on bound MSS.', in *BMQ*, vol.VII, 1932, pp.94–7
Shah, U.P. *More documents of Jaina paintings and Gujarati paintings of the sixteenth and later centuries*, Ahmadabad, 1976
Shah, U.P. *Treasures of Jaina bhaṇḍāras*, Ahmadabad, 1978
Shastri, H. *Indian pictorial art as developed in book-illustrations*, Baroda, 1936
Shastri, H. *Nalanda and its epigraphic material*, Calcutta, 1942
Shiveshwarkar, L. *The pictures of the Chaurapanchāśika, a Sanskrit love lyric*, Delhi, 1967
Siddiqi, M.I. 'An illustrated manuscript from Sind', in *PIL*, 1969, pp.172–86
Sircar, D.C. *Indian epigraphy*, Delhi, 1965
Skelton, R. 'Murshidabad painting', in *Marg*, vol.X, Bombay, 1956, pp.10–21
Skelton, R. 'The Mughal artist Farrokh Beg', in *AO*, vol.II, 1957, pp.393–411
Skelton, R. 'The Ni'mat nama: a landmark in Malwa painting', in *Marg*, vol.12, Bombay, 1958, pp.44–50
Skelton, R. 'Early Golconda painting', in *Indologen Tagung*, Wiesbaden, 1973, pp.182–95
Smart, E. *Paintings from the Babur-nama: a study of 16th century Mughal historical manuscript illustrations* [Ph.D. thesis, SOAS, Univ. of London, 1977]
Stchoukine, I. *La peinture indienne à l'époque des grands moghols*, Paris, 1929
Stchoukine, I. 'Quelques images de Jahângîr dans un Dîvân de Ḥâfiz', in *Gazette des Beaux-Arts*, vol.6, Paris, 1931
Stchoukine, I. *Les peintures des manuscrits safavis*, Paris, 1959
Stchoukine, I. 'Origine indienne d'un manuscrit persan achevé en 844 A.H.', in *Syria*, tome XLVI, Paris, 1969, pp.105–14
Stein, M.A. *Ancient Khotan*, Oxford 1907
Stein, M.A. *Innermost Asia*, Oxford, 1928
Stooke, H.J. 'An XI century illuminated palm-leaf MS.', in *OA*, vol.I, 1948, pp.5–8
Stooke, H.J., and K. Khandalavala *The Laud Ragamala miniatures*, Oxford, 1953
Sudhākara, Pandit 'Gaṇakatarangiṇī', in *The Pandit*, vol.XIV, Benares, 1892
Suleiman, H. *Miniatures of Bābur-nama*, Tashkent, 1970

Thompson, B. *The story of prince Rāma*, 1980
Titley, N.M. 'An illustrated Persian glossary of the 16th century', in *BMQ*, vol.XXIX, 1964–5, pp.15–9
Titley, N.M. *Plants and gardens in Persian, Mughal and Turkish art*, 1979
Tod, James *Annals and antiquities of Rajasthan*, ed. W. Crooke, 1920
Topsfield, A. *Paintings from Rajasthan in the collection of the National Gallery of Victoria*, Melbourne, 1980
Trehan, G.L. *Learning and libraries in ancient India – a study*, Chandigarh, 1975
Trier, J. *Ancient paper of Nepal*, Copenhagen, 1972
Tyulaev, S. *Miniatures of the Babur Namah*, Moscow, 1960

Vira, Raghu, and Lokesh Chandra *Gilgit Buddhist manuscripts (facsimile edition), vol.VI*, New Delhi, 1974
Vredenburg, E. 'The continuity of Indian pictorial art', in *Rupam*, vol.I, Calcutta, 1927
Warner, *Sir* George *Descriptive catalogue of illuminated manuscripts in the library of C.W. Dyson Perrins*, 1920
Welch, A. *Calligraphy in the arts of the Muslim world*, Folkestone, 1979
Welch, S.C. 'The Emperor Akbar's Khamsa of Nizami', in *Journal of the Walters Art Gallery*, vol.XXIII, Baltimore, 1960, pp.87–96
Welch, S.C. 'The paintings of Basawan', in *LK*, no.10, 1961
Welch, S.C. *The art of Mughal India*, New York, 1963
Welch, S.C. *A flower from every meadow*, New York, 1973
Welch, S.C. *Indian drawings and painted sketches*, New York, 1976
Welch, S.C. *Imperial Mughal painting*, 1978
Wilkinson, J.V.S. *The lights of Canopus, Anvār i Suhailī*, 1929
Wilkinson, J.V.S. 'A dated illustrated manuscript of Akbar's reign', in *JISOA*, vol.2, 1934, pp.67–9
Wilkinson, J.V.S. 'An Indian manuscript of the Shāh Jahān period', in *AO*, vol.II, 1957, pp.423–5
Wilkinson, J.V.S. 'A note on an illustrated manuscript of the Jog-Bāsisht', in *Bulletin of the School of Oriental Studies*, vol.XII, 1948, pp.692–4

Zetterstéen, K.V., and C.J. Lamm *Mohammad 'Asafi: the story of Jamāl and Jalāl*, Uppsala, 1948